Damned Hunchbacks

Italy's Forgotten Torpedo Bomber Units of the Second World War (1940–1943)

Paolo Morisi

Helion & Company

Helion & Company Limited
Unit 8 Amherst Business Centre
Budbrooke Road
Warwick
CV34 5WE
England
Tel. 01926 499 619
Email: info@helion.co.uk
Website: www.helion.co.uk
Twitter: @helionbooks
Visit our blog at blog.helion.co.uk

Published by Helion & Company 2023
Designed and typeset by Mach 3 Solutions (www.mach3solutions.co.uk)
Cover designed by Paul Hewitt, Battlefield Design (www.battlefield-design.co.uk)

ISBN 9-7-81804512-37-1

British Library Cataloguing-in-Publication Data.
A catalogue record for this book is available from the British Library.

For details of other military history titles published by Helion & Company Limited contact the above address or visit our website: http://www.helion.co.uk.

We always welcome receipt of book proposals from prospective authors.

Contents

List of Photographs

Introduction

As the struggle between Allied and Axis forces for control of the Mediterranean Sea reached its climax in August 1942, the Royal Navy launched one of the most formidable efforts to resupply the besieged island of Malta. Although under continuous assault, Malta was Great Britain's primary base in the central Mediterranean during the Second World War, and from this strategic position the British launched countless submarine attacks against Axis convoys headed for North Africa. Operation Pedestal, however, was heavily disrupted from the outset and amongst other Axis aerial and naval forces by Italian *Savoia-Marchetti* S.79 torpedo bombers, which inflicted damage on the British supply ships and escorts.

S.79 pilot *Capitano* Giulio Ricciardini recalled the hard fight that took place during Pedestal: "I started my attack and at about 800 meters range I dropped the torpedo just as a burst of 20mm cannon fire struck my aircraft. I initially thought that it had hit the right engine, but as soon as I saw the right wing fuel tank on fire, I ordered my co-pilot *Tenente* Nicola Titi to pull out the fire extinguisher as a precautionary measure, but the blaze soon grew in intensity and I decided to ditch at once."[1]

Although several S.79s were downed by accurate British anti-aircraft fire during Pedestal, the torpedo bombers still managed to carry out over 100 sorties, dropping close to 100 torpedoes and scoring several hits on merchant shipping while sinking the 1,880-ton destroyer HMS Foresight. The battle ended in a stalemate, but it furthered the Axis campaign to cordon off this most vital British base. Summer 1942 was the high point of the Axis war effort in the Mediterranean and North Africa where the combined German and Italian forces appeared to be en route toward an important victory. This was the result of multiple forces including the Axis Mediterranean air forces that had gained an edge over the Allies. To this success the torpedo bomber units had made significant contributions alongside the German and Italian naval forces and the *Luftwaffe*.

As the name implies, torpedo bombers were land based aircraft designed to deliver torpedoes against enemy ships. The torpedo bomber was originally envisioned to operate like a torpedo boat or a submarine by attacking by stealth and surprise and slipping past the enemy's anti-aircraft defenses to launch the warhead at close range against enemy shipping or warships. The concept was an old one. An Italian naval officer, for example, had experimented with launching torpedoes from a seaplane, while Britain had dropped a torpedo by an aircraft in 1914. However, forging a viable torpedo bomber and also specially trained crews that could carry out effectively

1 Marco Mattioli, *Savoia-Marchetti S.79 Sparviero Torpedo-Bomber Units* (Oxford: Osprey, 2010), p.56.

the warhead launches was altogether a different matter. A torpedo represents a very heavy load for an aircraft, often slowing down the latter and exposing it to enemy fire. Furthermore, the necessity of delivering aerial torpedoes from low altitude and close range and at a modest aircraft speed meant that even the fastest torpedo bombers, such as those introduced during the Second World War were vulnerable to enemy fire and to enemy fighters as they approached a battleship. In fact, torpedo bomber units always suffered heavy casualties when they attempted to penetrate a powerful anti-aircraft screen by battleships or if intercepted by a squadron of enemy fighters. Across different military organizations and national states, torpedo bomber crews often did not survive past their third or fourth operation. The longevity of a torpedo bomber crew depended upon many factors. Longevity could be supported by a durable aircraft that was also fast and well-armed. Or by an aircraft that could launch a warhead at a higher altitude than most bombers and from further away from the target thus limiting its exposure to enemy fire. Another factor that helped was the group's attack theory such as by dispatching into combat the torpedo bombers shortly after attacks by dive bombers and fighters that distracted the enemy and suppressed his anti-aircraft defenses, or by accompanying the torpedo bombers by a large number of fighters that could clear the skies and allow the torpedo bomber crews to attack with greater impunity. The latter was also increased if the torpedo bombers were able to fight at night and with the help of modern equipment such as radar and radios. Other technological innovations such as unmanned radio controlled torpedo bombers could also increase the efficacy of this discipline while preserving the life of torpedo bomber crews.

Developed from an airliner, the S.79 trimotor torpedo bomber emerged as Italy's most important attack aircraft in the Mediterranean during the Second World War. The torpedo bomber units were some of the most successful branches of the *Regia Aeronautica (RA)*, the Italian Royal Air Force, during the conflict and this book aims to retrace their origins, development and their operational history. Accordingly, chapter one will focus upon the pre-Second World War period to detail how the Italian air force came into being and prepared for war. Chapter two will detail the technical development of the torpedo bombers and the men and organizations behind their constitution. The third chapter will focus on the months preceding the war and how Italy prepared for it, while chapter four will focus on the latter part of 1940, the first year of the war when the torpedo bomber units reaped their first successes against British naval shipping convoys and bases in the Mediterranean Sea. The fifth chapter will detail their successes and failures during 1941, the torpedo bombers busiest year of the war. The sixth chapter will focus upon the crucial operations in 1942, while the seventh chapter will focus upon 1943, a year of external and internal conflict for Italy and of far reaching consequences. The final chapter will present an assessment of the effectiveness of the torpedo bombers in the Second World War on behalf of the aims of the Axis alliance.

Despite the fact that the torpedo bomber became one of the most important weapons in its arsenal, the RA at the beginning of the war had very low stocks of warheads, also it did not have a torpedo bomber unit ready for combat nor trained pilots and crews in the torpedo discipline. Initially, the RA aimed to interdict British or French naval convoys in the Mediterranean by mainly utilizing standard bombers squadrons. Once these units were shown to be ineffective during the June and July 1940 timeframe, the air force hastened the introduction of the first torpedo bomber unit pushing it into an early action that failed mostly due to the fact that the crews were not experienced or fully operational and the plan was too ambitious. The delay in introducing the torpedo bombers into the conflict hampered the Italian war effort as early surprise attacks against British naval bases such as Gibraltar and Alexandria or naval convoys could have paid huge dividends if the crews were experienced and ready to go into action at the start of the conflict. Despite the initial delay the introduction on a delayed, but still favorable, time scale of the aerial torpedo specialty during the war by the Italian air force was nevertheless a positive development and a sign of technical innovation which in the field of military performance/preparedness studies is an indicator of increased military effectiveness. The latter is defined as "the process by which armed forces convert resources into fighting power. A fully effective military is one that derives maximum combat power from the resources physically and politically available. Effectiveness thus incorporates some notion of efficiency."[2] During the first part of the war, the Axis powers appeared to have a cutting edge. Especially the German Army from 1939 to mid-1942 appeared to be unstoppable displaying superior combined arms tactics by deploying a mix of aerial, armored, mobile infantry and mechanized infantry power. However, after the battles of Stalingrad and El Alamein the Allied forces gained supremacy. From mid-1942 onward the Allied powers went on the offensive and never looked back. This was the result of two different aspects of military innovation. One was technological innovation with the introduction of large quantities of new, highly effective weapons such as for example the Soviet T-34 tank. The other was a willingness to change doctrines of warfare and tactics. Material superiority was a third factor that allowed the Allies to seize the initiative thanks in large part to the combined industrial might of the Soviet Union, Britain and its Commonwealth and the United States. Military innovation is usually a catalyst that manifests itself in two forms. It can determine a complete overhaul of how a national state deploys combat power such as for example the development of the atomic bomb by the United States in the latter stages of the Second World War.[3] This being a unique development that ushered in a new age of warfare. Or it can introduce incremental change such as the United States amphibious operations in the Pacific and in Europe or the development of blitzkrieg tactics by the German army during the early part of the Second World War. There is no single factor that social scientists agree upon that spur's military innovation. Technology industrial prowess, intelligence and ingenuity, are just some of the multiple factors that prompt military innovation. But usually innovation takes the form of learning from experience or improving upon an existing weapon or tactic. A rich historical legacy is key for making progress in military innovation. Defeat sometimes can be a catalyst for innovation as it sweeps aside an old order or an established bureaucracy and ushers in a new class of leaders and innovators. The German Army once again is a good case in point. General Heinz Guderian, for example, was able to introduce new combined arms tactics set around the tank in the 1930s even when Germany was not allowed by the Versailles agreement to establish and maintain armored divisions. Guderian did this by adopting innovative theories developed primarily in France and Great Britain regarding mechanized warfare and introducing and disseminating them to German staff officers, the majority of which had never ridden a tank.[4] Similarly, during the Polish campaign of 1939 the *Wehrmacht* implemented these combined arms tactics and once the fighting was over several officers reviewed what had

2 Allan R. Millett, Williamson Murray and Kenneth H. Watman, "The Effectiveness of Military Organizations", *International Security*, Vol. 11, No. 1 (Summer, 1986), pp.37-71.

3 Stephen Peter Rosen, "New Ways of War: Understanding Military Innovation" in *International Security* Vol. 13, No. 1 (Summer, 1988), pp.134-168.

4 R.L. Di Nardo, *Germany's Panzer Arm in World War II* (Mechanicsburg: Stackpole, 2006).

worked, what had not and most importantly spent considerable time thinking about how to improve upon past experience. This led to a rapid training program that encompassed all the new tactics of combined arms warfare in preparation of the campaign against France.

The Italian Army of the Second World War is generally considered by military historians not an innovative army.[5] But despite the general unpreparedness for the conflict, during the war itself the armed forces improved combat performance due to a multitude of factors. It can be argued that: "The army was unprepared for fighting a modern desert war, the doctrine of rapid course war notwithstanding. Its tanks were too few, too light and had inadequate firepower and the infantry did not have the training armaments or the tactics for fighting in such a theatre."[6] Still the army adopted to modern warfare and continued fighting in North Africa despite having obsolete equipment, especially artillery, until mid-1943. This capacity to improve upon combat performance can be associated to military innovation which in the Italian case manifested itself by adopting German tactics as well as bringing in better weapons such as for example the 90mm anti-tank gun and by a renewed focus on training. Even Italy's air forces were unprepared for a major conflict in 1940 since they possessed aircraft that had inferior engines to those of Britain and Germany and its organization leaned on a narrower aviation industrial base. But in some fields, such as for example the aerial torpedo, the Italian air force succeeded from a relatively early stage. The aerial torpedo was not a new concept when the Second World War erupted but prior it had not been used on a large scale. It was an adaptation of an existing concept made possible by developments in aircraft technology and in the technical developments specific to aerial warheads. In the early stages of the war between 1940-42 the deployment of this new weapon by the RA was a positive development which enhanced its military effectiveness, but in the long-term technical development stalled. For example, a new plane the S.84 which was intended to supersede the S.79 torpedo bomber was unsuccessfully introduced in 1941. Another attempt to partially supersede the S.79 with the S.79bis, although an improvement, was also not fully successful. Several new torpedo aircraft prototypes also failed (mostly because of a lack of initiative and funding) between 1942-43. Another factor that hindered further development was the lack of a more powerful warhead or the availability of aircraft that could carry more than one torpedo. Or innovation came too late into the war such as when in 1943 Italian air force officers introduced a smaller warhead, the 'silurotto' that could be launched by a fighter plane or the introduction of a radio-controlled warhead. This failure to innovate and to take stock of how the Royal Navy and the Royal Air Force (RAF) had blunted torpedo attacks by late 1942 were paid dearly by the RA as the threat posed by the torpedo bomber diminished overtime. Unlike the Soviet Union's experience with new tank technology, the Italian air force ultimately could not up its game: "The story of tank development during the Second World War illustrated a large truth. Armies in combat developed a dialectical relationship. Improvements in design on one side served only to encourage the other to redouble its own efforts to produce something better or to find other ways to nullify the enemy's advantage. In general and measured in terms of weapons, German mortars, machine

5 Mac Gregor Knox, *Hitler's Italian Allies: Royal Armed Forces, Fascist Regime and the War of 1940–1943* (Cambridge: Cambridge University Press, 2009).

6 Nicola Labanca, "The Italian Wars" in Richard Overy, *The Oxford Illustrated History of World War II* (Oxford: Oxford University Press, 2015), pp.208-09.

guns, artillery and anti-tank guns were probably more destructive than their American and British counterparts, although in the T-34 the Soviets undoubtedly possessed the war's best medium tank."[7]

The Soviet experience during the Second World War is most illustrative of the benefits of continuous innovation in warfare. The pre-war purges in the officer ranks ordered by Stalin was a most destabilizing factor for the Red Army. The poor showing of the Red Army during the Finnish Winter War of 1939-40 demonstrated the negative effects of an army being led by incompetent and politically nominated officers. Furthermore, during the initial stages of Operation Barbarossa the Red Army was constantly on the defensive and was losing high numbers of men and equipment. After losing more than 3.8 million soldiers, Stalin began to change course. He first surrounded himself with capable military leaders. He then loosened the grip of the political commissars on the Red Army. Then, Soviet industry went into full production mode through a massive organizational restructuring and the development of new technology. "Troops were issued with new, better, more robust equipment in the shape of the T-34 and KV-1 tanks, self-propelled artillery and multi barreled rocket launchers. But the Soviets did not merely equip their forces with more, newer and better weapons. The Soviet General Staff took a hard and objective look at the past performance of their forces, analyzed what had gone wrong in the battles of 1941 and 1942, and embarked on a programme to put this right." [8] First, the Soviet anti-tank defense was much improved by training special anti-tank defense units which were also better equipped with more powerful guns. This did much to blunt the *Wehrmacht*. Second, the formation of large tank divisions comprised of armor and motorized infantry units gave the Soviet Army the opportunity to go on the offensive. These were specialty trained units especially the officer ranks and the tank personnel that were well versed in combined arms warfare. Their effectiveness was further enhanced by improvements made in the communications tools used by units during operations. At the battle of Kursk, for example, the tank and mechanized corps of the Soviet Army gave an excellent account of themselves reversing the trend that historically had saw much higher numbers of Soviet casualties versus German ones. Soviet innovation did not end there has the military unveiled tanks with greater firepower and new aircraft with more powerful engines between 1944-45. Unlike the Soviet case, with regards to the Italian torpedo bomber units and its air force service, it can be argued that initially between 1940-42 there was innovation and even the British accounts, for example, point to the torpedo squads as being one of the most effective enemy units that their naval personnel encountered. But unlike the Soviet example and due to a host of reasons that will be illustrated further, the RA could not continue on the path of military innovation between late 1941 to the end of the conflict. As the conflict progressed innovation stalled or was not fully successful. Italy did introduce some very fast and technically competitive fighters, but it did so too late into the conflict and with production figures that were not very impressive. Concerning torpedo bombers, there was no major improvement over the S.79, although there were some interesting prototypes. The S.84 was largely a failure, while the S.79bis represented a marginal improvement. Prototypes such as radio controlled torpedo bombers, a fighter that could carry a torpedo and smaller warheads that would have permitted the pilots to launch them at greater altitude and distance also were developed. But unlike, the Japanese or American experience,

7 David French, "Fighting Power" in Richard Overy, *The Oxford Illustrated History of World War II* (Oxford: Oxford University Press, 2015), pp.208-09.
8 Ibid., p.218.

the Italians were not able to transform the prototypes into actual working weapons during the war that could be readily deployed. Faster British and American fighters proved to be too much of a match for the torpedo bombers units equipped with the S.79 which became more sluggish and more prone to being downed by these enemy fighters. The units themselves lost their initial cutting edge. The Royal Navy perfected its anti-aircraft defense proving to be a major obstacle to torpedo bomber attacks. This forced the torpedo bomber units to operate only at night or at dusk limiting the number and scope of their operations. Still representing a threat to British shipping convoys, the torpedo units would reap only partial successes between 1942-43. But their losses began to mount and as Italy's war effort vaned in late 1942 and 1943, the torpedo bomber fleet became smaller and smaller and industry could not produce enough new aircraft to replace the losses. Eventually when it surrendered on 8 September 1943, the once powerful torpedo bomber fleet was reduced to a shadow of its former self.

There are very few books in the English language that have analyzed the role of the *Regia Aeronautica* in the Second World War. Two works stand out: *Courage Alone* by Chris Dunning and the chapter by Brian Sullivan in the edited work *Why Air Forces Fail: The Anatomy of Defeat*. On the specific role of the torpedo bombers there are two excellent books. The first by Marco Mattioli, *Savoia-Marchetti S.79* which although does not begin with a section on aircraft development or on tactics and strategies of the Italian air force, offers an excellent account of the torpedo bomber units. A second exceptional work is Francesco Mattesini *Luci ed Ombre degli Aerosiluranti* which is only in Italian but delves deeply in the analysis of the torpedo bomber units and how effectively they fought alongside the Italian Navy in the great battles in the Mediterranean. Finally, several works by Mark E. Stille have described the role of the Japanese torpedo bomber units in the Pacific campaign which are interesting to read and compare with the operations of the Italian torpedo bombers. One question that often came up during the writing of this work was whether the Japanese and the Italians shared lessons learned, technical innovations, and combat tactics with regards to torpedo bombers during the war. In the Italian military archives there was almost no information regarding this topic which I hope future historians will one day address.

1

Birth of the Air Forces

First World War

At the start of the twentieth century, Italy was one of the many national actors in the development of civil and military aviation. The latter developed as early as the first decade of the century. During the colonization of Libya in 1911, for example, the Italian army used several aircraft to conduct reconnaissance missions and on 1 November of the same year aircraft were used to conduct a bombing raid.

In the First World War the *Corpo Aeronautico Militare*, which at the time was not yet a standalone branch of the Italian armed forces, supported the war effort with trained pilots, utilizing mostly French manufactured fighters and Italian bombers. The fighter pilots dueled their Austro-Hungarian and German counterparts for control of the skies over the Isonzo while *Caproni* bombers were deployed to terrorize Austro-Hungarian frontline and rear positions. Italy's most effective fighter pilot was the renowned ace Francesco Baracca, who would not only become the leader of Italy's most successful fighter squadron but would also be credited with 34 aerial victories. Alongside the creation of fighter squadrons, the *Corpo Aeronautico Militare* also issued "Regulations for Offensive Actions with Airplanes" in July 1915 which established the use of aviation for bombardments. Between 1915 and 1916, the new regulations began to be put into practice with the deployment of an aircraft mass to bomb enemy cities and military infrastructure. This was made possible by technological innovation, mainly the arrival of the heavy *Caproni* bomber airplanes which could carry several tons of explosives and allowed the Italian crews to carry out medium and long-range bombing missions. For example, in Slovenia in August 1915 an Italian crew struck the station of Ajševica and, on 7 October, another station (Kostanjevica) was successfully targeted. On 18 February 1916, seven tri-motor planes departed from the airfield of Aviano to conduct a raid on Ljubljana as retaliation for the bombing of Milan (which had taken place three days earlier) by the Austro-Hungarian air force. In the summer of 1916, the Italians conducted a massive bombing raid against the port of Fiume using twenty *Caproni*.

1: GABRIELE D'ANNUNZIO

Born March 12, 1863, Pescara,—died March 1, 1938, Gardone Riviera. A renowned poet and literary figure, D'Annunzio was also a man of action. When the First World War broke out, he became a key *interventista*, a member of the political faction that vigorously promoted Italy's entry into the conflict. In D'Annunzio's view Italy had the historical task of finishing up the project that the Risorgimento of Mazzini and Cavour had begun, mainly the political and geographic unification of the nation. The *interventisti* argued that war with Austria-Hungary was inevitable to liberate Trento and Trieste, the last two major Italian cities under Austrian rule. After Italy declared war, D'Annunzio plunged into the fighting by volunteering his services in several branches of the military to take on very dangerous tasks or missions. Offering his services to the Italian air force, D'Annunzio planned and then participated to a very dangerous mission which yielded a major propaganda coup. The 'Flight over Vienna' was an air raid conducted on 9 August 1918 with a squadron of Ansaldo SVA-1 aircraft (SVA stands for Savoia/Verduzio/Ansaldo, the first two being the last names of the aircraft design engineers and Ansaldo the manufacturer), from 87ª *Squadriglia*. The squadron was to fly for over 1,200 km in an eight-hour round trip from an airfield near Padua to Vienna to drop thousands of propaganda leaflets. Since aircraft technology was in its infancy and the long flight would test the aircraft endurance and also because there was the possibility that enemy aircraft could interfere, the operation was considered as extremely risky. From the onset, the squadron was faced with numerous challenges. Within the first hour three planes were forced to return to base due to technical difficulties, while another plane was forced to make a crash landing in Austrian territory after experiencing a technical failure while in proximity of Vienna. With only seven remaining single seated aircraft along with D'Annunzio and his pilot's Natale Palli two seated plane, the squadron finally reached its destination and dropped 50,000 leaflets on a three-colored card (green, white, and red: the colors of the Italian flag). The text was written by D'Annunzio himself and it read:

> VIENNESE!
>
> Learn to know the Italians. We are flying over Vienna; we could drop tons of bombs. All we are dropping on you is a greeting of three colors: the three colors of liberty. We Italians do not make war on children, on old people, on women. We are making war on your government, the enemy of national liberty, on your blind, stubborn, cruel government that can give you neither peace nor bread, and feeds you hatred and illusions.
>
> VIENNESE! You are famous for being intelligent. But why have you put on the Prussian uniform? By now, you see, the whole world has turned against you. You want to continue the war? Continue it; it's your suicide. What do you hope for? The decisive victory promised to you by the Prussian generals? Their decisive victory is like the bread of Ukraine: You die waiting for it.
>
> PEOPLE OF VIENNA, think of your own fates. Wake up!
>
> LONG LIVE LIBERTY!
>
> LONG LIVE ITALY!
>
> LONG LIVE THE ENTENTE!

The Italian airmen continued to support the war effort culminating with their massive deployment during the Battle of the Piave River in June 1918 where the army was able to blunt the enemy offensive and inflict grave casualties on an Austro-Hungarian army that simply ran out of steam losing the battle of material supply against a resurgent foe. In this phase of the war the fighter planes were used primarily to strafe the advancing enemy infantry units, while the bombers concentrated on the enemy's rear infantry and supply concentrations. The following furnishes some statistics regarding the air service contribution during 1917-18 to the war effort:

> In 1917, the Italian aviation completed 1,298 missions (fifty-two of which by airships) and dropped 254 tons of bombs, while 2,730 missions were carried out during 1918 (114 of which by airships) for a total of 491 tons of bombs. During the battle for the Piave alone, fought between 15-25 June 1918, the aviation of the Royal Army carried out 3,895 flights, using an average of 450 airplanes per day, and dropping a total of over ninety-eight tons of bombs. In 1917, the aerial duels between Italian and Austro-Hungarian planes amounted to 700, while between January and August 1918, no less than 2,225 duels took place. Overall, between 1915 and 1918, just the Royal Navy Aviation, subjected since 1916 to the Submarine and Aviation Inspectorate, carried out 2,177 bombing operations (fifty-six of which by airships), 3,467 reconnaissance and supply missions, 1,107 defense missions, 9,433 exploration missions and 10,385 operations to defend naval traffic, for a total of 26,569 missions, increasing from 305 in 1915 to 16,814 in 1918. At the end of the conflict, the air component of the Italian army was generally on the par with the other allied aviations and turned out to be decisive for the victory.[1]

2: FRANCESCO BARACCA

(Born on 9 May 1888 in Lugo– Died 19 June 1918 Montello)
Francesco Baracca the Italian ace among aces of the Italian First World War Army is one, if not the most, popular hero of the Italian people. Much like Richthofen, Guynemer or Bishop he was an aviator that excited the population with his heroic deeds. The son of a property owner and wine merchant, from 1907 to 1909, Baracca attended the Military Academy of Modena, and then the Cavalry Training School. On 15 July 1910, Baracca joined the prestigious 2nd Cavalry Regiment *Piemonte Reale*. In 1912 he attended flying school in Reims, France and gained his pilot's license and later in the same year Baracca became a pilot for one of the Italian army's first air force units. His first plane was a Nieuport 10 on which he trained extensively. When Italy entered the war Baracca was assigned to the 8° *Squadriglia Nieuport*, then the 1° *Squadriglia*, and, on 8 April 1916, the 71° *Squadriglia*. His first aerial victory took place on 7 April 1916 when he shot down an enemy plane. By 11 February 1917 Baracca had already five victories under his belt and became the most effective Italian fighter ace.

1 "Air Warfare Italy", *Encyclopedia 1914-18* <https://encyclopedia.1914-1918-online.net/article/air_warfare_italy> (accessed 2 May 2021).

On 20 March 1917, Baracca began flying the SPAD S.VII equipped with a synchronized machine gun and propeller. On 6 June 1917, he was given command of the 91° *Squadriglia*, Italy's most prestigious fighter unit. On 6 September, he gained his nineteenth victory and was promoted to *Maggiore* (major). By this time, he began to fly the SPAD S.XIII.

On 24 October 1917, Austria-Hungary and Germany launched the Caporetto offensive which resulted in a huge victory for the Central Powers on the Italian front. During the hectic and chaotic days of the offensive, Baracca and his squadron flew non-stop, daily missions to interfere and stave off the enemy offensive. Within forty days, Baracca shot down ten planes. For his courageous deeds he was awarded the gold medal of military valor, after having previously been awarded three silver medals and one bronze medal for military valor.

Baracca and his squadron were again involved in very hard fighting during Austria-Hungary's Piave River Offensive in June 1918, the last major offensive of the Dual Monarchy. On 19 June, at 1800 Baracca took off to strafe at low altitude the advancing enemy infantry with his machine gun, but he was shot presumably by an infantry sniper and crashed onto the Montello mountain. His popularity was so great that he was granted a very well-orchestrated and attended funeral. The main funerary oration was written and delivered by none other than Gabriele D'Annunzio.

In the 1920s Baracca became one of the icons of the fledgling *Regia Aeronautica* and a large statue was dedicated to him in the main square of his hometown, Lugo di Romagna. During the 1920s, the race car driver Enzo Ferrari was granted by Baracca's family the permission to use his personal emblem – the prancing horse – as a company logo. To this day this is the logo of the Ferrari car company.

Regia Aeronautica

The Italian air force became an independent service—the *Regia Aeronautica*—on 28 March 1923. Benito Mussolini's fascist regime seizing an opportunity for policy innovation, job creation and gross domestic product growth, created the new branch sensing that the air force could also be utilized for other less tangible purposes.

The creation of the new organization represented one of the first policies of the new government that wanted to promote the domestic aviation industry as well as use the air force for propaganda objectives to bolster its popularity. Another consideration behind the government's move was the growth of air power during the First World War and the necessity for Italy to be a player in the realm of military aviation in the post war era.

Initially, Aldo Finzi was nominated has its nominal head with two deputies, Arturo Mercanti responsible for maintaining relationships with the domestic industry and *Colonnello* Riccardo Moizo responsible for military relations. The decree of 28 March 1923 established that the RA would become an autonomous branch of the military with soldiers wearing its uniforms and subject to its authority.

The two other branches of the military, the Army (*Regio Esercito*) and Navy (*Regia Marina or RM*), did not welcome this new initiative since both considered the air force to be an auxiliary arm to be subjugated to them. Indeed, they originally opposed its creation, but when they saw that the regime was determined to establish an air force service and later a ministry, they abided to the directives of the political authorities. Rivalry amongst the services only intensified after 1923 and throughout the 1930s and 1940s as the three branches fought each other to protect their own turf, each always bargaining to gain a greater share of the military budget and each always opposed to inter-service collaboration.

At any rate, initially the RA was very small and not much of a threat, for example it had only seventy planes, but even if it was still in its infancy the other services were unwilling to help it in any way or to allow the use of their budgets to support its development. This policy stance by both the Army and the RM would later have important repercussions upon inter-service relations since for many years the RA also sought to not collaborate with the other services. For most of the period between the First and the Second World War the relationship amongst the three services would be predicated upon mutual distrust and intense competition for state financial resources. The most negative consequences of the infighting within the armed services would be primarily the inability to deploy truly combined arms tactics by the RM and RA especially during the early stages of the Second World War.[2] According to a renowned aviation historian the inability to cooperate effectively, for example, was a factor of greater importance than the lack of an aircraft carrier during the early reversals against the Royal Navy between 1940-41.[3] Meanwhile inter service collaboration was more established within the British military establishment, resulting in several early British military successes in the Mediterranean in 1940. Second, inter service rivalry prevented the constitution of a centralized state agency for the procurement of military goods and equipment which would have contributed to bring the cost of such goods down as well as rationalize equipment production. As a result, Italy faced the Second World War with aircraft that were generally technically inferior to Allied planes and that on average took longer and were more expensive to build.[4]

In November 1924 the government named *Generale* Pier Ruggero Piccio, a First World War fighter ace, as the head of the new discipline after Finzi was forced to resign due to the Giacomo Matteotti affair.

In 1925 the air service organization was further solidified with the creation of the ministry for aviation (*Ministero dell'Aeronautica*) with *Generale* Alberto Bonzani has its *sottosegretario* (undersecretary) and Mussolini has its first minister. On 6 November 1926 the head of government decided to make the new discipline a centerpiece of his administration by nominating the charismatic Italo Balbo as its *sottosegretario* (undersecretary or deputy), a title that he combined on 12 September 1929 with *Ministro dell'Aeronautica* when he became the minister of aviation. Balbo was a Blackshirt of the first hour and was also very driven and dynamic to the point that he was considered by many as Mussolini's political heir. In his new assignment, Balbo would be faced with numerous challenges mainly how to increase the organization's budget and how to develop an effective military fleet while not downplaying the importance of sportive events to improve the image of the regime. As minister Balbo was responsible for all aspects of aviation development from civil to military. When he took office, he noted that: "our Aeronautica was nothing more than an office for propaganda...Now it is necessary to begin building military aviation and its weaponry ..."[5]

2 Orazio Giuffrida, *Buscaglia e gli aerosiluranti* (Rome: Ufficio Storico, 1988).
3 Ferruccio Botti, "La Guerra aerea" in *L'Italia in Guerra, 1940* (Rome: Uffcio Storico, 1991), p.279.
4 Ibid.
5 Claudio G. Segre, *Italo Balbo* (Berkeley, California: Universty of California Press, 2004), p.152.

Balbo's tenure at the air force ministry was predicated upon expanding it at the expense of the other branches of the armed forces in order to build organizational autonomy and capacity. In 1931, in a speech to parliament Balbo stated that "the organic unity of the defense of the air space independently of the various theatres of operation and the necessity that this task is exclusively assigned to the Air Force necessitates that both offensive and defensive means are concentrated into one organization."[6] Thus, he continued to pursue a policy of independence versus the other services that conflicted with the need to enhance inter-service collaboration.

The budget of the air force would expand considerably under his tenure, but never to the point of overtaking the budget of the other two services. Despite Balbo's efforts the RA remained the smallest of the three military branches. Balbo was able to obtain more financial resources for the air force, but overall, its funding remained stable for seven years in relation to the share of the total military budget. With increased budgets by 1928 the RA had established an aviation academy, a school for airplane mechanics and an institute for the study of meteorology. By 1931 specialized schools had been established to train and raise pilots and observers for both bombing and fighter operations. The budget for the aviation ministry in the 1920s was approximately 13 percent of the total of military spending with the bulk of the money going to the Army and approximately 26 percent going to the RM. At the time, France and Britain, for example, dedicated greater resources to their respective air services. The French military budget for aviation in 1928 was the equivalent 1,348 million Lire, while Britain spent the equivalent of 1,900 million Lire. Meanwhile the Italian budget for the RA was of 663 million Lire. In addition, year over year the air force budgets of Britain and France grew exponentially at a much greater pace than the RA's budget reflecting the industrial and financial might of these two established national states.[7] In 1930 the Italian aviation portion of the military budget was 14 percent, while in France it was 22 percent and in Britain 17 percent.[8] Based on the comparison of Italy's budget versus France and Britain, Balbo remarked that "Italy was jousting with giants."[9] Balbo demanded more funding to build a greater bomber fleet but funding continued to remain within the financial confines of the Italian government, a medium sized power.

Table 1: Funding to the three war ministries (1925-1934) in Millions of Lire

	Ministero Aeronautica	Ministero Guerra	Ministero Marina	Total Budget
1925-26	558	2,795	1,080	23,000
1926-27	754	3,112	1,320	24,600
1927-28	663	2,705	1,210	29,650
1928-29	737	2,856	1,262	20,840
1929-30	744	2,943	1,298	20,860
1930-31	787	3,230	1,582	25,850
1931-32	775	3,067	1,626	25,230
1932-33	770	3,068	1,615	22,850
1933-34	770	2,700	1,440	28,140

Source: Annuario statistico italiano

6 Gianni Rocca, *I disperati* (Milan: Mondadori, 2003), p.25.
7 Claudio G. Segre, *Italo Balbo*, p.157.
8 Ibid., p.158.
9 Ibid.

Balbo was also a strong proponent of transatlantic flights not only as a propaganda tool but also as way to win contracts abroad for Italian manufacturers. Balbo's focus on using aviation as a propaganda tool produced benefits for the domestic industry as Italian aircraft and components were sold across the globe in large numbers and Italy became one of the top ten worldwide suppliers of aviation equipment. But this success came at a steep price with the establishment of monopolistic practices. Since the state desired to create industrial champions through state aid, contracts and trade policy, the industrial aviation companies not only became excessively reliant on state aid but also became national monopolies with Fiat being the top supplier of fighter aircraft, while Caproni became the primary supplier of bombers. As domestic monopolies that were protected and shielded by the state from competitive forces from abroad, these entities over time became less competitive and often passed the higher costs for building aircraft and components upon the state. Thus, while the industrial companies benefited from state policy, innovation, research and development suffered in the long term. Balbo's export led policy prompted his main rival, Francesco De Pinedo, to write a memorandum titled "Promemoria sulla situazione del materiale aeronautico", on 18 August 1929 that was very critical of the state of the Italian aviation industry: "The aircraft that are presently manufactured by the domestic industry are of low quality. The Cr. 20, for example, cannot even reach an altitude of 6,000 meters and even at 5,000 meters it does not perform adequately as a fighter and is definitively inferior to French fighters. Industry must be pushed to produce better quality aircraft and by transforming their production apparatus to one of mass production."[10]

De Pinedo, who was considered as a dangerous rival to Balbo, was sidelined politically by the regime for having made public his critique of the policies of the new ministry. His downfall produced a political vacuum and the absence of an opposition to the policies of the ministry ensured that no one for many years would challenge the close relationship between the state and the aviation industry. In short, Balbo, has a critical biographer asserts, was an innovator in his own right but he was unable to transform the domestic industry toward a more competitive position:

> During Balbo's ministry, Italy's aircraft industry, on which he relied to equip Aeronautica, developed and expanded. Italy became a major exporter of aircraft. One the surface these look like commendable achievements. Post-World War II however, the Italian industry has come in for some harsh criticism. No one questions the skill and inventiveness of individual designers such as Celestino Rosatelli, Filippo Zappata, Giovanni Pegna, Mario Castoldi, Giuseppe Gabrielli, Alessandro Marchetti, or Gianni Caproni. Individually they produced aircraft that won races and prizes and established a host of records. The industry as a whole, however, failed to deliver the critics argue.[11]

Another feature of Balbo's tenure was his effort to safeguard the autonomy of the air force at all costs. This stance, which was dictated by the intense rivalry between the air force and the other services, did not foster a climate of military and economic collaboration especially with the RM. For example, Balbo argued strenuously against the RM and the Army having any

10 Giorgio Rochat, *Italo Balbo aviatore e ministro dell'aeronautica 1926-1933* (Ferrara: Italo Bovolenta Editore, 1979), p.204.

11 Claudio G. Segre, *Italo Balbo*, p.165.

aircraft unit even for reconnaissance purposes under their control. In 1931 he issued a ministerial decree that limited inter service collaboration and killed a proposal to develop together with the RM an aircraft carrier.[12] Another victim of Balbo's corporate defense of his ministry were the shared testing conducted on the torpedo bombs for aircraft. [13] In 1932, for example, an air force research paper affirmed that: "tests on launching torpedoes have continued successfully to the point that the Regia Marina has compiled a manual of instruction on how to use them in an offensive capacity. This same manual is to be examined by the ufficio di stato maggiore della Regia Aeronautica."[14] That year, the domestic manufacturer of torpedoes had begun testing aerial torpedoes prototypes and made inroads in this promising field, but the RA had been lukewarm about the whole project because it entailed extensive collaboration with the RM. As a result, for many years the RA would leave the development of the torpedo bombs almost exclusively in the hands of the domestic manufacturer. In Japan or Britain, in contrast, the air force service and the Navy were both at the forefront of aerial torpedoes research and development to the point that they were the ones pushing the private industry and not the other way around. This different approach would yield important results during the war years.

From a strategy perspective Balbo maintained that the RA adhered to Giulio Douhet's notion of strategic bombing by building a large fleet of bombers. During the First World War Douhet was a colonel who focused on the notion of national preparedness. In his view, Italy should build an air force potent enough "to gain command of the air so that to render the enemy harmless."[15] He advocated production of 500 bombers capable of dropping 125 tons of ordnance per day on vital military and economic installations in Germany and Austria-Hungary. The head of the armed forces Luigi Cadorna was aware of Douhet's theory of air power but did not embrace it. Thus, Douhet remained a secondary figure throughout the war. In 1921, Douhet released *Il Dominio dell'Aria* (The Command of the Air), his principal theoretical work centered on the concept of strategic airpower. His main assumption was that future wars will be total wars fought between whole peoples. Such wars will be won by paralyzing the enemy by carpet bombing his vital centers of resistance and his main military installations. The aircraft, in his view, was the only modern weapon that could overcome the trench warfare of the First World War and carry out massive bombing attacks on military installations, fuel depots, key industrial plants etc... Douhet believed in a two-step offensive. First, that the air force's first task was to gain air supremacy by attacking airfields, parked aircraft, fuel depots and aircraft factories. Second, after having neutralized the enemy's aviation capabilities the foe would be unable to stop massive bombing raids against its cities and military installations. Air power, in Douhet's view, was therefore the key to winning future conflicts.

Although Balbo embraced Douhet's theory and use it to bargain for more state aid toward aviation and expand the size of the air force and especially the bomber units, his thinking was also influenced by Amedeo Mecozzi, a First World War ace fighter, that advocated a different strategy. The latter saw in air power an organization tasked with the support of large scale infantry advances and basically to be used as aerial artillery in support of land based objectives. For Mecozzi the two branches had to cooperate to further the territorial penetration

12 Ibid., p.91.
13 Ibid, p.129.
14 Ibid.
15 Robert S. Dudney "Douhet", *Air Force Magazine*, April 2011.

of the Army into enemy defenses and strongpoints. In his view the aerial service in order to favor such approach had to switch production toward fast, agile and light fighter aircraft that could support such efforts. Balbo maintained a flexible and pragmatic position that favored the strategic bombing approach but did not negate the relevance of Mecozzi's theory. He thus continued to expand the bomber force while also fostering the development of new fighters.

Despite the fact that Balbo expanded the organization of the air force, he did do so without overly strengthening either one of the two strategic options. Balbo was ultimately torpedoed by Mussolini who was jealous of the former's popularity as a result of his widely acclaimed trans-atlantic flights. Prior to being sacked, Balbo stated that the RA under his watch had grown to 1,824 operational aircraft, while the head of government had his technical experts review Balbo's claims and they could only locate 911 aircraft.

Thus, a new era began when Giuseppe Valle took the reins of the service in 1933. On 16 November 1933 Valle was promoted to *sottosegretario di Stato per l'Aeronautica* which was combined with his other position of *Capo di Stato Maggiore dell'Aeronautica* which he already held since 1928, while Mussolini took the ministerial portfolio. Valle was promoted because he was considered a capable administrator and, unlike Balbo, was content with following the Duce's guidelines. During his tenure, Valle, much like his predecessor, was also not able to fully transform the domestic industry toward greater efficiencies of scale, although he initiated several successful endeavors. Under his watch the aviation industry remained fragmented, largely artisan, or pre-industrial based in its production methods, but his insistence on modernizing the fleet paid some dividends.[16] In 1934, for example, the size of the aviation industry was quite modest with 10,000 workers employed by 27 companies, 17 of which made aircraft and engines, while the remaining 10 made parts and assembly components.[17] Even the big players like Fiat remained fairly small by international standards. They were domestic giants, but medium sized firms compared to some of the largest international aviation companies. Another factor was the excessive number of models of aircraft supplied by the domestic industry to the RA, which inhibited a consolidation of the industry. For example, there were more than twenty aircraft types at military hangars in 1939 prompting one official to state that the artisan, decentralized nature of the industry was to be overcome with standardization of production: "We are convinced of the necessity of working toward standardization of material, that is, of reducing to a minimum the number of standard planes, engines, arms, equipment",[18] Moreover, the *Comitato Mobilitazione Civile,* which was charged with developing economies of scale and centralizing procurement for the three branches of the armed forces, was never put in a position to coordinate industrial policy. One good example of its failure was the slow development of the torpedo bombers. In the 1930s the intensive inter service rivalry for the control of the financial means as well as for new disciplines, special units and weapons, that had characterized the Balbo years continued unabated. Thus, for many years the RM and the air force service fought over control of the torpedo bomber discipline since the former had more funding and had a history of working with underwater weapons, while the latter insisted that it had the responsibility for

16 Valle was much maligned after Generale Pricolo took command in 1939, but recent scholarship on the Italian aviation history has revisited Valle's role in modernizing the military fleet.
17 Maurizio Simoncelli, "L'Industria Militare Italiana nella seconda Guerra mondiale", *Disarmo*, No. 1-2, January 1996, p.1.
18 Ibid., p.4.

the training and the operational deployment of the new discipline.[19] The experience of Japan, Britain and the United States, for example, demonstrates that the development of aerial and naval torpedoes was a very expensive undertaking. In those countries torpedo development took place primarily because the national state backed private industry with funding the research and design effort as well as footed the bills to manufacture the torpedoes. Private industry was not willing to work alone in torpedo development since the undertaking was costly and also very risky. Thus private industry relied heavily on government funding and backing. In Italy, on the other hand, as a direct result of the RM and the RA unwillingness to put their differences aside with regards to torpedo development, private industry was the main actor in the development of torpedo warheads with only limited backing from either ministry. Without strong governmental intervention technological development was not linear and was heavily characterized by false starts and an overall more elongated timetable. This partly explains why the torpedo bombers were introduced after the war started.

One area in which Valle's tenure was partly successful was the fighter aircraft segment and the quest for more modern engines. For example, the original design for the *Macchi* C.200 was launched under Valle's tenure in the second quarter of 1935 as a response to a government issued bid that was awarded to *Macchi* and *Fiat* respectively. In the bid package, the ministry called for all metal monoplanes realizing that the mixed wood-metal construction of most Italian aircraft manufactured in the early part of the decade was obsolete. Given all metal construction, the ministry instructed industry to opt for more potent engines. In the original design the *Macchi* C.200, for example, was much more heavily armed than in its final form with five machine guns and a 1000 Hp engine, while the Fiat G.50 had in its original design a 20mm cannon and two machine guns. Both early prototypes adhered to the strict technical specifications issued by the ministry. Only later did the industry realize that it lacked a powerful engine to power a much more heavily armed, all metal, and hence heavier aircraft. Under Valle's leadership the Ministry in 1938 had requested that the aviation industry develop a 1,100 Hp engine and then in 1939 a 1,500 Hp engine. A public request for quote was issued asking Piaggio, Fiat, Alfa Romeo and Isotta Fraschini to participate. However, industry proved incapable of meeting the new requirements and the fallback position by the Ministry was to water down the specifications and performances required for a modern fighter and to have Alfa Romeo purchase the license to produce the German Daimler Benz DB 600 and 601 engines so that industry could fulfil the request for a fighter aircraft that could exceed 600 km/h and with an endurance of over 2,000 km. The decision by Valle to purchase German engines was sound, although it penalized to some extent future domestic aircraft design given its reliance on foreign licenses for the powerplant. The first contract for the *Macchi* C.200 was issued by the ministry in March 1939, but it would take the manufacturer and Breda until March 1940 to test the first four assembled planes while only three more came off the assembly line in April 1940 mainly because of "their inability to cope with series production of modern, stressed-skinned monoplane fighters."[20] Another issue that prevented a greater monthly output of the *Macchi* C.200 and that contributed to an exceedingly complex assembly process were its

19 Ibid., p.1.
20 Giorgio Apostolo and Giovanni Massimello, *Italian Aces of World War Two* (Oxford: Osprey, 2000), p.9.

exceedingly high number of components.[21] The same difficulties were experienced by *Macchi* and Breda when they were called to produce the more advanced *Macchi* C. 202, which did not make its operational debut until the fall of 1941. "With only meagre quantities of Macchi fighters made available to the Regia Aeronautica, the C.202 had little real impact on the North African air war. So slow was the production of this fighter that entire frontline units (such as the 8 Gruppo) were still flying the long obsolete C.200 when the armistice was signed in September 1943."[22]

During Valle's tenure the force was comprised of two main medium bombers the Fiat BR. 20, and the S.79. The RA in 1934 issued specification requirements for new bombers which were to be twin-engined, a maximum speed of 240 mph at 16,500 feet carrying a bomb load of 1,100 kg and armament comprised of three machine guns. The only design to meet these criteria was the BR.20 which the RA began to order into production in 1936, while the S.79 had been a commercial line production that was adapted to military use. Although the BR.20 was the clear winner the RA also placed orders for less effective aircraft like the *Caproni* Ca. 135. According to Sullivan: "These Italian bombers surpassed the early model He.111 and Do 17 in speed, range and bomb load, however they did so due to lighter partially wood and canvas structures and inferior defensive armament to compensate for their weaker engines."[23] In 1939 the RA began to receive in limited numbers the new medium bomber the Cant Z.1007 that had greater speed of the comparable German bombers because like the S.79 and the BR.20 it was comprised mainly of a wood and canvas construction. What plagued Italian bombers, and just like the fighters, was the engine. "All the aircraft were underpowered, primarily due to the unreliable1,000 hp Fiat A.80 and the 1,000 hp Piaggio P. IX radial engines; both had lower power to weight ratios than their foreign equivalents and required more frequent maintenance."[24] In 1938-39 *Generale* Valle demanded that industry introduce better armed bombers with more powerful engines and like the fighters the domestic industry was unable to go beyond the capabilities of the radial engine. His plan was to launch a largescale program to renew the fleet that was to last several years at least until 1943 when it was estimated by air force planners that Italy would have a force of 3,000 aircraft and at least a third were to be bombers. The war, however, which began more quickly than originally envisioned, would largely upset these development plans.

Valle, unlike Balbo, was also able to overtake the RM's with regards to the share of state funding which helped him to launch the revitalization and expansion of the aircraft fleet. State spending after 1933 for military expenses soared as the international context became very heated. The RA, like the RAF and the *Luftwaffe*, was fortunate to see a greater share of the military budget going for the purchase of aircraft and aerial weapons. In fact, between 1933-40 the RA's share rose to 25% of the total military budget versus the average of 13% of the Balbo years. This figure was still much less however, of the 36% received by the *Luftwaffe* in 1934 or of the 38% of total military spending received by the RAF. Both of these national states also had much larger budgets.

21 Andrea Curami, "Piani e progetti dell'aeronautica italiana 1939-1943 Stato maggiore e industrie", *Italia Contemporanea*, No. 187, June 1992, p.251-52.
22 Giorgio Apostolo and Giovanni Massimello, *Italian Aces of World War Two*, p.9.
23 Brian Sullivan, "Downfall of the Regia Aeronautica in Robin Higham (ed.), *Why Air Forces Fail* (Lexington, Kentucky: University Press of Kentucky, 2006), p.144.
24 Ryan K. Noppen, *Malta 1940–42* (Oxford: Osprey, 2018), p.22.

Outside Interventions and the Spanish Civil War

In 1935 the Italian army began a campaign in Ethiopia where Caproni bombers CA 113 and CA 101 were deployed along with CA 111 used for reconnaissance and surveillance. Most historians have argued that the campaign, especially for the air forces, resulted in a huge drain on resources and prevented further technological innovation and the rationalization of the aviation industry.[25] The latter was busy fulfilling the demand for more equipment and munitions and lost its focus upon innovation and the development of new weaponry.

By February 1937 the Italian army was fully committed to another campaign, the Spanish Civil War, with a force that included 49,000 soldiers, 248 aircraft, 542 guns, 756 mortars, 81 tanks and 4,000 trucks. During the Spanish campaign three new aircraft were widely deployed alongside older ones. The S.79 which was used as a heavy bomber, the Fiat BR 20 medium bomber and the *Breda* Ba 65 ground attack aircraft. All were heavily deployed especially in support of the land-based battles of Bilbao, Brunete and Santander. Between June and August 1937, the *Aviazione Legionaria* completed 1,971 sorties, 525 bombing missions dropping 453 tons of explosives and conducting 275 reconnaissance missions. These were undertook by experienced pilots such as Ettore Muti, Adriano Mantelli, and *Capitano* Ernesto Borro.

The Spanish campaign was very important for the Italian air force because its pilots gained first-hand experience fighting against Soviet aircraft and it allowed them to perfect high altitude horizontal bombing attacks on mostly stationary targets such as artillery parks, military buildings/barracks, fuel and infrastructure assets and infantry positions. On the flipside, the campaign was another great drain on resources yielding the loss of more than 100 planes. As Simoncelli as argued "the increase in state spending for defense (which were particularly steep in 1935 and 1937) was used to pay for the wars in Abyssinia, Ethiopia and Spain rather than to modernize the weapons supplied by the domestic industry."[26]

The decade of the 1930s saw an increase to the overall size of the industry which by 1938 employed 46,000 in 23 manufacturing companies.[27] The main problem, however, at the time of the Italian aviation industry appeared to be a lack of specialization. Since budgets were not unlimited and the air force had to compete with the other services for the allocation of state funds, many economists and military planners argued that Italy should have focused its domestic industry on one major branch of military aviation such as bombers or fighters, while procuring from abroad the other types of aircraft or components. This would have forced a reorganization of the domestic industry, the elimination of its quasi artisan-based machine shops and bring about a specific focus to the industry. Unfortunately, this did not occur, and industry remained fragmented and dispersed.

25 For example, see Lucio Ceva and Andrea Curami, *industria bellica anni trenta : commesse militari, l'Ansaldo ed altri* (Milan: Franco Angeli, 1992).

26 Maurizio Simoncelli, "L'Industria Militare Italiana nella seconda Guerra mondiale", *Disarmo,* No. 1-2, January 1996, p.1.

27 Fredmano Spairani, Un*a politica aeronautica* (Milan: Franco Angeli, 1995), p.247.

A New Chief of Staff

In September 1939, Chief of Staff Valle ran into trouble when at a meeting of the chiefs of staff of the armed forces chaired by Pietro Badoglio he opposed Italy's participation in another conflict by stating that the air service was not prepared for war. On that occasion Valle also proposed to suspend the sale of S.79 bombers to Yugoslavia, a practice that was fairly common during the 1930s whereby the regime aimed to increase state revenues by selling goods to foreign countries. His opponents, however, argued that it was necessary to improve Italy's balance of trade and his demand was not heard. The following month Valle was dismissed. As the new Chief of Staff (*sottosegretario di Stato per l'Aeronautica* and *Capo di Stato Maggiore*) Francesco Pricolo took the reins of the RA on 10 November 1939, he immediately ordered an inventory of combat worthy aircraft. The internal investigation into the RA revealed that of the 2,802 aircraft in service, there were only 536 bombers and 191 fighters that could be readily fielded for combat. The viable force was comprised of 388 S.79, and 148 Fiat BR.20 bombers, 143 Fiat CR.42, 19 Fiat G.50 and 29 *Macchi* C.200 fighters. Initially there were 24 *Stormi* bombers and eight fighters. The report concluded that compared to the RAF and the *Aéronautique Militaire,* the RA's modest force was not in a position to enter into a prolonged conflict for control of the Mediterranean Sea.

Upon learning of the survey results, *Generale* Pricolo accused his predecessor Valle of having run the organization into the ground. The accusation against Valle was unfounded but it lay bare some of the weaknesses of the air service, mainly a fragmented manufacturing base, a fleet comprised of over twenty aircraft models which varied widely in effectiveness and efficiency and some glaring gaps in weaponry such as the lack of long range bombers or torpedo bombers. Pricolo's accusations against Valle led to a trial in which ultimately the latter was acquitted. Pricolo in his memoirs wrote that upon taking the reins of the service he was shocked and surprised by the fact that the air service was so weak but being an insider, he was the former commander of the 2ª *Squadra Aerea*, it is likely that Pricolo was well aware of the general state of the RA prior to being elevated to the top. His accusations were primarily a means to deflect the blame on one individual rather than upon the entire organization.

Given the necessity to renew and enlarge the fleet, *Generale* Pricolo first order of business was thus to hasten the introduction of a new series of fighters that were powered by German engines thus continuing the work of his predecessor who had authorized the new weapons.

But the lack of aircraft was not the only problem that plagued the service. As Jack Greene asserts the Italian aviation industry and its wider base of sub suppliers was also largely unprepared for a major war. Specifically, the industrial base was not wide enough to support a prolonged struggle:

> On the whole, Italian aviation industry was badly organized and inefficient, producing a wide variety of aircraft types in small numbers. The various companies involved resisted manufacturing each other's more successful designs, and the almost artisan production methods resulted in production times that were more than 50 percent longer than for comparable German aircraft. The Italian air force largely depended on radial engines, but these low powered machines seldom exceeded 1,000 horsepower. Adoption of the bulkier but much more powerful German designed Daimler-Benz inline engine solved that problem. The fact that the Fiat CR.42, a wood and canvas biplane fighter with nonretractable landing

> gear was still in production in 1944 reveals the sad state of Italian aircraft production. Italian fighters were all under armed because of financial considerations and were poorly designed. Radios were not installed in all aircraft until 1942.[28]

Thus another objective by the new Chief of Staff appeared, at least in its intent to be a major overhaul of the industry to reorient production, eliminate obsolete aircraft models and, ultimately, hasten the introduction of new weapons. During the war this intent would take the form of an institutional special commission whose objective was to modernize the fleet by establishing new production criteria's and by closing down the production of older, obsolete aircraft models.

By 1939 the industry had grown but its size and industrial might paled in comparison to the monthly aircraft output of France, Britain and the United States. In 1938 the domestic industry was able to satisfy 76% of the total number of armored units requested by the army, 22% of artillery ammunition, 27% of the aircraft ordered by the RA and 22% of the number of aircraft engines requested by the service. Facing greater demand for armaments in 1939 the lag between demand and industry output became even greater than in 1938 in certain categories. In 1939 only 14% of the artillery ammunition demand was supplied, while industry met 42% of the number of aircraft and aircraft engines requested and 10% of machine guns ordered by the army.[29] In France, for example, industry in 1939 met 70% of production demand across all segments.[30] Second, Italy's industrial base was still fairly fragmented with sixteen companies that manufactured one or more aircraft model: Ausa, Breda, Cab, Cansa, Caproni-Taliendo, Caproni-Vizzola, Crda, Fiat Aviazione, Imam, Macchi, Nardi, Piaggio, Regggiane, Sai and Savoia Marchetti. In contrast, by 1939, Britain's government had significantly reduced the number of aircraft suppliers forcing the standardization of production around fewer models.[31] The Spitfire, for example, was preferred over other fighters while Italy's air ministry still entertained new fighter proposals from *Reggiane, Macchi, Fiat* and others. Third, most Italian manufacturers had plants that were still small and artisan in nature. These were labor intensive shops that did not follow an industrial process. Planes in the 1930s were mainly constructed out of wood and therefore to modernize itself Italian industry had to move away from wood and embrace steel thus overhauling the skills of its work force. Historian Brian Sullivan writes with regard to Italian pre-war production aircraft and engine methods that they were mainly artisanal in nature: "All constructed their products in relatively small batches using high skilled labor. These methods sprang from deep roots in Italian artisan culture. The Air Ministry favored such traditions and the regime's labor policies promoted them. Aircraft manufacturers favored them as well. But that reflected technological backwardness. Lack of sufficient machine tools left aviation firms highly dependent on the small number of highly skilled craftsmen who dominated the aviation industry workforce. Semi-skilled laborers could have been introduced into the system to expand production significantly only if they could have been put to work

28 Jack Greene, "Air Force, Italy" in Spencer C. Tucker, *World War II: The Definitive Encyclopedia* (New York: ABC-CLIO, 2016), p.871.
29 Maurizio Simoncelli, "L'Industria Militare Italiana nella seconda Guerra mondiale", *Disarmo*, No. 1-2, January 1996, p.1.
30 Ibid.
31 Keith Hayward, *The British Aircraft Industry* (Manchester: Manchester University Press, 1989).

running specialized machine tools."[32] Moreover, most companies were also reluctant to merge with their rivals to scale production and their relatively small size in many instances prevented them from purchasing expensive machine tools to automate aspects of the production process. Thus, they took longer on average than their counterparts in France, Germany, or Britain to achieve a finished, assembled product. For example it took 4,500 man hours to assemble the German Bf.109, while it took on average 21,000 man hours to complete the *Macchi* C.200.[33] Fourth, Italian aircraft radial engines were the industry's Achilles' heel being inferior to those made abroad. The engine being the main determining factor behind an aircraft design and performance, held back Italian aircraft development. For example, many aircraft were of mixed wood and metal construction because of the constraints of the radial engine that imposed limitations on the overall weight of the aircraft. Lacking a domestic aircraft engine manufacturer such as Rolls Royce or Daimler Benz, that acted as a magnet for aircraft design and production, the Italian aviation industry was always at a disadvantage versus its peers. As Andrea Curami asserts in relation to fighter aircraft: "A critical evaluation of the pre-war period demonstrates that the chiefs of *Stato Maggiore Regia Aeronautica* underestimated the importance of the engine. It was impossible to improvise engine design in six months and start its production in series in three months. The heads of *Alfa Romeo* of Pomigliano d'Arco, for example, could only manufacture 74 Db 601 engines in 1941 because it took the plant more than a year to set up the engines production line."[34]

Having a large scale design and manufacturer of engines of the likes of Rolls Royce, for example, would have likely led to the introduction of a fighter such as the *Reggiane* 2001 prior to 1942 and possibly have led to the introduction of a proper torpedo bomber to replace the S.79 that by 1943 had become obsolete. Thus, *Fiat, Piaggio* and *Alfa Romeo,* whose origins lay in the car manufacturing industry, were not able to advance aircraft design and manufacturing in such a speedy fashion like Rolls Royce or Daimler Benz could. Most importantly, they had to rely on foreign engines along with a costly overhaul of their production methods in order to do so.

Five, although Italy enjoyed a geographic advantage as the war against Britain was fought in the Mediterranean basin, the economic balance favored Britain, which possessed an economy several times larger than Italy's. Moreover, while Britain and its Commonwealth enjoyed a diverse and robust industrial infrastructure, Italy's was more limited. In 1940, for example, Britain produced 224.3 Megatons (Mt) of coal, 11.9 Mt of crude oil, 17.7 Mt of iron ore, and 13.0 Mt of steel, compared to 4.4 Mt of coal, 0.01 Mt of crude oil, 1.2 Mt of iron ore and 2.1 Mt of steel in Italy. Whereas Britain, in large part thanks to its Commonwealth, was largely self-sufficient in key resources, Italy relied on foreign sources of raw materials. Rome imported 75 percent of its steel, 80 percent of its coal, and all of its rubber, copper, and nickel. In 1940, approximately 80 percent of its crude and refined oil stocks came from German controlled plants. Whereas Italy received much of its war-supporting materials from Germany, Britain was not dependent on foreign sources, but primarily on the Commonwealth. The vast majority of the Italian workforce was employed in agriculture while only 3.8 million workers were employed

32 Brian Sullivan, "Downfall of the Regia Aeronautica" in Robin Higham (ed.), *Why Air Forces Fail* (Lexington: University Press of Kentucky, 2006), p.153.

33 Ibid., p.154.

34 Andrea Curami, "Piani e progetti dell'aeronautica italiana 1939-1943 Stato maggiore e industrie", *Italia Contemporanea*, No. 187, June 1992, p.256.

in industry compared to 8.7 million in Britain and 13 million in Germany. Unlike Britain or Germany, Italy had also fought two wars in the 1930s that had absorbed key resources.[35]

The economy did not improve significantly and this was a major limiting factor to the war effort. In 1940 and 1941 there was an uptick in production, but then it began to decline in 1942 due to material supply and fuel constraints in addition to Allied bombings of factories. Overall Italian industrial mobilization for the war turned out to be much weaker than during the First World War failing to provide the armed forces the weaponry and ammunition that was necessary for a multi-year conflict. A great indicator is artillery gun production by month. In 1939 industrial output was of 71 guns per month, while in 1918 it was 700 per month.[36] Another indicator is the demand versus the output of aircraft as Italy lacked adequate raw materials to develop a true air armada. In 1940, the air service requested 7,200 aircraft, but industry could provide only approximately 45 percent of that figure.[37] This was due to the lack of adequate state planning, the fragmented nature of the industrial base which limited centralized control, and lastly the cozy relationship between top industrial concerns and the state which hindered innovation. Aircraft production peaked in 1941 but declined in 1942 and 1943 given the lack of raw materials caused by the Allied stranglehold on the Atlantic, Italian plants dependency on German manufacturing components, fuel shortages, and work stoppages due to Allied bombings.

The poor state of the RA was not a singular deficiency of one branch of the armed forces. The other services, especially the army were also not ready for a prolonged conflict. As Burgwyn asserts: "The country was ill prepared to fight a modern war. The soldiers, many of whom were semi-literate and half-trained, bore equipment that was old and inefficient."[38]

Just a few months before the outbreak of the war Carlo Favagrossa, undersecretary of munitions, had submitted a report that on the state of the armed forces. In the report Favagrossa affirmed that the army had seventy-four divisions, of which only nineteen were combat ready in both men and weapons. The army faced shortages in fuel, artillery and ammunition. The armored units were only three and were equipped with tanks of three and a half tons compared with the twenty-ton tanks that equipped the German and British armored units. The state of motorization of the army and special forces was low. The army, for example, had no jeeps or armored vehicles. The navy had a strong force of 576 vessels of various sizes but it had glaring shortcomings such as the lack of radar, no air cover or aircraft carriers. The air force had approximately 1,900 aircraft but they were not as technologically advanced as those of the enemy and included no long range heavy bombers or torpedo bombers.[39]

35 Brian Sullivan, "Fascist Italy's Military Involvement in the Spanish Civil War", *The Journal of Military History*, Vol. 59, No. 4 (1995), p.711.
36 Carlo Favagrossa, *Perche' perdemmo la Guerra* (Milan: Rizzoli, 1946), p.12.
37 Ibid.
38 James Burgwyn, *Mussolini Warlord* (New York: Enigma, 2008), p.4.
39 Marco Innocenti, *L'Italia del 1940* (Milan: Mursia, 1996), p.66.

2

Torpedo Bomber Development

In 1922 the *Regia Marina* issued a request for quote for the construction of a seaplane that could drop two 500 kg bombs or launch a 1,000 kg torpedo. To procure the latter the RM signed a contract with the Whitehead firm based in Fiume, the largest naval torpedo supplier, for the development of an aerial warhead. The RM's interest in this subject matter derived primarily from experiments conducted before and during the First World War. In 1914 a Navy *Capitano* Alessandro Guidoni, for example, launched a dummy torpedo from a twin-engine Henry Farman Model 1910 plane. In 1917 the Italian air service with *Sottotenente Pilota* Luigi Ridolfi flew a *Caproni* CA.3 from the 201ª *Squadriglia* to launch a 600-kg torpedo against an Austro-Hungarian ship moored at Pola on the night between 2/3 October. The raid against the ship failed because the great anti-aircraft fire by the Austro-Hungarians prevented the pilot from launching the torpedo from a favorable distance but despite this setback the Italians continued to experiment with this technology. In March 1918 they created the *1ª Squadriglia Aerosiluranti* (first torpedo bomber squad) but it existed in name only. The unit was never brought up to full staff and it did not carry out torpedo launches given that it lacked dedicated equipment. After the war it was dissolved.

In the postwar period interest in the aerial torpedo was renewed mainly by the Navy. The following projects were considered in 1923 as a response to an RM's request for quote for a seaplane capable of launching a torpedo: *Macchi* M.24, *Savoia Marchetti* S.55, *Piaggio* P.4 and *Cantiere Navale Triestino* CS.800. These four projects by four different companies were proposed as a response to the quote request. At first all four were considered as potential candidates for the aerial torpedo application, but a final selection was made at the tail end of 1923 when the *Macchi* M.24 and the *SM* S.55 were chosen by RM planners. The reason was that both firms were further ahead in the design of the aircraft and also because they were more established players in aircraft manufacturing. In 1925 the first torpedo launches were made in Varese Lake and Lake Maggiore against stationary targets. Both sets of launches from the *Macchi* M.24 were made at approximately five feet from the water.

In 1926 the RM obtained the authorization to constitute a special experimental unit based in La Spezia devoted to the aerial torpedo bomber specialty. The agreement brokered with the RA called for the RM to supply the warheads and the personnel to load the torpedoes while the former to supply the planes and the crews. Meanwhile, tests were continued launching torpedoes from S.55 aircraft belonging to 187ª *Squadriglia* against moving targets at sea near La Spezia. Then for a few years little was done because of a lack of a viable aerial torpedo. The main problem was the dropping of torpedoes at very low altitudes which caused the warhead to suffer damage when impacting the water or to enter the water too steeply which caused the torpedo to dive very deeply and then take a different trajectory toward the target than the one originally anticipated. Some modifications were necessary which were finally made in 1933. A device that allowed the angled launch of the torpedo, mainly to cushion the impact of the aerial torpedo on the water, was successfully added to modify the basic design. This took the form of an aerodynamic tail with the addition of wood stabilizing fins for the air drop.[1] That year, having secured a new aerial torpedo prototype, the RM resumed trials with S.55 aircraft of 91° *Gruppo Idrobombardieri* which were held at Orbetello, Cadimare and then at Whitehead's headquarters in Fiume. The launches were taking place with the aircraft travelling at a speed of 180 km/h and the drop at an altitude of 30 meters above the water.

In order to further consolidate the gains that had been made the two branches of the armed forces agreed to constitute a torpedo bomber unit on 1 September 1935. The agreement was brokered by *Ammiraglio* Domenico Cavagnari and the head of the RA Valle. Under this agreement the latter was responsible for: securing a number of aircraft for the torpedo launches, executing the launches, and the purchase of aerial warheads that were to be produced by Whitehead. Meanwhile, the RM was responsible for funding an aerial torpedo prototype, the transfer of its torpedo technical personnel into the new unit, the purchase of the torpedoes to be used in the trial launches and lastly, the transfer of the warheads to the bases used for the launches. Following this agreement a prototype of a 450mm aerial torpedo was developed by Whitehead that could be launched at approximately 100 meters from the water by an aircraft traveling 300 km/h. The trial launches were made with a *Savoia Marchetti* S.81 carrying two torpedoes at altitudes between 80-100 meters above the water. For its time the development of such an aerial torpedo/bomber combination was quite an achievement as other national states were still much further behind. But despite these positive trials, the agreement suffered a major blow when RA representatives did not approve the new weapon since in their view it exposed their pilots to too many risks. While arguing that in general the air force was interested in the project, they also argued that a working torpedo bomber had to operate and especially be able to launch the torpedo at much higher altitude. The RA at the time and especially its Chief of Staff Valle was skeptical because the torpedoes were being released too close to the water, while it was believed that RA pilots could never operate successfully in that fashion. Valle insisted that Whitehead develop a torpedo that could be launched at 1,148 feet (350 meters) above the water and by an aircraft traveling at 311 mph (500 km/h). Unable to meet such stringent technical specifications, Whitehead was forced to put the project on hold while Valle stated that the "torpedo, as conceptualized today, is not a suitable weapon for the air force."[2] Similarly, *Generale* Ajmone Cat in a 1934 article had written that: "Contrary to public opinion, the air force will not develop the torpedo bomber as an offensive weapon."[3] He had also argued that since the funds available to the RA were not unlimited, the latter ought to continue investing in the development of new bombs for standard bombers rather than spending its funds on aerial torpedo prototypes which were very expensive and were also in an experimental stage. Despite the break-up of the agreement, the RM continued to purchase aerial warheads from Whitehead

1 Giuseppe Santoro, *L'aeronautica italiana nella seconda guerra mondiale*, vol. I, p.61.
2 Ibid.
3 Il Messagero, 27 March, 1934.

and to conduct torpedo bomber trials, while it has been hypothesized that the RA walked away from the agreement because its Chief of Staff *Generale* Valle feared that the torpedo bombers would wind up under RM control.[4] RM purchases were continued in batches of eight aerial torpedoes at a time, one of which was used in the trials with a S.81 flying out of Gorizia airport and launching the warhead against a stationary ship in the Gulf of Trieste. While the agreement between the two services languished Whitehead was busy patenting there aerial torpedoes, each with its own specifications and developed specifically for the use on aircraft. All were designed and manufactured at Whitehead's expense. Given that the air force had not placed at Whitehead's disposal one single aircraft to conduct experiments, the latter took it upon itself to fabricate and install a special catapult near the bay at Fiume, suitable to simulate the same dynamic forces that occur in real launches from aircraft. The catapult was used to conduct test launches for the three torpedoes. This appears to be a main difference between the Italian and the experience of aerial torpedo development in other national states such as the United States or Britain where the state was fully behind the endeavor providing financial backing to industry. In the Italian case there was interest on the part of the military services, but the state did not provide any major financial backing.

450 mm Silurificio Whitehead F5W Specifications

Ship Class Used On	Aircraft
Date Of Design	1938
Date In Service	1940
Weight	1,930 lbs. (876 kg)
Overall Length	17 ft. 9 in. (5.460 m)
Explosive Charge	374.5 lbs. (170 kg)
Range / Speed	3,300 yards (3,000 m) / 40 knots
Power	Wet-heater

Source: Petrucci (2018)

The warhead finally selected by Whitehead was the MAS 450/170 / 5.40 (diameter (mm) / weight of explosive charge (kg)/ length in meters) built exclusively in two locations: *Silurificio di Fiume Whitehead* and later by the *Silurificio Italiano* of Baia (Naples). The latter was called *Siluro Italiano* (SI). It also was a 450mm weapon and differed in length only from the Whitehead torpedo, being 5.25 meters or 17.22 feet long. The warhead had a range of 3,000 meters (or 1.86 miles) at 40 knots. The launch took place, as a rule, at a speed of 180-200 mph at an altitude ideally of 30-70 meters (100-250 feet) from the water, in these conditions the torpedo entered the water with an inclination of 30° degrees and stabilized after initially dropping on impact 10 meters or more into the water and travelling approximately 160 meters. The favorable distance to the target was approximately 1,000-700 meters (0.62-0.43 miles) from an enemy ship. At such a distance the torpedo had enough time to stabilize without the risk of passing under the enemy ship or falling short of the intended target. While the Navy continued experimenting

4 Jack Greene and Alessandro Massignani, *The Naval War in the Mediterranean* (Norfolk, Virginia: Naval Institute Press, 2011), p.89.

and continued to partner with Whitehead, between 1933 and 1937 the RA debated within its official monthly journal "*Rivista Aeronautica*" whether the service should focus its efforts at all on the torpedo bomber. Majority opinion was that the service should dedicate its limited budget in advancing the introduction of new weapons for high altitude bombing rather than the aerial torpedoes which were much more expensive to design and build. In one issue in 1934, for example, a RA planner argued that a comparative analysis of the costs related to build standard weapons versus torpedoes showed a great disparity. The latter were much more expensive to build and their effectiveness was doubtful.[5] The RM's reply appeared in one of the following issues arguing that aerial torpedoes trials had demonstrated their effectiveness.[6] In issue n. 10 one of the most well-known military aviators of the time, *Capitano* A. Trizzino, recommended that the RA continue to focus on 'its own weapons and tactics mainly bombs and horizontal bombings", whilst eschewing torpedoes.[7]

In November 1937 a Cant.Z 506B was delivered to the 35° *Stormo* to be used as a torpedo bomber, but the latter was inexplicably never used in the role. At the same time the first S.79 torpedo bomber prototype was also delivered:

> In 1937 the Air Force General Staff arranged for an S. 79 aircraft to be equipped for the launch of W-type torpedoes built by the domestic supplier. As a result, the first aircraft, equipped for launching a single torpedo, entered service in November 1937. In March 1938 it pushed for the S. 79 to be equipped to carry two torpedoes. In August this modification was completed by Savoia Marchetti, the manufacturer of the aircraft. The first tests revealed that the prototype was not ready, and some further modifications had to be made.
>
> In September 1939 the first S. 79 prototype with two warheads arrived on the field of Gorizia and, after tests and modifications, in October it was possible to begin its serial production. As can be seen from this brief chronology, the trials and experiments had been conducted very slowly, without a precise vision of the importance of the problem, and without a determined will to reach a solution quickly.
>
> Not only that, but for years between the air force and the navy a narrow minded and not edifying struggle took place to establish which service was responsible for the supply of torpedoes and who should pay for them.
>
> The outbreak of the conflict in 1939 found the question still unsolved.[8]

The choice of the S.79 for the torpedo bomber application was a fallback position. Since the early experiments conducted by the RM had been carried out with seaplanes, that were reputed to be too slow, and a purpose designed torpedo bomber was not designed, the fallback position in 1937-38 became the use of a modified S.79 in the torpedo bomber role. The aircraft was a trimotor medium bomber, much larger than American or Japanese torpedo fighter aircraft used in 1941 which therefore made it an unusual choice for the torpedo specialty which required high maneuverability and a limited silhouette to effectuate the torpedo launches in the face of concentrated enemy fire. According to RA planners the S.79, although not originally designed

5 Archivio Storico Aeronautica Militare: Rivista Aeronautica, "Aerosiluro o bomba?" ,N. 3, 1934.
6 Archivio Storico Aeronautica Militare: Rivista Aeronautica, "Il siluro", N. 7, 1934.
7 Archivio Storico Aeronautica Militare: Rivista Aeronautica, "I propri metodi", N.10, 1934.
8 Giuseppe Santoro, *L'aeronautica Italiana nella Seconda Guerra Mondiale*, p.134.

as a torpedo bomber, offered several outstanding specifications such as its top speed and its strong defensive armament, which made it the best choice amongst the aircraft available to *Regia Aeronautica* in 1937. Between 1937 and 1939, however, no major strides were made in training and arming a torpedo bomber unit within the RA which continued to show a limited interest in the discipline.

The issue came back with force to the fore when the Second World War broke out as Pietro Badoglio, the head of *Comando Supremo* (High Command), and his staff were driven by the necessity of introducing new and more lethal weapons.

On 26 January 1939 at a meeting of the armed forces chaired by Badoglio *Ammiraglio* Cavagnari argued that the RA should be equipped with a torpedo bomber force and a large number of its planes should be retrofitted to enable them to carry the torpedo. Valle's reply was the RA did not have the funds for the undertaking. The discussion then branched out to warhead production:

> Badoglio – This involves the purchase of 30 torpedoes for torpedo bombers. There is a divergence of views between the Navy and Air Force on this issue. The same has happened in Germany.
>
> Cavagnari – For me the problem of a torpedo for torpedo bombers is already solved. We made a type that can be launched from 120m altitude, at a speed of 300 km. No country has managed to make one that can be launched from more than 40-50m altitude and speed of 180-200km. Therefore, I can no longer consider our torpedo in an experimental phase and, therefore, I believe that I should no longer have to pay for experiments."
>
> Valle – For the Air Force, this type of torpedo cannot be used.
>
> Cavagnari – I repeat that the agreement established with the Air Force clearly states that the Navy will pay for the torpedo prototypes, and this the Navy has done. With the prototypes, the altitude and speed parameters set by the Whitehead company were brilliantly achieved in the tests in Fiume, as possible with the type of torpedo which has been realized. Therefore the current production of 30 prototype torpedoes is no longer relevant to the Navy and therefore I believe I do not have to pay anything."[9]

Meantime, *Generale* Valle of *Regia Aeronautica* continued to argue that the service did not have the budget to procure the torpedoes. Unable to compromise, the meeting adjourned with no decision taken on who should pay for them.

Valle was not a strong believer in the aerial torpedo based upon the fact that it could not be launched at higher altitudes and also because the air force had a limited budget. But when Valle was forced to resign on 31 October 1939 as *sottosegretario di Stato per l'Aeronautica* the new RA Chief of Staff *Generale* Pricolo took a more favorable position toward aerial torpedoes. On 12 November 1939 at a meeting of the heads of the armed forces Badoglio argued that the RM and the RA should put their past differences aside and work toward the common objective of developing a viable torpedo to be used by aircraft. On 18 November the issue of the torpedo bomber

9 *Verbali delle riunioni tenute dal Capo di Stato Maggiore Generale,* tomo I (Rome; Ufficio Storico, 1992), p.13.

was raised again by Badoglio at another meeting of *Comando Supremo* with the service chiefs. Here are Badoglio's recollections of the meeting that show that when the discussion turned to the issue of torpedo bombers both services still shifted the blame to each other:

> Badoglio: "We should no longer discuss if the bomb is more effective than the torpedo, these are opinions without any practical confirmation and should be examined from a more realistic point of view. We have too long of an exchange of letters at this point."
>
> Cavagnari: The principle is not on the table but only who pays for it. The Navy holds that this problem has been solved for 3 years. The Air Force must purchase them.
>
> Badoglio: "It is not useful to deal here again with the problem of aircraft torpedoes. I want to avoid discussions that would result in a waste of words. Who pays is always the state. Therefore, we should not become rigid on this question.
>
> Air Force representative: The question is already settled. The Air Force was unable to buy 30 torpedoes because the production plants are busy with the order going to Germany.
>
> Cavagnari: This is not true.[10]

The meeting minutes once again point to the ongoing rivalry between the two services and their inability to compromise on major issues of national preparedness. They also demonstrate that the Chief of the General Staff did not exert full control over the branches of the armed forces. Badoglio was in fact the Chief of the General staff of the armed forces but did not have a full planning staff to prepare for war, nor the power of the purse to coerce the services into doing what *Comando Supremo* desired. In the case of the torpedo bombers it is clear that his powers to force the service chiefs into a compromise decision were quite limited. His planners' span of control (C*omando Supremo* structure under Badoglio was based on six officers and their staff, each officer was drawn from one of the services along with the staff) was also limited as they exerted scarce influence upon the three service chiefs that organically were under Badoglio but were ultimately responsible to the head of the regime.

Moreover, the three service chiefs were very defensive of their own turf to the point that they challenged efforts by *Comando Supremo* to centralize power. This fragmented organization created loopholes as each service branch could develop its own war plans independently and conduct its own pre-war preparations without much coordination with the other branches.[11] The RM, for example, was preparing for a clash against the British fleet but it lacked both aircraft carriers and radar and had very few seaplanes for reconnaissance and no fighters under its control. Thus it was particularly lacking in the aerial protection of the surface fleet and was totally dependent on the RA for reconnaissance. The army had a doctrine for a rapid course war but not the means to achieve it since its infantry had a low rate of motorization and Italian tanks were light and without radio. Meanwhile, the RA was the weaker of the three services being without the adequate number of aircraft to face a long war of attrition. As far as the torpedo bombers were concerned the history shows that for many years both the RM and the RA showed only a modest interest in its development. No one owned the project, although the RM saw value in the development of aerial torpedoes through its trials

10 Jack Greene and Alessandro Massignani, *The Naval War*, p.61.

11 Giorgio Rochat, 'Lo sforzo bellico 1940–43: Analisi di una sconfitta', *Italia contemporanea*, N.160 (September 1985), pp.8–9.

and its collaboration with Whitehead. As a follow up to the 18 November 1939 meeting the newly appointed service head of *Regia Aeronautica Generale* Pricolo, prodded by Badoglio, in late November 1939 placed an order for an initial batch of aerial torpedoes: "Shortly after his appointment he had hastily ordered a batch of 30 aerial torpedoes from Whitehead. To further accelerate this process following Italy's entry into the war, Pricolo ordered a further batch of 50 aerial torpedoes (formerly allocated to Germany) for the air force's new role in July 1940. Thanks to his initiative, Italy at least had a modest quantity of torpedoes at its disposal during the first months of the war."[12]

German air force planners had by 1939 already commissioned a large order of torpedoes from Whitehead as stated by Petrucci: "The German armed forces (both Navy and Air Force) were particularly interested in the results of the tests on the airborne torpedo, and after having witnessed a cycle of trials specifically organized for their benefit, on 1 April 1939 placed an order for 300 torpedoes type W 170 x 450 x 5,46 , even before the Italian Navy and Air Force placed corresponding orders for their own use."[13] This German purchase was not a main factor in the RA decision which was influenced primarily by Badoglio's interest in aerial torpedoes and his push for the introduction of new weapons generally. The German interest in the Whitehead torpedo however, created production bottlenecks as the latter was not able to meet the demands of the Italian Navy, *Kriegsmarine* and the RA all at once.

In his diaries *Generale* Pricolo affirmed that the torpedo bomber concept was not new in 1939 at the time he placed the initial order as it had already been considered in 1932-33 after the RM had conducted drills with torpedo boats and seaplanes.[14] Furthermore, he stated the torpedo bomber in 1939 suited the RA's objective of introducing new weapons aimed at potentially halting British operations in the Mediterranean. Pushed by the crisis, it would ultimately be a key juncture such as the Second World War to force the RA and RM to compromise and finally take a decision on the constitution of a torpedo bomber unit. Given its relative effectiveness in the war it can be argued that both services underestimated the potential of the new weapon and their delay in launching the new unit after the war had already started was a major setback for Italian operations in the Mediterranean in 1940. As air force historian Ferruccio Botti asserts the availability of a well drilled torpedo bomber unit at the beginning of the conflict could have yielded some major dividends for Italy in the early naval/aerial clashes in the Mediterranean.[15]

There are several interpretations that explain how the torpedo bomber units came to be. The official historian of the service Giuseppe Santoro, for example, argues that the *RA* was the main proponent of the aerial warheads and that it worked on the project for more than a decade.[16] This explanation clashes with the RM's version of events. *Ammiraglio* Iachino on the other hand argues that: "After the experience of Punta Stilo everyone naturally agreed on the need for us to develop torpedo aircraft and this was accordingly done, but unfortunately precious months had

12 Marco Mattioli, *Savoia-Marchetti S.79 Sparviero*, p.5.

13 Bruno Petrucci, "The Italian period of the Whitehead Torpedo" <http://protorpedo-rijeka.hr/wp/wp-content/uploads/2018/04/22.pdf > (accessed 12 February 2021).

14 Francesco Pricolo, *La Regia Aeronautica nella seconda guerra mondiale* (Milan: Mondadori, 1971), p.21.

15 Ferruccio Botti, "La Guerra aerea" in *L'Italia in Guerra, 1940* (Rome: Ufficio Storico, 1991), p.277.

16 Giuseppe Santoro, *L'aeronautica Italiana nella Seconda Guerra Mondiale* (Rome: Ufficio Storico, 1957), p.63.

been lost in the meantime."[17] He also points to the fact that during the interwar years it was the Navy and not the air force that continued to advocate for aerial torpedoes

It can be argued that both interpretations are partially incorrect. The development of aerial warheads was undertaken primarily by the RM during the interwar years which used its budget to fund several technical modifications made by Whitehead to improve aerial torpedo performance and also conducted a number of trials despite a general lack of interest by the RA. The latter was lukewarm about the project up until *Generale* Valle resigned. Then, mainly through the directives of Badoglio did the new leader *Generale* Pricolo rehash the issue of aerial torpedo development in a forceful manner which led to the consequent constitution of a dedicated torpedo bomber unit. The unsatisfactory results of the Battle of Punta Stilo then hastened the development and introduction of the torpedo bomber units, although these units had already been in formation prior to this important aerial/naval battle of July 1940.

Following this RA about turn, Whitehead was commissioned to deliver aerial torpedoes on a steady basis, although its main responsibility remained the production of naval warheads for submarines and torpedo boats. Having secured a modicum supply of torpedoes the next step was the constitution of a dedicated air force unit that was to be trained and focused exclusively on specializing in the launching of aerial warhead. After several months on 25 July 1940 a new experimental unit called *Reparto Sperimentale Aerosiluranti* (Experimental Torpedo Bomber Unit) was assembled by Pricolo with order n. 46731 and headquartered at Gorizia airfield in north-east Italy. It was deployed to the 6a *Divisione Aerea Falco*. Command of the unit was handed over to *Capitano* Amedeo Moioli, replaced shortly after by *Maggiore* Vincenzo Dequal, a veteran of the Spanish Civil War, who was awarded two silver medals of military valor for his service as the commander of the *Squadriglia Cucaracha*. Initially, volunteers were not accepted as the Chief of Staff of the *Regia Aeronautica* wanted only the best pilots for this unit. The latter were thus handpicked directly by the Chief of Staff amongst the veterans of the air service. Those selected were *Maggiore* Enrico Fusco, *Tenenti* Carlo Emanuele Buscaglia, Franco Melley and Carlo Copello and *Sottotenenti* Guido Robone and Aldo Forzinetti. Two naval officers, *Tenente di Vascello* Giovanni Marazio and *Sottotenente di Vascello* Giovanni Bertoli, were also added to the newly formed unit given their experience with naval torpedoes and their ability to recognize enemy ships. The last real tug of war between the RM and the air force centered on these naval officers on board the torpedo bombers. Initially the RM insisted that its observers be given the command of torpedo operations since they knew how to distinguish British from Italian ships and also knew how best and when to attack them. The air force on the other hand, argued that the pilot of a torpedo bomber had to act quickly to aim and then disengage and that the naval observers could not reasonably demand that a pilot fly over the enemy ships multiple times in order to get a more accurate shot at the target. [18] Moreover that only the pilot was in a position to release the lever that launched the torpedo because of the cramped environment of the S.79. Ultimately, the RA prevailed primarily because the pilot controlled the aircraft and also because the communication instrumentation on board the S.79 was limited hence reducing the possibility of the RM observers to influence operations.

17 Angelo Iachino, *Guado e Matapan (*Milan: Mondadori, 1963), p.124.
18 Franco Pagliano, *Storia di 10,000 aereoplani* (Milan: Mursia, 2003), p.127.

For the next few weeks the newly formed group conducted extensive training exercises thus trying to make up for the time lost during the pre-war period. During the period between 30 July to 7 August 1940 the unit's war diary reports that twelve flight training sessions were held, three of which culminated with the launch of dummy torpedoes.[19] Some pilots such as Carlo Copello, for example, conducted only two torpedo drops given the relative short duration of the training. The launches took place above the waters near Pola harbor where the crews released dummy torpedoes against a First World War Austro-Hungarian ship (the *Cattaro*) which was located in shallow waters. This was a stationary target. No training was provided for moving targets. During this time flight training was integrated with instructions on how to spot and identify enemy ships. The trainees were given a booklet that included drawings and descriptions of Royal Navy ships by class and type so they could identify them during their reconnaissance operations. Shortly thereafter the unit was renamed *Reparto Speciale Aerosilurante* (Special Torpedo Unit) and placed again under the command of the 6ª *Divisione Falco*. As Greene and Massignani assert by this time: "The crews were skilled pilots, but they were still inexperienced in torpedo operations. Only two or three practice attacks against stationary targets had been made and they still had not worked out the optimum altitude to drop their weapons from."[20]

One of the trainees of the torpedo training, Martino Aichner, has left us with this recollection of what the practice flights entailed:

> Five or six kilometers before reaching the beach I had brought the plane down and very close to the water in order to spring the surprise attack. This was the tactic of the torpedo bombers which consisted in getting at a working distance of approximately two kilometers from the ship by literally almost brushing against the water a few meters above the sea and then suddenly pouncing upon the enemy. By flying so close to the water we were not only able to avoid getting spotted by the enemy, but we also went undetected by enemy radar.[21]

Order of Battle of the *Reparto Speciale Aerosilurante*, August 1940

Officers/Pilots:
1 – *Maggiore* Vincenzo Dequal Comandante.
2 – *Maggiore* Enrico Fusco Vice Comandante.
3 – *Tenente* Carlo Emanuele Buscaglia.
4 – *Tenente* Carlo Copello.
5 – *Tenente* Franco Melley.
6 – *Sotto Tenente* Guido Robone.
7 – *Sotto Tenente* Aldo Forzinetti.

19 Ufficio Storico Aeronautica Militare: Diario storico del 278ª *Reparto Sperimentale Aerosiluranti*, Gorizia, 7 August 1940.
20 Jack Greene and Alessandro Massignani, *The Naval War*, p.90.
21 Martino Aichner, *Il gruppo Buscaglia: Aerosiluranti italiani nella seconda guerra mondiale* (Milan: Mursia, 1990), p.15.

NCOs/Pilots:
1 – Sergente Maggiore Sirolli.
2 – *Sergente Maggiore* Ferrandi.
3 – *Sergente Maggiore* Pipitone.
4 – *Sergente* Deodato.

Officers/Observers *Regia Marina*:
1 – *Tenente* di Vascello Giovanni Marazio.
2 – *Sotto tenente* di Vascello Giovanni Bertoli.

On 3 September 1940 the unit's name was changed again to *278ª Squadriglia Autonoma Aerosiluranti* equipped with five S.79 aircraft already modified to carry torpedoes. By now it was deemed to be fully operational by the air force planners.

In conclusion it can be argued that the air service entered into the conflict in June 1940 without having constituted a torpedo bomber specialty even though it and the RM had experimented with the concept since the 1920s. According to the official historian of the force *Generale* Giuseppe Santoro the development of the discipline was characterized by many false starts and with great delay with respect to the demands of modern warfare. It was "conducted with great delay and without a precise vision and without the will to come to a resolution quickly....The Aeronautica and the Navy gave rise to a deplorable fight regarding which service would ultimately control the torpedo bomber discipline and also with regards to who would purchase the torpedoes and who would ultimately pay for them. This conflict was still unresolved when Italy declared war."[22]

Sparrowhawk

The aircraft selected for the new discipline was the *Savoia Marchetti* 79 that already had been converted as a standard bomber during the Spanish campaign. Prior to the adoption of the S.79 tests were conducted with numerous other planes such as the *Caproni* Ca.33, *Macchi* M.24, S.55, S.81, and the *Cant.* Z 506B. But none of these planes were found to be suitable for effectively carrying a heavy warhead at a reasonable speed. Originally developed as a commercial airliner by Alessandro Marchetti (chief engineer of *Societa' Idrovolanti Alta Italia* working in partnership with Umberto Savoia owner of *Savoia Marchetti*), the S.79 *Sparviero* (Sparrowhawk) would become one of the most formidable weapons of Italy's air force during the Second World War. The original prototype, the S.79P (P for passengers) completed its maiden flight on 2 October 1934. It was based on three 610-hp Piaggio radial engines and could accommodate eight passengers. By that time three engines transport planes like the S.79 (P) were fairly common. In 1935 the aircraft competed at international aviation events setting several world speed records. "The trimotor soon attracted the interest of the *Regia Aeronautica* and, bearing the military serial MM260, it was chosen to transport *Generale di Squadra Aerea* Giuseppe Valle, undersecretary and Chief of Staff, to East Africa to organize

22 Giuseppe Santoro, *L'aeronautica Italiana nella Seconda Guerra Mondiale*, p.134.

the invasion of Abyssinia. On 1 August 1935, flown by *Tenente Colonnello* Attilio Biseo and *Capitano* Gori Castellani, the aircraft flew from Rome for Massawa, in Eritrea, with an Egyptian stopover at Cairo, in just 12 hours. This performance was repeated on the return flight on 5 August, when the aircraft averaged 230 mph. This remarkable round trip made *Generale* Valle a strong supporter of the S.79, and he pressed for the development of a bomber variant, designated S.79M (M for military)."[23] The RA realizing that the plane could be used also in the bomber role began an evaluation of its benefits as a medium bomber. On 8 July 1936 the first S.79 prototype, MM20663, was tested successfully in several flights as a medium bomber.

Participation of the Italian contingent to the Spanish Civil War furnished the opportunity to deploy the S.79 as a medium bomber replacing the obsolete S.81. With this new aircraft, which in 1937 was considered to be state-of-the-art, it was hoped to not only strike at targets deep in Republican territory but also to do so with a plane that was fast and well-armed and more than a match for the Republican fighter aircraft. The first S.79s, belonging to the 12° Stormo, arrived at Palma de Mallorca on 14 February 1937 and shortly thereafter began to target Republican targets. Particularly noteworthy were the S.79 based in the Balearic Islands which were committed in several strikes against Barcelona, Valencia, Alicante and Cartagena, as well as interdiction sorties against maritime traffic aiding the Republicans. Along with the BR.20 the S.79 became one of the workhorses of the *Aviazione Legionaria* with a total of 99 aircraft deployed in the campaign and the loss of only four during combat. Since the S.79 was used extensively as a bomber in Spain prompting *Generale* Pricolo to state that the aircraft had a future as a bomber and possibly as a torpedo bomber despite the fact that it is: "A difficult airplane that performs well only during sunny days because it is utterly unstable. When it's cloudy and windy the pilot cannot take his hands off the steering wheel even for one instant."[24]

Generale Pricolo was not the only one to criticize the performance of the S.79, since during the Spanish campaign the aircraft was considered to be unsuitable by both pilots and crews especially during nighttime operations and while flying in bad weather conditions. Many pilots simply refused to operate it for night operations believing that it would not work effectively. In fact, only one nighttime mission was completed during the campaign when in late afternoon on 1 January 1938 one S.79 took off from Guidonia airfield near Rome to reach Barcelona at 2130 where it dropped eight 100 kilograms bombs and then returned to Rome after midnight. Some pilots as a result of their experience with the S.79 during the campaign were of the opinion that the plane ought to be ditched altogether and that Italy needed to develop a sturdier bomber with four engines along the lines of the most recent technological developments in Britain and America. Others were of the opinion that to be successful the S.79 not only needed to be better escorted by a number of fighters that could intercept enemy planes but also that it should be retrofitted with at least five weapons such as four machine guns and a cannon to protect the crew and fend off challenges from enemy aircraft. Finally, the plane had to be retrofitted with a working radio and the collaboration during flight between *piloti* and *puntatori* (observers and gunners) had to be enhanced.

23 Marco Mattioli, *Savoia-Marchetti S.79 Sparviero*, p.6.
24 Gianni Rocca, *I Disperati*, p.94.

With war clouds looming in 1939, additional S.79s were converted into medium bombers. The cockpit cabin was extended with a bulging top fuselage position that gave the bomber its nickname, *Gobbo Maledetto* (damned hunchback), and four and later five machine guns were mounted in various fuselage positions. Initially the defensive armament of the S.79 consisted of *Breda-SAFAT* machine guns. Three of these were 12.7 mm guns that were fast firing 900 rounds per minute, one of which was positioned in the cockpit, one was rearward firing and positioned in the dorsal hump, while the third was in the ventral position. In the first design there was also a 7.7 mm Lewis Gun that was later replaced first by one and then by two 7.7mm *Breda* guns located in the waist mounts. Of the five machine guns the one located in the dorsal hump was often considered to be the most important as, following the torpedo tactic of making low-level attacks, the *Sparviero* was attacked by enemy fighters typically from the rear and from above. The gun located in the dorsal hump was protected by an aerodynamic shield which gave the gunner some additional protection from the enemy gunfire. The nose of the plane and its front engine were well insulated by several inches of the outer layer thus offering some protection from enemy fire. Due to the fact that Italy had low stockpiles of steel only its main body was made of steel, while the wings were made of wood. This was somewhat acceptable in 1940 but by 1943 standards however, most advanced foreign bombers were made of steel, a factor that saw the *Sparviero* losing ground given its increased vulnerability. "The wood and canvas construction of the Italian bombers caused them to warp when exposed to moisture, offered no protection against machine gun and anti-aircraft fire, and made them easily flammable."[25]

In the 1930s the *Sparviero* was considered to be heavily armed especially because most enemy fighters were not usually fitted with any armor and had fewer machine guns. By the Second World War, however, the *Sparviero*'s vulnerability to newer fighters increased significantly mostly because the latter were faster and better protected. Compared to other bombers at the start of the conflict the *Sparviero* was also considered to be heavily armed but by 1943 things had changed. The defensive armament of the *Sparviero* had not kept up when compared to other more heavily armed bombers such as the Vickers Wellington that was equipped with six 7.69 mm guns, or the Heinkel HE.111 with a 20mm cannon and six machine guns or the American Boeing B.17 'Flying Fortress' equipped with thirteen 12.7mm guns. Other improvements to the S.79 beginning in 1940 included more powerful power plants, improved aerodynamics and retractable landing gear. Finally, the plane was retrofitted with an offset rack under the fuselage so that it could carry a 450mm Whitehead torpedo. Further retrofit work was conducted during the war, enabling the aircraft to carry two torpedoes, however it almost never completed operations carrying two warheads as the aircraft was too slow and less maneuverable with the extra load. The aircraft was operated by a six (sometimes five) men crew: Two pilots (*pilota* and *co-pilota*), a flight engineer (*primo aviere*), a radio operator (*aviere marconista*), a torpedo shooter (*aviere puntatore*), and one machine gunner (*secondo aviere*). After the warhead had been released one of the crew members would become the photographer trying to document the results of the torpedo attack.

25 Brian Sullivan, "Downfall of the Regia Aeronautica" in Robin Higham (ed.), *Why Air Forces Fail* (Lexington: University Press of Kentucky, 2006), p.144.

S.79 Sparviero Serie III Specifications
Engine: Three 780 hp Alfa Romeo 126 RC.34 9-cylinder air cooled radials.
Wingspan: 69 feet 6 2/3 inches
Wing Area: 664 sq. ft.
Length: 51 feet 3 ½ inches
Height: 14 feet 5 ¼ inches
Weight: 14,991 lbs. (empty): 23, 148 lbs. (maximum takeoff)
Maximum Speed: 267 mph at 13,150 feet (without the torpedo).
Climb Rate: 13,150 feet in 13 minutes and 9 seconds.
Ceiling: 21, 325 feet.
Range: 1,223 miles.
Crew: 4 to 6.
Armament: one forward firing fixed 12.7mm Breda-SAFAT machine gun, two flexible 12.7mm Breda-SAFAT machine guns (dorsal and ventral), two 7.7mm Breda-SAFAT machine guns firing from the beam hatches.
One Whitehead torpedo.
Source: Angelucci (1988)

The military version of the S.79 was thus a large, low-wing trimotor of metal and plywood construction. Originally equipped with three Piaggio engines (two at the wings and one at the nose) which were then replaced by three Alfa Romeo 126 engines (780 hp each), gave it a top speed of 267 mph (430 km/h). Carrying the torpedo, the aircraft had a reduced top speed of 200 mph (322 km/h). In 1943 the torpedo bomber's engines were swapped for new Alfa Romeo 128 engines, and its ventral gondola was removed, further improving performance. Although the *Sparviero* was considered as one of the fastest torpedo bombers between 1940-41, by 1943 foreign torpedo bombers with a newer design and technical platform such as the Japanese Nakajima B6N 'Jill' fighter/bomber were not only faster but could also launch the torpedo from a higher altitude than the *Sparviero* making it a less vulnerable aircraft against enemy naval gunfire. Moreover, the former's 1850 hp engine gave it considerably more power and improved performance also by way of its leaner design.

The *Sparviero's* cockpit was designed for two pilots seated side-by-side. The instrumentation panel included a clock, airspeed and vertical speed indicators, oil and fuel gauges, altimeters for low and high altitude, gyroscope, compass, turn and bank indicator. The instrumentation panel and instrument navigation tools were very crude by 1940-41 standards especially as compared to German bombers which also had much more precise aiming devices to aid the pilot in the torpedo launch. While German torpedo bombers were retrofitted with Siemens aiming devices, the *Sparvieri* initially had nothing but by 1941 they relied for accuracy on a custom built but rather crude device called the *grafometro* (graph meter) a tool that allowed the pilot to estimate the speed and distance of an enemy ship. The reduced instrumentation and communication versus a comparable German bomber was also the result of the fact that Italian medium bombers lacked the power of their German counterparts thus to compensate they had to be lighter by carrying less instrumentation. Furthermore, ground to air and air to air radio communication aids remained poor throughout the war. Radar was non-existent in the RA, while by 1943, one of every three Japanese B6N2 torpedo bombers was equipped with 3-Shiki Type 3 air-to-surface radar for detecting enemy ships. Given its limited instrumentation, for example, the

S.79 was considered to be inoperable at nights especially when the full moon was not present. In contrast, both German and British torpedo bombers could effectively fight at night with their more effective instrumentation.

From October 1936 to June 1943 1,217 *Sparvieri* came off the production line. While the majority were used as standard medium bombers it is estimated that up to a third or more were used in the torpedo launcher role.

The Torpedo Bomber Comes of Age

Although Robert Whitehead, the father of the torpedo, developed weapons mainly for naval applications, his firm by 1907 had redesigned a naval torpedo so that it could be dropped by plane. The first Whitehead naval torpedo was "four meters long and 35 centimeters in diameter, it was propelled by compressed air which drove a small engine and a propeller. The warhead was loaded with 8.2 kilograms of dynamite and there was an ingenious depth-regulating mechanism which was the heart of the device."[26] Whitehead was ahead of its times since in 1907 the first to propose a torpedo bomb for aircraft were two British naval aviators, Commander Murray Sueter and Lieutenant Douglas Hyde-Thomson that collaborated with the British domestic aviation industry to build a seaplane capable of carrying a torpedo and they also designed the drop mechanism. The partnership resulted in the first torpedo drop in history on 28 July 1914 by a Short seaplane. The torpedo was made by the Royal Gun Factory, a 14-inch, 800-pound Mark X. Britain was also the first to drop a torpedo during wartime when on 17 August 1914 Flight Commander Edmonds dropped a warhead on a Turkish vessel from a Type 184 torpedo plane.

Throughout the conflict the Royal Navy, working with Sopwith Aviation Company, began to investigate the possibility of designing planes carrying aerial warheads that could operate from battleships. Meanwhile, the Imperial Japanese Navy, based on technical evaluations conducted in collaboration with the Royal Navy, in 1922 built the Hosho, its first carrier equipped with torpedo planes. The United States shortly after also entered the fray with the design of a new torpedo-carrying aircraft, the PT-1, which became the basis of the Navy's first torpedo squadron. During the 1930s the American, Japanese and the Royal Navy continued technical evaluations on improved aircraft carrying torpedoes for use on aircraft carriers. The United States Navy was in the vanguard when, for instance, it developed the Mark XIII in 1938. This was a 22.5-inch diameter aircraft torpedo, 161-inch-long, with a speed of 33.5 knots, a range of 6,300 yards and a 600-pound warhead.

The Royal Navy employed the Fairey Swordfish[27]to good effect several times between 1939-41. In June 1940, six Swordfish successfully targeted with aerial torpedoes the German battleship Scharnhorst near the coast of Norway. On 12 July 1940 a Swordfish squadron took off from the carrier HMS Ark Royal to successfully torpedo the Vichy French battleship Dunkerque at Oran. Then on 22 August of the same year a strike force consisting of three Fairey Swordfish of No. 824 Squadron/Fleet Air Arm took off from HMS Eagle and attacked during the afternoon and sank the *Monte Gargano*, damaged the *Calipso* and, most importantly however, struck

26 Ian Hogg, *The Weapons that Changed the World* (New York: Arbor House, 1986), p.68.

27 Swordfish were single engine biplanes used as torpedo bombers or fighters with a maximum speed of 139 mph, and a range of 528 miles.

Iride. The latter carried the men and equipment of the Italian naval frogmen unit X MAS, who were set to attack ships at Alexandria. Thus this preemptive action not only may have saved the battleships but also "greatly influenced the British high command about the possibilities of airborne torpedoes."[28]

Fairey Swordfish Mk. II Specifications
Engine: 750hp Bristol Pegasus 30 radial engine
Wing span: 45 feet.
Length: 36 feet.
Height: 12 feet.
Empty weight 4,690 lbs., max. take-off weight loaded 7,493 lbs.
Max speed 138 mph (224km/h at 1525m).
Service ceiling 10,690 feet (3260m).
Max. range 1,028 miles (1658km), range with a torpedo 885km.
Crew: Pilot
Armament: One fixed forward-firing Browning .303 machinegun, and one .303 Vickers K gun in the rear cockpit. An 18-inch torpedo (731kg), a 681kg mine, bombs, or four depth charges could be carried. Racks under the wings for eight 3-inch rockets.
Source: R. Jackson (2015)

On 11 November 1940, HMS *Illustrious* launched twenty Fairey Swordfish torpedo planes in a daring night attack against the Italian fleet at anchor in Taranto. Despite its intricate defenses, the British aircraft achieved a tremendous success sinking one battleship, damaging two battleships and three cruisers. Only two aircraft were lost during the attack. This well planned and executed operation demonstrated the effectiveness of aerial torpedoes (each plane could carry an 18-inch torpedo-731kg) as a cutting-edge weapon for naval warfare. From a tactical perspective the Taranto attack, conducted in 1940, when the aerial torpedo tactics were in their infancy, was of primary importance for the development of torpedo group tactics. As naval historian A. J. Smithers asserts in his study of the Taranto operation, the coordinated and synchronized attack by a large number of torpedo bombers was a prelude to Pearl Harbor, in other words it offered a blueprint for advanced torpedo bomber tactics.[29] The plan entailed the use of torpedo bombers in an attack to be delivered by two waves, spaced about one hour apart. Each wave consisted of three combat elements: two aircraft whose task was to illuminate the enemy battleships by dropping flares, standard bombers to target ships in the inner harbor and to create a diversion, and finally the torpedo bomber forays. It was based on solid intelligence work conducted prior to the attack. For several days reconnaissance planes took photographs of the location of the battle ships in the harbor. The details of the principal defenses, including the number of guns, their locations, the locations of anti-torpedo nets and the numerous barrage balloons were gleaned by these preliminary operations. It was also estimated that the harbor was approximately 60-80 feet deep and a special device was invented to ensure that the torpedoes did not drop precipitously in the seabed. "British armorers attached a wire cable to the nose of the torpedo. The

28 Thomas P. Lowry, The *Attack on Taranto* (Mechanicsburg: Stackpole, 1995), p.115.
29 A.J. Smithers, *Taranto 1940* (Annapolis, Maryland: Naval Institute Press, 1995).

rest of the wire was wound around a drum attached to the Swordfish torpedo bomber. As the torpedo dropped, the wire played out. As it did so, however, it kept upward resistance on the nose of the torpedo, preventing the nose from rotating down too much."[30] Then on the day of the attack everything came together:

> Shortly before 9 p.m. the first wave of twelve Swordfish from Nos. 813, 815 and 824 Squadrons, led by Lieutenant-Commander K. Williamson, was formed up and away, having been flown off from a position 170 miles to the south-east of Taranto. Two hours later, as they were approaching the target area from the south-west, the flash of anti-aircraft guns showed them that the defenses were already alert. Just before 11 p.m. the flare-droppers and bombers left the formation to carry out their respective tasks, while the torpedo-bombers made off to westward to get into position for the final approach. The two sub-flights of three then dived towards the anchorage in the face of intense fire from the shore batteries supplemented by the close range weapons in the warships. The aircraft came down as low as 30 feet above the water to launch their torpedoes. The moon was three-quarters full, and to the eastward the flares were outlining the battleships perfectly. The leader attacked the southernmost battleship, the Cavour, and his torpedo struck home under the foc's'le as the aircraft, badly damaged, crashed near the floating dock. One minute later the Littorio was struck under the starboard bow by a torpedo dropped by the second sub-flight, and a few moments afterwards she was hit again on the port quarter. The other torpedoes either missed, exploded prematurely, or failed to go off, though they were all dropped from close range. Meanwhile, the flare-dropping aircraft, their main task completed, bombed the oil storage depot before making out to sea, and the other bombers attacked vessels in the inner harbor and started a fire in a hangar. In spite of the heavy fire all the aircraft of the first wave with the exception of the leader, who with his observer was made prisoner, were safely back 4½ hours after taking off.
>
> The second wave from Nos. 813, 815, 819 and 824 Squadrons, reduced in strength to eight, led by Lieutenant-Commander J. W. Hale, appeared in the target area shortly before midnight. The tactics were the same, and once again the targets were successfully illuminated by the flares. From about 4,000 feet the five torpedo-bombers began their dive, and as before they continued it to a very low height above the water. One torpedo struck the Duilio on the starboard side and another hit the damaged Littorio, which was then hit for the fourth time by a torpedo that failed to explode. The Vittorio Veneto and the 8-inch cruiser Gorizia were unsuccessfully attacked, the latter by an aircraft which was then shot down. In the inner harbor the cruiser Trento was attacked, and another fire was started ashore. By three o'clock in the morning the second wave arrived back, having, like the first, lost one aircraft.[31]

30 Ray Panko, "Pearl Harbor: Thunderfish in the Sky", *Pearl Harbor Aviation Museum Magazine*, December 28, 2015.

31 Major-General I.S.O. Playfair, *The Mediterranean and Middle East Volume I: The Early Successes against Italy (to May 1941)* (London: HMSO, 1954) <http://www.ibiblio.org/hyperwar/UN/UK/UK-Med-I/UK-Med-I-12.html > (accessed on 12 May 2021).

The operation was a great success and it demonstrated the early acquisition, prior to many other air services, by the RAF and the Royal Navy/Fleet Air Arm of several key capabilities including the ability of the pilots, crews and support personnel to conduct a large scale coordinated night operation, the availability of aircraft carriers to transport the torpedo bombers near the attack site so that the latter could operate with greater fuel autonomy, and the use of a mass of torpedo bombers (up to six at a time) in a coordinated attack against multiple targets. For example, the pilots ability of flying in formation and then attacking the battleships without some of the planes crashing into each other was a major success in and of itself during a night attack. During the course of the war Britain continued in the path of innovation by introducing two land base torpedo bombers (Vickers Wellington GR.Mks VII and Bristol Beaufort Mks X) which represented a vast improvement over the Fairey Swordfish. The former, for example, was slightly slower than the S.79 but could carry a heavier warhead and was fully capable of operating at night. Whereas the latter was faster, with a top speed without the warhead of 318 mph (512 km/h), and well-armed with four 20mm forward firing cannons and one rearward firing machine gun.

Unlike the British Fleet Air Arm, in the fall of 1940 the fledgling Italian torpedo bomber unit did not possess, for example, the capability to conduct night operations. Large scale torpedo bomber tactics such as the group attack method were not possible because of the paucity of the torpedo bomber fleet and pilots and their lack of training in flying and conducting large scale operations. Moreover, because of long standing infighting between the RM and the *Regia Aeronautica*, Italy did not have an aircraft carrier. This represented a major handicap to Italian torpedo bomber operations as the aircraft could not be launched from deep enemy waters for attacks against Gibraltar, Malta or Alexandria. Another feature that aided the British torpedo bomber and standard bomber operations was a set of technological developments during the war which brought about improvements in the search and strike procedure. From mid-1941 onwards, Air to Surface Vessel radar sets became available to the British. These instruments greatly aided in locating enemy aircraft and allowed an even greater emphasis to be placed on night strikes, thus further exacerbating the differences with the Italian squadrons that lacked radar. Lastly, another feature differentiated the British from the Italian torpedo bomber units. Whereas the Fleet Air Arm units had been placed in 1937 under Royal Navy so that it controlled all naval aviation, in Italy reconnaissance planes and torpedo bombers remained under air force command. Both organizational set-ups had their strengths and weaknesses. The British organization, for example, had an integrated naval command for torpedo bomber operations thus eliminating the dualism between the two services that characterized Italy's experience.[32] In 1941 the British torpedo units continued to have success against the German *Kriegsmarine* and the RM. In April 1941, for instance, Bristol Beaufort torpedo bombers inflicted grave damage to the German battleship *Gneisenau* and two months later they torpedoed the battleship *Lutzow*.

Japanese experience with torpedo bombers was probably one of the most, if not the most, successful of the Second World War. It all began with principled leadership, sound tactics, extensive training and an integrated system were naval aviation was under the control of the Imperial Japanese Navy. Interest in aerial and naval torpedoes began early within the ranks of the Imperial Japanese Army, whose basic doctrine was predicated on always making the first

32 Lowry, The *Attack on Taranto*, p.113.

strike against the enemy. The torpedoes fit well within this aggressive strategy because they were considered quintessential offensive weapons. A pioneer of torpedo technology was the aviator Lieutenant Kawazoe Takuo, who in 1919 wrote "On Torpedo Attacks", a work that had widespread influence upon the thinking of the Japanese naval aviation arm. Rear Admiral Jisaburo Ozawa[33], who during the war was in charge of aircraft carriers, also had a life-long interest on torpedoes. His tactical and strategic emphasis was on "the importance of concentrated air attacks launched from aircraft carriers, as well as unified command."[34] By the early 1930s when aircraft technology had made important strides, the Imperial Japanese Navy began to view aircraft carriers as launching platforms for attacks against the larger United States Navy battleships and carriers. Since the American forces were much larger, Japanese strategic thinking hinged upon attacking the enemy first and possibly by surprise. First, bombers, fighters and torpedo bombers were to strike at the enemy in surprise attacks to weaken the American carrier fleet. Second, having debilitated the carriers, the Imperial Japanese Navy was then to face the American battlefleet in a major naval encounter.

The torpedo bomber specifically interested the Japanese upper echelons and the specialists because it offered the Navy another weapon or tactic to purse its "offensive tradition."[35] Initially training was carried out with wooden, dummy torpedoes as the Navy did not have viable torpedoes. It would take the domestic industry several years to develop one, in the form of the Type 91. It had a range of 7,000 feet (2,000 meters), a speed of 42 knots and an explosive charge of 331 pounds (150 kilograms). Against capital ships at sea the torpedo could be launched at an airspeed of 115 mph (85 km/h) and at a height of 330 feet (100 meters) and at a distance of 4,000 feet (1,200 meters) from the target.[36] In shallow waters attacks the torpedo could be launched from an altitude of 66 feet (20 meters) and at a speed of 185 mph (300 km/h). In April 1941 Japan was able to introduce the Type 91 Model 2 torpedo fitted with a 452lb warhead and a speed of 43 knots, while in early 1942 the Mod 3 was introduced with a slightly larger warhead. "Thanks to extensive experience that led to constant development, the Japanese Type 91 torpedo was by far the best aerial torpedo in the world in December 1941. It was reliable at a time when most aerial torpedoes were fragile and quick to stop, sink, or turn away from their targets. Under water, its depth-keeping limits were plus or minus 18 inches. Its yaw limits were a mere 1 percent of the range. Its warhead was big enough to sink even battleships. Perhaps best of all, from the bomber crew's point of view, it could be dropped at

33 Jisaburo Ozawa graduated from the Imperial Naval Academy in 1909. He was a professor at the academy in the 1930s. Between 1935 and 1937, he served as the commanding officer of light cruiser Maya and then battleship Haruna. He was promoted to the rank of rear admiral in 1936. Between 1938 and 1940, he served as commanding officer of various naval units. He was promoted to the rank of vice admiral in 1940. He was considered as a first rate tactician. Despite his naval academy education, Ozawa was a proponent of building an aviation arm in the Imperial Japanese Navy – he was the first high-ranking officer to recommend that the Japanese aircraft carrier forces be organized into an air fleet so that they could train and fight together. Toward the end of the war he was nominated as the commander in chief of the Combined Fleet.

34 Mark Chambers and Tony Holmes, *Nakajima B5N Kate and B6N Jill Units* (Oxford: Osprey, 2017), p.11.

35 Mark R. Peattie, Sunburst: *The Rise of the Japanese Naval Air Power, 1909-1941* (Annapolis, Maryland: Naval Institute Press, 2001), p.35.

36 Ibid., p.36.

considerable speed and from considerable height. This made torpedo attacks more survivable for the air crew."[37]

Type 91 Model 2 Torpedo Specifications
Type: Aerial Torpedo
Diameter: 17.7 inches
Length: 18 feet
Weight: 1,841 lbs
Warhead: 452 lbs
Speed: 41-43 knots
Range: 2,200 yards
Source: Mark E. Stille (2020)

The torpedo bomber also took several years to develop. Finally, the Japanese naval aviation arm settled on the specifications of the Nakajima B5N 'Kate' bomber armed with a Type 91 aerial torpedo. In the words of a prominent naval historian: "The Mitsubishi A6M Zero fighter was superior to any U.S. fighter at the outbreak of the war, and the Nakajima B5N Kate torpedo bomber at the outbreak was generally superior to contemporary American designs."[38] It took Japan over ten years to develop such a bomber/fighter, single engine, three seater aircraft that could carry one torpedo or two bombs. The final version, the improved B5N2, was introduced in 1941 equipped with a more potent engine (one 1,000 Hp Nakajima NK 1B Sakae), a top speed of 235 mph (378 km/h), and a range of 1,240 miles. According to naval historian Mark Stille: "These aircraft, combined with well-trained and experienced air crews and deck crews, combined to make the Imperial Navy's carriers into formidable striking platforms."[39]

B5NS Type 97 Model 12 Specifications
Engine: 1,000 hp Nakajima NK 1B Sakae 11 Radial Engine
Span: 50 feet and 11 inches
Length: 33 feet and 10 inches
Height: 12 feet and 2 inches
Wing area: 406 square feet
Weight empty: 5,024 lbs.
Weight Loaded: 8,378 lbs.
Max Speed: 235 mph at 11, 810 feet
Range: 1,240 miles
Ceiling: 27,100 feet
Payload: Type 91 torpedo
Armament: One 7.7mm rear firing machine gun
Crew: Three
Source: Mark E. Stille (2020)

37 Ray Panko, "Pearl Harbor: Thunderfish in the Sky", *Pearl Harbor Aviation Museum Magazine*, 28 December 2015.
38 Thomas G. Mahnken, "Asymmetric Warfare at Sea: The Naval Battles off Guadalcanal, 1942–1943", *Naval War College Review*, Vol. 64, No. 1 (Winter 2011), p.118.
39 Mark E. Stille, *Imperial Japanese Aircraft Carriers* (Oxford: Osprey, 2005), p.5.

Having the basic technology in place by the late 1930s, the Imperial Japanese Navy began to develop specific tactics and drills. In 1939, for instance, the Combined Fleet Command undertook drills to better coordinate carrier and land based torpedo operations. In addition, training for night operations was critical to Japan's preparation for the war since the United States Navy was primarily trained to fight in day-time operations. "The point of a night assault is, first detection of the enemy by the reconnaissance squadron, followed by the dropping of flares by the lighting squadron and finally launching of torpedoes by torpedo bombers. This operation will not succeed unless coordination among the three squadrons is done with perfect precision."[40] Night assault drills were conducted almost a year prior to the assault on Pearl Harbor and they took inspiration from various theories as well as from the November 1940 attack by the British torpedo bomber units against Taranto. For example, the Japanese naval officer stationed at the Japanese embassy in Rome travelled to Taranto after the British strike to gain first-hand information on how the attack was conducted and to gauge its results. Information such as this was instrumental in putting to the test the Japanese torpedo group attack theory launched from aircraft carriers.

Moreover, the Imperial Japanese Navy had a number of aircraft carriers whose flight decks had been modified to launch and land the torpedo bombers. Experienced Navy personnel as well as air support crews and pilots were plentiful and most importantly, they were trained to fight in the most difficult conditions: "The Japanese navy sought to improve the quality of its fighting forces to offset the U.S. Navy's quantitative superiority. The navy leadership believed that the toughness, morale, and fighting spirit of the Japanese fighting man would give a marked advantage in a war with the United States. To hone their skills, Japanese forces trained ten months out of the year in exercises that were arduous and sometimes fatal. Because exercises emphasized combat at night and in poor weather, crews learned to operate effectively under even the harshest of conditions."[41]

Another tactic refined by Japan was the shallow water attack. This called for modifications to the basic design to improve the torpedo's trajectory in shallow waters to limit the initial plunge so that it would not strike the bottom mud. An early modification took the form of a wood extension to the fins. Then in 1939 and 1940 extensive drills were conducted with the modified torpedo in a bay that had very shallow waters. Prior to the Pearl Harbor attack, the Japanese had to further modify their Type 91 Model 2 aerial torpedoes. The additional design change was represented by small wooden fins near the front of the tail cone that ensured that the torpedo dropped without rolling. This change was achieved only a few months prior to the attack against Pearl Harbor.[42] This permitted the Imperial Japanese Navy to order fifty of these modified torpedoes prior to the attack.

Finally, the Japanese also developed the group attack tactic by designing a protocol that saw different types of aircraft attacking in simulated operations. It was based on the premise that an air attack by different types of aircraft could achieve many more hits than one conducted by only one specialty. As far the torpedo bombers were concerned they would press forward an 'anvil and hammer attack,' or an attack from dual flanks of the ship or convoy to ensure one or more hits on the target. As Mark Peattie argues:

40 Ibid, p.16.
41 Ibid., p.100.
42 Ray Panko, "Pearl Harbor: Thunderfish in the Sky", *Pearl Harbor Aviation Museum Magazine*, 28 December 2015.

> Out of the research devoted to the problem of coordinating massed air attacks by carrier aircraft there emerged an air doctrine that called for closely phased operations by various types of aircraft. In the scheme that the navy began to work out, the attack would be launched about 200 miles from the enemy. As it approached the target, the strike force, organized into vanguard and rear elements, would divide. Some fighters would provide direct cover for the attack group racing in to hit their targets from predetermined altitudes. Other's would sweep the enemy's combat air patrols from the sky. Still others would strafe the bridges and decks of enemy carriers, an idea that derived from the experience of navy fighter pilots in ground attacks in China. The fighters would have barely swept past when high level horizontal bombings attacks would be delivered … to be immediately followed by dive bombing sorties … Almost simultaneously, a succession of torpedo attacks would be delivered…[43]

The Japanese Navy was an integrated organization. Japan did not have a stand-alone air service and the naval aviation arm was strictly under naval control. This organizational set up eschewed the rivalry between the navy and the air force that characterized the Italian or German experience and it ensured a continuity in torpedo development and tactics to furnish the aircraft carriers a multitude of attacking weapons.

The Japanese military employed torpedo carrying aircraft to deliver the opening blow against the United States Navy at Pearl Harbor. On 7 December 1941, the Imperial Japanese Navy effectuated a surprise attack with 353 aircraft, a portion of which were carrying torpedoes. The first wave of Japanese aircraft, for instance, included forty torpedo bombers, forty-nine high level bombers and fighters. The torpedo bombers came in low 100 feet above the water and struck moored battleships. United States Navy battleships Oklahoma, Nevada, California, and West Virginia, the crews of which had been caught in complete surprise, were all severely damaged by this daring attack. Meanwhile, the Arizona was sunk by a combination of torpedoes and bombs. According to the American Official History of the war the plan of operation against the American base at Pearl Harbor was long in the making:

> Plans for the strike had been initiated during the previous summer, completed by early November. In September picked crews--with pilots who averaged better than 800 hours' flying time--from the Japanese First Air Fleet had begun a period of intensive training in horizontal and dive bombing and in the technique of torpedo attack in shallow waters. En route to the rendezvous above Oahu, with the ships under radio silence, the pilots were briefed on their coming mission. The primary target was the naval base of Pearl Harbor, the design to cripple the Pacific Fleet. It was hoped that at least four aircraft carriers and four battleships could be sunk or rendered useless for a long period. Postwar interrogations of enemy personnel indicate a lack of precise information as to U.S. naval vessels then at Pearl Harbor, but each pilot received charts marking off definite areas of attack.[44]

43 Mark R. Peattie, *Sunburst: The Rise of the Japanese Naval Air Power, 1909-1941*, p.146.
44 Wesley Frank Craven (ed.), *The Army and the Air Forces in World War II, Vol. I: Plans & Early Operations* (Washington DC: Office of Air Force History, 1983), p.195.

The success of the operation relied upon good intelligence of the enemy ships disposition within the harbor and on the pre-war drills conducted by the Imperial Japanese Navy and its overall advanced state of preparedness.

The Japanese used again torpedo units to sink the British battleships Repulse and Prince of Wales shortly thereafter. During the early stages of the campaign in the Pacific, Japanese torpedo squadrons benefited from the superiority of their torpedo warhead, their reliance upon an excellent torpedo fighter aircraft, and their extensive training which made them adept at coordinating their attacks. The only major issue faced early on by the Japanese torpedo bomber units was related to the fragile nature of their lightly armed and designed aircraft which were in essence fighters adopted to the torpedo bomber role. Speed had been favored over armor and firepower. They were increasingly vulnerable to anti-aircraft fire especially as the United States Navy personnel became more experienced at confronting the torpedo bomber threat. Deadly at first, the Japanese torpedo squadrons became less effective in 1943 as the average skill of Japanese pilots, due to high losses of experienced personnel in combat, diminished while American fighters tactics and anti-aircraft fire steadily improved. This development happened even in the face of improvements made by the Japanese such as the introduction of a faster torpedo bomber and improved accuracy in torpedo launches.

American resurgence was fully vindicated at the Battle of Midway where United States torpedo aerial and standard bombers squads exacted their revenge against the Imperial Japanese Navy. The Japanese forces, in a desperate gamble to reverse their Pacific campaign, then reverted to two things. First, Japan sought to improve its combat effectiveness and revert the trend of losing battles against the United States Navy through technical innovation. One of the ways this occurred was through the deployment of a successor to the BN5 torpedo bomber, development of which had started in December 1939 when the Imperial Japanese Navy issued a specification to Nakajima for a new, faster aircraft capable of carrying the same external weapons load as the B5N. The new torpedo bomber was to be operated by a crew of three including the pilot, the navigator/bombardier and the radio operator/gunner. It took the form of a versatile fighter/bomber aircraft with low wing and all-metal construction, the Nakajima B6N. Further requirements included a top speed of 290 mph (460 km/h), a cruising speed of 230 mph (370 km/h) and a range of 1,200 miles (1,900 km) with an 1,800 lbs. (816 kg) bomb load. Most importantly the new aircraft, which was placed into service in 1943, allowed torpedoes to be launched at a higher altitude and a greater distance from the target thus improving the chances of survival of the crew during an attack. Despite this major technical innovation in torpedo bomber technology the Imperial Japanese Navy could not revert the long term trend of American power slowly gaining the upper hand in the Pacific. By 1944 Japan had lost a significant number of battleships and carriers and hence the torpedo bombers squadrons had to be increasingly launched from land based pads. This had an impact on the operating endurance of the aircraft whereby launches could not be made from aircraft carriers in striking distance of American battleships. Moreover, the quality of the pilots and crews had diminished considerably due to the high losses of experienced personnel sustained between 1941-43.

Second, Japan turned to the desperate tactic of the suicide attack when faced by the overwhelming combat power of the American Navy. Although, suicide attacks remained three to four times more effective against surface vessels than conventional torpedo and bomb attacks, they were an indication of how desperate Japan's forces had become in 1944 in their prolonged struggle against the might of Unites States military.

It can be argued that Japan's experience with torpedo bombers was much more comprehensive than those of Italy or Germany, although ultimately it lacked the resources of its more powerful enemy to sustain a long war of attrition. Japan's development of torpedo bomber technology and tactics began in the 1910s where preliminary torpedo drops were held and a torpedo bomber tactic was first developed. In the 1920s Japan's Navy set specifications for a torpedo bomber and a warhead that could be launched from an aircraft carrier. Japanese torpedo bomber development benefitted tremendously from the fact that the naval aviation arm was under Navy control, thus giving the discipline the continuity and the necessary funding to develop innovative solutions. By 1939, well before the war broke out, Japan possessed the basic doctrine of an integrated group attack tactic. Unlike Italy, Japan not only had the torpedo bomber squadrons in place but also possessed the most advanced tactics before the outbreak of the Pacific Campaign. Even some of the smaller details had been flushed out prior to the war such as wooden extensions to the torpedo fins so that the torpedo would better perform on impact with the water. Most importantly, torpedo bomber technology was advanced during the war with the introduction of a new aircraft and with modifications to the torpedo to make it more effective. This technologically driven approach allowed the Japanese to make early surprise strikes against the United States Navy possible but also to continue to up the game during the Pacific campaign by introducing more deadlier weapons.

The American experience with torpedo bombers was different from that of Japan. In America torpedo bombing was a natural outgrowth of naval weapons design, which had placed the torpedo at the center of the United States Navy's range of available weapons since the late 1890s. Since the Navy had a long history of operating with naval torpedoes, it was natural that its naval aviation arm would dedicate time and effort toward the design of an aircraft capable to deliver these weapons and that the focus in aircraft design be placed on the mechanisms to carry torpedoes (which weighed more than 1,000 pounds) and operational range.

During the antebellum period however, torpedo bomber development had its share of detractors within the Navy. The thinking of many planners and strategists within the Navy was that torpedo bombers, due to the fact that they had to carry such a heavy load, were sluggish by nature and hence vulnerable to anti-aircraft fire. To combat this view the United States had a key proponent of aerial torpedoes, Brigadier General William Mitchell,[45] who many consider to be the founder of American air power. Mitchell fought in the First World War and had a

45 In June 1917 Mitchell was named air officer of the American Expeditionary Forces, with the rank of lieutenant colonel. In May 1918 he was promoted to colonel and nominated as the air officer/I Corps. In September 1918 he commanded a mass bombing by a joint Franco-American force of 1,500 planes during the St Mihiel offensive. In October 1918 Mitchell was promoted to temporary brigadier general. After the war, in March 1919, Mitchell was appointed as assistant chief of the Air Service. Mitchell became an outspoken proponent of an independent air force and continued working on developing an American combat aircraft force. He claimed that the rise of air power had made the battleship obsolete and, to press his point, in 1923 he led field tests by sinking several captured battleships from the air. Mitchell strongly criticized the Navy and the Army by arguing that they held back the growth of the air force. His very public pronouncements put the issue of combat aircraft power on the agenda but they also alienated him from the top brass of the U.S. military. This led Mitchell to a transfer to the minor post of air officer of the VIII Corps. Following heated controversy against the Navy he was forced to resign from the military in 1926. He died ten years later.

long standing interest in military aviation. In the 1920s, as assistant chief of the Air Service, he argued that that an airplane could sink any surface ship by bombs or torpedoes and that the United States should not build new warships but focus upon the development of its military aviation arm. His views were obviously opposed by the United States Navy which refused requests for a test launch of aerial torpedoes against naval vessels. Mitchell consistently advocated for air power: "He taught that with pursuit and attack planes an air force could establish air supremacy over a fleet, neutralize its antiaircraft defenses, and in low level attacks dispose of light warships and merchantmen. Bombers, equipped either with bombs or torpedoes, could sink the most heavily armed ships."[46]

When the United States entered the Second World War, however, its Navy was very powerful with its large fleet of carriers and battleships, but the torpedo bomber and dive bomber units were not as well trained as their Japanese counterparts. Torpedo bomber squadrons were present within Carrier Aviation and Escort Carriers. American Carrier aviation had its main offensive force in its fast-carrier striking forces. The functions performed by the fast carriers included offense, defense, and reconnaissance against enemy aircraft, warships, merchant vessels, and harbor/naval base targets. Fighter, dive-bomber and torpedo-bomber squadrons were organized in carrier air groups and trained to operate together as coordinated striking units. Fast carriers were normally operated in task groups of 3 to 5 carriers, 4 to 6 battleships and cruisers, and 12 to 20 destroyers, all under a single command. Two to five task groups composed a fast-carrier task force, such as, for example, Task Force 58 which operated at Midway. The standard carrier air group in 1942 was comprised of four squadrons. The fighter squadron was equipped with twenty-seven F4F Wildcat fighters. Two squadrons were equipped with Douglass SBD Dauntless dive bombers which each squadron having twenty aircraft. Lastly, the torpedo bomber squadron was assigned between 12-15 TBD Devastator aircraft. Escort carriers provided air and antisubmarine defense of invasion convoys and beachhead areas and close support of seaborne invasion troops. The carriers themselves were smaller, slower ships of about 30-plane capacity, on which were based squadrons of fighters and torpedo bombers. In amphibious operations escort carriers were normally employed in formations of 4 to 7 carriers with 6 to 12 destroyers and destroyer escorts but single carriers with fewer escorts were used for specialized antisubmarine or convoy-escort operations. The invasion of Leyte, for example, was supported by a task group of 18 escort carriers in 3 task units with a total of 500 planes. Whereas the group for the Lingayen landings had the same number of carriers but was divided into a larger number of units with a total of 570 planes. The sheer number of carriers and of aircraft deployed by the United States compared to the biggest deployment of Axis aircraft in the Mediterranean during Operation Pedestal in 1942 makes the latter look like a very paltry and limited force.

Initially, United States Navy torpedo bomber tactics were less advanced that their Japanese counterparts suffering from coordination problems and by the inferior quality of their torpedo bomber versus Japan's torpedo aircraft:

> Since torpedo bombers were so vulnerable, the ideal tactic was to conduct a coordinated attack with the dive bombers to split the target's defenses. As described above, the Devastator was forced to conduct an attack at very low speed because of the limitations of

46 Craven (ed.), *The Army and the Air Forces in World War II, Vol. I: Plans & Early Operations,* p.39.

> the Mark XIII torpedo. As with the Imperial Japanese Navy, the preferred tactic was an anvil attack with aircraft attacking from both bows simultaneously so that whatever direction the target maneuvered it would be exposed. If the pilot judged his approach correctly, the torpedo would enter the water 1,400 yards from the target.[47]

Initially the American carrier air groups were equipped with the Douglas TBD Devastator torpedo bomber which was had a maximum speed of 206 mph (331 km/h), a limited defensive armament consisting of a 7.62 mm Browning machine gun for the rear gunner and a 12.7 mm M2 Browning machine gun. "The Devastator was forced to employ the unreliable Mark XIII torpedo that had to be dropped from 120 feet or less and not above 100 mph if there was any hope of it running a true track to the target. These limitations made the Devastator exceedingly vulnerable".[48]

But American industrial prowess together with the ingenuity of naval and aviation engineers made significant improvements to torpedo bomber technology during the conflict to turn from a position of weakness to one of strength. These efforts led in June 1942 to the replacement of the Devastator with the Grumman TBF-1 Avenger, which was a more sophisticated aircraft. With a top speed of 271 mph (436 km/h), three machine guns, and greater endurance than its predecessor, the TBF-1 Avenger became a powerful tool in the arsenal of the fast carrier task forces. The latter was a definite improvement over the Devastator which had a range of 805 miles with a 1,000-pound torpedo, while the Avenger carried 1,600 pounds of ordnance out to 1,381 miles. The first six TBF-1 Avengers to come off the production line were deployed in the Battle of Midway where unfortunately they did not have a determining influence on the final results of this major naval/air engagement. The TBF-1 Avenger was then deployed at the Battle of the Eastern Solomons in August 1942 where its crews took part to effective coordinated attacks against the Imperial Japanese Navy with dive bombers. The aircraft played also a role in the anti-shipping campaign when TBF-1 Avenger squadrons based at Henderson Field on Guadalcanal, heavily interfered with Japanese re-supply convoys known as the "Tokyo Express." On 14 November 1942 TBF-1 Avengers flying from Henderson Field sank the Japanese battleship Hiei which had been disabled during the naval Battle of Guadalcanal. Avenger torpedo squads remained the United States Navy's primary torpedo weapon for the remainder of the war. While seeing action at key engagements such as the Battles of the Philippine Sea and Leyte Gulf, the TBF-1 Avenger also proved an effective submarine killer. During the course of the war, Avenger squadrons sank around 30 enemy submarines in the Atlantic and Pacific.

As the Japanese fleet was greatly reduced later in the war by American power, the TBF-1 Avenger's role began to diminish as the United States Navy shifted to providing air support for operations ashore. These types of missions were more suited to the fleet's fighters and dive bombers such as the SB2C Helldiver. During the war, the TBF-1 Avenger was also used by the Royal Navy's Fleet Air Arm.

Not only did the United States Navy during the course of the war became armed with an improved torpedo bomber but it also advanced its capacity to fight at night, which at the beginning of the war was not well developed. In 1943, Japanese night torpedo attacks indicated a

47 Mark E. Stille, *Pacific Carrier War: Carrier Combat from Pearl Harbor to Okinawa*, (Oxford: Osprey, 2021), p.36.
48 Ibid., p.37.

need for night fighters, but the United States Navy lacked suitable radar-equipped planes. As a stop gap solution, given that the United States Navy could not afford to wait for the completion of the new planes, it equipped a number of its standard Hellcats and Corsairs with the necessary instruments and developed special training for pilots operating at night. Shortly after the United States Navy had night fighters on all large carriers and at land bases. Thus it can be argued that while the American experience with torpedo bombers began from a position of weakness, it steadily built upon its increasing combat experience of its pilots and crews and on the introduction of a world class torpedo bomber.

The Italians in 1940 on the other hand, were further behind the United States, Britain and Japan with regards to aerial torpedo units development. During the First World War they did some technical evaluations and tests launching a dummy torpedo from a twin-engine Farman plane. In the post war they conducted several tests by dropping aerial warheads from several types of seaplanes and aircraft. But as Italy entered the war its air force did not have a functioning *reparto aerosilurante* mainly as a result of the competitive nature and the uneasy relationship amongst the branches of its military. Unlike Japan, where the Navy spearheaded torpedo development, in the 1930s the responsibility for developing a warhead for the Italian air force had been assumed primarily by a private company (*Silurificio Whitehead di Fiume*) who had spent considerable time and resources on a weapon that the air force had been lukewarm about for many years. The RM too had not been fully behind the development of the aerial torpedo, even though it had continued periodic trials and launches. Luckily, with Whitehead working behind the scenes and out of the spotlight, when the war erupted the Italian air force was able to place a limited order for a small batch of aerial torpedoes and it possessed a bomber (S.79) that could be readily deployed in the torpedo role.

In the Italian case the air force had traditionally favored the standard bombers approach mainly because of the influence of Douhet and the experience of the Spanish Civil War. Majority opinion within the air force in 1940 stressed the same point made by Colonel Koller chief of staff of the *Luftflotte* 3 who argued: "Why drop a missile (in the shape of a torpedo) into the water in front of the ship, when as a bomb it can be dropped straight on to it?"[49] The poor results of this strategy based on standard bombers at the battle of Punta Stilo (Battle of Calabria 9-11 July 1940) made the RA reassess its anti-shipping tactics bringing to the fore the torpedo bomber as an alternative and/or a complementary tactic to be deployed against enemy ships. The advocates of the standard bombers overlooked two factors: 1. The effectiveness of the British anti-aircraft guns in preventing low level bombings from being pressed home from favorable positions; 2. "The far more lethal effect of a torpedo hole below the water line than a bomb exploding amongst the superstructure, as it usually did."[50] Since standard bombers during the first months of the war scored few lethal hits against enemy merchant and battleships, the RA was forced to introduce other weaponry including the torpedo. Its first dedicated unit, *Reparto Sperimentale Aerosiluranti*, was established on 25 July 1940 in Gorizia when the war had already begun. During the course of the war the RA would form an additional twelve torpedo bomber squadrons and convert several standard bomber units into torpedo carrying units. The newly formed units included: 278ª *Squadriglia Autonoma Aerosiluranti* (278th Autonomous Torpedo Bomber Squadron), 279ª

49 Cajus Bekker, *The Luftwaffe War Diaries* (Garden City: Doubleday, 1968), p.266.
50 Ibid.

Squadriglia Autonoma Aerosiluranti, 280ª *Squadriglia Autonoma Aerosiluranti*, 281ª *Squadriglia Autonoma Aerosiluranti*, 283ª *Squadriglia Autonoma Aerosiluranti*, 284ª *Squadriglia Autonoma Aerosiluranti*, 34° *Gruppo Autonomo Aerosiluranti* (34th Autonomous Torpedo Bomber Group), *41° Gruppo Autonomo Aerosiluranti*, 130° *Gruppo Autonomo Aerosiluranti*, 131° *Gruppo Autonomo Aerosiluranti*, 132° *Gruppo Autonomo Aerosiluranti*, 133° *Gruppo Autonomo Aerosiluranti, 32° Stormo Aerosiluranti, 36° Stormo Aerosiluranti and 46° Stormo Aerosiluranti.* Most of these units were originally formed in Italy in an airbase such as Ciampino, Catania, Gorizia, Borgo Panigale (Bologna) or Elmas and were then transferred to Sicily, Sardinia, Rhodes, or North Africa at air bases closer to the frontline and the Mediterranean Sea. Meanwhile, the *Gruppi* and *Stormi* were mostly former standard bomber groups based in Italy and converted to the torpedo bomber role. In total between 1940-43 the RA would deploy an estimated 300-350 S.79 torpedo bombers, plus approximately an additional 100 S.84. A *stormo* (flock) was the largest formation in the RA normally operating a single type of aircraft or carrying out a special discipline. *Stormi* were usually sub-divided into *gruppi* of twelve or more aircraft, each *gruppo* being sub-divided into two *squadriglie*. The standard *Sparviero squadriglia* had five aircraft, sometimes six.

Aerial Torpedo Tactics

When carrying a torpedo, the S.79 had a top speed of only about 200 mph and was thus vulnerable to being shot down by enemy fighters or by anti-aircraft defenses. Despite its machine guns the *Sparviero* was vulnerable to enemy fire especially because of its relative speed and its part wood construction. This meant that fighter escorts were essential for its survival especially when a large *Sparviero* force was deployed that hence could be easily detected. The torpedo bombers generally attacked at dawn or dusk to make a low and unobserved approach toward the target. During daytime operations they attacked with the sun behind them so that it would blind the enemy's vision. During nighttime operations, which were seldom conducted until 1943, the torpedo bombers could only operate on nights with full moon since they lacked radar and other equipment to improve visibility. The use of torpedoes made these type of operations particularly hazardous, as they forced the aircraft to come down very low and make a straight approach to release the torpedo in the water and therefore exposing itself to close range enemy fire. Torpedo operations were triggered by two factors. First, the operations required a reconnaissance aircraft to search an area where targets were calculated to be, based on intelligence. The aircraft would take the laborious approach of flying sweeps in an area until a target was located and night operations were even much more time consuming. When spotting an enemy target the reconnaissance aircraft would signal for the dispatch of the S.79s. Second, the S.79s conducted regular reconnaissance sweeps of their own gathering intelligence. Often these sweeps would lead to attacks on convoys or lone ships. Both searching methods were fairly laborious and rudimentary lacking for most of the war enhanced instrumentation. Since the target had to be located visually, night strikes were not easy to execute.

Once having approached a target the attack could be carried out by a single aircraft or by two or more. To begin the descent upon the target the S.79 pilot typically stood the aircraft on his nose. The latter began to accelerate heading straight down until it reached very close to the water. The aircraft then assumed a horizontal position as it made its way toward a target. Flying at a range of 40 to 120 meters above the water the *Sparviero* rushed over the waves at a considerable speed. As the pilot drove toward the target, the silhouette of the ships became visible. The latter opened fire with tracer bullets. Fire by rapid fire guns started whizzing about the *Sparviero*. Ignoring the crisscross of tracer, the pilot continued the approach toward the enemy ship. In the most perilous seconds of torpedo bomber operations the pilot pulled the release and a few seconds later the aircraft leapt up free of the weight of the warhead to make its escape. The following is how an experienced torpedo bomber described the typical lining up of a target:

> The warhead had to be released at an altitude between 60-80 meters from the sea level and at a speed of between 300-350 kilometers per hour and with the aircraft in a perfectly horizontal position versus the target.... The warhead had very delicate components that had been designed by Antonio Trizzino to improve precision and ensure that it hit the target. If the torpedo launches took place at different distances and position from those above indicated it could misfire often by passing below the ship or by failing to reach the ship. If launched at the proper altitude and distance even a very fast and highly maneuverable ship could not escape the deadly warhead.[51]

The launch was made by the first pilot by pulling a lever that released the warhead. This often occurred at an estimated optimum distance of about 700 to 1,000 meters feet from the flank of the enemy ship. This distance was needed to overcome the "dolphin" trajectory of the torpedo at the first impact with the water until it would stabilize itself. At times, given the ample enemy fire, the distance at which the launch was made was greater, and only in few cases it was successful. After releasing the warhead, the pilot would make his escape. Torpedo bomber operations were dangerous because the pilot had to come down in altitude to release the warhead while after the launch he had to fly over the enemy guns in order to speed away. "I got the plane down low almost grazing the water", writes torpedo bomber pilot Giuseppe Cimicchi in his memoirs. "My enthusiasm led my aircraft to the point of almost crashing against the flank of the ship I was supposed to attack. At that point I realized I had pushed too far as the towers of the ships appeared to be so close. The torpedo began its flight rapidly. At that distance it was impossible to miss the target. I flew over the enemy ship through the columns of smoke that surrounded it while my machine gunner unleashed fire on the ship's bridge."[52]

After the release of the torpedo, the aircraft began to climb away from the enemy ships. The pilot took evasive action by twisting the aircraft to avoid the tracer, while the observer took photographs of the damage produced by the warhead. This was probably one of the most dangerous aspects of a torpedo bomber attack since the plane had to fly over the ship that it had just released the torpedo against. Flying over meant receiving fire from relatively close range from the warship that had been attacked as well as from other destroyers or cruisers nearby. *Tenente* Giulio Cesare Graziani recalls in his memoirs the results of a flyover: "When I had escaped the hellish enemy fire and the aircraft was out of range of anti-aircraft weapons, with a quick glance I realized the trauma my crew had been through. I saw the co-pilot *Maresciallo* Riso slumped on the right side, and his chest bloodied. I heard primo aviere Pavese behind me

51 Martino Aichner, *Il gruppo Buscaglia: Aerosiluranti italiani nella seconda guerra mondiale* (Milan: Mursia, 1990), p.108.

52 Giuseppe Cimicchi, *I siluri vengono dal cielo* (Milan: Longanesi, 1964), p.31.

complaining about a hand wound, I saw *Sergente* Venuti who, all soiled with blood, informed me that primo *fotografo* Di Paolo had died. Meanwhile primo aviere Galli, who was also wounded, told me the torpedo release mechanism had failed … Primo aviere Di Paolo was standing leaning outside the window of the plane in order to take a photograph during the attack when he was struck by machine gun fire to the point that his brains splattered all over the wing of the plane……Maresciallo Riso had his lungs perforated by two splinters. He lost lots of blood and remained unconscious during the return flight. Pavese sitting behind me had lost two fingers, while aviere Galli, who had been hit in the thighbone lay at the back of the plane."[53]

Torpedo bomber pilot Martino Aichner described that while on a combat mission both pilots and crews were generally calm and, in the thick of the action seldom felt pressure or fear. Fear and apprehension were more common during the time taken to prepare for the mission which was typically more stressful:

> The difficult moments for us torpedo bombers pilots were not those when we were conducting a combat action which generally were the most dangerous times. What really was difficult for us were the preparations for the combat actions where we had all the time in the world to think about the operation we were to undertake. For example, the difficult moments were when we were warned that a combat action was going to take place or when we were below the wings of the aircraft waiting for the command to board and then depart. From that moment on the life of the pilots, of the radio transmitter and of the motorista was fine. On the other hand, the gunner and the photographer lived with great concern and apprehension those few moments in which an enemy ship was located and targeted. In short for an aerosilurante the time when he had to show courage and determination was when he volunteered to enter into the torpedo discipline. This was the crowning moment and the first step toward a dangerous life.[54]

Likewise torpedo bomber ace Giuseppe Cimicchi also states that the preparations for a combat action were full of trepidation while the combat action generally was not:

> We settled quickly at Gadurra airbase (Rhodes). Just outside the airfield, shielded by the shade of the olive trees, we built a shack used as an office for our squadron, inside it we frequently gathered to talk and to elaborate plans for combat actions. Sometimes to smoke a cigarette in peace and away from the noise and the preoccupations in the airfield. It was fitted with a table, some chairs and a telephone that was both our hope and our nightmare at the same time. Through that microphone, in fact, orders, reports and communications from the Air Command were transmitted to us. The ringing of that telephone excited everyone present beyond belief.
>
> The scene was always the same. An officer collected the communications transmitted by a distant voice while the others waited anxiously. In the silence of those minutes, everyone tried to imagine what the new mission that was being assigned could be. Once the riddle was solved, everyone gathered around the table where plans were quickly made, and routes

53 Ibid.
54 Ibid, p.109.

> were drawn to follow. That shack was our little Pentagon. With each of those phone calls the airfield changed. Orders went from one hut to the other, from the officers to their wingmen. The crews began refueling the planes without delay and promptly transferred them from the hangar to the runway. In a few feverish moments the officers got dressed. They left the base with their heads down, deep in thoughts and taking their head gear and the flight papers with them. In the moments prior to take off they tried to rearrange their ideas while waiting to get on the planes, overcoming that sense of anguish and dismay that grips each of us when we get on board the aircraft. Then we would take off. After hooking up the life jacket and the parachute, the pilot took the controls and drove, taxiing, to the take off point. Those who remained on the ground greeted us, waving their hands and caps, and screaming out: 'In bocca al lupo!'
>
> The roar of the engines quickly drowned out their voices. The pilot was now alone with his machine and with the unexpected. Every preoccupation or trouble disappeared at that point. When the aircraft takes off towards the sky, the pilot always overcomes doubts to strongly believe in himself. From what I remember from my personal experiences, an Olympic calm took over me the instant I took off.[55]

Torpedo bomber attacks could also be made against stationary targets such as ships in harbor or against moving targets such as warships and merchant transports at sea. Both types of operations presented challenges. Attacks against harbors faced not only the threat posed by the anti-aircraft fire but also had to overcome the specific harbor defenses such as balloons and net obstructions, and for this reason not more than a few torpedo-bombers could be used at a time. Anti-shipping attacks typically faced the anti-aircraft defense as well as the interference of the enemy's aerial fighter escort whose job was to disrupt the torpedo launches. During the first year of the war, the Italian torpedo bombers attacked individually or in pairs, but by mid-1941 several planes flying at a comparatively close range would attack together. Against individual ships or convoys the sole torpedo bomber had to contend with the evasive tactics of the ships which often foiled attacks especially those put forth by less experienced torpedo bomber pilots. For this reason during the interwar years and during the Second World War itself, planners developed the group attack method. This was a new tactic that "showed that losses could be minimized if surprise was achieved and the attack carried out simultaneously from different directions. Still better was a combined attack by both bombers and torpedo aircraft."[56] Bombers were frequently dispatched into the attack first to create disarray in the enemy defenses with high altitude or dive bombing forays. At times new weapons would also be unleashed. Then a flight of ten or more S.79s, escorted by fighters, would press home an attack by launching several torpedoes at their targets. Often the flight commander would lead the attack by targeting the largest enemy naval vessel, while the remaining members of the unit would target both warships and merchant ships. Buscaglia's own 132° *Gruppo* formed in spring 1942, for example, was comprised by thirteen S.79s and usually accompanied by either *Reggiane* Re.2001 fighters commanded by *Tenente Colonnello* Quarantotti 2° *Gruppo Autonomo Caccia Terrestre* or *Macchi* C.202 from 51° *Stormo* of *Tenente Colonnello*

55 Giuseppe Cimicchi, *I siluri vengono dal cielo*, p.19.
56 Cajus Bekker, *The Luftwaffe War Diaries*, p.266.

Aldo Remondino. In the fierce aerial and naval battles of the summer of 1942 the stepped up cooperation between fighter units and torpedo squadrons was made necessary to counter the increasingly larger scale deployment of enemy fighters which became more successful in downing S.79s. The RAF squadrons equipped with more reliable and generally faster fighter aircraft such as the Supermarine Spitfire Mk IX and the Hawker Hurricane, were called upon to intercept the *Sparvieri* before they got close to their targets. The RAF squadrons would take off from base or from aircraft carrier and quickly try to climb above the *Sparvieri*. With their silhouette shielded by the sun, the RAF fighters would pounce upon the adversaries from above, often with great force. To check the RAF threat, the *Reggiane* and *Macchi* fighter escort would forcefully intervene to ensure that the torpedo bombers strike force could get a clear shot at their targets. Their role was to either engage any aerial enemy escort present or attack the escorting vessels of the convoy tying up their anti-aircraft units as the strike force made the attack.

The Japanese torpedo bomber units were reputed to be the most skillful from a tactical perspective. An American intelligence assessment, for example, describes the Japanese group attack tactic in the following way. "Approximately 25 Japanese torpedo planes attacked one of our convoys in the following manner: The planes came in at angles of about 45°, covered with three levels of fighters up to 20,000 feet. The planes dropped their torpedoes from heights of 20 to 50 feet, while flying at about 250 miles per hour. The fighters strafed several of our ships during, and after, the period when the torpedoes were being dropped."[57]

By 1943 the Japanese had the fastest torpedo bomber that also allowed for torpedo bomber launches at higher altitudes than comparable Italian or British aircraft. This allowed the pilots to press home more successful attacks while also minimizing losses.

Beginning in 1941 the Italians would take on group attack tactics following the examples set out by RAF Fairey Swordfish attack on Taranto and later by Japan's attack on Peral Harbor, despite the fact that Italian pilots were not experienced fighting at night which somewhat limited the effectiveness of such tactics. These tactics, although sound, allowed the Italian torpedo bomber units to achieve some measure of success, although not the scale of success enjoyed by the British or Japanese torpedo bomber units.

Often the torpedo bomber pilots' offensive tactics were successful as evidenced by the following assertion by the authors of the British Official History of the war:

> The Italian Air Force had made repeated attacks on British ships, mostly from high-level, sometimes with great accuracy but on the whole with surprisingly little success. The chief threat to the British ships was from torpedo-bomber attacks, a type of action which the Italians had not fully developed when they came into the war, and which therefore did not figure very largely for some time. But in addition to their successes against the Kent and the Liverpool, already mentioned, torpedo-bombers scored two hits on the cruiser Glasgow in Suda Bay early in December; all three cruisers had to leave the Mediterranean for repairs.[58]

57 US Military Intelligence Service, "Notes on Air Tactics Used by Japanese", *Intelligence Bulletin*, December 1943.

58 Major-General I.S.O. Playfair, The Mediterranean and Middle East Volume I: The Early Successes against Italy (to May 1941) (London: HMSO, 1954) <http://www.ibiblio.org/hyperwar/UN/UK/UK-Med-I/UK-Med-I-16.html > (accessed 12 May 2021).

British Counter-Measures

The new threat represented by the torpedo bombers in 1940 initially forced the Royal Navy and the RAF to take countermeasures such as strengthening considerably port defenses as well as increasing the protection of naval convoys which resulted in a greater tie up of resources that were dedicated to the anti-torpedo defense rather than to support offensive actions or other functions. In some instances British convoys were rerouted to the longer route through the Cape of Good Hope so that they would avoid the shorter, but much more dangerous route through the Mediterranean. This was another costly inconvenience of the enemy attacks.

Port Defences – As far as the increased port defenses the British official history outlines some of the countermeasures taken by naval and artillery commanders to check the torpedo bomber threat:

> The air defense of the fleet base caused Admiral Cunningham particular anxiety, primarily on account of the mixed nature of the organization which the Rear-Admiral commanding the fortress had to control. The guns on shore were maimed by British, Maltese, and Egyptian gunners, while all the searchlights were manned by Egyptians. Low-flying aircraft armed with mines or torpedoes constituted a great threat to ships in harbor because the radar could not detect them, which meant that they were most unlikely to be intercepted before delivering their attacks. This was countered to some extent by the rigging and flying of various obstructions, but it was clearly essential for all the guns and searchlights to be most efficiently operated. During November the Italians made a number of night attacks and showed more persistence and determination than hitherto, and this, coupled with the lack of success on the part of the anti-aircraft defenses at night, caused Admiral Cunningham to press strongly for the standard to be improved. Accordingly an Anti-Aircraft Defence Commander was appointed to help the Fortress Commander with the training, supervision and co-ordination of the anti-aircraft defenses; eight of the searchlight positions were taken over by the Royal Wiltshire Yeomanry, who had recently been trained in this work; and British liaison officers were placed with the Egyptian units. It was decided to strengthen and extend the searchlight layout as soon as more equipment and trained men were available.[59]

By the spring of 1941 British harbor anti-aircraft defenses had improved markedly as they increasingly met the challenge posed by both German and Italian aircraft, including torpedo bombers. The British guns located at Malta's main harbor, for example, were centrally controlled. Fifty or more went off at once and the Axis planes had little time to react in maneuvering to alter height and direction. In a matter of minutes, if not less, a multitude of explosions trailed the bombers and torpedo bombers. The gunners, now much better trained than during the first few months of the war, were capable of rapidly adjusting fire at multiple altitudes. As the planes descended to press forward their attack, the heavy guns would light up the sky at aim at 9,000,

59 Major-General I.S.O. Playfair, *The Mediterranean and Middle East Volume I: The Early Successes against Italy (to May 1941),* (London: HMSO, 1954) <http://www.ibiblio.org/hyperwar/UN/UK/UK-Med-I/UK-Med-I-12.html> (accessed 12 May 2021).

6,000 then 4,000 feet. Then the light flak guns, the guns on the ships anchored at harbor and the machine guns would also intervene. An Italian torpedo bomber observer recounted the reception that greeted his squad during an attack on Malta: "Even before the first Sparviero had dived down toward the harbor, the roar of the anti-aircraft guns followed by the volcanic eruption of the battleship guns prevented the aircraft from getting into the range for the torpedo launch. Then the cruisers also opened fire. This concentrated fire was enough to shred to pieces our low flying aircraft."[60] Increasingly it became very difficult for the pilots to launch torpedoes from favorable ranges. Similarly, the gunners on warships also harnessed their skills to fight off torpedo bomber attacks which by their nature "rendered them vulnerable to defensive fire."[61] A British technical report stated that "the control systems in themselves were inadequate to enable controlled fire to be brought to bear on low flying torpedo aircraft and barrage was the normal method of fire used against this form of attack."[62]

Anti-aircraft – At sea the Royal Navy achieved considerable success against standard and torpedo bombers as early as 1941 but particularly great successes were made in mid-1942 mainly because the service adopted early warning systems and it improved the effectiveness of the anti-aircraft gunnery. The first warning signs of the weak or unprepared anti-aircraft defense were witnessed during the Norwegian campaign which brought losses to the British fleet. As Stephen Roskill asserts during the campaign "Forbes himself became very critical about the ineffectiveness of his ships anti-aircraft gunnery; and it was in those months that the mistakes made by the Admiralty before the war in the design of such weapons and their control systems came home to roost."[63] In 1941 increasing challenges to the Royal Navy's position in the Mediterranean made the development of more effective anti-aircraft weapons and tactics on the ships an even greater imperative. Churchill himself was at the forefront pushing the Royal Navy to introduce more effective weapons.[64] The result of this prodding was the introduction of a tachymetric system of fire control that actually measured both the course and the speed of an enemy aircraft and furnished this operational data to a central control system. "the outcome was the long overdue decision to form a Gunnery and Anti-Aircraft Warfare Division, and to appoint a new Assistant Chief of Naval Staff to supervise all aspects of weapons development…..the most important result was to expedite the fitting of the new short wave radar sets to all ships weapons systems."[65] The Tiger convoy of 1941, for example, is offered by the British Official History of the war as a good example of a well escorted and defended convoy which relied on the tactical improvements made primarily by the Royal Navy but also by the fighter escort in fighting off torpedo and standard bomber attacks. This was achieved through a combination of good work by the British fighters, and heavy and concentrated anti-aircraft fire from warships that had been retrofitted with more effective long range guns. Both initiatives had done much to protect the Fleet and the convoy from aerial threats especially from the torpedo bombers. Both the British fighters and the artillery crews on the ships were helped by the fact that more ships by 1941 were fitted

60 Fabio Bianchi, "Gli aerosiluranti italiani", *Storia Militare*, No. 14, June 2014.
61 Vincent P. O'Hara, *Six Victories* (Annapolis Maryland: Naval Institute Press, 2019), p.64.
62 Ibid.
63 Stephen Roskill, *Churchill and the Admirals* (New York: William Morrow, 1978), p.119.
64 Ibid.
65 Ibid, p.181.

with radar. Moreover, the radar sets had been improved from a technological standpoint and there was more experience in using them. By 1942 and especially with Operation Pedestal both the RAF and the Royal Navy would further improve their tactics by fielding more technically advanced fighters and larger range guns operated by experienced personnel on the ships which helped to mitigate the Axis torpedo threat. A few examples will be used to demonstrate the improvements made by the Royal Navy and the RAF to check the Axis aerial threat during the course of the conflict. HMS Warspite, for example, was one of the ships the Royal Navy had reconstructed before the outbreak of the war and was further equipped during the war to improve its anti-aircraft defense. "The range of her armament was increased to 32,000 yards by increasing the elevation of the gun mounts from 20 to 30 degrees and she was also fitted with improved range finding equipment. Weight saving reductions were made and her propulsion system was upgraded, giving her a best speed of approximately 23 knots. Limited improvements were made to her horizontal protection and anti-aircraft armament, which would be further augmented during the war, and radar would be added later."[66] Its most important modifications during the war were the single 4 inch anti-aircraft guns replaced with twin mounts, four additional 2 pounders were added, and a quad 0.5 inch machine gun mount was fitted to the top of the turret. Subsequently the two new High Angle Director Control Towers were fitted with a Type 285 Air Radar, a Type 271 (surface warning) radar was fitted at the top of the lower foremast, a Type 286 (aircraft warning) radar at the masthead, and a Type 284 (Surface Warning) radar was also added. In addition, 20mm Oerlikon cannons were added as a response to the rise of dive and torpedo bombers. The latter enjoyed a high reputation amongst both British and American Navy gunners as an effective short range anti-aircraft weapon.[67] 40mm Bofors guns were also effectively used against dive and torpedo bombers.

Aircraft Carriers – The Royal Navy not only strengthened its anti-aircraft arm but also its aviation support force used to intercept torpedo and other bombers. In another example, the strength of the Fleet was augmented by the arrival in the Mediterranean of ships such as HMS Illustrious whose capabilities strengthened the Royal Navy preparedness against an RM that did not have aircraft carriers: "Her effective low-angle radar and her Fulmar fighters, had greatly increased the freedom of action of the fleet and had given it a high degree of local command of the air. The activities of the Fleet Air Arm were, however, not entirely confined to its primary function of operating from the carriers, for No. 830 Squadron (Swordfish) was used from Malta for attacking enemy shipping, and Swordfish of No. 813 Squadron had been operating with the Royal Air Force in the Western Desert, in attacks upon coastal shipping. Others had attacked targets in the Dodecanese from Crete."[68]

Radar – During Operation Hats in August 1940, for example, the Royal Navy not only attacked Italian bases on the coast of Sardinia but also forced through the Mediterranean a major convoy to resupply the beleaguered island of Malta. According to the British Official History one

66 Greene and Massignani, *The Naval War,* pp.46-47.
67 Mark E. Stille, *US Navy Ships Vs Japanese Attack Aircraft* (Oxford: Osprey, 2020), p.7.
68 Major-General I.S.O. Playfair, *The Mediterranean and Middle East Volume I: The Early Successes against Italy (to May 1941),* (London: HMSO, 1954) <http://www.ibiblio.org/hyperwar/UN/UK/UK-Med-I/UK-Med-I-16.html> (accessed 12 May 2021).

aspect behind the success of the operation was that the "four ships with the Force were equipped with radar made it possible not only to detect the enemy's shadowing aircraft but also to direct fighters on to their targets; with the result that during the first two days fighters claimed to have shot down some of the shadowers and no bombing attacks developed."[69]

Fighters – The RAF also further improved its capability to escort naval convoys at sea or when attempting to intercept torpedo bombers targeting port infrastructure. Special fighter units were specifically organized to check torpedo attacks, then fighters with improved speed and armament were progressively introduced. The *Sparvieri* in the early stages of the war faced Fulmar fighters, for example, which were very good airplanes but could still reasonably be dealt with by the weapons and speed of the S.79. With a top speed of 272 mph (438 km/h), the Fulmars still had an edge over a torpedo carrying S.79, but the latter could deploy ample defensive fire. The Blenheim IF were then introduced in the Mediterranean theatre and although they were well armed with four .303 inch machine guns and had a very good range they were found to be slow and would be vulnerable to enemy fighter attack aircraft. Similarly, the Beaufighter Mark IC long-range fighter, although faster than the S.79 was still considered a threat that could be reasonably be dealt with. But in 1942 the RAF began to deploy much faster fighters such as the Hawker Hurricane and the Supermarine Spitfire Mk IX with a top speed of 404 mph (650 km/h) which were more than a match for the S.79. The number of downed S.79 in 1942 is a testament of the increased competition faced by the Italian torpedo bombers. Still, the multiple machine guns on the *Sparviero* were also effective when the aircraft was challenged by these faster enemy fighters, although *Sparviero* losses continued to increase in 1942 and 1943. The following are the recollections of *Tenente* Giuseppe Cimicchi of a close encounter between two *Sparvieri* and some much faster enemy fighters. Although the S.79 operated at a lower speed than the Spitfires, its defensive fire was fairly concentrated and could produce a large volume of fire that was often fatal for the enemy aircraft. Its numerous machine guns could sometimes offset its lack of speed and overtake the much faster and more difficult to pin down enemy planes.

> Thirteen Spitfires now are vomiting all their firepower at my aircraft and at Caresio's and we close in on each other as if seeking protection and go low zigzagging over the surface of the water to avoid the enemy's attacks. But 13 Spitfires like a pack of dogs excited by the smell of blood are more aggressive than ever. Are they invulnerable? No, at last one of them struck by our gunfire catches fire and plunges into the sea. Flying as we are a few meters above the sea's surface we see the water seething with spray under the hailstorm of fire. One Spitfire has threaded its way between Caresio's aircraft and mine. Caresio is challenged to a duel. At the machine gun is wireless operator airman Aldo Manca, a brave good boy. He has good aim, for the British fighter is hit and breaks away, its tail smoking. But Manca too is fatally hit. He will be awarded a posthumous silver medal.[70]

69 Major-General I.S.O. Playfair, *The Mediterranean and Middle East Volume I: The Early Successes against Italy (to May 1941),* (London: HMSO, 1954) <https://www.ibiblio.org/hyperwar/UN/UK/UK-Med-I/UK-Med-I-10.html#Page201> (accessed 12 May 2021).

70 Marco Mattioli, *Savoia Marchetti S.79 Sparviero*, p.66.

Nevertheless, the material air superiority of the Allied air forces achieved in 1942 increased the vulnerability of the S.79. By late 1942 the umbrella-like protection provided by Allied fighters of the naval convoys barred *Sparviero* daylight operations. The latter were forced to conduct combat actions primarily at dawn or dusk thus reducing the overall number of operations that could be carried out.

Improved port defenses and naval convoys with more robust air force escort made the job of the torpedo bombers much more dangerous and difficult. By late 1941 the Royal Navy was also in a much-improved position to anticipate the arrival of the torpedo bombers thus denying the enemy the element of surprise. This was achieved through the use of radar and by deploying more reconnaissance aircraft. The first line of defense against torpedo bomber attacks was the dispatching from aircraft carriers of fighters to interfere with Italian air force operations. These were also supported by Malta or North Africa based fighters. Then, as soon as an S.79 was spotted the anti-aircraft defense would open up a hellish fire even at a distance of 6,000 meters from the plane. Then they would also fire the weapons just above the water, then 50 feet higher and then 100 feet higher. Finally the 20 mm Oerlikon guns would open up fire alongside the machine guns. This curtain of fire would make the life miserable for a *Sparviero* pilot attempting to release the torpedo at close range. "Although aircraft torpedoes were brutally effective weapons, they had to be delivered at very close ranges; it took brave, dedicated men to fly directly into the concentrated fire from a capital ship to drop a torpedo. Torpedo planes of all nations experienced very high losses during World War II, and flying torpedo planes was an extremely hazardous occupation. In the attack on Pearl Harbor, the Japanese "Kate" torpedo planes inflicted the most damage, but they also suffered the highest percentage of losses during their attacks on the battleships."[71]

At the end of the war the Italian military statistics indicated that a *Sparviero* crew would on average carry out three missions before being shot down. It was an extremely dangerous job, almost to the point of being quasi-suicidal especially for units that had less experienced pilots and crews. In 'Operation Pedestal' British historian Max Hastings reports that during the attacks on the convoy: "The torpedo carriers had taken off in low spirits. Martino Aichner kept unhappily repeating to himself a statistic avowed by his squadron, that a pilot might hope to survive no more than three attacks on enemy shipping."[72]

Decline of the S.79 and attempts to go beyond it

As historian Jack Greene asserts the Italian torpedo bomber units could have been even more effective if the air force and the domestic industry had collaborated to design a true torpedo bomber:

> One area in which the Italian air force excelled was the torpedo bomber. Although use of this plane was hindered by inter service rivalry before the war, the torpedo bomber was deployed to units by late 1940. German air units later successfully emulated Italian torpedo

71 Arthur Burke, *Torpedoes* <https://apps.dtic.mil/dtic/tr/fulltext/u2/1033484.pdf> (accessed 21 May 2021).

72 Max Hastings, *Operation Pedestal* (New York: Harper Collins, 2021), p.157.

bomber tactics and purchased torpedoes from Italy. Yet Italians chose simply to adapt a three engine S.79 level bomber for torpedo bombing rather than design a true torpedo bomber.[73]

A true torpedo bomber was not available in 1940 as industry and the armed forces at large were caught unprepared with Italy's sudden entry into the conflict. The services had by that time developed multi-year goals and objectives and they were not anticipating intervening in a conflict prior to 1943.

The industry did attempt beginning in 1939 to develop a successor to the S.79 in the form of the *Savoia Marchetti* S.84. The basic technical concept behind this new plane was to use the technical design platform of the S.79 and improve upon it. S.84 had the same wing design of the S.79 but had more powerful Piaggio engines and the defensive weapons were rationalized to 4 x 12,7 mm machine guns. But unfortunately, the plane did not meet expectations. Although faster, it had many performance issues during takeoff, and it had a much-reduced maneuverability than the S.79. The S.79 was eventually rendered obsolete by the Italian industry's failure to design and manufacture a faster torpedo bomber and by Italy's capitulation on 8 September 1943. For a brief time the tri-motor upgraded version of the Cant. Z.1017bis was then sought as a replacement to the S.79 because it combined speed and high maneuverability. However, only one prototype was tested extensively as a torpedo bomber and then the project was dropped. Similarly, the *Reggiane* Re.2001 was also evaluated for the torpedo bomber role and matched to a smaller torpedo than the standard Whitehead torpedo. Unfortunately also in this case only one prototype was developed and briefly evaluated before Italy exited the war.

Despite its many strengths, the S.79 became less successful as the war progressed, especially after the Allies introduced more technologically advanced fighters. The Royal Navy also conducted extensive training for its gunners to spot, identify and shoot down the torpedo bombers. Radar played a big role in improving the defense of naval convoys.

As more warships were retrofitted with radar torpedo bomber operations became much more complicated. In addition to up gunned and more technologically sophisticated defenses in British warships, the S.79 lost ground also because some of its major flaws were never addressed during the war. The *Sparviero* lacked stabilizing gyroscopes and modern electrical devices for the pilot and the bombardier to communicate with each other during an attack. If the bombardier wanted to talk with the pilot, he was forced to crawl up to the cockpit. This rather cumbersome system of communication caused delays that often led to unsuccessful operations. Likewise the instrumentation panel remained poor especially with regards to tools to aid the pilot in launching the warhead. German torpedo bombers, for example, were fitted with more precise tools and aiming devices, but during the war no attempts were made by the RA to secure such state of the art equipment for its aircraft. Another limitation of the S.79 was its limited endurance of 2,000 kilometers which hindered its effectiveness against the furthest British bases in the Mediterranean such as Gibraltar and Alexandria. *Capitano* Carlo Emanuele Buscaglia and aviation engineer Carlo Baudazzi in 1942 worked on a special project to increase the endurance of the S.79 by adding an additional fuel tank without hampering the plane's performance.

73 Jack Greene, "Air Force, Italy" in Spencer C. Tucker, *World War II: The Definitive Encyclopedia* (New York: ABC-CLIO, 2016), p.871.

Baudazzi was able to redesign the fuel tank compartment adding an overload of 1,100 liters of fuel, but the modified S.79 was only built as a prototype. "If industry and the R&D department of Guidonia had had the drive of Buscaglia, we could have deployed already in 1940 S.79s with greater endurance to strategically bomb British bases. This could have achieved much more strategic results."[74] Another negative factor was its tri-motor design with the third motor in the nose of the plane which "reduced the forward vision of the pilot and accuracy of the bombardier."[75] The Italians also lacked adequate service facilities, and it was not unusual at any given time during the war for up to a third of the *Sparviero* fleet to be unfit for military operations. Historian Marco Mattioli, for example, gives us a snapshot of *Sparviero* fleet overall efficiency in 1943. At the time of Operation Husky there were approximately 100 S.79 available to the torpedo bomber units, but only 41 were airworthy, while most S.84 had already been retired as torpedo bombers.[76] A report by *Regia Aeronautica* published a few days before the launch of Operation Husky also gives an indication of overall fleet efficiency when it mentions the presence of 110 S.79s at operational bases, of which only 80 were airworthy.[77] The enemy intelligence services, for example, during the planning phase of Operation Pedestal in the summer of 1942 estimated the serviceability of the Italian air forces to be around 55%.[78] Therefore it is fairly safe to assert that overall fleet efficiency during the campaign was not very high. It was probably higher in 1940-41 or early 1942 when the Italian war effort was at its highest and industry was at its peak, but it steadily declined after. Lack of spare parts and slow production rates of new S.79s also greatly limited the Italian war effort. In spite of the *Sparviero*'s design flaws and poor service capabilities, Allied intelligence continued to issue reports warning naval personnel about the dangers posed by the a*erosiluranti* well into 1943. U.S. intelligence reports on Axis torpedo squadrons (see below), for example, singled out the S.79 as one of the most powerful aircraft deployed by the *Regia Aeronautica* and noted that its pilots had the highest morale of any unit in the Italian military. Their effectiveness against enemy ships was recognized even by the generally better-equipped *Luftwaffe*, which in 1941 had dispatched bomber pilots to Italy for instructions in torpedo tactics. Several German bomber squadrons also flew S.79s.

As with the torpedo bomber warhead technological innovation also stalled, or was not successful in time, during the war contributing to the decline of the *Sparviero*. One of the pitfalls of the Whitehead torpedo was that it could not be regulated during flight. It's under water depth while travelling against a destroyer or an aircraft carrier could not be differentiated according to the intended target of the attack. This factor hampered launch efficacy especially when it was made against smaller targets. Pilot Giulio Marini had developed a system to regulate the torpedo's bathymetric valves during flight. But since there were two types of torpedoes (*Whitehead* and *Siluro Italiano*) it could not be adopted since it only worked for the Whitehead torpedo. Extensive studies were also conducted to develop a smaller torpedo (*silurotto*) that

74 Martino Aichner, *Il gruppo Buscaglia*, p.98.
75 Brian Sullivan, "Downfall of the Regia Aeronautica" in Robin Higham (ed.), *Why Air Forces Fail* (Lexington: University Press of Kentucky, 2006), p.147.
76 Marco Mattioli, *Savoia Marchetti S.79 Sparviero*, p.72.
77 Ufficio Storico Aeronautica Militare: "La situazione al 9 luglio 1943", 4° Reparto di Superaereo n. 7025077, 9 July 1943.
78 TNA ADM 223/341: Mediterranean Dispositions, 22 July 1942, p.2.

could be transported and released by faster fighter aircraft such as the *Reggiane* Re.2001. But this effort although successful came too late in the war to have any impact.[79]

Radio directed torpedoes were also extensively designed and tested but also could not be introduced until mid-1943. On 28 March, during the celebrations for the 20th anniversary of the creation of *Regia Aeronautica*, a presentation of this new weapon was made in Pisa. Mussolini and his entourage reviewed the 41° *Gruppo* armed with several S.79 equipped with radio-controlled torpedoes, which due to the worsening of the conflict for Italy never saw action.[80]

Another missed opportunity was the failure to introduce in time a deadlier warhead to replace the standard Whitehead torpedo. At the end of 1941 industry together with the R&D facility of Guidonia had modified the head, which was capable of about 200 kg of explosive, in place of the 170 kg of the standard Whitehead torpedo. But by the time Italy exited the war, industry had not been able to mass produce this more lethal warhead. According to a notable historian of the Italian air force the domestic industry's main pitfall, however, remained the failure to follow up with an improved bomber during the conflict: "For the aerosiluranti unit only one plane, with the exception of one Stormo that flew S.84s, the S.79 was used during the conflict. This plane had won many international competitions in peacetime, was used extensively as a bomber in Spain, and as a bomber and reconnaissance plane during the war. Undoubtedly the S.79 was a successful aircraft, but it could not maintain its primacy for a period of over ten years without much needed modifications. If by the end of the conflict our pilots were still flying this plane made of canvas, wood and steel, then industry failed to develop a more modern, technically superior successor to the S.79."[81]

3: AMERICAN INTELLIGENCE SERVICES REPORT ON ITALIAN TORPEDO BOMBER

Torpedo Bomber (Italian SM-79)

The land-based Savoia-Marchetti (SM-79) bomber is the most widely used of several types of aircraft employed by the Italian Air Force. This aircraft has long been the mainstay of the bomber squadrons, and has been adapted successfully for torpedo-carrying purposes.

The SM-79 is a large, low-wing, tri-motored monoplane of metal and plywood construction. The engines, approximately 1,000 horsepower each, give the aircraft, when used as a bomber, a speed of almost 300 miles per hour. When a torpedo is carried, the plane has a top speed of about 200 miles per hour. The SM-79 normally carries a crew of four—two pilots, a radio operator, and a bombardier.

The depth settings of the torpedoes carried vary according to the size of the target. When employed against convoys, the aircraft carry torpedoes with several settings, the planes with deeper settings always attacking the larger vessels. These settings are adjusted by special torpedo mechanics and cannot be altered in flight.

79 Franco Pagliano, *Storia di 10.000 aeroplani* (Milan: Mursia, 2003), p.83.
80 Ibid., pp.83-84.
81 Ibid, p.77.

An attack by torpedo bombers is usually made at dawn or dusk. Dusk is considered preferable since the aircraft may make a low, unobserved approach toward the target, which is silhouetted against the horizon. The attacks are always made from the east since this is the direction of poorest visibility. Daylight attacks are suicidal and are very seldom attempted.

Early in the war Italian aircraft torpedo attacks were usually made by individual aircraft and were not pressed home. Recently, however, these attacks have been better coordinated and many of them have been made at comparatively close range.

Torpedo squadrons are believed to have the highest morale of all units of the Italian Air Force. Their efficiency is such that Germany has sent squadrons to Italy for instructions in torpedo tactics. Italian aircraft torpedoes are believed to be superior to those of German design and are probably used by the German Air Force.[82]

82 Intelligence report on the Italian Savoia-Marchetti (SM-79) torpedo bomber and its tactics. See *Intelligence Bulletin*, United States Army, Washington DC, January 1943.

3

Approach to War

Despite the RA's and, most importantly the entire military apparatus, utter unpreparedness for total war, Mussolini in May-June 1940 was eager to enter a conflict that in his view would be short because Germany was on the verge of defeating France and thus forcing Britain to sue for peace.

As the mighty German war machine was overcoming French defenses one by one, on 9 April 1940 the Italian politicians and the upper echelons of the military met to discuss a potential entry by Italy in the war. While the politicians were optimistic, the generals were skeptical. The head of the armed forces Pietro Badoglio detailed the military's lack of tanks, artillery pieces and equipment. In his view the country given the lack of modern weaponry was not prepared to fight until at least 1943.[1] RM Chief of Staff Domenico Cavagnari stated that the "enemy fleet will place itself at Gibraltar and at the other end of Suez and we shall choke in between."[2]

Meanwhile RA Chief of Staff Pricolo was also doubtful of military intervention into the conflict stating that many in the upper echelons of the army had "too many illusions about aero-naval offensives, the possibilities of which are few."[3] In essence, Italy's entry into the war presented its armed forces with significant challenges. First, Italy had to keep the Central Mediterranean free from British and French military interference. Second, its armed forces had also to maintain open the sea lanes to East and North Africa to supply its military and civilians based in Libya and Italian East Africa. These dual objectives were likely to present challenging tasks since the French and the British had very powerful naval and aerial forces and possessed bases such as Gibraltar, Corsica and Malta from which they could launch their military assets to intercept Italian convoys or interfere with the battlefleet. From the onset to some military planners the biggest obstacle for the Italians appeared to be the British base of Malta which was located a few miles from Sicilian shore. Malta's importance during the war grew tremendously and rested on it being an advanced air and submarine base against Axis shipping in the central Mediterranean. Moreover, Malta-based aircraft could also provide fighter escort necessary for British naval operations as well as conduct strikes against Italian air bases in Sicily and Sardinia. With a central operational base in the center of Italian convoy routes, Royal Navy submarines and destroyers based in Malta could gain a strategic advantage. Unfortunately, during the

1 Pietro Badoglio, *Italy in the Second World War* (London: Oxford University Press, 1948), p.1.
2 Ibid., p.4.
3 Ibid.

period of non-belligerence little had been done mainly by the RM to study the Malta problem and to plan a seaborne and airborne invasion of the island fortress. A fortress that at the beginning of the war was almost inviting an invasion given that it had no real defenses, few troops and guns on the ground, five aircraft and few small naval vessels. Moreover, during the initial stages of the conflict Malta lacked basic military infrastructure such as submarine pens against aerial attack or underground hangars for the RAF. Both the RM and the RA during the pre-war period had recognized Malta's decisive importance to the conduct of war in the Mediterranean but had done very little planning. In 1938, for example, naval advisers proposed to *Comando Supremo* a preliminary plan for the capture of the island which was based on a joint initiative between the RM and the RA and was based on close air support to the fleet. But the plan did not go beyond the initial preliminary stages because the air strategists expressed a reluctance to cooperate in a combined land-sea operation and argued that Malta could be eliminated by air attack alone. Since the RM was unwilling to undertake further planning without full cooperation from the RA and the plan was shelved.[4]

On 5 June 1940, just a few days before Italy would enter the war, a meeting was held by the heads of the three armed services in which *Maresciallo* Rodolfo Graziani, Chief of Army General Staff, raised the issue of Malta and whether its takeover was being planned only to be confronted by the RM Chief of Staff Cavagnari who objected that his organization had no experience nor the required capabilities related to a seaborne and airborne take-over of an island fortress.

Moreover, he argued based on faulty intelligence that "given the exceptional difficulties that an invasion requires and the large deployment that it would call for, a takeover of Malta would be justified only if the British intend to make it their firm base in the Mediterranean. But having the British given up on Malta, it appears that the island will not represent a serious obstacle to our sea routes and our naval bases."[5] The RM believed that Malta in 1940 was of "secondary importance"[6] to the British overall strategy in the Mediterranean and that the British army would not concentrate large numbers of forces and weapons there.

Meanwhile, RA Chief of Staff *Generale* Pricolo was of the belief that his service had enough bombers to subdue the island fortress if that goal became a priority. Evidently even the air forces head had underestimated the task of taking Malta or merely even temporarily subduing it. This became evident once the war began and the RA alone would reveal itself unable to subdue Malta.

The meeting adjourned with Badoglio merely urging the two services to begin a detailed study on the feasibility of the takeover of Malta. Thus, it can be argued that the minutes of the meeting demonstrate that Italy entered the war with no predetermined plans for the capture of Malta, and its major efforts to subdue it relied primarily upon the air service to neutralize the threat of British employment of the island as an offensive air and naval jump off platform. The underestimation of Malta's importance to the British strategy in the Mediterranean would prove to be one of the major blunders by the Italians during the war. Equally the lack of a plan to take the island fortress in the early months of the conflict would also represent a major handicap to a strategy aimed at dominating the Mediterranean. Throughout the month of June, the RM began to evaluate the Malta problem and came up with a rudimentary plan for a takeover of the island fortress. "In June 1940 the navy examined the task of taking Malta and concluded that

4 M.A. Bragadin, *Che ha fatto la Marina?* (Milan: Garzanti, 1947), pp.15-20.
5 Gianni Rocca, *I Disperati*, p.114.
6 Ufficio Storico: Regia Marina, "Investimento di Malta," 18 June 1940.

it would have to be weakened by protracted air action and submarine blockade after which a force of at least 20,000 men would effect a landing helped by parachute troops. The RM would bombard defenses, not risking the two Littorios, but doubted whether it would be able to dominate the eighty-odd batteries of guns, most of which were sited in caverns. It would, the sailors concluded, be an arduous undertaking. "[7] The RM plan relied heavily on massive bombardments by the air forces to soften the island and hence pave the way for a seaborne landing. Thus its plan was dependent on the effectiveness of the bombings by the RA. At the time, it can be argued, based on the achievements of the first year of the war, that the air force units did not possess the resources to carry out a sustained and effective bombing campaign against Malta.

Not only did the plan call for inter service collaboration but it also called for the deployment of special troops such as the paratroopers that Italy did not have at the time. It was evident that a planned invasion of Malta would take time mostly in the buildup of the force necessary for a successful operation. Moreover, fundamental considerations such as the amount of fuel necessary to conduct the operation, for example, were not even examined once again demonstrating that the strategic takeover plan of the fortress was in June 1940 in its infancy.

On 10 June 1940, when the French were about to fall and the conflict appeared to be virtually over, did Italy enter the war in the hope of sharing some territorial and material spoils with the German ally. The die was cast. With French collapse, British isolation, and Germany triumphant, a window of opportunity for Mussolini and the Italian government appeared to have opened. The collapse of France altered the balance of naval power, but it did not change Italian naval policy in the Mediterranean. Specifically, the Italian naval staff continued to adhere to a conservative policy that its forces were to remain on the defensive at each end of the Mediterranean; only in the center were they to act offensively and engage the enemy fleet especially when they enjoyed superior forces. Since the RM had no prospect of receiving newly built battleships during the war to replace losses, the overall policy was to engage in battle sparingly and only when the Italian naval formations held a numerical advantage over the enemy. Meanwhile traffic to and from Africa had to be safeguarded to maintain control of Libya and East Africa. As naval historian Mark Stille argues: "In almost every major battle involving cruisers, Italian on scene commanders were handicapped by restrictive orders that they were not to engage a British force unless a clear superiority was evident. Given the difficulties of coordinating air reconnaissance with the Italian Air Force, and the almost universal unavailability of accurate and timely reconnaissance reports, the RM rarely fought sustained actions, even when it possessed superior strength."[8] The Italian Navy saw its main role as the entity that could guarantee the free flow of goods and armaments between Italy and its colonial possessions. As Vincent O'Hara states at the beginning of the conflict the Allies aimed to flex their muscle by way of challenging the Italian fleet to a major encounter battle in the Central Mediterranean, while the Italians planned to respond by deploying primarily their small craft fleet (torpedo boats, submarines, etc..) in cooperation with the air force to ambush the enemy battleships.[9] Despite its conservative policy, the RM at the beginning of the war had a significant force, especially in light of the fact that the British fleet was involved in multiple theatres of operation.

7 John Gooch, *Mussolini's War* (New York: Simon and Schuster, 2020), p.193.
8 Mark E. Stille, *Italian Cruisers of World War II* (Oxford: Osprey, 2018), p.5.
9 Vincent O'Hara, *In Passage Perilous: Malta and the Convoy Battles of June 1942* (Indianapolis, Indiana: Indiana University Press, 2021), p.11.

The RM had six battleships with which to contend for control of the Mediterranean, while the French and British had 12. Two (*Littorio* and *Vittorio Veneto*) battleships were received after the war broke out and these were the most modern ships at the disposal of the RM. Each displaced 45,000 tons, were 780 feet long and had triple turrets each mounted with three 381 mm guns. The four older ships included the *Cavour* class ships (*Cavour* and *Giulio Cesare*) which had originally been built in 1911 and could do twenty-seven knots and mounted 305 mm guns. The other two main battleships were the *Doria* class ships: *Andrea Doria* and *Caio Duilio* which were built in 1913 and could do twenty-six knots. In addition, to the six capital ships, the Italians had 21 cruisers, 54 destroyers, 67 torpedo boats, and 116 submarines against the twenty-seven cruisers, and seventy-four destroyers of the combined British and French fleet force. Its main cruisers were the *Trento* and *Trieste* both 13,000 tons and equipped with eight 203 mm guns and four 14,000 tons ships equipped with 203 mm guns (*Fiume, Gorizia, Pola and Zara*). Though the RM had a number of fast new cruisers with good range in their gunnery, the older classes had weak defensive armor. The Italian fleet was fairly large, but it included a number of older vessels, and its crews were generally not experienced. Its biggest limitations, however, were tactical in nature. The ships lacked the latest technological advances such as radar and sonar. No RM battleship or cruiser had radar at the beginning of the war and only a few received it by 1943, just a few months before the Armistice. This meant that in night engagements or foul weather, the Italian ships were unable to detect the approach of their British adversaries. When engaged, they could only range their guns if they were able to visually locate their targets.

In order to carry out its main tasks the RM had to rely on air reconnaissance and air cover. But having no aircraft carriers and equipped with only a few reconnaissance seaplanes the RM was dependent upon the air force who operated all other aircraft for the support of naval operations. The fact that the RM was to be supported mainly by aircraft under air force command called for a close collaboration between the two branches which at the start of the war was not very strong, mainly because of the history of inter service rivalry that stemmed back seventeen years. "Combined operations call for cooperation and coordination, but interservice rivalries and jealousies blocked close liaison, rapid communication and shared responsibilities."[10] In light of the rivalry between the two services, it would take some time for them to establish a modicum of interservice collaboration, which was only enhanced after several trials and errors. A rudimentary but procedurally complex communication system that inhibited radio communication between warships and aircraft also did not facilitate such close collaboration. The RA at the time had no experience of collaboration with the RM although since the start of the war it was tasked with providing coverage for the naval convoys and for the battlefleet.

10 Thomas P. Lowry, The *Attack on Taranto* (Mechanicsburg, Pennsylvania: Stackpole, 1995), p.44.

4

War

Overall Military Situation

Italy declared war against France and Britain on 10 June 1940. After the very brief campaign against France ended in late June 1940, the Italian government opened another theatre of operations in North Africa by building up the capabilities of the X Army for a planned offensive against the British army in Egypt. This was to be led by generals under Italo Balbo, Governor General of Libya. But after the death of Balbo in a friendly fire incident on 28 June 1940, *Maresciallo* Graziani, who at the start of the Second World War was the Chief of Staff of the *Regio Esercito* was appointed as Commander-in-Chief of Italian troops in North Africa and as Governor General of Libya. The latter was instructed to plan the invasion of Egypt and was initially given a deadline of 8 August 1940 to start the operation by the Italian government. Graziani, based on the feedback received from his planners, soon began to ask for more time to amass more resources arguing that his large but non-mechanized force was not in a position to go on the offensive. However, pressured by the political authorities, Graziani's X Army invaded Egypt on 9 September. In a brief offensive the Italians achieved only modest gains in Egypt arriving at Sidi Barrani where they then prepared a series of fortified camps to defend their positions. Meanwhile, after a further buildup of troops and tanks, Graziani wowed to launch another leap forward in November. By October 1940 the Italian armed forces, but especially the air forces, were further stretched when the government decided to launch the invasion of Greece, which ultimately led to a major redeployment of forces of all kinds including medium tanks, bombers and torpedo bombers as the Greek Army put up a gallant defense and the Italians were forced to deploy a greater number of soldiers and arms in the campaign. This caused the rerouting of tanks and equipment of all kinds including aircraft from Italy to Greece rather than to North Africa. On 8 December 1940 the British, seeing a favorable circumstance with Italian troops deployed both in North Africa and in Greece, counterattacked and pushed back the X Army into Libya during Operation Compass thus dealing a serious blow to their enemy. In addition, at this time Italy had also dispatched an air force of 200 aircraft to help the *Luftwaffe* in the Battle of Britain and had also undertook an offensive in East Africa against British Somaliland.

During the early stages of the war Malta had still not build up a decent strike force to interdict Italian supply convoys destined to North and East Africa and although the RA began to bomb the island almost on a daily basis, In mid-1940 Malta appeared to not represent a major threat to Italian interests abroad. But in November the Royal Navy had conducted a brilliant raid against Italian battleships moored at Taranto inflicting serious damage.

The RA in 1940

In addition to providing escort coverage for the Italian Navy when it deployed its battlefleet or for when it escorted convoys to Africa and Albania, the RA had also other tasks to carry out at the onset of the war. A key objective was to act aggressively in the central Mediterranean by interfering with the Royal Navy convoys destined to Malta and Alexandria and by subduing a threat close to home, such as Malta with pinpoint bombardments. Lastly, the RA was expected to be a part of the *guerra di rapido corso* by supporting the infantry and the mechanized columns as they advanced in major offensives against the enemy in Europe or abroad.

To carry out all of the tasks assigned to the air service by the summer of 1940 *Generale* Pricolo had increased the number of modern bombers and fighters to 995 and 574 respectively, but only 573 bombers and 368 fighters across the entire Mediterranean basin were deemed operational.[1] The bomber force was comprised primarily of medium bombers since there were no dive bombers, torpedo bombers or heavy, long range bombers. Whereas, the fighter *Stormi* were primarily equipped with Fiat CR.42 biplane fighters, that despite incorporating some modern elements of fighter design, were lightly armed. More modern, all metal monoplanes such as the *Macchi* C.200 and the Fiat G.50 were only introduced in greater numbers in 1941 when they became the fighters of choice of the *Stormi* of the RA. In addition, fighter pilots training for metal monoplanes aircraft was still in an embryonic state in 1939-40, as generally pilots preferred to fly the biplanes which were light and sleek and allowed them to perform stunts and evasive maneuvers typical of the tactics adopted during and after the First World War.

This force from the onset was not considered to be strong enough for a protracted war against the British. Its standard bomber fleet had performed well against the Spanish Republicans, but fighting against the RAF was an altogether different story. Delays in planning and production were mainly responsible for the RA's modest force at the beginning of the war. Other delays had been caused by inter service rivalries especially with regards to the torpedo bombers. Giuseppe Santoro, the RA's official historian, has stated that "technical evaluations were conducted very slowly without a precise vision of the problem, and without a determined will to quickly reach its solution." And this was also because "between the Air Force and the Navy a struggle took place to determine which of the two administrations was to pay for the procurement of torpedoes and on which of the two budgets should this expense be recorded." A question that, as General Santoro asserted, at the beginning of the conflict unfortunately was "still unresolved."[2] The same state of unpreparedness was prevalent in other sections of the RA. For example, the service had no long range, heavy bombers that had the endurance to target enemy capitals such as London, or the Suez Canal or the oilfields. In the medium bomber realm the service was reliant on three aircraft models whose frame was composed of a mixture of wood/canvas/steel, while in the fighter realm a large section of the fleet was still constituted by CR.42 biplanes.

1 Brian Sullivan, "Downfall of the Regia Aeronautica," in Robin Higham (ed.), *Why Air Forces Fail* (Lexington, Kentucky: University Press of Kentucky, 2006), p.152.
2 Giuseppe Santoro, *L'aeronautica italiana nella seconda guerra mondiale*, p.45.

Torpedo Bomber Units Organization

The fledgling torpedo bomber organization was established with the formation of the *Raggruppamento Sperimentale Aerosiluranti* formed in Gorizia on 25 July 1940, a month and a half after the start of the war and posted shortly thereafter at El Adem airbase in Libya where it began to undertake its first operations with only five torpedo bombers. On 3 September 1940 it was converted into the 278ª *Squadriglia Autonoma Aerosiluranti* and was headquartered in Cyrenaica, Libya. The only other torpedo bomber unit established in 1940 was the 279ª *Squadriglia Autonoma Aerosiluranti* which was founded in Gorizia on 26 December 1940, whereby this time a torpedo bomber school had also been set up (28 October 1940) and led by *Tenente Colonnello* Carlo Unia of *1º Nucleo Addestramento Aerosiluranti*. This training branch of the discipline would provide the teaching foundation to help establish five newly formed *Squadriglie* of torpedo bombers during the first half of 1941. Since the first torpedo bomber unit was fairly effective against the Royal Navy, one question that emerged periodically in the second half of 1940 was what was being done to expand the discipline. At a meeting of the *Comando Supremo* in December of 1940, Chief of Staff of the *Regia Aeronautica* Pricolo was pressed by Badoglio about why there were so few torpedo bombers available when Italy entered the war and why there were only twenty-five S.79 torpedo bomber planes in service as of December 1940. Replying to the critique, *Generale* Pricolo argued that only one prototype was available in June 1940 and since then the domestic industry had done an above average job of retrofitting existing S.79s for torpedo bomber service and had readily replaced the losses.[3] As of December 1940, he reported, one torpedo had been lost during the Alexandria raid and three had been destroyed by enemy fire. Moreover, he stated that his main worry at the time was not with how many aircraft the domestic industry could convert for torpedo bomber service but with the dwindling supply of warheads. Thirty-seven torpedoes had been dropped with at least 3 confirmed targets between August and December 1940.[4] These were manufactured at only two plants (Fiume and Naples) and the Germans were also seriously contributing to a dwindling inventory with their steady monthly torpedo purchases. A July 1940 purchase of a batch of aerial torpedoes for the *Regia Aeronautica* had clearly not solved the long term steady supply problem since Whitehead by the fall of 1940 was already at maximum productive capacity while trying to meet demand for both naval and aerial torpedoes. Its modest monthly output had prompted *Generale* Pricolo on 28 September 1940 to write a letter to *Ammiraglio* Cavagnari, undersecretary and Chief of Staff of the RM to demand that the latter provide the flintlocks for the warheads, which up to that point had been procured solely by the RM. In addition, *Generale* Pricolo had asked for a batch of 20 additional torpedoes under production for the Germans to be re-assigned to the RA. While the RM initially balked at the demand to provide flintlocks to the RA, on 29 September the *Kriegsmarine* agreed to the demand to provide some aerial torpedoes by stating: "We are in agreement that the Whitehead firm of Fiume deliver 20 aerial torpedoes to Italy. Whitehead will receive a communication with regards to this matter."[5] The German agreement allowed torpedo bomber operations to continue for at least a few months. On 21 November the

3 Gianni Rocca, I *disperati*, p.151.
4 Marco Mattioli, *Savoia-Marchetti S.79 Sparviero*, p.12.
5 Francesco Mattesini, *Luci ed ombre degli aerosiluranti italiani e tedeschi nel Mediterraneo* (Rome: Ristampa SRL, 2019), p.33.

issue related to a ramp up in production of torpedoes by Whitehead was addressed at a joint meeting between the Italian and German Navy in Munich. The meeting, chaired by Admiral Beckenkchler, put forth two ideas for increasing production. One was to license production of naval and aerial torpedoes to German firms, while the second was to provide Whitehead with twenty new tool machines that were to be paid by the Italian state so that the former could increase production.[6] Accordingly, it was envisioned that production could be increased from the current 55 torpedoes per month to an estimated 100 by early 1941. On 24 November the RM finally agreed to the demands of the RA by committing to furnish the latter with its share of flintlocks and of warheads so that aerial torpedoes units: "Having shown their ability to inflict damage to the enemy…can be expanded and utilized fully and to the largest extent possible by devolving to them the resources and the men that it needs to carry out its tasks." It concluded by stating that the RM was ready to "provide all the weapons that could be readily utilized."[7] Thus, ultimately the RA prevailed against the RM because of two reasons: First, the first set of successful torpedo bomber operations between September and December 1940 had given credibility to the new discipline. Second, the RM after the 11 November 1940 battle with the British East Mediterranean Fleet at Taranto was in a situation of crisis with many of its activities paralyzed by the losses sustained. The twenty aerial torpedoes reassigned to the RA represented another stop gap solution to keep torpedo bomber operations alive, while the concessions made by the RM to the air force were more structural in nature but still did not guarantee a steady supply.

Initially the torpedo bombers were deployed primarily at El Adem, Libya to carry out operations against British battle and transport ships in the Mediterranean. When Italy invaded Greece in October, the British responded by installing troops and weapons in the island of Crete. In addition, the RAF came to the aid of the Greeks by deploying bombers and fighters in the Aegean. This forced the RA to also deploy its assets in the region and by early 1941 bombers and torpedo bombers were deployed in Gadurra, a base in the island of Rhodes. The *34° Gruppo Autonomo* (*67ª and 68ª Squadriglie*) was converted to the torpedo bomber role in 1941 but initially in late November 1940, still as a standard bomber unit, it was headquartered in Rhodes. At the time, it possessed four S.79 torpedo bombers and newly trained crews under the command of *Capitano* Giorgio Grossi. This commitment in the Aegean Sea/Balkan region further stretched the already thin resources of the Italian air forces and especially of the fledgling torpedo bomber units.

Operations 1940

Battle of Punta Stilo – The first major naval/aerial battle in the Mediterranean

The strategic situation in mid-1940 in the Mediterranean Sea saw the Italians strong in the central Mediterranean, while the French and the British on both the eastern and western flanks. Starting with the western half of the Mediterranean, Britain controlled Gibraltar at the entrance

6 Ibid.

7 Archivio Storico Aeronautica Militare "Costituzione dei reparti aerosiluranti", lettera n. 4073/op dell'ammiraglio Domenico Cavagnari.

from the Atlantic, while France held Morocco, Algeria and Tunisia. Malta at the center was a British base. In the eastern half, Britain held Egypt and the Suez Canal, Palestine and Cyprus. In the Levant, Lebanon and Syria were French. Italy stood in the central basin and held Libya with its provinces of Tripolitania and Cyrenaica to the south. Albania on the Adriatic Sea and the Dodecanese Islands in the southern Aegean were also under Italian control. With the collapse of France and the consequent loss of the French Fleet it was imperative for the British to maintain control of the Middle East and this depended primarily upon the retention of a large-scale presence by the British fleet in the Eastern Mediterranean. In order to safeguard such a presence Commander of the Mediterranean Fleet Admiral Andrew Cunningham's fundamental aims were thus to seek out and destroy Italian naval forces and to disrupt the supply line from Italy by which the Italian forces in Libya were being built up. This latter aim was to be achieved by systematically attacking the sea-borne traffic and by bombarding the concentrations of enemy troops and supply depots located in harbors or cities near the Libyan coast. A second objective was to protect the free flow of goods, soldiers and armaments being dispatched from Britain or the Commonwealth to the Middle East to build up the British Army presence. As historian Vincent O'Hara asserts both Italy and Britain had to exert some control over the Mediterranean in order to achieve their stated goals: "For the British, sea power (was measured in order of importance) by the ability to supply the army in North Africa from outside the theatre; to maintain maritime traffic within the theatre, particularly to frontline ports; and to supply Malta from inside and outside the theatre. For the Italians sea power consisted of maintaining maritime communication along the Italian coast and between the mainland and Sicily, Sardinia and Albania; supplying North Africa and ensuring the maritime traffic to the Western Mediterranean (particularly Spain) and the Aegean and Black seas. For both sides it also included the ability to interfere with enemy traffic and to conduct offensive operations – such as bombardments and amphibious landings as required."[8] The principal units of the Eastern Mediterranean Fleet based in Alexandria were battleships: *Warspite*, *Valiant*, *Malaya*; carriers: *Eagle*, *Illustrious;* 8-inch cruisers: *Kent*, *York;* 6-inch cruisers; *Gloucester*, *Orion*, *Neptune*, *Liverpool*, *Sydney*; A.A. Cruisers: *Calcutta*, and *Coventry*. Whilst the other major force in the Mediterranean in mid-1940 was Force H based in Gibraltar with battlecruiser: *Renown*; battleship: *Resolution*; carrier: Ark Royal; and 6-inch cruisers: *Sheffield* and *Enterprise*.

The principal tasks for the RAF in the Mediterranean were: reconnaissance for all three services, air defense of naval convoys and land-based installations, and the support of offensive action. Particular importance was attached to striking at the Italians early and prior to any potential buildup of the Italian air forces in Libya. It was therefore decided to strike quickly at aircraft and airfield installations and ports. The RAF, however, was also, like the RA, understrength in 1940 in the Mediterranean as its force was limited to eighteen Fairey Swordfish of the FAA onboard the aircraft carrier HMS *Eagle* and the RAF Middle East command force that had fewer than 260 combat ready aircraft many of which were second-rate such as Gloucester Gladiator biplane fighters and Vickers Wellesly bombers.[9] Moreover, the main supply port of Benghazi was out of reach of the Mark I Blenheims. The subsidiary port of

8 Vincent P. O'Hara, *Six Victories*, p.7.

9 Richard Hammond, "Air Power and the British Anti-Shipping Campaign in the Mediterranean, 1940-1944," *Air Power Review*, Vol. 16, No. 1, 2013, p.52.

Tobruk and the nearby airfields thus became the main target area for the RAF bombers, while bases in Southern Italy were also attacked.[10]

The first aerial clashes and bombing operations in the Mediterranean demonstrated the determination by both sides to attack aggressively naval installations and airport hangars despite their inadequate air fleets. The first bombing operations were conducted by the Italians against Malta which in June alone committed 630 planes dropping 170 tons of bombs hitting Maltese targets such as port facilities, ships, artillery and anti-aircraft batteries and also bomb La Valetta to undermine civilian morale. On 16 June 11° *Stormo* S.79s damaged HMS *Diamond* off Malta. The first RAF attack was conducted the same week that Italy declared war on 10 June. The first sortie struck the airfield at El Adem with 26 Blenheims of No. 45, 55 and 113 Squadrons: some enemy planes were damaged, but three bombers were lost. The attack was repeated during the same day and in all 18 aircraft were destroyed or damaged on the ground. At dawn next day nine Blenheims of No. 45, 113 and 211 Squadrons attacked Italian transport ships at Tobruk and managed to drop a bomb that damaged the cruiser *San Giorgio*. In early July Farey Swordfish biplanes conducted a daring mission over the port of Tobruk by torpedoing three Italian destroyers. On 3 July Hawker Hurricanes[11], flown to Malta to strengthen the British garrison, checked an Italian bomber attack by downing a S.79 bomber and a reconnaissance plane, despite being escorted by CR.42 fighters. The Italians of 9° *Gruppo* responded by damaging a Hurricane and forcing it to crash land. On 4 July a CR.42, piloted by *Sergente Maggiore* Agostino Fausti, during its second sortie of day, was downed by a Gloster Gladiator.[12] On 5 July the RAF conducted a successful attack upon Catania's airport by machine gunning at very low altitude an officers mess and killing fifteen soldiers.

Between 8-11 July both contenders were involved in the Battle of Calabria (Battle of Punta Stilo for the Italians) which resulted in the first major naval confrontation in the Mediterranean of the Second World War. But despite favorable conditions such as the close proximity of the fighting to Italian air bases and the consequent ability to deploy a large number of aircraft, the Italian air forces failed to inflict significant damage upon the British battle fleet.

On the 7th, Admiral Cunningham sailed from Alexandria with the battleships HMS *Warspite,* HMS *Malaya*, HMS *Royal Sovereign* and carrier HMS *Eagle*, cruisers and destroyers to cover convoys between Malta and Alexandria and possibly to challenge the Italians to action. Next day – the 8th – two Italian battleships, 14 cruisers and 32 destroyers were spotted in the Ionian Sea covering a convoy of their own to Benghazi in Libya. At dawn on 8 July Italian reconnaissance planes spotted south-east of Crete the presence of Admiral Cunningham's fleet which triggered the air attacks. From 1000 to 1900[13] seventy-two standard bombers, mostly S.79s and a few older S.81s, were deployed by the Italians which dropped 433 100 kg bombs on the British ships. Despite the large deployment the results were poor exposing the

10 Major-General I.S.O. Playfair, *The Mediterranean and Middle East Volume I: The Early Successes against Italy (to May 1941),* (London: HMSO, 1954) <http://www.ibiblio.org/hyperwar/UN/UK/UK-Med-I/UK-Med-I-6.html> (accessed 12 May 2021).

11 These aircraft were single engine monoplanes used as fighters with a maximum speed of 342 mph and a range of 970 miles with auxiliary tanks.

12 Gladiators were single engine biplanes used as fighters with a maximum speed of 245 mph and a range of 523 miles.

13 The description of the combat actions in this book reflect Italian time when referring to Italian post battle reports. This may differ from British accounts used throughout the book.

limits of horizontal high altitude bombings. The few positive results were a hit against HMS *Liverpool* resulting in a small damage to the ship and twenty dead, and one on HMS *Gloucester* which killed fifteen including its captain, while the majority of bombs failed to strike a target. Undeterred by these inconsequential air attacks, Admiral Cunningham's naval forces continued on their route to Malta. While en route to the British base, Cunningham gleaned from intelligence reports that the Italian fleet was returning to Taranto, after having escorted a convoy to North Africa. Determined to engage the enemy at sea the British Admiral gave orders to the crews to head in the direction of Taranto to attempt to cut off the Italian warships before they anchored. The move was very bold potentially exposing his battle fleet to the aerial threat of the RA which had bombers and fighters at hangars nearby in Sicily and Puglia. *Generale* Pricolo in fact saw this British naval movement as an opportunity to pounce again upon the British fleet from favorable jumping off platforms and ordered immediately the deployment of all available aircraft to intercept it. On 9 July however, things did not go as planned since for most of the morning Italian reconnaissance aircraft failed to locate the British fleet. Moreover, *Ammiraglio* Campioni, the commander of the Italian warships headed to Taranto, was unaware of the presence of the British fleet due to a lack of communications with the RA and the other services. The British would make their presence felt suddenly at 1315 when several torpedo bombers took off from HMS *Eagle* and launched their warheads at the Italian fleet. At 1330 a Cant 501 was able to finally spot the British ships but the delay in doing so meant that only at 1535 the first units of Italian aircraft would take off from their Sicilian airbases to hunt for the enemy ships. Due mainly to the inability to locate the British ships in the morning, the Italian air force had lost its opportunity to engage and degrade the British warships prior to the clash with the Italian naval force. By the time the bombers arrived at sea the naval battle had already taken place. At 1505 an Italian cruiser spotted the British fleet and the combat action commenced at 1520 when the Italian ships opened fire at 23,600 yards. At 1550 HMS *Warspite* spotted the battleships *Giulio Cesare* and *Cavour* and shortly thereafter opened fire. At 1559 the battleship *Giulio Cesare* received a hit by a 15-inch shell that struck the starboard side. At 1612, as the Italian cruisers closed in on HMS *Warspite* in an attempt to come to the aid of *Giulio Cesare* which had slowed to 18 knots, *Bolzano*, the leading cruiser in the formation, was hit sustaining small damage. After this brief naval engagement, the Italian battleships turned back toward Taranto. As the Italian ships were retreating to port, the British force chased them approximately 30 miles from the coast of Calabria. Then, 126 Italian bombers intervened beginning at 1643 dropping 514 bombs but they were not very effective and also dropped some bombs by mistake on the Italian ships. "By 1700 not a single enemy ship was in sight and the coast of Calabria was clearly visible 25 miles to the west. More high-level bombing attacks now developed on the British Fleet and lasted for four hours, during which the Italian aircrews distributed a large number of bombs on their own fleet also, even after the ships had begun to enter the Straits of Messina."[14] Thus, a stalemate ensued after a promising start due to the initially favorable conditions that could have helped the Italians. But not having any torpedo bombers ready for action or more lethal standard bombs or dive bombers, the RA on the 9th missed a viable opportunity to target the enemy near its home turf. The torpedoes or the dive bombers would have likely been more effec-

14 Major-General I.S.O. Playfair, *The Mediterranean and Middle East Volume I: The Early Successes against Italy (to May 1941),* (London: HMSO, 1954) <http://www.ibiblio.org/hyperwar/UN/UK/UK-Med-I/UK-Med-I-8.html > (accessed 12 May 2021).

tive weapons than the high-altitude bombings on the enemy ships. Moreover, the operation would not have tested the S.79's endurance, but rather furnishing the crews the opportunity to carry out multiple attacks and the pilots the time to properly line up their targets.

Between 11 and 13 July the Royal Navy headed back to Alexandria, but it was challenged once again by the bombers, over 300 of them dropping hundreds of bombs. Most failed again to hit a target and landed in the sea. Only one bomb struck HMS *Eagle*. In total during the Battle of Punta Stilo the RA had deployed 639 aircraft, which in 74 sorties had dropped 2,366 bombs of which less than 1 percent had hit a target. Seven aircraft failed to return to base. The lack of coordination between the two services especially in the realm of intelligence sharing and the fact that both bombers and the naval cruisers and destroyers had launched attacks from too far away against the British ships were some of the most glaring shortcomings of the battle of Punta Stilo.

This first major engagement revealed that standard bombers had experienced difficulties hitting moving targets with high level bombing attacks. Italy in fact lacked effective dive bombers and its 100 kg bombs proved ineffective against the sturdy British ships. For many years and based upon the experiences of the Spanish Civil War, RA planners had maintained that the 100 kg bombs were effective against both land-based targets and against ships, even large aircraft carriers moving at sea. The RA post battle report highlighted that the drop mechanism of the standard bombers had not functioned effectively dropping bombs vertically rather than horizontally because of the way the bombs were stored on the S.79 which had a cramped fuselage. This had caused many of the bombs to roll and disperse beyond the targets. Meanwhile, some of the bomb drops had been made from disadvantageous, high altitude positions. The bomber crews showed that some of its personnel lacked training in proper ranging and that they operated aiming equipment that did not allow for precision bombing. Moreover, the crews, lacking training, in some instances could not clearly identify enemy from friendly ships. The S.81, for example, had demonstrated to be obsolete for pinpoint bombardments, while the bombsight on the S.79 "was complex and difficult to use." Finally, the lack of effective radio communications between the bomber squadrons and their headquarters had also negatively influenced operations.[15] The squadrons unable to receive any feedback during the sorties couldn't alter tactics on the go or to concentrate their forces more effectively. *Sottotenente* Giuseppe Cimicchi, who would later become a torpedo bomber ace, summarized effectively the shortcomings faced by the RA crews during the Battle Punta Stilo in a detailed report. In his insightful report Cimicchi wrote:

> The poor effectiveness of our naval bombing revealed itself after the first actions against the British ships. Early in the war it was firmly believed that our aircraft would inflict severe damage on the enemy fleet. And I believed that the English feared such a possibility. The care they displayed regarding their movements confirmed this. We were mathematically convinced of the possibility to sink ships using classic bombing tactics. Later, the facts proved the opposite. Many factors made it difficult to strike the target. First of all, the target's speed, then the lack of an aiming device that would assure certain precision and, finally, the bombs' poor destructive effect.[16]

15 Ibid.
16 Marco Mattioli, *Savoia-Marchetti S.79 Sparviero*, p.59.

Similarly other bombing operations had been made such as eight raids against Gibraltar, seven raids against the refinery in Haifa and Alexandria was targeted seven times. All had inflicted some damage but had not been severe enough to disrupt operations for a long period of time. As Greene and Massignani assert: "By 21 July Comando Supremo was aware that, despite the reports of the aircraft crews, the air attacks against the British Fleet had been largely ineffective … Comando Supremo concluded that the addition of just eighty dive-bombers would enable the Italians to impose a heavy toll on the British forces and proposed to buy these aircraft from the Germans immediately, and one hundred Ju87 would shortly be supplied by Germany to Italy. No mention was made of torpedo aircraft, an area affected yet again by inter-service rivalry."[17] *Generale* Pricolo also placed an order for 500kg and 250kg anti-shipping bombs to complement the inventory of 100kg and 50kg bombs and to ensure effective harm against the battleship.

Torpedo Bombers Pressed into Service

Due to the poor showing of the standard bombers at the Battle of Punta Stilo with their established tactic of high level horizontal attacks on enemy battleships, a battle whose real results were covered up by the regime's propaganda which extolled in the newspapers the deeds of the air forces, *Generale* Pricolo decided to rush the torpedo bombers into service with the expectation of a spectacular and sudden victory. His other two objectives were to showcase what his branch was capable of and lastly to hit back at the enemy. Thus rather than attempt a more limited operation against British naval convoys in the Mediterranean, the RA command in August 1940 aimed to achieve a spectacular victory by torpedo bombing the port of Alexandria. The plan was extremely ambitious, but also very dangerous since the newly formed *aerosiluranti* unit would be pitted against the established strong port defenses of one of the largest British bases in the Mediterranean. Under order n. B/17955 the operation entailed a first high altitude bombing of the northern end of the port by 8-10 standard bombers of 10° *Stormo* charged with creating a diversion for the torpedo bombers. This first action was to be followed a half hour later by the sudden arrival of the five torpedo bombers split up into two groups. A first group of three aircraft under *Maggiore* Dequal was to be followed by the arrival of two more planes after a 15 minutes interval under the command of *Maggiore* Enrico Fusco. After having reached the position for the attack at approximately 100 meters of altitude from the port both teams were to release their torpedoes "at a preset altitude at the entrance of the port between its western and eastern embankment."[18] The planned torpedo attack against stationary targets such as battleships and merchants moored at Alexandria was considered to be more feasible than targeting ships steaming at sea since the first batch of torpedo bombers were delivered without any guiding devices to aid the pilot in the torpedo launch. After the torpedo bombers had completed the mission, the plan entailed a final attack by three Cant Z.506 of 35° *Stormo* that were to drop special bombs that spiraled once they hit the water named *Motobomba* FFF. The latter was a circular torpedo and its designation FFF was derived from the last names of the three engineers involved with its original design: *Tenente Colonnello* Prospero Freri, *Capitano* Gaetano Filpa,

17 Greene and Massignani, *The Naval War,* p.80.
18 Archivio Storico Aeronautica Militare: fondo LT2, cartella 19.

and *Colonnello* Amedeo Fiore. The weapon was a 500mm diameter electric torpedo which was dropped on a parachute, on entering the water it was designed to create concentric spirals of between 500 and 4,000 meters until it found a target. It weighed 350 kg, had a 120 kg warhead, a speed of 40 knots and an endurance of 15–30 minutes.

On 10 August the five torpedo bombers of the *Reparto Speciale Aerosilurante* took off from Gorizia and landed at Ciampino airport near Rome where Pricolo's staff briefed the pilots on the operation that they were about to undertake. The crews then travelled to Tobruk's T5 airfield on 12 August. On the 14th they moved to El Adem airfield, still near Tobruk. On the morning of the 15th *Maggiore* Dequal and the two RM observers attached to the unit conducted a reconnaissance of the port of Alexandria where they spotted several warships and some transport ships at anchor including a large cruiser. On their return to the airfield the plan of action was further refined and it was decided that in order to overcome the port defenses (torpedo nets) and to avoid the torpedoes getting stuck in the shallow waters, the torpedo drops were to occur only once the aircraft had past the dam in the section of the port where the water depth was higher. It was also decided that the flight would occur at an altitude of 1,500 meters hoping in this way to avoid getting spotted by the enemy. On the evening of the 15th the torpedoes (5 x 450mm Whitehead warheads) were affixed to the S.79s and by 1928 the planes were ready to go. The torpedoes had been transported a few days before from Catania airfield on S.82 planes. They were accompanied by a special armorer technician team from Whitehead that prepped the torpedoes to operate in the sandy and humid conditions of North Africa and who also affixed them to the aircraft. The first two planes to take off were those of *Maggiore* Dequal and of *Tenente* Buscaglia. The former had Franco Melley as co-pilot, *osservatore* Giovanni Marazio, *motorista* Guerrino Comisso, and *marconista* Armorino De Luca. The latter's crew was comprised by co-pilot Eugenio Sirolli, *motorista* Leonardo Beccececi, *marconista* Dionello Danielli and *armiere* Narciso Munari. Shortly thereafter, *Sottotenente* Robone's plane took off, followed by *Tenente* Copello and *Maggiore* Fusco's aircraft. Robone's crew included co-pilot Corrado Deodato, *motorista* Ulderico Sabatini, *marconista* Umberto Mauri and *armiere* Antonio Origlio. Meanwhile, Copello's crew was comprised by co-pilot Camillo Pipitone, *motorista* Fosco Neroni, *marconista* Giuseppe Dondi, and *montatore* O. Moretto. Finally, Fusco's crew was comprised by co-pilot Attilio Ferrandi, *osservatore* Giovanni Bertoli, *motorista* Guido Franco, and *marconista* Renato Vanelli.

It was estimated that the *Sparvieri* had limited endurance of five hours and given that the round trip would take approximately 4 hours and 20 minutes there were approximately only 30-35 minutes to identify the targets and launch the weapons. Initially, the flight progressed smoothly as the small squadron travelled undetected and did not experience any mechanical failures. By this time the standard bombers led by *Colonnello* Giovanni Benedetti of 10° *Stormo* had already completed their task at 2050 dropping their bombs (32 of 100kg and 9 of 250 Kg) on the port and sinking the mooring vessel HMS *Moorstone*, which went under in less than three minutes after being struck and wounding several soldiers and killing one. The torpedo bombers of Dequal and Buscaglia finally reached Alexandria at 2130. They encountered very low clouds that obstructed their views and shortly thereafter they were spotted by the search lights and were put under fire by the anti-aircraft defense. Despite intense enemy fire, the planes managed to make their way near the port and dropped their weapons against HMS *Gloucester*, a light cruiser. Both torpedoes would miss their target mainly due to the shallow waters of the port of Alexandria which was only 11 meters deep while the torpedoes initially upon impact with the water typically dropped 10 meters or more before stabilizing. While misfiring his weapon Buscaglia would from the onset demonstrate his great abilities as a pilot by managing a successful landing to base with almost no fuel left in the tank and with only one operating landing gear/wheel in working order since the second one had been damaged by the British guns. The other three aircraft reached the objective at 2145, but they too would also be unable to hit their targets. *Sottotenente* Robone's plane was unable to press home the attack because of the dense clouds and also because it had already flown beyond the port. To make another attempt against the port infrastructure would have been impossible given the aircraft's limited endurance. Robone was thus forced to ditch the torpedo at sea and make a safe return home. Meanwhile, Fusco and Copello were less fortunate arriving at Alexandria when the port defenses were already in full alert and they were greeted by very intense enemy fire. The first pilot flew over the port three times in order to find a suitable target but was unable to find one. Copello too would attempt unsuccessfully three times to locate the target. With little fuel autonomy remaining both then make a speedy return to base.

Primo Aviere Marconista (wireless operator) Giuseppe Dondi, a crew member on board Copello's plane, left us the following description of the memorable night action:

> 600, 500, 400 meters and these damned clouds are even lower, here is the trick! At last we emerge at less than 100 meters, and straight as a spindle we find ourselves over a deserted enemy beach. One right turn to the left brings us over open sea again. Alexandria cannot be far. The damned clouds want to trick us. We head in again, and as if by magic, one, two, ten, thirty searchlights switch on, their beams combing the sky, crossing one another, pursuing us, lifting and lowering in a possessed dance. We are again immersed in cloud and find ourselves in a hellish pit that even Dante could not have remotely imagined. The fireworks of Venice and Naples are nothing by comparison. Intersecting tracers rocket into the sky, forming the most beautiful hieroglyphics that one could imagine. They are white, red, blue, all colors. They whistle, as if to give us our first greeting. Much higher up, strange flashes switch on and off. The anti-aircraft artillery is welcoming us. We are perfectly in the harbor's center, at the wavetop level, but the drop is impossible. The white houses of Alexandria stand out neatly in the darkness, and the pier as a long arm stretches out into the sea, almost as if it were enfolding the vast number of ships in the harbor in a protective embrace. Beyond the harbor there is a second circular basin, and on a strip of land dividing the two harbors the batteries are doing their duty, illuminating the waters with their sinister flashes. We nose up, make a perfect turnaround, and again find ourselves out of range. The searchlights continue their futile effort. It is useless trying again, instead, we will begin the return flight home and the drama.[19]

Copello was lucky to be able to reach an Italian advanced base, while Fusco, whose plane had been damaged by enemy fire and no longer had operating landing gear, was forced to crash land. Luckily, Fusco's adroit maneuvers landed the plane safely but in enemy territory. The crew had survived the precipitous landing but was about to be captured. Their split-second decision was

19 Marco Mattioli, *Savoia-Marchetti S.79 Sparviero,* p.8.

to set the plane on fire. The flames attracted the attention of an enemy motorized platoon that would later arrive on the scene and capture the crew.

Dondi, the crew member on Copello's plane, recorded the following recollection of the *Sparviero* landing on a friendly base:

> We are hoping for a lucky and smooth landing. Where, how and when? For the moment and for our own safety, we are forced to release the torpedo at sea. Let's go back to the coast. An illuminated airport!? I scream out loud: where? Over there! A light in fact can be seen in the distance in the clouds. Our hope is reborn. But a little later we notice that it's just a big bluff. The red and green lights are distinctly visible, and they are nothing more than those of another aircraft. A device that perhaps like us is looking for a nearby location to land safely. Commander Copello tries to approach him but the aircraft disappears in a sea of clouds. These cursed ones are on the ground and give us no respite. We go down even further to find a suitable place for landing and we barely manage not to get shot down by enemy fire. A valley appears in front of us, black, interminable, it seems an enormous gorge ready to swallow us. But soon after the pilots steady hands take control of the plane. A resolute maneuver and a brush 90-degree angle change of direction followed by a slight bump tells me that we landed. A truly problem free landing, that only a very experienced pilot can make.[20]

The first to make it back to base at El Adem was Robone's plane at 2430. After landing, it was observed that the plane had been hit several times by the anti-aircraft fire while none of the crew members had been wounded. He was followed by Buscaglia's aircraft with the pilot making an emergency landing due to the crippled right wheel. The other two planes would make it back in the following days, making pit stops along the way. Thus, the first deployment on the night of 15 August 1940 of the *Reparto Sperimentale Aerosiluranti* team of five S.79s had failed. Instead of raiding British ships stationed at the port of Alexandria the crews had to make a hasty return home due to the *Sparviero*'s limited endurance. The crews' inexperience in ranging and firing torpedoes also ensured that the first mission ended in failure. The operation was probably dead on arrival as it was far too ambitious and dictated more by a desire to raise the morale of the home front, which had hitherto been somewhat depressed, than by careful planning. Like most improvised actions, it could not be successful. The reasons for its failure were the long flight pushing the S.79 endurance beyond what was technically feasible, the predictable north west direction of the attack which was the only possible way to attack Alexandria, and the low depths of the port which were unsuitable for an effective torpedo launch. Nevertheless, the pilots had gained valuable experience and would shortly thereafter score their first hits. RA's post battle report acknowledged the risky decision to go for broke instead of authorizing a more limited plan given that the crews were not experienced: "The operation was not perfectly planned, but it was not an improvised action either. Probably it would have been better safe to wait and to encounter the enemy ships at large in the middle of the Mediterranean. But at the time the service was dominated by a desire to know as quickly as possible if it was possible to succeed with the torpedoes." It also asserted that the planes and their weapons had demonstrated their

20 Archivio Storico Aeronautica Militare: fondo LT2, cartella 19.

potential to inflict damage upon the enemy. It concluded by stating that it was only a matter of time before the *Sparvieros* would fully unleash their destructive potential.[21]

On 23 August the operation was repeated on a much smaller scale by dispatching a single aircraft to attack the port. The S.79, flown by *Tenente* Robone, was unable to approach the intended target and launch the warhead from a favorable distance due to intense anti-aircraft fire. Based on these two unsuccessful operations, *Generale* Felice Porro, who had assumed command of the newly formed 5ª *Squadra aerea* operating in Libya after Balbo's death, and his staff decided to shift the efforts of the torpedo bombers against isolated ships at sea and avoid attacking ports infrastructure for a time.

On the 26th *Maggiore* Dequal and *Tenente* Robone scrambled from El Adem in order to attack a British convoy at sea. This was the first torpedo bomber operation aimed at moving targets. The pilots and their crews were aware of the difficulties this type of attack presented since the aircraft did not have proper aiming devices and the torpedo launch was to take place only when the RM observer on board gave the order to release the warhead. The bad weather on that day did not allow to test the RM's observer's timing abilities, as both aircraft returned to base with their torpedoes still attached. The *Sparvieri's* fourth operation was conducted on 27 August 1940 when a lone *S.79* flown by *Tenente* Buscaglia spotted 60 miles north-east of Bardia a British convoy heading to Port Said. The latter was comprised of two cargo ships and escorted by HMS *Kent* and HMS *Gloucester*. Buscaglia launched the warhead against HMS *Kent* but he misfired. Upon reading the post-action report, *Generale* Pricolo issued a new order to the *5ª Squadra Aerea* based in Cyrenaica which read as follows: "Torpedo bombers are to be deployed solely against battleships and not against transport ships."[22] Presumably, this warning was triggered by the low stock of warheads, which made it necessary to go after significant targets.

On 30 August two torpedo bombers flown by *Maggiore* Dequal and *Tenente* Robone were deployed to interfere with the Mediterranean Fleet which was involved in Operation Hats that entailed escorting the MF2 convoy (transport ships *Cornwall* and *Volo* and the tanker *Plunleaf*). The escort consisted of the aircraft carrier HMS *Illustrious* (Nos. 815 and 819 Squadrons—22 Swordfish, and No. 806 Squadron--12 Fulmars), the battleship HMS *Valiant,* and the anti-aircraft cruisers HMS *Coventry* and HMS *Calcutta.* They were supported by four destroyers due to return to Gibraltar. In support was also Admiral Somerville's Force H: HMS *Renown*, HMS *Ark Royal*, HMS *Sheffield* and seven destroyers. The plan was for Force H to turn back to Gibraltar when it reached Sardinia, while the reinforcements proceeded through the Sicilian Narrows to join the main body of Admiral Cunningham's fleet. HMS *Valiant* and two anti-aircraft cruisers would enter Malta to discharge guns, stores, and ammunition for the fortress, while the destroyers would refuel. The strengthened fleet would then return to Alexandria, carrying out one or two offensive operations against Italian bases on the way. On 30 August the torpedo bombers failed to spot the convoy after having spent most of the fuel in a wide sweep over the Mediterranean. The same operation was conducted again by the torpedo bombers on 31 August but with the same result. In an independent action standard bombers struck the 11,288 tons steamer Cornwall with three bombs while the bulk of the convoy was unscathed. As a result of the failure of the RA to substantially interfere with the operation, the precious

21 Giuseppe Santoro, *L'aeronautica italiana nella seconda guerra mondiale*, p.121.
22 Archivio Storico Aeronautica Militare: fondo LT2, cartella 19.

cargo of MF 2 convoy arrived safely at Malta. Operation Hats represented a significant success for the Royal Navy because it was the first major attempt to make the first through passage in the Mediterranean to Malta that had been attempted since Italy entered the war.[23] Both the RM and the air forces were unable to halt or significantly degrade it.

On 3 September the torpedo bomber unit assumed a new name 278ª *Squadriglia Autonoma Aerosiluranti* (278th Autonomous Torpedo Squadron). The squadron number (black) and the individual number (red) were stenciled on the fuselage of the S.79s. At this time, the units nickname and emblem became the *Quattro Gatti* (the four cats because of the loss of Fusco's plane), that in time became closely associated with the torpedo bomber units. Its meaning was that it was a unit of few but very skilled aviators: "From the initial number of aircraft in the squadron, *Capitano* Erasi one day said that we are the usual 4 cats. The name stuck and the unit's emblem was thus born. The gifted hand of S*ottotenente* Garat Maffei drew four cats (two white and two black) sitting on a torpedo. As per tradition the white cats bring fortune to the attackers, while the black cats bring bad luck upon the enemy. The unit's motto *pauci sed semper immites* ("Few but always dangerous") was penned by Francesco Pastonchi."[24]

By this time the unit also had a new commander (*Capitano* Massimiliano Erasi) as *Maggiore* Dequal was transferred to a standard bomber unit.

First Successes

On 4 September *Generale* Porro issued a new order which reiterated *Generale* Pricolo's directives and urged the unit to focus their efforts on British shipping especially those convoys operating along the Sicilian channel. "Torpedo attacks", it stated, "are to be carried out exclusively against battleships. When targeting an enemy convoy, the primary target should be the aircraft carrier. If the latter is not deployed then the biggest battleships should be targeted. The attack must be made simultaneously by two aircraft targeting the ship from opposite directions."[25] The directives by both Pricolo and Porro were dictated by two factors: one was to conserve the dwindling stock of warheads for major targets and second by the need for something big to happen such as scoring a major hit against an enemy battleship to lift the morale of the home front. Striking moving targets was a complete novelty for the torpedo bomber pilots since their training had always been conducted against stationary targets. Moreover, during 1940 the S.79 did not have any measuring instruments to guide the pilot and increase accuracy when launching the torpedo which further complicated these types of operations. Therefore in their reconnaissance actions at sea the pilots still had a lot to learn in order to be successful bombers. Another action was conducted by *Tenenti* Franco Melley and Buscaglia on 4 September. The two S.79s took off at 1015 from El Adem to locate the Mediterranean Fleet involved in the closing stages of Operation Hats. Instead they were intercepted by two Hurricanes and forced to turn back. The two aircraft would land safely at 1455 almost at the limit of their endurance at El Adem. On 13

23 Major-General I.S.O. Playfair, *The Mediterranean and Middle East Volume I: The Early Successes against Italy (to May 1941)*, (London: HMSO, 1954) <https://www.ibiblio.org/hyperwar/UN/UK/UK-Med-I/UK-Med-I-10.html#Page201> (accessed 12 May 2021).
24 Orazio Giuffrida, *Buscaglia e gli Aerosiluranti* (Rome: Stato Maggiore Aeronautica, 1975), p.32.
25 Archivio Storico Aeronautica Italiana, fondo LT2, cartella 19.

September *Tenenti* Buscaglia and Copello took flight to reach Mersa Matruh but were forced to turn back after failing to locate viable targets. During the afternoon of 17 September two S. 79s, flown by *Tenenti* Buscaglia and Robone attacked 40 miles west of Mersa Matruh, the British ship Ladybird. Both pilots passed untouched through a rainstorm of fire from the anti-aircraft batteries and sent both torpedoes in the direction of the enemy ship. Both torpedoes ran on a quarter of a mile further than the ship. On the night of 17 September, *Tenente* Buscaglia (and his crew Copello as *secondo pilota*, *primo aviere* Fosco Neroni, and Giovanni Tesi as *primo aviere marconista*) flying again with *Tenente* Robone and his crew (Corrado Deodato as *secondo pilota*, *osservatore* Giovanni Marazio, *primo aviere marconista* Umberto Mauri, and *primo aviere marconista* Ulderico Sabatini) carried out another attack against British ships that were besieging the Italian fortress of Fort Capuzzo at Bardia and achieved their first hit. This operation by the Royal Navy was a repeat action. The British fleet had been deployed to engage concentrations of Italian troops assembled at Bardia. On 17 August the Commander-in-Chief of the Royal Navy in the Eastern Mediterranean led a force consisting of three battleships and an 8-inch cruiser (HMS *Kent*) screened by twelve destroyers for the purpose of inflicting casualties on the Italian troops garrisoned at Bardia and destined for an advance against the Egyptian frontier. As the British Official History asserts, the operation had caused severe damage as the ships had bombed: "The target area was well plastered and the opposition was weak and ineffective."[26] A month later the Royal Navy had ordered a second naval raid against Bardia. This time cruiser HMS *Kent* (traveling at 18 knots) along with two destroyers HMS *Mohawk* and HMS *Nubian* were approaching the port of Bardia (approximately 40 miles out) when they were challenged at 2240 by two torpedo bombers. As the two S.79s began their descent toward the enemy ships, they were illuminated by a full moon and the British naval crews opened up with a hellish machine gun and artillery fire. The first plane flown by Buscaglia dove down quickly skimming past the two destroyers that fired at the aircraft from very close range and barely missing their target. Flying very close to the water, Buscaglia released his warhead. Similarly, from the opposite direction Robone also brought down his plane. He too passed untouched through the curtain of enemy fire and finally released his torpedo at HMS *Kent*. They released their torpedoes from approximately 700 meters out, with one torpedo striking HMS *Kent*. Buscaglia's torpedo struck near the stern of the ship on its starboard side and wreaking havoc to the propeller shafts to the point that the cruiser stopped operating at once. The blast killed 33 crewmen (including two officers), and damage to the 9,850-ton heavy cruiser was so severe that it was disabled. The ship then caught fire and had to be rescued by HMS *Nubian* which at 1120 of 18 September began towing it to Alexandria. Traveling at 11 knots per hour HMS *Nubian* successfully brought HMS *Kent* to Alexandria on 19 September so that extensive repairs could be done. It was then transferred to Portsmouth where it stood under repairs for a year. Meanwhile, the two *Sparvieri* managed to make their way back to the airbase at El Adem by 2330 with only minor damage from some ack-ack fire.

"We had a low torpedo-bomber attack on our starboard beam", recalled Lt. Cmdr. George Blundell, who was aboard *Kent* that night: "I saw the splashes, enormous ones, as the torpedoes were dropped. Shortly afterwards there was a tremendous blow aft. The whole ship reeled,

26 Major-General I.S.O. Playfair, *The Mediterranean and Middle East Volume I: The Early Successes against Italy (to May 1941)*, (London: HMSO, 1954) <http://www.ibiblio.org/hyperwar/UN/UK/UK-Med-I/UK-Med-I-8.html> (accessed 12 May 2021).

then suddenly went dead, and we could feel on the bridge as if her tail had dropped—a sort of bending, dragging feeling. The ship wouldn't steer. We were then machine gunned by aircraft that came in from ahead. I didn't realize what it was at first, except that there were loud cracks, just like one hears when standing in rifle butts, whilst red worms seemed to fly all around us. At first, I thought they were sparks from the funnel. It was too fascinating to be in the least frightening, but when I realized they were bullets I knelt down to present a smaller target."[27] The British naval officer's testimony reveals the twin threat of the *Sparviero* attacks: torpedoes followed by machine gun fire as the planes overflew the enemy ship.

The daring attack against HMS *Kent* had some repercussions. According to the British Official History the new threat posed by the *Sparvieri* opened a new phase in the conflict and became one of the biggest concerns to the commanders of the Eastern Mediterranean Fleet and Force H:

> A bombardment of Bardia by the cruiser Kent and destroyers was unfortunately prevented by an attack on the cruiser by torpedo-bombers just as she was taking up her position. One hit with a torpedo was scored in her stern. Protected by the Royal Air Force she was brought into harbor two days later so badly damaged that she was unfit for further service in the Mediterranean. This was a serious matter, as only one other 8-inch cruiser, the York, had been assigned to Admiral Cunningham and she was not due to reach Suez for another week. The incident marked the beginning of a new phase in the encounter between the British Fleet and the Italian Air Force; from now until the arrival of the Luftwaffe the torpedo-bomber was to be the principal cause of anxiety and damage.[28]

On 22 September an unsuccessful patrol action was undertaken by *Tenenti* Buscaglia and Copello. On 28 September *Generale* Pricolo reiterated his earlier directives with a newly issued order that stated: "The deployment of torpedo bombers should be made against battleships that are located at sea and not too far from air bases. This will avoid that the aircraft fly at the limit of their endurance to launch torpedoes. Since torpedoes are scarce and few aircraft have been converted to the torpedo role, battleships should be the primary targets, while large transport ships should also be a secondary target."[29] On 29 September at 1535 pilots Dequal, Robone, Buscaglia and Copello attacked a cruiser from opposite directions, but were not able to damage it severely mainly because they were challenged by Fulmars which interfered with the launches. Two warheads were lost.

After the daring but unsuccessful maneuver of 29 September, S.79 pilot *Capitano* Massimiliano Erasi made several unsuccessful attempts to close with HMS *Liverpool* on 14 October 1940 before he finally emerged from the clouds and pounced on the cruiser at 1855. HMS Liverpool had escorted a Malta bound shipping convoy as part of Operation MB 6 when it was spotted by an Italian reconnaissance plane 60 miles south of Crete. As HMS *Liverpool* together with other vessels (HMS *Illustrious*, HMS *Warspite*, HMS *Valiant*, HMS *Malaya*, HNMS *Eagle*

27 Marco Mattioli, *Savoia-Marchetti S.79 Sparviero*, p.10.

28 Major-General I.S.O. Playfair, *The Mediterranean and Middle East Volume I: The Early Successes against Italy (to May 1941)*, (London: HMSO, 1954) <http://www.ibiblio.org/hyper war/UN/UK/UK-Med-I/UK-Med-I-11.html> (accessed 12 May 2021).

29 Archivio Storico Aeronautica Italiana, fondo LT2, cartella 19, foglio n. B/00672, "Criteri d'impiego."

and HMS *Gloucester*) from the Mediterranean fleet were making their way back to base in Alexandria, the reconnaissance aircraft notified base that it had spotted the British fleet south of Crete. This prompted Erasi and his crew (co-pilot Robone, observer Marazio, *marconista* DeLuca and *motorista* Comisso) to immediately take off from El Adem airfield at 1550.

After three excruciating hours of searching for the ships, the crew finally spotted the British fleet. The full moon enabled the crew to follow the enemy initially without being detected but the clouds made it difficult for them to aim and to have a clear shot at any of the ships. The pilot steered the plane above the ships twice while attracting considerable enemy fire from the anti-aircraft batteries but was unable to get a clean shot. On the third attempt, Erasi pressed home the attack by bringing down the plane almost hugging the water to avoid the anti-aircraft fire. At an altitude of 70 meters above the ship and at a distance of approximately 700 meters the warhead was finally released. It struck HMS *Liverpool,* a Town class 9,394 tons cruiser mounting twelve six-inch (152 mm) guns, right under the forward tower causing an immediate explosion. The huge blaze that resulted from the collision then caused a second explosion which split into two pieces the bow of the ship causing irreparable damage. Thirty were killed and forty-two were wounded. HMS *Orion* was tasked with towing the crippled ship to Alexandria. Travelling at a speed of nine knots both ships arrived at Alexandria at midnight on 16 October. The ship would stay under repair for more than a year. Two days after the strike *Comando Supremo* issued bulletin number 132 that announced the torpedoing of the cruiser and even mentioned its name. The latter was most likely revealed by a *Servizio Informazioni Italiano* (SIM) spy in Alexandria.

The following is the hour by hour description of what happened that night according to a Royal Navy officer that was on board HMS *Liverpool*:

> At 1853, an aircraft was sighted crossing and re-crossing our bows. As there was only one pom-pom crew closed up, they rushed from one side of the ship to the other trying to get a shot at the machine. In a few minutes, the aircraft steadied up to come in on the starboard beam, and the starboard pom-pom fired four rounds at it. The ship swung around hard to starboard as a torpedo was seen to fall from the plane. Only one was seen to fall, but another was reported to have passed astern, and at 1856 we were struck on the starboard side abreast the center line capstan. The ship gave a sickening lift under the force of the explosion. The D/F pole snapped off at the topmast, and the bridge and pom-pom decks were showered with petrol. Petrol fumes began to seep through the entire ship by way of the ventilation trunks, and the engines had to be stopped.
>
> In the HACP we heard the pom-poms open fire and guessed immediately that torpedo bombers must have been attacking. After a horrible few seconds of waiting, an explosion rocked the compartment like a full broadside with no recoil. I tested communications after ordering the crew to the top of the hatch and, on finding all correct in spite of the shaking up, I ordered the crew back down. Petrol fumes started coming down the ventilation trunks so I ordered the men to put out their cigarettes. Here I might add that the men remained perfectly calm and silent through these horrible moments of doubt.
>
> I found out later that Illustrious and Valiant were attacked at the same time as Liverpool by two aircraft on each ship. They had received RDF warnings on these aircraft well in advance of the attack, so when the planes came in, the whole armament of both ships was trained on them and they were riddled with shot before they had an opportunity to drop their torpedoes. It is thought by some that those planes were German. RDF reports were

> also received in Liverpool, but the rating on watch in the remote control office was new to his job and, not knowing what the reports were, failed to pass them up to the compass platform. This episode is a glaring example of a ship's dependence upon the individual ... the chain suddenly grew taut and broke at a weak point.
>
> We waited in the HACP. "A" turret's crew was cleared from the turret. Ammunition supply numbers were ordered up from below. "A" and "B" magazines and shell rooms were flooded, and fire and repair parties were piped forward.
>
> At 1920, the petrol compartments exploded with a blast like ten torpedoes. The two ton armored top of "A" turret was blown sixty feet in the air. The turret itself was whipped around from a starboard to a port bearing, with the right gun aimed at the moon, the center gun bent and trained on Arcturus, and the left gun dropping into the sea. The whole of the deck became a blazing inferno of twisted metal that hung limply to the ship, rising and falling with the swell--a beacon for enemy aircraft. Hands were ordered to fall in by divisions, so we vacated the HACP. On coming up from below, I passed the sick bay where the most ghastly sight I have ever seen presented itself. The dead and wounded were lying about on stretchers. The sick bay was full, and many had to be left on the deck while those still coming in were being moved aft to the wardroom and gun room flat. Dazed men were wandering about with all the clothes burned off their blistered and bleeding bodies. The smell of burnt flesh and the groaning and suffering were so horrible, I cannot write about it.
>
> Boats and Carley floats were ordered out so I went up to the four-inch gun deck to see that my number thirteen float was correct. On finding the float correct, I went aft to the quarterdeck where the majority of the ship's company was fallen in and watched the preparations for being taken in tow astern. By this time the ship was down by the bows with a list to starboard. The fire cast an ugly glow on the sea, and we expected another attack at any minute. The pinnace and motorboat were hoisted out by the crane. The power had not failed and the lights continued to burn brightly.
>
> At 2000 a destroyer arrived and in the next hour, Gloucester, Orion, Calcutta and Coventry also came to our assistance. We commenced to go astern in order to swing the ship around to get better control of the fire and also to have our stern roughly in the direction of Alexandria. Ongoing astern, the motorboat, pinnacle and two Carley floats broke adrift and were lost. A large fire was burning forward with intermittent explosions in "A" turret. At 2230 Orion came up to take us in tow. At 2300 the tow was passed, and at 2330 she commenced towing astern on a course 135 degrees at 9 1/2 knots. By this time the wardroom and gun room flat had become veritable hospitals. I wandered among the injured doing what I could to alleviate suffering, but finding my stomach too delicate, was forced to return to the quarterdeck for some fresh air.[30]

The action was described as follows in the British Official History: "Air attacks with bombs and torpedoes developed as the fleet proceeded to Alexandria, and on the evening of October 14th

30 Extract From The Journal of Midshipman W. P. Hayes, RCN Aboard HMS Liverpool, October 1940 <https://web.archive.org/web/20120224025032/http://www.noac-national.ca/article/hayes/returntoalexandria_bywphayes.html > (accessed 21 March 2021).

the cruiser Liverpool was hit by a torpedo and severely damaged. With part of her bow torn off she was eventually towed safely into harbor."[31]

On 2 November the hunt for British ships resumed as four S.79s flown by *Capitano* Erasi and *Tenenti* Robone, Buscaglia, and Copello attacked the Mediterranean Fleet that had been spotted at sea by an Italian reconnaissance plane at 0940. The four aircraft, however, at 1230 failed to press home their attacks due to violent anti-aircraft fire and the deployment of Fulmars that took off from HMS *Illustrious* to chase the *Sparvieri* away. The pilots claimed one hit but were unable to observe the results of their operation as the Fulmars forced them to hastily turn back to base.

As a result of these multiple operations, the Italian command began to take notice of the torpedo bomber units by awarding the ranks of this emerging specialty its first military awards. On 7 November 1940 *Maggiore* Dequal, *Tenenti* Buscaglia, Melley, Robone, Copello and Galimberti and other co-pilots of 278ª *Squadriglia* were decorated with Italy's second highest honor, the *Medaglia d'Argento al valor militare* (silver medal). On the same occasion several other NCOs received the bronze medal of military honor.

Despite the success of the torpedo bombers it appears that the domestic industry was still challenged in meeting the weapon production requirements of the armed forces. In December 1940 there were only ten aerial torpedoes in stock. This prompted another order: "The Chief of the air staff ordered his commanders to conserve their forces and avoid undue risk when selecting and carrying out operations as planes were difficult to replace. They were not to send aircraft against the enemy fleet if aircraft carriers were present and must prioritize using the limited supply of aerial torpedoes against enemy warships."[32]

Lack of warheads was not the only problem troubling the torpedo bomber squad. The dwindling supply of *Sparvieri* was another. A planned attack by the RAF against El Adem airbase was particularly effective. On 9 November several bombers flew over the airfield and dropped their lethal bombs destroying three S.79s which further reduced the *Squadriglia*'s ability to wage an effective campaign.

On 11 November the Mediterranean Fleet achieved an important victory over the RM which had most of its battle fleet anchored at Taranto. The Taranto raid occurred on the night of 11–12 November 1940. The Royal Navy launched a massive all-aircraft naval attack by deploying twenty-one Fairey Swordfish biplane torpedo bombers from the aircraft carrier HMS *Illustrious* which had navigated deeply into enemy territory to approximately thirty miles from Taranto. The attack struck the battle fleet of the RM at anchor in the harbor of Taranto, using aerial torpedoes despite the shallowness of the water. Extensive damage was inflicted against the battle ships *Cavour*, *Littorio* and *Duilio*, whilst British losses were minimal. On 12 November *Generale* Pricolo issued order B-03123 which committed the torpedo bombers to vindicate Taranto: "Torpedo bombing units in the Aegean and Libya have been given the responsibility of vindicating Taranto. I am sure that the crews will work tirelessly and if needed until the ultimate sacrifice to attack the enemy ships."[33] *Capitano* Massimiliano Erasi and *Tenente* pilota Melley would take off from El Adem to hunt for the Mediterranean Fleet on the afternoon of

31 Ibid.
32 John Gooch, *Mussolini's War*, p.125.
33 Francesco Mattesini, "La notte di Taranto," Bolletino dell'archivio della Marina Militare, December 1998, p.108.

the 12th but were unable to proceed with the operation because of extremely dangerous weather. The next day two S.79s flown by *Tenenti* Buscaglia and Copello were dispatched in the morning to pursue the Mediterranean Fleet but wound up attacking the British convoy AS5 which was comprised of eight transport ships escorted by HMS *Wryneck* and HMS *Fiona* and *Chakla*. The two torpedo bombers flew several times over their target before attacking it. Finally, at 1423 they came down and released their torpedoes. The pilots mistakenly asserted in the post battle report to have scored hits against the convoy, but the latter entered Port Said on 15 November without having suffered any losses. In the afternoon *Capitano* Massimiliano Erasi and *Tenente* Robone took off from El Adem to pursue the British battleships but were unable to launch the torpedoes. The two S.79s patrolled over the Mediterranean sea until late at night but were unable to locate the British ships. The latter finally reached Alexandria at 0700 on 15 November without suffering any losses from Italian aerial attacks. At 1730 on 17 November two S.79s flown by *Tenenti* Melley and Robone attacked a British ship that was navigating a few miles from the port of Alexandria. The pilots asserted in the post battle report to have scored one hit against a light cruiser. According to SIM the pilots had slightly damaged HMS *Hasty*, an H class 1,350 tons destroyer. On 24 November the torpedo bombers failed in their attempt to score a hit against an enemy aircraft carrier at Suda Bay. *Capitano* Massimiliano Erasi's plane had to turn back because it was at the limit of its endurance, while *Tenenti* Buscaglia and Robone were forced to turn back due to strong winds.

On 27 November another major naval engagement took place in the Mediterranean with the Battle of Cape Spartivento (for Italian historians it was the Battaglia di Capo Teulada). While the Italian battle fleet returned to base between 1200 and 1215, an Italian cruiser division sighted enemy ships and opened fire. After gunfire was exchanged between British and Italian cruisers, HMS *Berwick* was struck twice by Italian 8 inch shells and received severe damage while the Italian destroyer *Lanciere* became immobilized by a British shell. During this gun battle the RA was only tangentially involved as only the standard bomber units were deployed. The battle of Cape Spartivento was an inconclusive action although the RM had inflicted slightly greater damage on its rival. It showed that the Italians were unable to interfere on a large scale with British operations and within the Italian military leadership the impression was that they had missed a significant opportunity especially because a well-coordinated combined aerial and naval action did not take place despite the fact that the Royal Navy was engaged close to Italian air and naval bases.

The 278ª *Squadriglia* was to achieve its third major success on 3 December 1940. At the time the Royal Navy was supporting the decision by Churchill and his top military advisors of strengthening the Malta garrison as well as bringing more heavy supplies such as 25-pdr field batteries, tanks, anti-aircraft batteries, ammunition, coal, fuel and soldiers to Alexandria in order to sustain Operation Compass. These convoys left England and made pit stops at Gibraltar. From there they would typically travel to Malta escorted by Force H and then from Malta to Alexandria escorted by the Eastern Mediterranean Fleet. The naval operations began in November and continued the next month. Every convoy brought troops or equipment to the Middle East. Typically, the destroyers carried as many soldiers as possible, while guns, tanks and other vehicles followed by merchant ships. According to the British Official History, the Italian Navy, still reeling from the initial clashes with the Royal Navy, did not forcefully challenge the convoys and mainly kept its ships at bay in Taranto or Naples, while Italian bombers were dispatched to intercept the convoys but had little success since the bombings took place from altitudes where it was very difficult to hit targets. The only success was the hit on the 6-inch cruiser HMS *Glasgow*, one of the ships used to ferry soldiers over to Malta or the Middle East, by torpedo bombers. HMS *Glasgow* and HMS *Gloucester* were spotted anchored at Suda Bay during the late morning of 3 December 1940 by a RA reconnaissance plane, a Cant.Z.506. Two S.79 planes (number 2 and 6 of the 278ª *Squadriglia*) took off from El Adem airfield at 1315. The first aircraft was piloted by *Tenente* Buscaglia, while the second by *Capitano* Erasi. Approximately two and half hours later the two planes flew over the island of Crete and began to circle the harbor of Suda Bay. The British ships were at anchor and were protected by the light anti-aircraft defense consisting of eight Bofors 40 mm guns and eight light guns as well as by balloons and anti-torpedo nets. The planes at first attempted to wear down the anti-aircraft defense by fainting attacks repeatedly by flying over the harbor but without pressing the final attack. After approximately forty minutes of using this tactic they attacked simultaneously from opposite sides of the harbor. The first torpedo, released by Erasi at 1548, struck HMS *Glasgow*, a Southampton-class light cruiser of 9,100 tons, almost immediately making a large hole in the starboard side forward causing the ship to begin to be flooded by water. The second torpedo came in soon after and struck at 1551 hitting starboard side aft and damaging two propeller shafts. One officer and two soldiers were killed while three soldiers were wounded. The cruiser hit by both torpedoes had to be towed to Alexandria escorted by HMS *Gloucester*, HMS *Hasty* and by HMS *Calcutta*. It remained out of service for almost a year. Admiral Cunningham stated that "Glasgow was hit by two aircraft approaching from the entrance of the bay. They were greeted by a fury of anti-aircraft fire but nonetheless managed to release their torpedoes."[34] The attack had been conducted with extreme precision and the experienced pilots had shown their worth by avoiding the enemy fire and pouncing at the right time emerging from the clouds almost undetected. They had also by this time gained considerable experience in ranging and aiming the warhead in order to hit their target from an angle so that they could overcome the harbor defenses. The 278ª *Squadriglia's* war diary concisely reported that: "Torpedo action against enemy vessel at Suda Bay. Enemy unit hit by torpedoes. Violent enemy anti-aircraft reaction."[35]

As a reprisal for the action against Suda Bay the RAF on 9 December targeted once again El Adem airbase. Four S.79s were damaged lightly by low level bombings. But in less than eight days they were made operational again by the special technicians of *Servizio Riparazioni Aeromobili e Motori* which were flown from Italy. As a result, on 22 December the S.79s of 278ª *Squadriglia* were back in action. One aircraft flown by *Tenente* Rinaldo Galimberti attacked and damaged a destroyer near Sollum at 2100. On 25 December the S.79s made two attempts to hunt down the aircraft carrier HMS *Illustrious* which had been spotted by a reconnaissance plane navigating between Alexandria and Mersa Matruh. *Tenenti* Buscaglia and Copello took off at 0430 from Ain el Gazala and flew toward Mersa Matruth but were unable to locate the target. After having returned to base and after refueling both pilots scrambled a second time from the airbase at 1700 to search for HMS *Illustrious,* but once again returned to base empty

34 Major-General I.S.O. Playfair, *The Mediterranean and Middle East Volume I: The Early Successes against Italy (to May 1941)*, (London: HMSO, 1954) <http://www.ibiblio.org/hyper war/UN/UK/UK-Med-I/UK-Med-I-11.html> (accessed 12 May 2021).

35 Ufficio Storico Aeronautica Militare, Diario storico 278ª *Squadriglia*, Rapporto n. 3825, 5 December 1940.

handed. Two days later Robone and Copello carried out a successful mission when they sunk a motorboat and light destroyer anchored in Sollum Bay.

At the end of November, the *34° Gruppo Autonomo* (*68ª Squadriglie*), based in Rhodes, began operations as a torpedo bomber unit. It was initially equipped with four S.79 under the command of *Capitano* Giorgio Grossi. Its first operation was conducted on 19 November in the area north of Crete when three S.79s attacked without success a destroyer. The next operation took place on 24 November when again three S.79s unsuccessfully pursued an enemy convoy near Suda Bay. Its first success was achieved on the night of 16 December when it took part of a wider operation which aimed to target British ships that were bombing Bardia. Two S.79s flown by *Capitano* Grossi and *Tenente* Umberto Barbani attacked two Australian destroyers (*Vampire* and *Voyager*). The two pilots were able to observe the results of the operation and they reported having hit at least one destroyer which was observed being engulfed by large columns of fire and smoke. The damage to one of the destroyers is unconfirmed by the Royal Navy post battle report. On 29 December one S.79 from the same unit launched a torpedo against a British destroyer that was able to avoid it by making an evasive maneuver.

From a tactical perspective the first few months of torpedo bomber operations had highlighted several factors that could yield further success. First, combined bomber and torpedo bomber operations could be more successful if better synchronized during the first and the last phase of the attack. Second, the two units could benefit from improved coordination in the joint planning of operations. Third, the need for navigation devices especially when the crews had to travel in the open sea were keenly felt. Finally, the introduction of a proper aiming device for the torpedo launches was of critical importance to achieve further successes.[36] The support infrastructure comprised of aircraft mechanics, hangar workers and torpedo specialists was also to be expanded to allow for the execution of more operations. By the end of the year the support infrastructure for the torpedo bombers had been significantly expanded to support a greater number of operations. Initially Whitehead personnel had been flown in from Italy to oversee the preparation of the aircraft and the warheads for operations. This was of special importance at El Adem airfield given the special operating conditions. When affixed to the S.79 the warheads had to be covered by special blankets to conceal them from the sand. Then when the planes were ready to take off the torpedoes had to be washed down and then dried with compressed air pumps. Whereas it took on average thirty minutes in Italy for a warhead team to load the torpedoes, in Libya it took much longer. Also the torpedoes had to be stored in a very particular way from sandstorms and the sun. The Whitehead personnel had also been authorized by the RA to construct a special bunker/hangar to stock the torpedoes since it was too dangerous to house them in the airport hangar which was subjected to daily bombings. According to the head of the Whitehead personnel based in North Africa, who was initially responsible for fixing the torpedoes to the planes and preparing them for action, life in North Africa was extremely harsh and it had tested his workers: "Life in the desert is full of inconveniences of all kinds including the lack of food and water. The wind and the sand try our patience, while the fact that we are located 60 miles from the Egyptian border is a cause of almost daily concern. These conditions have further burdened the mental and physical condition of my personnel which have worked tirelessly though daily bombardments, emergencies of all kinds and without one full night of sleep.

36 Orazio Giuffrida, *Buscaglia e gli aerosiluranti* (Rome: Ufficio Storico, 1994), p.86.

Our life here is relegated to our refuge and is extremely dangerous. A rotation of the personnel is therefore necessary to give some of the technicians the time to rest and recuperate."[37] The solution to the lack of specialized armorers was found by training RA personnel at Whitehead's headquarters which in the fall of 1940 began to rotate its personnel out of the North African theatre. The training lasted a week and it involved primarily instructions on the assembly of aerial torpedoes. A second week of training at El Adem focused specifically on the cure of the torpedoes prior to affixing them to the aircraft and once they were affixed to the aircraft. By November of 1940 Whitehead personnel retained a nominal presence in Libya and the servicing aspect of torpedo bomber operations was taken up almost entirely by RM and RA armorers who had undergone the training at Fiume.

Summary and Conclusion

1. In the July-December 1940 period the Italian army suffered several reverses of fortune mainly in North Africa and in Greece, while the RM suffered a significant defeat at Taranto. Despite the lack of success against the Royal Navy, the RM was still able to carry out its main role which was to guarantee the safe passage of supply transports to North and East Africa. Italy, for example, shipped 304,467 tons of supplies to North Africa between June and December 1940 and lost only 2.3 percent of them.[38] During these six months Malta, which was still under strength, did not pose a major threat to Italian naval operations.
2. The RA entered the war with a fleet that was not large enough to sustain multiple operational deployments or campaigns. It could only carry out limited campaigns centered around the Central Mediterranean. When the Italian government in October 1940 opened another front in Greece, the air service's shortcomings became more apparent. Perhaps its biggest pitfall was its entering the war unprepared and without any special units being trained and equipped to conduct preemptive strikes against the Royal Navy or its bases. The lack of a viable torpedo bomber, dive bomber or heavy bomber units in mid-1940 represented some of the most evident gaps of a force that had been designed around medium bombers. Without such capabilities the RA missed several opportunities to influence the course of the conflict. If for example, attacks by dive bombers or by torpedo bombers had been planned against large capital ships in the Mediterranean by experienced pilots in the summer/fall of 1940, the convoy war and the early confrontations between the British and the RM might have had different outcomes. At the time torpedo attacks represented a novelty that the Royal Navy crews were not prepared for. The lack of torpedo bombers, for example, was one of the main factors in the lackluster results during the battle of Punta Stilo. Similarly, the lack of heavy and dive bombers had prevented meaningful attacks against Royal Navy installations.
3. Overall, British efforts to bring troops and supplies to Malta and the Middle East were also successful as the Italians between November and December only managed to intercept less than ten percent of the cargo. "The month of December showed clearly what a large

37 G. Getti and R. Capinacci, "Relazione sulla missione in Africa," Silurifico Whitehead, October 1940.
38 John Gooch, *Mussolini's War*, p.194.

measure of control the Royal Navy was able to exercise in the Mediterranean. Warships and important convoys had completed the through passage in both directions; other convoys had passed freely up and down the Aegean; places as far apart as Rhodes and Tripoli had been attacked; and the fleet had even swept into the Adriatic. Fifty-five ships (totaling over 235,000 tons) had been escorted during the month—all without damage."[39]

4. While the Royal Navy had been free to move between the Eastern and Western Mediterranean, one bright spot for the Italians had been its torpedo bomber unit, a weapon that caused some harm against the Mediterranean Fleet. This is recognized by the British Official History of the War when it states that: "The Italian Air Force had made repeated attacks on British ships, mostly from high-level, sometimes with great accuracy but on the whole with surprisingly little success. The chief threat to the British ships was from torpedo-bomber attacks, a type of action which the Italians had not fully developed when they came into the war, and which therefore did not figure very largely for some time. But in addition to their successes against the Kent and the Liverpool, already mentioned, torpedo-bombers scored two hits on the cruiser Glasgow in Suda Bay early in December; all three cruisers had to leave the Mediterranean for repairs."[40] On one hand, standard S.79 medium bombers had achieved twenty-seven successful strikes against the Royal Navy between June- December 1940. Although their tally was higher than that of the torpedo bombers, medium bomber strikes were less lethal.[41] On the other, S.79 torpedo bombers had struck only three times, but in all three cases their strikes caused the cruisers to leave the Mediterranean and be under repairs for more than a year.
5. One consequence of these first successes of the torpedo bombers was the change in tactics by the RA which began to disband some of the standard bomber units in order to transform them into new torpedo bomber squadrons. This along with the formation of the new torpedo bomber squads represented one of the primary changes for the air forces in late 1940 and throughout 1941. Even standard bombers, although less effective and lethal, commanded some degree of respect because they interfered with operations. Admiral Cunningham "gave the Hawk full marks. He described the efficiency of Italian reconnaissance and noted that the Italians seldom missed finding and reporting British ships at sea. Without fail the Sm-79 Hawks, each carrying 2,500 pounds of bombs, arrived within two hours. The usual attacks were made at 12,000 feet, keeping in tight formation even under heavy anti-aircraft fire. The bombers were unusually precise."[42] A second consequence was that between late 1940 and 1941 some British ship convoys, because of the threat posed by the RA, were rerouted and had to sail round the Cape of Good Hope rather than through the Mediterranean, thus making elongated sea voyages and spending more resources to deliver supplies to British bases. These convoys were out of reach of the Italian aircraft but were much more burdensome for the Royal Navy.[43]

39 Major-General I.S.O. Playfair, *The Mediterranean and Middle East Volume I: The Early Successes against Italy (to May 1941),* (London: HMSO, 1954) <https://www.ibiblio.org/hyperwar/UN/UK/UK-Med-I/UK-Med-I-16.html> (accessed 12 May 2021).

40 Ibid.

41 Marco Mattioli, *Savoia-Marchetti S.79 Sparviero,* p.91.

42 Thomas P. Lowry, *The Attack on Taranto,* p.48.

43 Andrew Cunningham, *A Sailor's Odyssey* (London: Hutchinson and Company, 1951).

4: ETTORE MUTI

Born in Ravenna on 22 May 1902 and died on 24 August 1943 in Fregene near Rome. At 14 he left school and ran away from home in order to volunteer his services during the First World War, but was caught by the Carabinieri and returned to his parents prior to seeing any action at the front. The next year (1917) he ran away again and this time he was able to join the 6° *Reggimento Fanteria Brigata Aosta.* He later volunteered into the *arditi* battalions by joining the 1° *reparto d'assalto.* During the Caporetto Offensive he saw combat between October and December 1917 on Col Beretta and Col Moschin near Mount Grappa. In 1918 he joined the 20° *reparto d'assalto* and saw combat in June during the large scale Austro-Hungarian Piave Offensive. After the war Muti participated to Gabriele D'Annunzio's takeover of Fiume. During this time, Muti carried out a number of secretive missions on D'annunzio's behalf as the latter attempted to negotiate with the army as well as seek support in Rome for his political project. During the Fiume experience, he was also part of the buccaneer Uscocchi group, a trained unit under D'Annunzio that raided ships to capture foodstuff and other resources to feed the population and military units of Fiume. Once the Fiume experience ended, Muti returned to Ravenna and worked in a bank for a short time. He then joined the fascist movement as a leader of the action squads in the Ravenna area. In this capacity his unit would frequently be involved in violent clashes against the Socialist Party organizations and the labor unions. Muti then became involved with the MVSN, the fascist militia, on 1 February 1923 and went on to hold several positions within the organization. In December 1931, for example, he joined the Ports Militia in Trieste and was nominated *Console* and then commander of the III *Legione Portuaria* between 1933 and 1935. In the mid-thirties Muti became fascinated with airplanes and gained his pilot license in 1934. Muti volunteered as an officer in the Italian air force joining the 15a *Squadriglia Bombardieri* in 1935 and saw action during the campaign in Ethiopia. During the Spanish Civil War, he distinguished himself for carrying out several daring bombing operations gaining the rank of *Maggiore*, a gold medal and four silver medals. In 1938 Francisco Franco awarded Muti with a medal of military valor. He became party secretary of the PNF (fascist party) between 31 October 1939 to 30 October 1940. His tenure did not last long however, mainly due to his efforts to clean up the party by outlining cases of political corruption and ousting several corrupt leaders of the old guard. His mentor Galeazzo Ciano was quick to distance himself from Muti who was then substituted as party leader by Adelchi Serena. During the Second World War he again joined the RA and in the summer of 1940 was awarded another silver medal for conducting a daring operation against an enemy operated petrol refinery. The combat action consisted in four S.82 bombers flying over Bahrein in the Persian Gulf to drop bombs on a British refinery. The pilots took off from Rhodes on 18 October 1940 for a long winded mission of over 4,100 kilometers that tested the endurance of the aircraft. The small unit was able to drop 135 bombs on the refinery which procured damage to the plant. The four pilots then terminated their journey landing in Italian East Africa. In 1941 he was promoted to *Tenente Colonnello* and nominated commander of the 41° *Gruppo* based in the Aegean, which was transformed into a torpedo bomber unit. During his tenure as commander he wrote two very interesting reports outlining the weaknesses of the air service and pointing out the need for updated weapons, mainly fighters fitted with 20mm cannons and a new torpedo bomber. He then retired from the force due to eyesight issues and carried out a number of espionage/secret operations on behalf of the Italian intelligence service. Muti's last mission encompassed recovering components of an American radar system in Spain in June 1943. He died during the night of 23/ 24 August 1943, a month after the fall of the regime, in a planned assassination at the hands of Prime Minister Pietro Badoglio's secret police. Badoglio and his entourage saw him as a threat to the stability of their government.

5: CARLO EMANUALE BUSCAGLIA

Born on 22 September 1915 in Novara and died on 24 August 1944 in Naples. Buscaglia was one of the most famous Italian pilots of the Second World War. He entered the *Accademia Aeronautica* (air force academy) in October 1934 and by February 1937 Buscaglia had earned his military pilot license and was made *Sottotenente* (2nd Lieutenant). Initially assigned to a standard bomber unit (50ª *Squadriglia*/ 32° *Stormo*) Buscaglia would see brief action against France in June 1940. Shortly thereafter he would be one of only five hand-picked pilots to join the newly formed 278ª *Squadriglia Aerosiluranti* torpedo bomber unit based in Gorizia as a *Tenente*. After his successful strike on HMS *Kent*, he badly damaged the cruiser HMS *Glasgow* on December 3, 1940. The following year Buscaglia achieved further successes and was made *Capitano* and his name became closely associated with the S.79. His promotion to *Capitano* on 5 March 1941 would also give him command of the 281ª *Squadriglia Aerosiluranti*. In less than two years, Buscaglia became one of the most respected pilots of the RA, earning five Silver Medals of Military Valor and the German Iron Cross second class. On August 12, 1942, Italian leader Benito Mussolini personally promoted him to *Maggiore* (major) commanding the 132° *Gruppo Autonomo Aerosiluramti*.

Promotions and daring missions had made Buscaglia a well-known national figure. Thus, it was with great apprehension that the Italian people learned on November 12, 1942 that his plane had been shot down by a Supermarine Spitfire and that Buscaglia was missing. Declared killed in action, he was awarded a Gold Medal of Military Valor. But while Buscaglia had been wounded and badly burned, he survived and was captured by Allied troops. Sent to a prisoner of war camp in the United States, he later flew for the Allies, only to die while attempting to take off in a Martin Baltimore on August 23, 1944.

5

1941 and the Establishment of the Torpedo Bombers

Overall Military Situation

At the beginning of 1941 the Italian military's war efforts were in a poor state. The Italian army in September 1940 had attacked in North Africa advancing toward Sidi Barrani in British held Egyptian territory but then the infantry units had been instructed to take a defensive position while a buildup of tanks and guns was taking place in order to prepare the next leap forward to Mersa Matruh. Meantime, in Greece, the Italians had deployed eight infantry and *alpini* divisions along with an armored division to put forth an attack in the Epirus mountain region in late October 1940. For several days the Italians advanced into Greek territory but were later stalemated by the Greek counteroffensive and the horrible weather conditions whereby in November the heavy rains mixed with snow made the mountain roads almost nonnegotiable. To make matters worse on the night of 11–12 November 1940 the Royal Navy made its surprise attack against Italian battleships anchored at Taranto. The Royal Navy deployed Fairey Swordfish biplane torpedo bombers launched from the aircraft carrier HMS *Illustrious* which struck by surprise the RM battle fleet striking with aerial torpedoes. The attack was highly successful causing heavy damage to a number of Italian battleships. As a result, for several months the latter either remained at anchor for long periods of time or else it only sailed in large numbers to escort convoys. These convoys allowed Graziani to launch his initial offensive and then commence the build up for a further advance. But the British army preempted Graziani's build up by launching a mobile counter-offensive of their own. In December 1940 the Western Desert Force in North Africa began Operation Compass on the Egypt-Libya border, a major mobile operation undertaken by armored units and infantry traveling on lorries which overcame Italian infantry defenses at Sidi Barrani and then pushed them back to Tripolitania.

The Germans alarmed at what was happening in North Africa and in Greece and with an increasing concern for the Axis position in the Mediterranean began to ponder what to do. "The Italian defeat had removed at a stroke the threat to Egypt and hence to Britain's entire position in the Eastern Mediterranean, which had now been firmly consolidated. The British would be able to send strong forces from Egypt to Greece—in fact the process had already begun. The naval staff considered that the British had gained a great strategic success; their fleet could not now be driven from the Mediterranean, although this was a step which, in the opinion of Admiral Raeder, was vital to the favorable outcome of the war."[1]

In early 1941 the Germans decided to intervene in North Africa to prop up their ally. Not only did General Erwin Rommel's *Afrika Korps* come to aid the Italians but also the *X Fliegerkorps*, a veteran air group of the Norwegian campaign that was well trained in operations at sea against enemy shipping convoys, was transferred from Norway to Sicily consisting of bombers and twin-engine fighters. By 8 January 1941 ninety-six German bombers had been transferred to Sicilian airfields along with twenty-five twin-engine fighters. By mid-January the figure had risen to 186 aircraft of all types. The *Luftwaffe's* objectives were to subject Malta to aerial bombardments, support with the protection of Axis naval convoys to North Africa, disrupt British supply convoys and attack ports and unloading docks on the coasts of Egypt and Cyrenaica. According to Chief of Staff, *Generale* Pricolo, the German air units arriving in Italy were to play a joint role in the escalating air and naval struggle in the Mediterranean basin.[2] Along with the neutralization of Malta, the other objectives for the Axis in the Mediterranean were to interdict British supply efforts, to safeguard Tripolitania and to stabilize the Greek/Albanian front and then launch an offensive in the spring. Thus began a new phase in the Mediterranean campaign with the involvement of German troops. *Kriegsmarine* Grand Admiral Erich Raeder, for example, perceived the importance of the theatre to winning the war and weakening Britain by taking control of the oil supplies in the Middle East. Others within the German High Command favored other strategies while the political leadership in a few months' time would launch Operation Barbarossa against the Soviet Union which became the Axis main drain of manpower and resources of the war. This pulled the Axis effort to a new direction and the Mediterranean became a secondary theatre.

The RA in 1941

In the first quarter of 1941 the position of the RA, despite getting help from the *Luftwaffe*, had become more precarious mainly because it was overstretched fighting in too many theatres with an inadequate number of aircraft. Initially when Italy entered the war, 313 aircraft were based in Libya and the Aegean and 325 in East Africa. British intelligence assessments stated that the Italian air force would move aircraft from one theatre to another as the fighting demanded—from Italy to Libya or from Italy to East Africa for example. But these movements were not as widespread as the RA maintained a large force in Southern Italy were it could easily deploy aircraft in the Central Mediterranean. A large deployment of aircraft had been made in Rhodes to assist with the Greek offensive, while during Graziani's offensive a buildup of the air forces in North Africa had been made to sustain the infantry. Once the British Army went on the counteroffensive several advanced airfields were overrun leading to the loss of aircraft. Losses had also been caused by the improper use in some cases of the fleet. For example, S.79 standard bombers and other planes given the extremely precarious situation on the ground were

1 Major-General I.S.O. Playfair, *The Mediterranean and Middle East Volume I: The Early Successes against Italy (to May 1941),* (London: HMSO, 1954) <http://www.ibiblio.org/hyperwar/UN/UK/UK-Med-I/UK-Med-I-19.html> (accessed 12 May 2021).

2 John Gooch, *Mussolini's War,* p.145.

deployed to strafe at very low altitudes the attacking enemy infantry and their lorries in an effort to stave the British offensive. This resulted in a high loss rate of aircraft and by the end of Operation Compass: "By early February 1941, however, the RA in Libya lost nearly 700 aircraft to all causes, some 400 abandoned or burned to prevent capture, 140 destroyed by RAF attacks, 100 lost in aerial combat and the rest to unknown causes."[3] By March 1941 its overall fighting force outside Italy had declined with approximately 73 bombers and 137 fighters in Libya, and 37 bombers and 46 fighters in the Aegean, whereas the fleet in East Africa had been completely lost. Commanders were also changed. The air forces in the Aegean were now commanded by *Generale* Ulisse Longo, while the *5ª Squadra* in Libya was commanded by *Generale* Mario Aimone-Cat, who had replaced *Generale* Porro.

The objectives of the RA in early 1941 were thus to reorganize its ranks, replenish the losses of pilots and aircraft through advanced training and support an increase in aircraft production, sustain the aerial bombardment of Malta and rebuild the force in North Africa. The high losses in the field were partly compensated for by an uptick in domestic production. The second year of the war, for example, would be the best year for the Italian aviation industry as it produced 3,503 aircraft, an increase of 250 more planes than 1940. The major manufacturers of aircraft supporting the rise in production were *Caproni* (20,000 employees), *IRI* (24,000), *Fiat* (16,000) and *Piaggio* (12,000). These were followed by smaller more specialized entities such as *Breda, Reggiane, Savoia Marchetti* and *Macchi*. Each company at one point in 1941 or 1942 had to cease production for some time as a result of enemy air attacks or lack of fuel. Aircraft industry employment in 1941 had reached a total of 180,000 employees and it would peak in 1943 when there were 200,000 employees primarily working for thirty-two major companies.[4] The average monthly output of aircraft was 150 in 1939, 271 in 1940, 292 in 1941, 235 in 1942 and 241 in 1943. Similarly, aircraft engine production also increased in the first years of the war but then began to decline. In 1940 industry produced 4,150 engines, by 1942 production peaked to 6,507, but after it began to decline.[5] The major engine manufacturers such as *Alfa Romeo, Fiat, Isotta Fraschini* and *Piaggio* also expanded their capacity in 1941 while supporting the war effort, but by the end of 1942 they began a steady decline in production. Despite the modest rise in production of 1941, demand for aircraft outpaced production throughout the war. Between 1939 and 1943 the Ministry ordered 13,586 aircraft while industry was able to produce only 11,774. Of the 9,000 fighters requested industry was able to produce approximately 4,500, while of the 3,000 bombers and torpedo bombers requested, industry was able to manufacture approximately 2,000.[6] Another factor that hampered steady production was that by 1941 Italian aircraft industry became strongly dependent upon German supply chains for both its raw materials supply and components, especially engine parts. In its factories making German designed engines under license, for example, work depended upon the flows of components and machinery coming from Germany. As the war progressed Germany necessitated more raw materials and components to substitute its own losses, and Italian factories suffered these constraints consequences. Another factor contributing to dampen productivity was the slow evolution toward

3 Brian Sullivan, "Downfall of the Regia Aeronautica", p.162.
4 Maurizio Simoncelli, "L'Industria Militare Italiana nella seconda Guerra mondiale", *Disarmo*, No. 1-2, January 1996, p.6.
5 Ibid.
6 Ibid. p.7.

mass engine assembly production. It would take *Alfa Romeo*, for example, a year to set up the assembly line to produce German engines and equally slow was the transition of the industry toward one where workers were experienced in production aircraft primarily comprised of wood to one primarily based on steel. The majority of workers, for example, had to acquire new skills related to the production of steel based aircraft. This transition caused numerous delays as well as worker shortages. Italian production figures, even while seeing a modest rise in 1941, paled in comparison to the yearly production figures of the United States or Britain which were ten times greater. Germany for example would have an output of 15,600 planes in 1942, 25,000 in 1943 and 40,000 in 1944. The United States manufactured 18,466 aircraft in 1941, 46,907 in 1942 and a staggering 84,853 aircraft in 1944. Britain also had a very strong production output during the Second World War. Its industries manufactured 15,049 aircraft in 1941. In 1942 the aircraft manufacturing production reached 23,672 units and 26,263 in 1943. Finally, in 1944 aircraft output was 26,461 and 12,070 in 1945.[7]

The state of aircraft serviceability in the RA was also a recurring concern as indicated from the scale of Italian air operations where portions of the aircraft fleet could not be deployed at any given time due to a lack of spare parts and of technically experienced personnel. For example, just prior to the start of Operation Halberd in September 1941 the 36° *Stormo* had a force of approximately forty torpedo bombers at its base in Sardinia but could only deploy eleven due to the fact that a large number of its crews had not yet been trained for torpedo operations while a few aircraft required extensive service. Another concern for the Italian air force was the pace of introduction of new and improved aircraft. When Italy entered the war on 10 June 1940 there were approximately only 150 *Macchi* C.200 *Saetta* (Arrow) available for operations. At the time, this was the most advanced fighter plane that the Italians could field representing an improvement over the CR.42 and the G.50. The *Saetta*, the brainchild of Mario Castoldi who had previously designed several award winning seaplanes, was a low wing monoplane of all-metal construction. "Mario Castoldi had drawn widely on the experience he had acquired during the construction of the seaplane racers, especially as far as the aerodynamic solutions were concerned. In fact, in the model 200 the designer succeeded in combining the massive front section of the radial engine with an agile fuselage of reduced dimensions."[8] The wings and the tail of the fighter were its most innovative design features and its highest aerodynamic qualities to the point that they remained unchanged in the design of the successor of the *Saetta*, the *Folgore*. Its powerplant was based upon one Fiat A.74 RC.38 radial engine of 870 hp. The *Macchi* C. 200 had a top speed of 303 mph (503 km/h), a range of 350 miles (563 km) and a service ceiling of 29,200 feet. This was probably its biggest downfall, an engine that was not particularly powerful. While its speed was modest, the *Saetta* was extremely maneuverable giving the pilots a fighting chance against the most technologically advanced RAF fighter planes. Its other major downsides were that it was weakly armed (only two 12.7mm machine guns) and the first series of *Macchi* C.200 produced had a closed and rather uncomfortable cockpit. This was later modified as the pilots requested an open cockpit to facilitate ejection with the parachute. Over 1,151 *Saetta* aircraft were produced between 1939 to July 1942. It operated on all fronts, and until

7 National WW2 Museum, "Out-Producing the Enemy: American Production During WWII" <https://www.nationalww2museum.org/sites/default/files/2017-07/mv-education-package.pdf > (accessed on 10 March 2021).

8 Enzo Angelucci, *World War Two Combat Aircraft* (New York: Military Press, 1988), p.220.

late 1941 it was the main fighter plane of the RA. It first saw deployment in the brief campaign against France where it often prevailed against French fighter planes putting approximately seventy enemy planes out of action. The *Saetta* then saw deployment in bombing campaigns against Malta and Greece escorting bombers and torpedo bombers.

In the spring of 1941 *Saetta* units were deployed in North Africa. Here they supported Rommel's recapture of Cyrenaica by engaging the Hawker Hurricanes of the Western Desert Air Force and in targeting enemy troops on the ground. In its dogfights with the British planes the *Saetta* proved to be an equal opponent. By late 1941 the *Saetta* began to suffer from the introduction of faster British fighters especially because its engine was no longer competitive. The upgrade to the *Saetta* was the *Macchi* C.202 *Folgore* (Thunderbolt). This solution was to take the *Saetta* airframe and basic design to develop an improved fighter. While its armament was somewhat light (two 12.7mm Breda-SAFAT machine guns), several improvements made it a very competitive plane. The cockpit was remodeled and enclosed. Its fuselage was redesigned and characterized by carefully studied aerodynamic lines. The most important improvement, however, was the design changes to accommodate a more powerful licensed built Daimler-Benz 601A engine. It was a game changer for Italian aircraft as these more effective engines began to be made under license in Italy by Fiat and Alfa Romeo. By swapping the Fiat radial engine which was massive and cumbersome and limited in the amount of power produced for the German-designed inline Daimler-Benz, the *Folgore* could reach a top speed of 372 mph (599 km/h) at an altitude of 5,600. In ascent it could reach 19,735 feet (6,000 meters) in five minutes and 55 seconds. The choice of the new engine was revolutionary as the partnership with Daimler Benz later made the creation of the new 5 Series class of fighters possible with the adoption of the new engine beyond *Macchi* and expanded to the *Reggiane* Re.2005 and the Fiat G.55. Regarding the *Folgore* an aviation historian has argued that: "The aircraft is generally remembered as the best Italian fighter to go into service with the RA during world War II, due to its characteristics, the numbers that were built, and the extent to which it was used."[9] Approximately 1,100 aircraft were produced during the war. The aircraft was first introduced during the campaign in North Africa in November 1941 and then they were rolled out in the Balkans, and then in Russia. Between late 1941 and 1942, the *Folgore* was more than a match for Allied fighters such as the Hawker Hurricane II and Curtis P-40, but eventually lost some of its edge against the Supermarine Spitfire Mark IX and the Mustang.

By 1941, therefore, both Italian bombers and torpedo bomber units could count upon more effective fighter escorts to take on the various enemy fighter squads that increasingly interfered with their operations. This was a huge benefit for the *Sparvieri* squadrons which enabled more effective operations.

A big disappointment for the RA, however, was the S.84 which was meant to replace the S.79 torpedo bomber. It had ordered 246 S.84s but from the onset the aircraft did not live up to its high expectations. The S.84 project was launched in 1939 by Alessandro Marchetti of the same firm (*Savoia-Marchetti*) that had launched the S.79 and later in the same year a prototype was unveiled and tested extensively.

The plane had a similar platform to its predecessor the S.79 retaining the same wings design while the fuselage, the engine and the tail assembly were modified. The fuselage had more

9 Ibid., p.221.

innovative lines and lacked the hump on its back which was a key design characteristic of the S.79. The aircraft was powered by three Piaggio P. IX RC40 engines each generating 1,000 hp and driving three bladed variable pitch metal propellers. The rear section of the plane was an expanded version of the S.79. The other sections of the aircraft were characterized by low wings and the same frame of wood, and steel tubes and with an insulation layer made of fabric, plywood and dialuminium. The plane was equipped with four 12.7mm machine guns. One was installed in the belly of the aircraft, a second one in the turret and two more on the sides of the fuselage. The aircraft could carry both standard bombs and torpedoes. The bomb load was housed either under the wings or inside the belly. The fuselage's maximum bomb load was 1,001 kg (2,207 lbs.), while the belly could carry a maximum of two torpedoes or four bombs weighing up to 1,602 kg (3,532 lbs.).

As previously mentioned, despite a deep revamp and a new powerplant, the S.84 did not meet the needs of the torpedo bomber units:

> Prior to the prototype's maiden flight several tests had been carried out with a modified S.79 provided with double empennage and 860 hp Alfa Romeo engines and the aircraft's performance and potential proved to be generally satisfactory. This was not so when the prototype of the S.84 began its evaluation tests: it immediately proved to have a series of problems, especially during takeoff and landing, principally caused by the weight of the wings and by the inadequacy of the vertical empennage. Moreover, the Piaggio engines proved to be unreliable and difficult to build.[10]

The first prototype was tested extensively at Guidonia in mid-1940 and according to a secret report by the RA, the trials had furnished: "Overall […] unsatisfactory results"[11] due to poor directional stability.

On 1 June 1941 Ettore Muti, the commander of the *41° Gruppo,* wrote a damning report on the shortcomings of the new plane to *Generale* Pricolo. His unit was one of the first units to receive the S.84 in the torpedo bomber version. Muti, after flying the plane, made four critical points: 1) During takeoff the plane veered too much to the right and was very difficult to maneuver especially for more inexperienced pilots, 2) the plane had experienced technical difficulties when it carried onboard extra fuel for operations that involved longer flights, 3) the S.84's powerplant was mediocre because at an altitude of 5,000 meters or more the plane became unstable and dangerous to fly, 4) since it was unstable at certain altitudes, the *Squadriglie* could not fly in tight formations which were necessary to check the threat of enemy fighters, nor could they accurately launch warheads. Given the mediocre performance of the S.84 Muti advised sticking to the S.79 albeit with a few modifications.[12] In the post war the Italian air force historian Giuseppe Santoro would lodge the same critique against the S.84's performance as a torpedo bomber by arguing that: "Besides the S. 79 aircraft, the S. 84 were later equipped for the launch of the torpedo; but, due to the reduced visibility for the pilots and the poor handling,

10 Gianni Rocca, *I disperati*, p.124.

11 Archivio Storico Aeronautica Militare, *Verbali delle riunioni tenute dal Capo di Sm Generale*, vol, 2 (Rome: Ufficio Storico, 1985), p.23.

12 Francesco Pricolo, *La Regia Aeronautica nella seconda guerra mondiale* (Milan: Mondadori, 1971), p.165.

these aircraft did not give good results."[13] Initially these critiques were not well received by the heads of RA because on 28 August 1941 the latter issued dispatch n. 515789 which stipulated that "Gruppi equipped with S.84 shall assume the denomination of Stormi aerosiluranti"[14] and that given their specific characteristics these units shall be employed exclusively in the torpedo bomber role. By mid-1941 the RA had already ordered 246 S.84 aircraft as part of the first commission with *Savoia Marchetti* and a year later an additional 63 planes were purchased and delivered. Apparently in 1941 the S.84 appeared to be a real alternative to the S.79, whose production was to be slowly phased out. But the numbers alone for 1942 demonstrate that the S.84 was ditched just a year later after it was introduced thus giving credence to the opinions of experienced pilots such as Muti that found the S.84 unworkable. The plane was first utilized by the 41° *Gruppo* in February 1941 and then it equipped the 36° *Gruppo* which was transformed into a torpedo bomber unit shortly thereafter. Until the summer of 1942 the fleet of S. 84s was used primarily in the torpedo bomber role. But given its poor maneuverability which hampered precision launching of the torpedo, in the summer of 1942 the remaining aircraft were used only for standard bombing operations.

In 1942 a limited attempt was made to improve upon the S.84 with the bis version which included design changes to the cockpit and the wings as well as increased ventilation to the engine. These changes however did not alter completely the initial design flaws and the engine troubles of the Piaggio XI. Thus in 1941 the RA's problems were clearly noticeable. It had a more modest fleet compared to Britain and the United States that was operating in numerous theatres of action and it also had a less technologically sophisticated set of aircraft. While the quality of the fighters improved dramatically but it still trailed developments in Britain and the United States, the torpedo bomber, did not. The failure to introduce a successor to the S.79 would become clear in late 1942 when Italian torpedo bombers had fewer successes. Two other main issues in 1941 were the lack of a domestic dive bomber and of a heavy bomber.

Torpedo Bomber Units Organization

The torpedo bomber discipline was further augmented in 1941. In recognition of the emerging importance of the torpedo bomber units, *Generale* Pricolo established in February 1941 an *aero-siluranti* office within the RA General Staff. This office took charge of all the technical, logistical, operational and organizational activities of the discipline. In essence it centralized all torpedo bomber activities into one organization and it also regulated the use of aerial torpedoes with the drafting of a handbook for operations. One of the principal tasks of this office was to streamline torpedo bomber operations by ensuring that each torpedo bomber airfield had a modicum number of warheads to carry out operations or in cases this could not be achieved due to production or logistical constraints, it organized the swift delivery of torpedoes at bases were none or few were available in anticipation of major aerial/naval battles. "S. 82 aircraft were equipped for the rapid transport of torpedoes, in whose belly it was possible to stow, in addition to the other components making up the weapon, such as the slings, tripods, cranes, test

13 Giuseppe Santoro, *L'aeronautica italiana nella seconda guerra mondiale,* vol. I, p.63.
14 Ibid.

benches, spare parts, assembly tools, compressor, reserve compressed air tank, etc. Sometimes it was possible to ship from Italy to Rhodes or Tobruk on a single S. 82: 3 torpedoes, 3 loaded warheads, 3 torpedo guides, 3 tail ends, 3 loaded pistols, 3 gyroscopes, and relative packaging; all for a total weight of about 4,000kg."[15]

In preparation of a major battle, for example, the S.82s[16] were used to transport warheads to bases in the Mediterranean based upon intelligence reports detecting the movements of British naval forces at Gibraltar, Malta and Alexandria. "Then as the air and naval actions progressed following the movement of the convoys, the residual torpedoes were transported by means of the S. 82, for example, from Sardinia to Sicily, from here to Libya and finally, possibly, to the Aegean; and vice versa."[17]

Torpedo bomber operations were complex from a logistical perspective but equally complex was the timely deployment of the aircraft for combat. This required highly skilled personnel to ready them for action. For example, to affix a torpedo to the belly of a S.79 it took over 30 minutes and a special custom trolley had to be used to carry the torpedo from the base warehouse to the plane. These trolleys were in short supply but *Capitano* Buscaglia was able to break the red tape of the bureaucracy when he had them custom designed and built for use at his base.[18] After Buscaglia's initiative the *aerosiluranti* office took the lead in ensuring that all torpedo bomber operational bases had a modicum amount of trolleys. The task of selecting and training the specialists that could take care and affix the torpedoes was another key responsibility of the new office. Often at bases in Libya and the Aegean, for example, the skilled personnel were drawn directly from Whitehead or from *Savoia-Marchetti*. Operating in Libya was particularly difficult given the challenges presented by the desert climate which influenced the storage, preparation and servicing of the warheads and the aircraft. "The high temperature, the sand, the poor quality of the oils, the lack of electricity or the non-correspondence of the characteristics of these to the types of compressors used very often determined very challenging situations, in which all the initiatives and resolution skills of the staff responsible for preparing these very delicate weapons were involved."[19] Here key personnel was trained to progressively replace the private industry contractors which after having established the service units were rotated out of service.

Another responsibility of this office became the conversion of former standard bomber units into torpedo bomber. This entailed the training of their personnel into the torpedo bomber discipline as well as the retrofitting of the aircraft so they could carry the warheads. Torpedo bomber production was also overseen by this office which was also responsible for maintaining a stockpile of warheads. In August 1940 only 30 torpedoes were furnished to the RA since the bulk of torpedo production was taken up by the RM and the *Luftwaffe*. In December 1940 the RA had only few torpedoes available having used up more than 15 torpedoes during operations, meanwhile it was expecting to receive 40 more by early 1941. In May 1941 there were a total of 70 torpedoes available and the goal was to have 100 torpedoes available at any one time for

15 Ibid., p.62.
16 The Savoia Marchetti aircraft, S.82 were triple engine monoplanes used as bombers or transport aircraft with a maximum speed of 205 mph and a range of 2,200 miles.
17 Giuseppe Santoro, *L'aeronautica italiana nella seconda guerra mondiale*, vol I, p.62.
18 Martino Aichner, *Il gruppo Buscaglia*, p.106.
19 Ibid., p.92.

operations, while monthly production was of only 15 aerial warheads out of a total of 50-60 torpedoes. According to the report issued by *Comando Supremo* the situation "was not brilliant but was not desperate either."[20] By August 1942 production of aerial warheads had increased to 50 per month.[21] In September 1942, RA was in possession of approximately 250 aerial torpedoes and production continued at a steady pace of 50 per month for several months. Torpedo output increased in 1941 and 1942 but so did the fleet of torpedo bombers, which necessitated the uptick in production. At the time an inquest by the *aerosiluranti* office was conducted regarding potential sabotage after Buscaglia's squadron had carried out several combat actions that even while releasing the warheads from favorable positions had failed to produce any damage against enemy ships. The inquest lasted over a year and revealed that several workers at the Capodichino (Naples) factory had purposely modified SI warheads so that they would not explode. The inquest, although finding the workers guilty, formally acquitted them because by late 1943 Italy had switched sides and had negotiated a peace treaty with the Allies. Throughout the conflict it can be argued that industry continued to produce enough torpedoes to keep the squadrons active, although there was never an abundance of torpedoes and at multiple times pilots were instructed to launch them only when the likelihood of success was fairly high. Otherwise, crews were not to waste torpedoes. This conservative approach dictated by the need to safeguard torpedo inventory likely reduced the number of successful operations as some opportunities were clearly missed because some pilots were exceedingly cautious.

In 1941 the organizational growth of the torpedo discipline continued. A third torpedo bomber unit, 280ª *Squadriglia Autonoma Aerosiluranti* was formed in Gorizia on 8 February 1941 and it saw operational deployment at Elmas in Sardinia. A fourth unit, 281ª *Squadriglia Autonoma Aerosiluranti*, was formed in Grottaglie (Apulia) on 5 March 1941 and subsequently was deployed in numerous theatres of operation including a long stint at Rhodes.[22] It had five working S.79s.[23] 283ª *Squadriglia Autonoma Aerosiluranti* was the fifth torpedo bomber unit formed at Ciampino near Rome on 4 July 1941 to then be deployed at Elmas airfield in Sardinia and then North Africa.[24] Finally, 284ª *Squadriglia Autonoma Aerosiluranti*, also originally based at Ciampino, was the sixth unit formed on 7 November 1941.[25] It was transferred first to Sicily and then to North Africa. It was placed under the command of *Capitano* Erasi. The conversion of standard bomber units into torpedo bomber ones was initiated in 1940 but it continued to evolve in a more significant way in 1941 with the training of the crews to the new discipline. The *34° Gruppo Autonomo Aerosiluranti*, for example, was a former bomber unit (*67ª and 68ª Squadriglie*) that was converted to the torpedo bomber discipline and equipped initially with four then later six S.79 aircraft. The *Gruppo* was officially formed as torpedo bomber on 21 April 1941 and based in Rhodes at the command of *Tenente Colonnello* Vittorio Cannaviello. Its two squads were later disbanded in June 1941 and its personnel was placed into the 279ª and 281ª *Squadriglie*, which acted autonomously. Another standard bomber unit to be transformed into a

20 *Verbali dellle riunioni tenute dal capo di stato maggiore generale*, vol. II (Rome: Ufficio Storico, 1983), p.59.
21 Ibid., Vol. 3, p.747.
22 Marco Mattioli, *Savoia-Marchetti S.79 Sparviero*, p.88.
23 Giuseppe Santoro, *L'aeronautica italiana nella seconda guerra mondiale*, Vol. 1, p.211.
24 Marco Mattioli, *Savoia-Marchetti S.79 Sparviero*, p.88.
25 Ibid.

torpedo one was 41° *Gruppo Autonomo Aerosiluranti* which was comprised of the 204ª and 205ª *Squadriglie*. It had seen service since the beginning of the war operating standard S.79 bombers mainly against Malta and Greece. Then in January 1941 it was headquartered in Littoria near Rome and shortly thereafter received the first S.84s, the new torpedo bombers set to replace the S.79 fleet. After spending some time training as a torpedo bomber unit in Italy it was posted in Rhodes on 5 May 1941 where with a fleet of S.84 and a few S.79 torpedo bombers it began to conduct a number of operations against British shipping headed to and from Malta. In January 1942 it received more experienced torpedo bomber pilots and crews from the two former *Squadriglie* (281ª and 282ª) and when the S.84s were retired it received S.79 torpedo bombers. This unit was commanded by *Tenente Colonnello* Ettore Muti who was one of Italy's most well-known aviators and a highly decorated officer. On 28 August 1941 *Aeronautica della Sardegna* issued a communique that established the 36° *Stormo* from a standard bomber to a torpedo bomber unit based on two groups: 108° *Gruppo* (256ª and 257ª *Squadriglie)* and 109° *Gruppo* (258ª and 259ª *Squadriglie*). It was initially equipped with four S.79 and twenty-nine S.84 (only nineteen were operational at the time). It was headquartered at Borgo Panigale (Bologna) were it undertook the training in the new discipline. The unit then saw deployed for combat in Sardinia. Finally, the same command unit on 1 September 1941 announced the formation at Elmas airport in Sardinia of the 130° *Gruppo Autonomo* with 281ª and 283ª *Squadriglie* under the command of *Maggiore* Enrico Bianchi and set to fly exclusively with S.84 torpedo bombers. It was the first newly formed torpedo bomber group unlike other groups that were transformed into the torpedo bomber role.

According to a memorandum titled "Incremento linea aerosiluranti" written by *Superaereo* to outline the expansion of the torpedo bomber organization there were 99 torpedo bombers by the end of August 1941 while there were only 33 in March of the same year. The total was further broken down by aircraft type: 53 S.84 and 46 S.79 with approximately 85 warheads available.[26] In contrast, at roughly the same time (data from July 1941), the British in the Mediterranean could count upon the following: the RAF had 67 maritime strike aircraft available that included a mix of types including new Bristol Beaufighters and the FAA had approximately 99 strike aircraft distributed around the theatre at the same point. These aircraft were not purely dedicated to anti-shipping operations, but the number of torpedo strikes in the region was increasing at a steady pace each month in 1941.[27] The data reveals that the Italian torpedo bomber discipline had been expanded considerably but it was still shy of the goals set by *Comando Supremo* on 15 May 1941. At the time, the goal was to have 184 torpedo bombers available for combat along with 206 warheads by August 1941.[28] The latter goal was to be achieved by increasing domestic aerial torpedo production as well as reorienting some naval to aerial torpedo production. As can be seen by the August torpedo bomber and warhead tally the initial plans for expansion were very unrealistic in light of the difficulties associated with expanding domestic production and the high losses of both aircraft and warheads sustained in combat operations. A very realistic number was furnished on 23 August 1941 regarding the combat readiness of the torpedo bombers (not the total number of aircraft) for an enemy anti-shipping operation to be

26 Francesco Mattesini, *Luci ed ombre*, p.101.
27 Richard Hammond, "Air Power and the British Anti-Shipping Campaign in the Mediterranean, 1940-1944", *Air Power Review*, Vol. 16, No. 1, p.55.
28 Ibid.

conducted in the following days. This number did not take into account newly formed torpedo bomber units equipped with S.84s nor the total number of torpedo bombers available at bases in the Mediterranean but it looked only at the aircraft that could be deployed the next day. By looking at the fleet in such a strict fashion, there were only thirty-eight torpedo bombers deemed combat ready (mostly S.79) and forty-eight aerial torpedoes. The dislocation of the aircraft was as follows: Sardinia-12, Sicily-11, North Africa-4, Aegean-11, mainland Italy 10.[29]

By early 1941 two additional torpedo bomber training schools had been established (one in Capodichino near Naples and one in Pisa), again demonstrating that the RA desired to make the torpedo bomber specialty one of its foremost elite units. The *2° Nucleo Addestramento Aerosiluranti* was established on 25 November 1940 at Capodichino airport near Naples, while *3° Nucleo Addestramento Aerosiluranti* was formed on 15 January 1941 at Pisa airport. The schools were located near the training grounds or where the torpedoes were manufactured. The first school in Gorizia, for example, was located near Fiume where Whitehead was headquartered, while Capodichino was located near the *Silurificio Italiano*, the second torpedo assembly works. The schools were jointly led by a RA instructor and a RM officer observer and their main purpose was to train new crews. Most of the crews learned the trade by conducting flight training but they also experienced torpedo operations first-hand: "In the most bitter air and naval battles that took place in the Mediterranean, often the instructor staff and the students, would assist to the combat actions of the operational torpedo bomber units comrades using the school's aircraft."[30] A secondary task was to conduct research and tests relating to torpedoes and torpedo aiming instruments.

To further the training of the new recruits into the disciple a further reform was adopted in mid-1941 which sought to create a training team at each base to ease in new pilots or crew members into the role. It was recognized that flight training was not fully adequate to prepare the pilots for the vicissitudes of torpedo bomber operations and that further hands on training was needed to compensate for the lack of combat experience. This was provided by a selective team at each base which furthered the training regimen of the new recruits.

1941 Operations

The new year brought further losses to an already depleted torpedo bomber fleet. On 1 January a raid against Ain El Gazala airbase by four Blenheims damaged beyond repair one S.79. On 2 January *Capitano* Erasi carried out a lone wolf attack against a destroyer at 2130 near the Gulf of Sollum. Despite the fact that the combat action was well executed and the torpedo was released from a favorable distance (500 meters from the enemy ship), the warhead dropped down unexpectedly into the seabed. Apparently, a technical failure was the cause of the unsuccessful operation. Another technical failure was experienced the next day by a pilot from the same *Squadriglia* (278ª). The operation was carried out against a destroyer in the same area but a fault in the torpedo drop mechanism caused a misfire and the ship was unscathed. Then on 4 January two S.79s from the same unit attacked in the Gulf of Sollum a British destroyer. But the

29 Verbali delle riunioni tenute dal capo di Stato Maggiore Generale, Vol. 2 (Rome: Ufficio Storico, 1995), p.98.
30 Ibid.

scarce visibility and the strong anti-aircraft fire by Royal Navy gunners prevented a successful outcome. On 9 January the newly formed 279ª *Squadriglia* carried out its first operation of the year when two S.79s canvassed at night the coast of Malta. At 2200 they spotted a steamer and one of the S.79s launched the torpedo at a favorable distance but was unable to verify whether a hit had been made.

The first combined action between Italian and German aircraft against British shipping convoys took place on 10 January 1941 south of Pantelleria Island. The five ships convoy of Operation Excess began their journey from Clyde in Scotland, had made a stop at Gibraltar and were then headed to Malta and finally Greece. The *Essex* ship carried 4,000 tons of ammunition, 3,000 tons of food stuffs and twelve Hurricanes which were destined for Malta. The other ships, N*orthern Prince*, *Empire Song*, *Clan Cumming*, and *Clan Macdonald*—were destined for Greece with supplies, and ammunition. 800 soldiers and airmen for Malta were distributed among these five ships. The convoy was first escorted by Force H and then in the middle of the Mediterranean it was picked up by Admiral Cunningham's force consisting of HMS *Warspite*, HMS *Valiant*, HMS *Illustrious*, and seven destroyers. The first attack on the convoy was made by two Italian torpedo bombers flown by *Capitano* Orazio Bernardini and *Tenente* Angelo Caponetti of *279ª Squadriglia* on 10 January at 1223 just southeast of Pantelleria island, as the convoy made its way through the Mediterranean Sea south of Sicily. The latter had taken off from Catania airfield near Palermo and pressed forward their attack, but facing a hellish fire they could not get close to the ships and dropped their torpedoes at long range (2,500 meters) and did not reach the convoy. Of their attack the Royal Navy post battle report states: "At 1223, two S.79s dropped two torpedoes which missed astern of VALIANT. These aircraft were engaged in good time by the close range weapons of the battlefleet, without effect."[31]

Shortly thereafter, a nasty surprise awaited the two S.79s. Pursued by four Fairey Fulmar fighters, one of which badly damaged *Tenente* Caponetti's aircraft, the two planes were forced to make a hasty retreat back to base. Caponetti's battered plane, unable to continue the flight, was forced to crash land at Catania airfield. But while the two Italian planes were being pursued by the enemy fighters thirty Ju.88s and 87s (Stuka dive-bombers) sprang a surprise attack upon the convoy. Without the RAF fighters in a position to intervene to defend the convoy, the German (3° Stukas) and Italian pilots (96° *Gruppo Bombardamento a Tuffo*) quickly split up into three groups concentrating particularly on HMS *Illustrious.* According to the British Official History: "The attacks were made with great skill and determination and were quite unlike anything the fleet had experienced at the hands of the Italians."[32] *Illustrious* was struck six times. Several Royal Navy soldiers were killed or wounded and the ship's flight deck along with nine aircraft were destroyed. For many months she was out of action. The following are the recollections of an officer on board that records when the ship was struck as well as the eerie feeling of death and destruction that followed the attack:

31 James Somerville, "Mediterranean Convoy Operations ", *Supplement to the London Gazette*, n. 38296, 10 August 1948, p.4471.

32 Major-General I.S.O. Playfair, *The Mediterranean and Middle East Volume I: The Early Successes against Italy (to May 1941* (London: HMSO, 1954) <http://www.ibiblio.org/hyperwar/UN/UK/UK-Med-I/UK-Med-I-17.html> (accessed 12 May 2021).

> There was a blinding, staggering crash and a great thousand pounder struck the flight deck right in the center line. It burst through the armored deck and the hangar deck below, hit the after ammunition conveyor and exploded killing badly and wounding everybody in the wardroom flat. All the officers taking a hasty meal were wiped out. The whole after part of the ship went dark and dead. The fire took hold everywhere and raged through the torn and shattered components where men lay trapped. A smashed petrol pipe sprayed streams of liquid flame through the dark smoke filled passages.[33]

Despite the damage, HMS *Illustrious* was towed to Malta. In the next few days both Italian and German bombers continued to cooperate and pressed forward several forays into Malta in order to sink the embattled HMS *Illustrious*, but even though they managed to drop bombs on target the damage was not enough to sink the ship. Toward the end of January, HMS *Illustrious* made a successful night voyage to Alexandria where she would be better protected from enemy attack while undergoing repairs.

The new threat posed by the *Luftwaffe* with its powerful striking force ended the period in which the Royal Navy was able to bring supply convoys through the Central Mediterranean to Malta and to Alexandria with only some degree of interference from the Axis air and naval forces. The *Luftwaffe's* new cutting edge together with the forces deployed by the RA forced the Royal Navy to voyage primarily by night and to provide more escort protection to its convoys. The RAF in turn was tasked to step up its efforts to preempt the Axis air forces with interfering with the naval convoys by increasing the number of preemptive bombing raids against enemy airfields. The Royal Navy now also demanded that more RAF resources be deployed in the Middle East to gain aerial superiority and safeguard supply convoys and that Malta be strengthened. In the new context of a highly contested anti-shipping campaign by both sides, by early 1941 Malta's fortress assumed a role of vital importance for the British position in the Mediterranean and the Middle East by making the line of Axis supply to North Africa much more precarious. Churchill had stated that: "…the primary duty of the British Mediterranean Fleet…to stop all sea-borne traffic between Italy and Africa… Every convoy that gets through must be considered a serious naval failure. The reputation of the Royal Navy is engaged in stopping this traffic."[34] This led to the installation in Malta of a special force of light cruisers and destroyers (Force K) and the 10th Submarine Flotilla which became a constant menace to Italian shipping operations. In this effort they were aided by an intelligence coup of major proportions. In June 1941 the Italian C38m cypher was broken by ULTRA decryption. This gave the British advance warning of the departure dates of Italian convoys, often including the composition and projected routes as well. Another threat posed by Malta was its aerial striking force deployed both in anti-shipping operations as well as preemptive strikes against Axis bases. Malta's air strength was also augmented. In March for example, seven Bristol Beauforts were transferred to Malta and formed a joint reconnaissance/strike squadron (No. 69) with newly arrived Glen Martin reconnaissance aircraft. The first victims of these new units deploying the RAF's preventive strategy were Axis bases and supply depots. Two Italian air bases (Gadurra

33 John Withson (ed.), *The War at Sea* (New York: William Morrow, 1968), p.91.
34 Richard Hammond, "Air Power and the British Anti-Shipping Campaign in the Mediterranean, 1940-1944, p.55.

and Maritza), for example, were attacked by Wellington bombers on the night of 10 March which resulted in the destruction of one S.79 torpedo bomber and severe damage to two others.

The 34° *Gruppo* was in action on 31 January when one of its S.79s attacked 20 miles north of Suda Bay convoy AN14 which was destined to sail to Greece. The aircraft was able to launch from a favorable distance a torpedo against a British destroyer which was missed due to a malfunction of the aiming device. The same result took place on 23 February when at Suda Bay another British destroyer was missed. Both operations demonstrated that the crews of this unit were still green and inexperienced in the torpedo bomber disciple. Its war diary reported that between November 1940 and March 1941 the unit had carried out 37 torpedo bomber operations, of which only in 11 operations enemy ships had been located and targeted. Of these 11 operations only one had been successful (16 December) while in the other ten the torpedo bombers crews had misfired.[35]

On 5 March 1941 recently promoted *Capitano* Buscaglia was given command of newly formed 281[a] *Squadriglia* initially based in Grottaglie, but by 20 March it was posted to Rhodes under the command of the 34° *Gruppo*. Its role was to target enemy battlefleet and shipping convoys in the eastern Mediterranean and the Aegean Sea.

Between 27-29 March 1941 a major naval battle took place in the Eastern Mediterranean when the Italian battle fleet clashed with the East Mediterranean Fleet in the Battle of Cape Matapan. The battle was the result of pressure from the Italian government and from the *Kriegsmarine* upon *Supermarina* to seek out and engage in a decisive battle the Royal Navy battlefleet to avenge Taranto. The actual encounter battle at sea began at 0812 on 28 March when *Vice-Ammiraglio* Luigi Sansonetti's III *Divisione* cruisers were ordered to attack a group of eight Royal Navy ships that had been spotted by aerial reconnaissance two hours before. The RM admirals and the intelligence services were "totally unaware that Enigma had given Admiral Cunningham many key details including the exact date of the operation in advance."[36] As a result they fell into a well prepared trap by the Royal Navy which dispatched a destroyer division and the battle fleet. At 1056 the Italian battleship *Vittorio Veneto* opened fire on the enemy formation comprised of eight cruisers and destroyers. Other Italian cruisers also joined the fight, but they failed to hit the targets. Fearing torpedo attacks the Italian warships under the command of *Ammiraglio* Iachino retired. But in the afternoon a series of aerial attacks by the British damaged the *Vittorio Veneto*. Then at twilight another attack severely damaged the cruiser *Pola*. As several Italian cruisers were attempting to rescue the *Pola*, they came under heavy attack from Admiral Cunningham's three battle ships which severely damaged another two cruisers (*Fiume* and *Zara*) and two destroyers (*Vittorio Alfieri* and *Carducci*). The latter parts of the battle were conducted in late afternoon/early night where British radar capabilities enabled the Royal Navy to outmaneuver the Italian battleships. The naval engagement once again saw the British fleet prevail over the Italians given the former's superior all-arms strategy using airpower for both advanced early reconnaissance and for attacking the Italian fleet. Incidentally, the Italian battle fleet had been warned of the presence of the East Mediterranean fleet by *Capitano* Buscaglia who had spotted it on the morning of the 27th and had notified *Supermarina:* "One of them was piloted by the soon to be famous Carlo Emanuele Buscaglia, who reported a battle-

35 Francesco Mattesini, *Luci ed ombre*, p.40.
36 John Gooch, *Mussolini's War*, p.196.

ship, carrier, six cruisers and five destroyers steaming at 18 knots. But Admiral Iachino did not receive this report for some time, as it followed the complete chain of command, before being passed to the fleet....In contrast, the X Fliegerkorps reports were passed directly to the German liaison team aboard the Vittorio Veneto thus allowing for closer cooperation."*37* At 0100 two S.79s, Buscaglia and a companion, attacked HMS *Formidable,* which had become separated from the British battleships. The action was well conducted with the two planes attacking from separate direction and at low level, but ultimately HMS *Formidable* avoided the torpedoes. In the post battle report by *Ammiraglio* Iachino, Buscaglia was accused however, of not properly warning the RM in time and of delivering his intelligence report only later in the morning. His report also stated that RA had not provided any air support and that the latter failed to back up the RM with bomber and torpedo bomber attacks. At any rate, Cape Matapan once again showed the lack of extensive pre-war training and collaboration between the RM and the aviation forces as lack of intelligence sharing was one of the causes that led to defeat. As the naval battle was unfolding, the RA utilized its torpedo and its standard bombers against the British fleet but no major hits were scored.

The most notable aerial torpedo action during the battle of Cape Matapan took place on 28 March 1941 when the newly formed 281ª *Squadriglia* led by *Capitano* Buscaglia conducted its first major operation of the war. At 0745 an Italian reconnaissance plane spotted the Italian fleet (*Vittorio Veneto, Trieste, Trento and Bolzano*) at sea while it was pursuing Force B comprised of eight destroyers and cruisers. The former ships were mistakenly identified as British and the air force command of the Aegean dispatched three S.79s to interfere with its passage through the Aegean Sea. The planes took off at 0930 and were fortunate enough to spot the British ships at sea led by the aircraft carrier HMS *Formidable*, HMS *Warspite*, HMS *Valiant* and HMS *Barham*. At 1255 a squad of three S.79s (*Capitano* Buscaglia in the lead supported by *Tenente* Pietro Greco and *Tenente* Giuseppe Cimicchi) began to maneuver in order to target the East Mediterranean Fleet. After circling over the fleet, a mechanical issue experienced by Cimicchi's plane forced the latter to abandon the mission. The other two pilots pressed on and attempted to attack HMS *Formidable*. They cautiously advanced toward their objective despite very intense anti-aircraft fire. After having bypassed unscathed the curtain of enemy fire, they were challenged by two Fulmars from No. 803 Squadron. The S.79s maneuvered around the Fulmars avoiding them altogether and finally pressed home the attack by launching torpedoes at distances of 800 and 1,000 meters. In the post battle report the pilots detailed how the ship most likely had been hit by the warheads, but their evaluation was erroneous as HMS *Formidable* by taking precautionary action skillfully avoided them. Another attack was made against it by *Maggiore* Vittorio Cannaviello at 1730 but it was also unsuccessful. The pilot reported that "a dense column of black smoke"[38] could be observed coming in the direction of HMS *Formidable*, but once again it was an erroneous assessment. On 29 March *Aeronautica della Sicilia* also intervened in the hunt for the East Mediterranean fleet by dispatching four torpedo bombers of 278*ª* *Squadriglia* while another six S.79s were kept combat ready at base. Out of the four aircraft deployed only two were able to spot Royal Navy ships at sea. Accordingly, *Capitano* Orazio Bernardini and *Tenente* Rodolfo Guza attacked a number of destroyers at 1630 but they both

37 Jack Greene and Alessandro Massignani, *The Naval War*, p.154.
38 Francesco Mattesini, *Luci ed ombre*, p.53.

misfired. One of the enemy destroyers took evasive action to avoid the torpedo and also fired back at the bombers seriously wounding three crew members of *Capitano* Bernardini's plane.

On 2 April at 0900 an Italian reconnaissance plane spotted convoy ANF 24 comprised of seven merchantmen and protected by destroyers HMS *Nubian* and HMS *Hereward* south of Mersa Matruth. Immediately after, four torpedo bombers took flight from Rhodes (*Tenenti* Girogio Sacchetti and Giuseppe Cimicchi from 281*a Squadriglia* and M*aggiore* Vittorio Cannaviello and *Tenente* Umberto Barbani from 34° *Gruppo*) to interfere with its passage. They were followed by three standard bombers from the latter group. The combat action against the convoy took place at 1140 as the British ships put up considerable anti-aircraft fire which interfered with the torpedo bombers forcing the pilots to release the warheads from disadvantageous distances. In their post action report all four pilots asserted that they had hit targets but as the British post battle report indicated none of them did. The only hit was scored by the second wave of standard bombers which bombed the steamship Devis killing seven onboard and wounding fourteen. In a lone operation at night *Capitano* Buscaglia also attempted unsuccessfully to target the convoy. In his post battle report, he reported having hit a cargo ship but no strike was made.

On 18 April 1941 the torpedo bombers of 281ª *Squadriglia* and 279ª *Squadriglia* mounted an attack against Royal Navy vessels taking part in Convoy AN 27 that had left Alexandria with a destination of Piraeus, Greece. The first attack was made at midday when two S.79s torpedo bombers from *279a Squadriglia* piloted by *Tenente* Umberto Barbani and *Tenente* Angelo Caponetti struck a tanker (British Science 7,138 tons carrying a cargo of benzine, kerosene and naphtha) damaging it slightly. As the tanker was making its way onto Suda Bay at reduced speed because of the torpedo hit, it was targeted again at 1430 by two more S.79s torpedo bombers (the first piloted by *Tenente* Cimicchi of 281ª *Squadriglia* and the second by Orfeo Fiumani of 279ª *Squadriglia).* Converging from two directions, the *Sparvieri* approached low down on the sea and by avoiding the huge columns of water raised by the projectiles fired by the Royal Navy guns they pressed home their attack. *Tenente* Cimicchi recalled in his autobiography the dramatic events that led to the destruction of British Science:

> As we appeared near Kasos Strait we could well observe the enemy vessel, already hit by a torpedo traveling alone and at a reduced speed toward Suda Bay. While Fiumani's plane provided cover to my aircraft, I made a determined approach toward the enemy ship. As I got closer to the vessel all hell broke loose as the enemy was firing all that he had in order to immobilize my plane. Enemy fire was zig zagging all around the plane, some shots slightly damaged the plane, some bouncing off. Despite the hellish fire, I brought the plane within shooting range and dropped the warhead at the appropriate time. We could see that the torpedo had hit the ship and it was later reported that it had sank.[39]

Despite having achieved its stated aim, the RA lost one S.79 during the operation when the first two S.79 were attacked by Blenheim IF fighters from No. 30 Squadron. Barbani's plane was making its return trip to base when it was intercepted by an enemy fighter which fired in rapid succession a hail of bullets that damaged the S.79 forcing the pilot to ditch it. The crew, with two members wounded by the enemy fire, were stranded at sea in their small boat until

39 Giuseppe Cimicchi, *I siluri vengono dal cielo* (Milan: Longanesi, 1964), p.87.

they were fortuitously rescued by an Italian floatplane ten hours later. The second plane was also targeted by the enemy fighters but Caponetti's crew fired back vigorously damaging an enemy Blenheim which was forced to break off the pursuit and later crash landed on Crete's Maleme airfield. Another lively firefight between Italian S.79 torpedo bombers and British No. 803 Squadron Fulmars took place in the afternoon when the Italians attempted a second raid against the enemy convoy. This time the torpedo bombers were intercepted and chased away well before they could get close to the ships by the enemy fighters. The two planes of 279ª *Squadriglia* (*Capitano* Orazio Bernardini and *Tenente* Rodolfo Guza) were struck by a hail of fire but fought back. "Return fire from the trimotors was effective, however, hitting Fulmar 6J and wounding its pilot, Lt Donald Gibson, in the arm. His crippled fighter crashed on Formidable' s flight deck when he attempted to land, sending it plunging into the sea. Gibson was quickly picked up by the destroyer HMS *Hereward*, but his observer Sub Lt Peter Ashbrooke, lost his life."[40]

The attack was followed up by a subsequent torpedo bomber foray on 21 April 1941 by two aircraft from 278ª *Squadriglia* flown by *Tenente* Robone and *Capitano* Oscar Cimolini. Both took off from Berka airfield in late afternoon (1625) to pursue Convoy AS 26 in the eastern Mediterranean. While *Tenente* Robone sighted the enemy British Lord 6,098-ton ship as it was being attacked by high-altitude bombers at 1840, he decided to also attack it head on. Flying low, his plane was soon spotted and began receiving a very powerful barrage. Disregarding the heavy fire, Robone's plane like lightning came down rapidly and the crew dropped the torpedo at a very favorable distance of 600 meters from the enemy ship. A tremendous explosion soon rocked the vessel. The first strike was followed by *Capitano* Cimolini's aircraft which dropped his torpedo twenty minutes later also striking British Lord. The post battle reports however, are contradictory. The British post battle report asserts that the torpedo attack did take place but that the damage was done by a German Ju.88 aircraft. Meanwhile, The Italian 278ª *Squadriglia* report states that it was Robone's torpedo that disabled the ship. An even bigger mystery surrounded the disappearance of *Capitano* Cimolini's plane which never made it back to base. Its return flight straight across the desert caused fear for the crew. They had to battle a storm of at least 65 mph and there were no noticeable landmarks to guide them. After calculating that it would take approximately two hours to reach their base, the aircraft traveled aimlessly across the desert. More time passed. Finally, with few drops of fuel remaining, Cimolini was forced to make a belly landing on the desert. Seeing that the plane never returned, the next day several Italian reconnaissance planes were dispatched to locate its remains, but all attempts were unsuccessful. The mystery was finally solved in July of 1960, nineteen years later, when an Italian oil and gas exploration team stumbled upon the wreck of the *Sparviero* in the desert. The remains were found 250 miles south of Benghazi. Further research determined that the pilot had been forced to land on the desert due to the fact that the compass had malfunctioned along with the radio and the crew had lost its way. The forced landing due to lack of fuel caused two of the crew members to sustain fractures. While the two injured crew members remained at the crash site, two other, gunner Gianni Romanini, and an unidentified companion whose remains were never found, began to walk north in order to seek assistance. After three days of walking in the desert and after having run out of water, Romanini collapsed and died in the desert.

40 Marco Mattioli, *Savoia Marchetti S.79 Sparviero*, p.16.

Operation Tiger

Operation Tiger took place in the first half of May 1941 and it was one of the major supply convoy operations that was organized to bring newly built tanks to the British Army in Egypt. The latter aimed to launch a major counterattack to halt Rommel's forces that were besieging Tobruk and necessitated reinforcements. As the British Official History asserts: "The plan for operation Tiger was soon made. A convoy containing large, armored reinforcements was about to leave the United Kingdom for Egypt. Instead of going round the Cape the fast tank-carrying ships of this convoy would turn off at Gibraltar on 5th May and take the short cut, with a saving of nearly forty days. This would be the first attempt to run a convoy through the Mediterranean since January, when the Luftwaffe had made its dramatic appearance."[41]

The convoy, which consisted of five 15-knot merchant ships: Clan Chattan, Clan Lamont, Clan Campbell, Empire Song and New Zealand Star transporting 295 tanks and 53 Hurricanes, was to be protected by Force H from Gibraltar to Malta and then from Malta to Alexandria by the entire Mediterranean Fleet. Thus, for the first leg of the trip the escort would be provided by the warships HMS *Renown*, HMS *Ark Royal*, HMS *Sheffield*, and nine destroyers all attached to Force H. This fleet was to be reinforced by elements of the Mediterranean Fleet, namely the battleship HMS *Queen Elizabeth* and the cruisers *Naiad* and *Fiji*, and from Malta HMS *Gloucester* and the 5th Destroyer Flotilla. Meantime, the second leg escort included HMS *Warspite*, HMS *Barham* and HMS *Valiant*, the carrier HMS *Formidable*, the cruisers *Orion*, *Ajax* and *Perth*, the minelayer *Abdiel* and all available destroyers. The mighty force deployed by the Royal Navy was evidence of the importance of the convoy for the continuation of the British campaign in North Africa. The news of the departure from Gibraltar of Force H, which took place on the morning of 6 May, was brought to the attention of the Axis commanders by SIM intelligence officers stationed in observation posts along the coasts of the Strait, on the shores of Spain and Spanish Morocco. This sighting then lead Axis commanders to order a number of reconnaissance operations in both the western and eastern Mediterranean. One of these sweeps yielded another precious piece of intelligence when elements of the Mediterranean Fleet were observed steaming in the eastern Mediterranean. This made it clear to Rome that it was likely that a double convoy operation was underway. The intelligence gathered forced *Superaereo* to further strengthen aerial reconnaissance while the air squadrons that were destined to attack the convoy could ready their aircraft. Part of these preparations also involved strengthening the torpedo bomber units in Libya. Thus, 279ª *Squadriglia* was transferred from the Aegean to Cyrenaica, in the Benghazi area with six S.79s on 7 May, while 281ª *Squadriglia* remained stationed in Rhodes.

On the 8th a lone S.79 reconnaissance plane from 49ª *Squadriglia*/32° *Stormo Bombardieri* took off from Decimomannu airbase in Sardinia. While the crew successfully spotted the convoy midday, it failed to return to base as it was shot down by an enemy fighter. Its pilot *Capitano* Armando Boetto, one of the most able pilots of 32° *Stormo*, was awarded a gold medal of military valor. The plane was shot down a few minutes after it had communicated its sighting of the enemy convoy.

41 Major-General I.S.O. Playfair, *Mediterranean and Middle East, Volume 2: The Germans Come to the Help of Their Ally, 1941* (London: HMSO, 1954) <http://www.ibiblio.org/hyperwar/UN/UK/UK-Med-II/UK-Med-2-6.html> (accessed 2 June 2021).

Based on the intelligence provided by the crew of the lone reconnaissance aircraft, the commander of the *Aeronautica di Sardegna, Generale* Ottorino Vespignani, decided to initially deploy a limited force of five S.79s from 280ª *Squadriglia* escorted by fifteen CR.42 of 3º *Gruppo Caccia* to pursue the convoy. This reduced force was due to the bad weather that prevailed which induced the commander to not risk dispatching a larger force. In light of the total force in Sardinia on 8 May which consisted of: six S.79 standard bombers from 28° *Gruppo Bombardamento*, thirty-two S.79 standard bombers from 32° and 8° *Stormo Bombardieri*, thirteen Cant.Z.1007 bis from 16° *Stormo Bombardieri*, five S.79 torpedo bombers from 280ª *Squadriglia*, thirty-two CR.42 from 3° *Gruppo Caccia*, and fifteen seaplanes (9 Cant.Z.501 and 6 Cant.Z.506), it can be argued that indeed a very limited force was initially deployed to counter the convoy.

The torpedo bombers led by *Capitano* Mojoli of 280ª *Squadriglia* came to the fore in the early afternoon. According to the war diary of the Italian air force: "The first to sight the enemy ships, at 1242, were the torpedo bombers of the 280ª *Squadriglia*, three of which were flying in formation and the other two aircraft were aligned on the flanks while protection was provided by fifteen CR.42 fighters of the 3° *Gruppo.* Heading towards the enemy, the S.79s were flying at a low altitude, some even flying only 10 meters above sea level, due to low clouds, and heavy rain and banks of fog. After having entered an area of higher clouds, the navigation continued at an altitude of 200-300 meters, and at 1245 the first enemy units were sighted on the starboard at a distance of 30,000 meters. Maneuvering so to attack the enemy formation from the south, in order to surprise the Royal Navy by making the attack from the African coast, at 1248 the torpedo bombers descended in altitude, spread out and headed against the most coveted target, the aircraft carrier HMS *Ark Royal.* As the ship opened fire raising high water columns, the bombers climbed in altitude to avoid the barrage."[42]

After being fired by the screen provided by the anti-aircraft defense four out of the five planes were chased away by Fulmars from No. 808 Squadron which had taken off from HMS *Ark Royal* to defend the transports. Meanwhile disregarding the enemy fire *Tenente* Franco Cappa's[43] S.79, one of the wingmen on *Capitano*'s Amedeo Mojoli's squad, flew on toward HMS *Renown*. Just has he was about to drop in altitude to release the torpedo, the aircraft suffered a direct hit that tore an enormous hole in his right wing. The aircraft began to drop precipitously and then crashed into the sea killing all crew members. But seconds before dropping into the sea, the crew had managed to launch the torpedo which although released at a considerable distance from the ship, missed it by barely ten yards. Admiral Somerville, on board the flagship HMS *Renown*, recounted seeing the torpedo fast approaching but then seconds later it sank barely a few yards from the ship. The courageous and determined effort by *Tenente* Cappa and his crew (*Maresciallo Pilota* Lamberto Giovagnoli, 1º *aviere marconista* Michele Scafa, *aviere scelto motorista* Antonio Flamini and 1º *aviere armiere* Antonio Luciani) was recognized with a

42 Archivio Storico Aeronautica Militare: "Comando 280ª Squadriglia, "Relazione attacco aerosiluranti alla formazione navale nemica nel mare di La Galite alle ore 12.50 dello 8-5-41." 5 August 1941.

43 Tenente Franco Cappa began the war as the pilot of a standard bomber unit. On 23 November 1940 he asked to be part of the new *aerosiluranti* specialty. He began training at Gorizia airport with the *Nucleo Addestramento Aerosiluranti* where he completed his first torpedo bomber flight on 3 December 1940. On 30 January 1941 his unit began the trial exercises in launching torpedoes. These ended on 8 February 1941. Tenente Cappa on 10 February 1941 is transferred to Elmas in Sardinia with the 280ª *Squadriglia* Autonoma Aerosiluranti, led by *Capitano* Amedeo Mojoli.

post-humorous gold medal for the pilot and silver medals for the other brave crew members. His motivation reads almost as a suicide attack:

> As the pilot of a torpedo bomber aircraft who had already distinguished himself in other combat actions as a standard bomber and had also participated in a prior attack on a powerful enemy naval formation, with supreme audacity and decision, he managed to penetrate through a violent barrage of anti-aircraft fire in order to remain true to his objective. Prior to take off he had told his comrades that he aimed to get as close as possible to an enemy ship so the torpedo would not misfire. While carrying out the action with this intent, enemy fire struck his heroic wings. Undeterred, he released the torpedo while the plane crashed into the sea.[44]

The British account of the action stresses how the torpedo bomber attack was halted by a combination of anti-aircraft fire and interference by British fighters:

> At 1345 hours, eight aircraft were seen approaching very low, fine on the starboard bow. These were engaged as they approached, but the AA fire appeared to be not very well directed. Torpedoes were dropped from outside the destroyer screen, which was roughly 3000 yards ahead of the convoy and extended to starboard to cover Renown, Ark Royal and Queen Elizabeth. The four Fulmar fighters on patrol at this time were engaging CR. 42 fighters that had accompanied these torpedo aircraft.
>
> Torpedoes were evidently aimed at Renown and Ark Royal but by very skillful handling by the Commanding Officers of these two ships all tracks were combed or avoided. Two torpedoes passed close to Renown. A third which was being successfully combed made a sudden alteration of 60° towards Renown and a hit forward seemed inevitable when the torpedo reached the end of its run and sank. Two torpedoes passed to port and two to starboard of Ark Royal.[45]

The lone S.79 attack was followed by a dogfight that ensued between the remaining four S.79s and the Fulmars squadron that pursued them as they were making their return to base. One *Sparviero* flown by *Sottotenente* Marino Marini was forced to land on the water at 1300 near Galite Islands, a group of islands near Bizerte in northern Tunisia, because of the damage it had sustained from enemy fire, but the crew was unhurt and later was saved by a French Vichy ship. The plane, however, could not be salvaged. Meanwhile, *Capitano*'s Mojoli's aircraft was also attacked by the Fulmars but his crew replied to the enemy fire and shot one down after a quick thinking gunner targeted his enemy's aircraft fuselage. *Tenente* Ugo Rivoli's S.79 was also targeted by the Fulmars which shot at it from several positions. Although the British pilots had damaged the plane, the crew was able to make it safely back to base. Finally the Italian escort fighters also exchanged fire with the Fulmars resulting in the unit's Commanding Officer's

44 Medaglie D'oro <https://italianiinguerra.com/2020/05/08/medaglie-doro-della-2a-guerra-mondiale-tenente-pilota-franco-cappa-mediterraneo-occidentale-8-maggio-1941/> (accessed on 23 March 2021).

45 Uboat.net, Allied Warships: HMS *Fortune* <https://uboat.net/allies/warships/ship/4227.html > (accessed 23 March 2021).

(R. Tillard) plane being shot down while three more suffered damage. During the confrontation two CR.42 were damaged. Between 1600 and 1900 three high altitude bombing attacks were pressed forward by the Axis air forces but failed to inflict any damage. The third attempt involving up to twenty German bombers was particularly unsuccessful.

As the convoy passed beyond Sardinia in the early evening the initiative passed to the Sicilian based units. At 1815 the commander of *Aeronautica della Sicilia Generale* Renato Mazzucco, based on the sightings of the enemy convoy by reconnaissance planes of 192ª *Squadriglia*, ordered the takeoff from Pantelleria of four S.79 torpedo bombers from 278ª *Squadriglia*. This was one the most experienced torpedo bomber units having reaped several successes against Royal Navy ships in 1940. It fielded four *aerosiluranti* led by *Tenente* Mario Spezzaferri, who had as wingmen *Tenenti* Mario La Guercia, Carlo Copello and Guido Robone. The latter was reputed along with Buscaglia to be one of the most able of the torpedo bomber pilots. Unfortunately, he had to turn back almost at the beginning of the mission as his plane experienced engine trouble.

The remaining torpedo bombers made several attempts to pursue the convoy. At 1910 three 278ª *Squadriglia* aircraft escorted by fourteen CR.42 from 1° *Stormo* attacked HMS *Ark Royal* but all missed their targets. This was mainly due to the heavy anti-aircraft fire which damaged but did not down the aircraft and most importantly prevented them from getting a clear shot from a favorable position. By this time, HMS *Renown*, HMS *Ark Royal*, HMS *Sheffield*, HMS *Harvester*, HMS *Havelock* and HMS *Hesperus* turned back for Gibraltar after having left the convoy in the hands of the Mediterranean Fleet after having reached the Sicilian Narrows. Only one torpedo bomber flown by Mario La Guercia overcame the curtain of fire of the enemy barrage managing to get within a range of 1,200 meters from HMS *Renown* but missed it by only 10 meters.[46] Despite the successful maneuver to avoid the torpedo HMS *Renown* suffered collateral damage when one of her port-side 4.5-in (114.3mm) gun mountings suffered a control failure and fired into the rear of another gun mounting, killing six and wounding 26 gunners. Finally, Copello's S.79, the last one to attack from this group, also misfired. Carlo Copello's plane, the hardest hit of the three, was forced to make an emergency landing at Sciacca. The other two aircraft returned safely to base.

The British account of this attack stresses how the torpedo bombers attacked with determination but the great volume of anti-aircraft fire together with a degree of fortitude fought back the air attack: "The turn to the west was just being completed when 'Force B' was attacked at 2030 hours by three torpedo-bombers which came from right ahead. The destroyers were still maneuvering to take up their screening positions and did not sight the enemy aircraft in time to put up a barrage of AA fire. This attack was pressed home by the enemy with great determination. All three aircraft were heavily engaged and two were seen to be hit. Renown combed the torpedo tracks, two passing close down the port side and one down the starboard side."[47]

Meanwhile the main convoy continued moving east escorted now by HMS *Queen Elizabeth*, HMS *Naiad*, HMS *Gloucester*, HMS *Fiji*, HMS *Faulknor*, HMS *Fearless*, HMS *Foresight*, HMS *Forester*, HMS *Fortune*, HMS *Fury*, HMS *Kashmir* and HMS *Kipling*. The failure of the daylight attacks prompted the air command in Sicily to launch a lone wolf operation on the night of 8 May to spring a surprise attack on the convoy. At 2245 *Tenente* Guido Robone

46 Archivio Storico Aeronautica Militare: Diario Storico del Comando dell'Aeronautica della Sicilia 1941.

47 Uboat.net <https://uboat.net/allies/warships/ship/4227.html> (accessed 2 November 2021).

(278ª *Squadriglia)* took flight one more time in an attempt to torpedo one of the biggest battlefleets of the Tiger convoy. Upon spotting the British ships he brought down his S.79 to a very exposed position above the battleship HMS *Queen Elisabeth.* Robone pressed home the attack at 2400, but the warhead narrowly missed the target. Regarding this operation the British Official History states: "The chief danger to the 'Tiger' convoy during the night was expected to be from mines in the Narrows, but the brilliant moonlight favored attacks by torpedo-bomber aircraft and motor torpedo boats, and—clear of the enemy minefields—by submarines as well. The remaining warships therefore formed in close support around the convoy. At midnight a mine exploded in the paravane of the New Zealand Star. This was followed by two mine explosions in rapid succession close to the Empire Song. Damage to the New Zealand Star was slight, but after half an hour the Empire Song reported that she had a fire in the ammunition hold. She began to drop astern and at 4 a.m. blew up and sank, but not before a destroyer had taken off her crew. With her went 57 of the 295 tanks and 10 of the 53 Hurricanes. During the night there was one attack from a torpedo-bomber aircraft on the Queen Elizabeth and she only narrowly avoided the torpedo. There were no other signs of the enemy."[48]

On the same day in a separate operation 281ª *Squadriglia,* with three S.79s piloted by *Capitano* Buscaglia, *Tenente* Carlo Faggioni and *Tenente* Pietro Greco, targeted convoy AN 30 in the Aegean Sea which was steaming to Suda bay. It was comprised of four transports and the escort. While the planes made their approach and then dove down, the British ships opened up a blistering fire to prevent the torpedo bombers from getting any closer. As the pilots then levelled out just above the water they could observe the vast hulk of the enemy ships which were becoming more and more visible. Despite great anti-aircraft fire the pilots kept on their steady course and when the distance had narrowed to only 800 meters they dropped the torpedoes into the water. After they pulled into a steep climb and sped away. During the operation all three aircraft took direct hits to the wings and the fuselage, but managed to release their warheads at favorable distances. This resulted in severe damage to the 5,000-ton vessel Rawnsley as the torpedo tore a large hole on the starboard bow of the ship. The Royal Navy rescue crews initially attempted to salvage it. Four days later however, it was sunk by German bombers. Faggioni would be awarded a silver medal of military valor with the following motivation: "Having already distinguished himself in previous operations, he participated to two daring attacks against well protected enemy convoys by fighter aircraft. Torpedoing a tanker and a transport ship, on both occasions he displayed extreme calmness and utter contempt for the danger encountered."[49]

On 10, 11 and 12 May no major attacks were attempted against the convoy in the eastern Mediterranean or Force B which was returning to Gibraltar. The only operations of note were a half fainted attack on the convoy on the night of 10 May where torpedo bombers, endeavored to attack the convoy and battlefleet but a very heavy blind barrage of anti-aircraft fire however kept them from getting close to the battleships. The other item of note was the bombing of HMS *Fortune* which was part of Force B. The bombing, still on the 10th caused a bent shaft and flooding in several compartments aft, and minor flooding in the engine room.

48 Major-General I.S.O. Playfair, *Mediterranean and Middle East, Volume 2: The Germans Come to the Help of Their Ally, 1941* (London: HMSO, 1954) <http://www.ibiblio.org/hyperwar/UN/UK/UK-Med-II/UK-Med-2-6.html> (accessed 2 June 2021).

49 Medaglie D'oro <https://www.quirinale.it/onorificenze/insigniti/13144> (accessed on 11 March 2021).

The Tiger convoy, bearing much needed weapons and munitions, represented an important victory for the Royal Navy when on 12 May it arrived at Alexandria. Losses were considerable but on the whole the Royal Navy had brought to Egypt 80 percent of tanks and 81 percent of the Hurricanes that had been embarked in England. Throughout the journey the Royal Navy, despite being under continuous attacks, had been able to check the Axis attempts to interfere with the convoy thanks to several factors. "Good work by the British fighters and the heavy anti-aircraft fire from warships had done much to protect the Fleet and the convoy from air reconnaissance and attack. Both aircraft and guns were helped by the fact that more ships were now fitted with radar; the sets themselves had been improved and there was more experience in using them."[50] This is what the commander of the 280ª *Squadriglia Capitano* Amedeo Mojoli wrote on the effectiveness of the enemy's anti-aircraft fire during the operation:

> During the approach flight we were spotted by the enemy. Almost immediately our fighter escorts were engaged in combat while the torpedo bombers were attacked by two Hurricane fighter patrols that attempted to break our formation and split us up. At a distance of 8000 meters a cruiser, the Renown spotted the torpedo bomber formation and immediately opened fire with the heavy guns. Then almost immediately the other British Navy units began to target our formation with both large guns and anti-aircraft guns. The fire was intense and well directed. At a distance of 4000 meters from the enemy cruisers all the machine gunners opened fire. At this time the torpedo bombers were flying at an altitude of 200-150 meters from sea level. There was intense and very rapid fire also from the aircraft carrier. The fire continued unabated and even when we began to turn back. The heavy naval guns continued to fire at us even at a distance of 25-30,000 meters.[51]

Whilst the torpedo bomber attacks had been stymied by accurate anti-aircraft fire, the Axis forces had demonstrated poor cooperation amongst the services. The RM, with only two available battleships, the *Doria* and Giulio *Cesare,* was not willing to force an encounter battle with the Royal Navy. The former had also failed with regards to reconnaissance for the convoy was spotted moving eastward through the Mediterranean too late for surface ships to have any meaningful chance to pursue it.[52] In a post operation report *Superaereo* lamented that: "Ideally our Navy should have barred the Canal of Sicily and forced a naval battle with the British fleet."[53] But the concerns of the RM heads of only forcing a battle when the Italian fleet had a clear numerical advantage had dissuaded any offensive action. The air forces themselves had not been effective. The RA's bomber units were deployed from Sardinian bases but they could not inflict any significant damage, while the *Luftwaffe's* units were also ineffective. The main potential threat to the Royal Navy had come from the torpedo bombers and *Tenente* Cappa's near miss weighed heavily upon the course of the fighting. Although they had failed during

50 Major-General I.S.O. Playfair, *Mediterranean and Middle East, Volume 2: The Germans Come to the Help of Their Ally, 1941* (London: HMSO, 1954) <http://www.ibiblio.org/hyperwar/UN/UK/UK-Med-II/UK-Med-2-6.html> (accessed 2 June 2021).

51 Archivio Storico Aeronautica Militare, "Comando 280ª *Squadriglia*, "Relazione attacco aerosiluranti alla formazione navale nemica nel mare di La Galite alle ore 12.50 dello 8-5-41".

52 M. A. Bragadin, *Che ha fatto la Marina?* (Milan: Mondadori, 1950), pp.196-8.

53 Francesco Mattesini "L'operazione Brittanica Tiger", *Bollettino Marina Militare*, p.74.

Operation Tiger, in the first five months of the year, torpedo bombers had heavily damaged a tanker and a motorship, they had conducted numerous operations, dropped forty-six torpedoes and lost seven aircraft.[54] Although very risky, the *Sparvieri* operations represented one of the main threats to British shipping operations that guaranteed some degree of success for the RA.

6: COLONNELLO CARLO UNIA

Born in Torino on 10 March 1906. Died 20 March 1990.
In 1929 he graduated from the RA academy gaining his pilot license. He was promoted to *Squadriglia* commander in 1935. In the same year he received a promotion to *Capitano.* In October 1940 he was promoted to *Tenente Colonnello* and assumed command of the *1° Nucleo Addestramento Aerosiluranti* in Gorizia, the first torpedo bomber training school. Shortly thereafter he was promoted to *Colonnello* mostly for his achievements in setting up the torpedo bomber training center. On 9 September 1943 while holding the position of commander of a air unit in Salon de Provence, Unia was accused by the Germans of sabotage and sent to a prison in Germany.

After the war he continued his career in the Air Force and retired in 1966 as a general. One of his most important achievements during the war was the development of the grafometro (graph meter) a tool that allowed the torpedo bombers to aim at their targets with more accuracy. This is how a torpedo bomber pilot described the device: "The aiming instrument was a primitive device shaped like a horseshoe with several nails sticking out of it. As I saw the ship, I was to estimate its speed. The only clue I had for this was the length of the wake; if it was equal to the length of the ship, the speed was estimated at 20 nautical miles per hour. For a wake half the length of the ship, the speed was estimated at 10 miles per hour; any other length of the wake would give me a corresponding estimated speed of the ship. Once the speed had been estimated, I would aim the corresponding nail of the horseshoe at the ship and launch the torpedo in the direction of the front nail of the device. This would create a triangle where the ship and the plane were at the two lower points and the torpedo would hit the ship at the third, higher point."[55]

Crete

The month of May 1941 saw the Axis forces preoccupied in the takeover of the island of Crete. The planning for the operation entailed the deployment of airborne forces first taking over the main Maleme airfield and then progressively expanding the Axis hold on the island by overcoming machine gun and artillery posts with dedicated paratrooper and infantry units. Both the Italian and German air forces were to provide their support to the operation and the torpedo bomber units were tasked with challenging Royal Navy convoys that came to the aid of the island's garrison.

54 Marco Mattioli, *Savoia Marchetti S.79 Sparviero*, p.18.
55 Commando Supremo, "S.M. 79 Torpedo Tactics", <https://comandosupremo.com/forums/index.php?threads/s-m-79-torpedo-tactics.62/> (accessed on 13 February 2021).

The 41° *Gruppo Autonomo* conducted its first operation as a torpedo bomber unit on 17 May when it carried out a sweep over Crete by two S.84s. But the torpedo bomber pilots were unable to find the enemy ships and the S.84s returned to base with the warheads attached to their offset rack. On 20 May the Axis airborne operation Merkur got underway and two Italian reconnaissance planes spotted at sea elements of Force C that were tasked with challenging seaborne Axis forces headed to Crete. In order to attack Force C the *Comando Aeronautica dell'Egeo* mustered together the bombers of 41° *Gruppo,* two S.79s from 281ª *Squadriglia* and ten CR.42 fighters from 163ª *Squadriglia.* These units finally spotted Force C at 2040 and the torpedo bombers were the first to pounce by pressing forward with their attack. Due to intense enemy fire the attack failed mainly because the torpedoes were launched from well over 3,000 meters from their targets. Both pilots *Maggiore* Vittorio Cannaviello and *Capitano* Guglielmo di Luise claimed in their post battle report of having hit a destroyer, meanwhile HMS *Juno,* the target of their attack, had been unscathed. The attacks were resumed the next day when five Cant.Z.1007 bis bombers of 50° *Gruppo* successfully put out of action HMS *Juno.* On that same day several S.84s from 41° *Gruppo* launched several attacks against Force C but all were unsuccessful given the ample anti-aircraft fire. Due to the heavy response from the anti-aircraft personnel the pilots were never in a favorable position to launch the warheads. On 23 May three S.84s from 41° *Gruppo* were tasked with finding 5th Flotilla destroyers (Kelly, Kashmir, and Kipling) but once again had to return to base with their warheads tied securely to the offset rack given the intense enemy fire. On 25 May two S.84s from the same unit conducted a sweep over Crete and the Aegean Sea but were not able to spot any enemy ships. Their operation tested the endurance of the S.84 aircraft to the point that they could not find their way back to base due to bad weather. The two pilots were forced to land in Turkey were they were taken into custody and held for a year. As Francesco Mattesini asserts with regards to the torpedo bombers of 41° *Gruppo* "the pilots that had recently been shifted toward the torpedo bomber role were not up to task. They were evidently not trained into the torpedo bomber role and this explains the numerous miss fires in the face of enemy anti-aircraft fire."[56]

On 26 May a lone S.79 of 279ª *Squadriglia* flown by *Capitano* Mario Frongia took off from Benghazi airfield after two German reconnaissance planes had spotted two British destroyers and a troopship, the HMS *Glenroy* traveling toward Crete transporting 800 soldiers that were to be reinforcements for the besieged island. At 1500 *Capitano* Frongia spotted the enemy ships and began his attack at a distance of 8,000 meters. At 3,000 meters from the enemy ships the *Capitano* was forced to turn back due to violent enemy anti-aircraft fire. A while later he reiterated the attempt to attack the troopship HMS *Glenroy* and this time the pilot was able to get to a distance of approximately 2,000 meters then he released the torpedo. This second attempt was only partly successful as the warhead grazed the target causing some damage to the ship which then triggered a fire. In addition, as the S.79 flew over the troopship the crew machine gunned at close range the upper deck killing eleven ratings.[57] The following is the dispatch report of the Royal Navy: "A final attack by low flying torpedo bombers occurred at 2050 GLENROY avoided the torpedoes but received slight damage and 11 casualties from near misses and machine gun attacks. Three of her landing craft were holed and a large dump of

56 Franceso Mattesini, *Luci ed ombre*, p.53.
57 Marco Mattioli, *Savoia-Marchetti S.79 Sparviero*, p.15.

cased petrol on the upper deck caught fire. The fire lasted for one and a half hours, during which time the ship had to steer south in order to bring the wind aft. One of the landing craft at the davits had to be cut adrift owing to the proximity of the flames."[58]

While the damage to HMS *Glenroy* was not substantial enough to halt the troopship it did cause it to abort the operation. After the fire was put out HMS *Glenroy* resumed its northerly course for Crete. But approximately an hour later the troopship was turned back to Alexandria. Glenroy's commander decided that the operation of landing the troops at Crete had to be cancelled due to the delay caused by the aerial attack, the reduction in available landing craft and unsuitable weather for landing on the beach.[59]

On the afternoon of 28 May Italian torpedo and standard bombers from 41° *Gruppo* were already whizzing around Crete to hunt down Force B when they encountered a strong enemy force. The latter had been dispatched from Alexandria so that the British infantry could evacuate from the island and it was comprised by three cruisers (Orion, Ajax, and Dido) and six destroyers (Imperial, Hotspur, Kimberly, Hareward, Decoy, and Jack). At 1755, when the convoy was approximately 90 miles from Scarpanto the waves of attacks began and culminated with the bombing of HMS *Imperial* at 1820 which severely damaged the helm of the ship. The damage was so extensive that the next day the Royal Navy was forced to scuttle it. Three S.79 torpedo bombers from 281ª *Squadriglia* were up next in pursuing Force B. All three planes were able to get within shooting range at 1958 of the enemy ships, but none recorded a successful hit. According to the post battle dispatch by the Royal Navy during this attack which occurred one hour and thirty minutes after HMS I*mperial* was bombed: "At 2100 AJAX had a close miss which started a small fire, -seriously wounded twenty men and caused slight damage to the ship's side.-a near miss caused slight damage and some casualties in HMS *Ajax*"[60] which was forced to cancel the mission and was then detached to Alexandria. It is not completely clear to this day whether the damage was the result of a bomb from a German Ju.87, a number of which were operating at the time, or it was caused by one of the three torpedo launched. This was the last operation aimed at interfering with Royal Navy operations in Crete. The Italian effort proved very wasteful as too many torpedoes had been fired but few successes were achieved. The post campaign memorandum penned by *Comando Aeronautica dell'Egeo* recognized the failure of its aircraft to inflict severe damage upon the Royal Navy.[61]

Still smarting over the defeat of the Italian fleet at the battle of Cape Matapan together with the inability by the torpedo bombers and standard bombers to inflict severe damage to the Royal Navy during Operation Tiger, *Generale* Ugo Cavallero, who had been appointed on 5 December 1940 *Capo di Stato Maggiore Generale* (Chief of Staff of *Comando Supremo)* by replacing Badoglio and thus inheriting a number of emergency situations, asked the services to come up with a plan for a combined arms operation against the Royal Navy in the Mediterranean. Unlike Badoglio, Cavallero intended to elevate the competencies of the *Comando Supremo* and to effectively direct the activities of the service chiefs of the three

58 James Somerville, "Mediterranean Convoy Operations ", *Supplement to the London Gazette*, n. 38296, 10 August 1948, p.3122.

59 Ibid.

60 Ibid., p.3115.

61 Francesco Mattessini, *Luci ed ombre*, p.68.

branches of the military, including the power to dismiss them.[62] On 27 June 1941 a law was approved that gave him full powers to direct the armed forces and this allowed *Comando Supremo* to coordinate the war effort more effectively. Given Cavallero's enhanced powers, the committee responsible to draft the operative plan, co-chaired by *Ammiraglio* Giuseppe Fioravanzo and *Generale* Umberto Coppa, could effectively bind the two services to a set of operational plans. The final product was presented to *Comando Supremo* on 28 May 1941 and one of its main recommendations was that standard bombers units along with three *squadriglie* of torpedo bombers were to support the battlefleet in a major naval clash with the Royal Navy by committing to takeoff an hour after the reconnaissance planes had spotted the location of the enemy fleet. Bombs and torpedoes were to degrade the enemy fleet prior to its encounter with the Navy. The standard bombers, but the torpedo bombers in particular, were expected to eliminate the enemy's aerial threat by harming the aircraft carrier. If an aircraft carrier was not present, the RA forces were to focus their efforts against the largest battleship. This entailed that for such combat action to take place the RA had to guarantee "the availability of the highest number possible of torpedo bombers. Therefore, several bases equipped with warheads and the special equipment necessary to prepare the aircraft for combat must be established across the Mediterranean. This will allow the torpedo bomber units to readily takeoff from the nearest base of operation."[63] Here the main concern was the limited supply of warheads which brought to the fore the unsolved problems related to the logistics of torpedo bomber operations. "Until the stock of warheads has not been expanded significantly, it is necessary to provide for the rapid movement of our modest force across the launching platforms in the Mediterranean."[64] Torpedo bombers and their warheads, in the absence of a larger force and greater stocks of warheads, had to be moved rapidly from base to base to conduct attacks by updating the S.82 fleet. The role of the torpedo bombers was further refined by stating that while the RM had to go out at sea to engage the Royal Navy: "The torpedo bombers have the main attacking role since they must strike first and it this can only be guaranteed by concentrating a large number of aircraft at specific bases. The combat action has to be carried out in coordination with standard bombers and fighters and should be restricted to the operative range of our aircraft especially the fighters. In some cases when bad weather prevails, the aerosiluranti can also be deployed in lone wolf operations. The latter will operate without fighter escort especially against enemy ships that have been already damaged by our forces."[65] Overall, the plan entailed reconnaissance of the enemy fleet followed by concentrated air attacks to weaken it, and finally followed by more low level torpedo and standard bomber attacks focused upon the ships that had been damaged by the first major strike. Throughout the air operations fighter escort was to be provided in case the enemy battlefleet also deployed aircraft carriers. Finally, the RM was to intervene in a largescale engagement against the surviving Royal Navy warships. This required a degree of coordination and cohesiveness from the services as well as enhanced communication. One of the aftermath reforms of Operation Tiger, for example, was to improve

62 Ibid. p.69.
63 Ibid. p.69.
64 Ibid. p.69.
65 Ibid., p.70.

interservice communication which was obtained with the battle fleet admiral having a direct radio connection to *Superaereo*.[66]

Another consequence stemming from the loss of Crete and the Axis occupation of Greece was a change in the camouflage of the torpedo bombers. During this period most S.79s underwent an overhaul as the theatre of operation moved further south after the completion of the campaign in the Balkans. S.79 pilot *Tenente* Cimicchi recalled that:

> After the fall of Greece and Crete our operational range widened to the South. The British ships had no more need to sail near Rhodes. To find them, we had to fly towards Alexandria and along the African coasts. [...] Enemy fighters were always on the look-out, but most times we could avoid them. We had camouflaged our aircraft based on the new prevailing environment.....The camouflage colors were matched with light azure blue, white and grey that blended in well with the sea waves, which were very light near the coasts of Egypt and Cyrenaica.[67]

Operation Substance

After the occupation of the island of Crete by the Axis forces, the British military's priority became to reinforce even more strongly than before the island of Malta so that it could better defend itself against a potential Axis invasion. At the end of July 1941 the Royal Navy thus led another major operation to supply the besieged island codenamed Operation Substance. This was to be the largest effort to supply Malta since the beginning of the war. The GM1 convoy was comprised of six transports (Melbourbe Star, Sidney Star, City of Pretoria, Port Chalmers, Durham and Deucalion) and one troopship, the Leinster. The most valuable component of the convoy was one light and one heavy anti-aircraft regiment equipped with thirty field guns to strengthen Malta's garrison against a combined seaborne and airborne Axis assault. The Royal Navy assigned the convoy escort to Force H which was comprised of the aircraft carrier HMS *Ark Royal* with twenty-one Fairey Fulmars and carrying seven Fairey Swordfish to be flown off as reinforcements to Malta, HMS *Renown* and seven destroyers (*Hermione, Faulknor, Foresight, Fury, Forester, Lighting*, and *Duncan*). To strengthen the force, the Royal Navy also provided to the convoy escort elements of Force X such as the battleship HMS *Nelson*, two cruisers such as HMS *Edinburgh* and HMS *Manchester*, the minelayer *Manxman*, the *Arethusa* and ten destroyers (*Cossack, Maori, Sikh, Nestor, Fearless, Foxhound, Firedrake, Farndale, Avon Vale* and *Eridge*). The RAF would provide reconnaissance and anti-submarine patrols from Gibraltar and Malta, and Beaufighters were assigned the task of protecting the convoy from air attack. The two naval units were set to travel separately until they reached south of Sardinia where they were to jointly escort the convoy.

On 12 July the British convoy began its voyage sailing from Scotland. On 21 July the convoy and its escort left Gibraltar but Leinster experienced difficulties almost at the beginning of the journey and had to turn back to port. Initially since convoy was intentionally split into

66 James Sadkovich, *The Italian Navy in World War II* (Westport: Greenwood Press, 1994), p.168.
67 Giuseppe Cimicchi, *I siluri vengono dal cielo* (Milan: Longanesi, 1964), p.65.

two naval units that were navigating separately the Italian intelligence services did not know whether their purpose was to escort a convoy or to attack Italian coastal installations. The RM decided outright not to deploy its fleet mainly because it feared the deployment of aerial torpedo bombers launched from HMS *Ark Royal* and took the more conservative route by deploying mainly torpedo boats, submarines and destroyers to intercept the convoy. This implied that the RA would be doing the bulk of the work while attempting to stop the British operation. Due to the numerous operations sustained by the S.79s in May through July the torpedo bomber airbases in Sardinia and Sicily had low stockpiles of torpedoes and this forced the *Squadriglia* heads, prior to the start of operations, to instruct the crews to only release their warheads when it was certain that a hit be made.[68] The units involved with Operation Substance were the 278ª *Squadriglia* based in Sicily and the 280ª and the 283ª *Squadriglie* based in Elmas, Sardinia. According to the war diary of *Aeronautica della Sardegna* on 20 July 1941 there were available twenty S.79 standard bombers from 32° *Stormo*, seven Cant. Z. 1007 bis bombers from 51° *Gruppo*, six S. 79 torpedo bombers from 280ª *Squadriglia*, five S. 79 torpedo bombers from 283ª *Squadriglia*, fifty-nine fighters from 24° *Gruppo* (35 CR.42, 7 *Macchi* C.200 and 17 G.50). Torpedo bomber strength in Sicily prior to the start of Operation Substance is unknown.

The first attack on the convoy was made on the 22nd when the Italian submarine Diaspro launched torpedoes against HMS *Renown* but missed the target. In the morning at 0920 Force H was sighted by an Italian reconnaissance plane at a distance of approximately 150 miles from Algiers which triggered the first aerial torpedo attempt. Between 1730 and 1750 on 22 July fifteen S.79 standard bombers from 32° *Stormo*, eight S.79 torpedo bombers from 280ª and 283ª *Squadriglie* escorted by seven G.50 from 24° *Gruppo* took flight to bomb the convoy. After two hours of attempting to locate it this force was unsuccessful and had to turn back.

By 0800 of 23 July Force H was approximately 70 miles from Galite Islands and had its destroyers navigating in two groups aligned in two semicircles surrounding the convoy ships. *Aeronautica della Sardegna* orders were that both standard and torpedo bombers were to attack the convoy simultaneously and they were instructed that priority should be given to the merchant ships. This tactic differed somewhat from previous torpedo bomber operations where the S.79s had acted primarily as lone wolfs or in small groups to achieve surprise, flying undetected and in order to press forward more unpredictable attacks made by experienced pilots. Whereas the new approach was of the mass attack by a squad size or an even greater force of torpedo bombers, it was based not so much on the element of surprise or the pilot's abilities but on the quantity of the torpedoes released all at once or in a swift sequential order.

At 0655 on 23 July a Cant.Z.506 spotted the convoy and the escort communicating back to base that: "The enemy formation includes two aircraft carriers, a battleships, and destroyers. These forces are escorting 18 transports. It is estimated that by tonight the convoy will have reached Cape Bon and by 24 July it will have reached Malta."[69] At 0657 HMS *Renown* reported a shadowing aircraft in sight and fighters were sent to down it but due to the low sun and mist were unable to find it. Meanwhile in response to the intelligence received from the shadowing aircraft, the Sardinian air force command ordered its aircraft to scramble at 0830. The first to take flight from Decimomannu were ten S.79 bombers from 32° *Stormo* (T*enente Colonnello* Antonio

68 Ufficio Storico Aeronautica Militare, Ali di Guerra, N. 5, August 1941.
69 Francesco Mattesini, *Luci ed ombre*, p.82.

Fadda), followed by six S. 79 torpedo bombers from 283ª *Squadriglia* (C*apitano* Giorgio Grossi), and six S.79 torpedo bombers from 280ª *Squadriglia* (C*apitano* Amedeo Mojoli) that took off from Elmas. Finally, twelve G. 50 fighters from 24° *Gruppo* (C*apitano* Vincenzo Dequal) and Cant. Z. 1007 bis bombers from 51° *Gruppo* (M*aggiore* Angelo Manfredini) provided the escort.

HMS *Ark Royal* was the first Royal Navy ship to go into action upon spotting the Italian planes with its radar by dispatching eleven Fulmar to intercept the enemy aircraft at 0910. The latter (32° *Stormo* bombers with G.50 escort) were first challenged approximately twenty miles from the convoy and suffered the loss of one S.79 that was shot down. The remaining bombers then dropped their load but at disadvantageous distances of 3,000 meters above the convoy and scored no hits. Next up were the *Sparvieri* of 283ª *Squadriglia* (*Capitano* Giorgio Grossi) and the Cant. Z. 1007 bis that were presented with a more favorable situation as the Fulmar fighters from No. 807 and No. 808 Squadron were busy fighting off the bombers of 32° *Stormo* and later the S. 79s from 280ª *Squadriglia* (C*apitano* Amedeo Mojoli) which were also heavily engaged. During the head to head encounter, the British fighters targeted mainly the six S.79s of 280ª *Squadriglia*. A wild dogfight developed as the faster Fulmars challenged the torpedo bombers; two S.79 were damaged while one was shot down. However, the remaining torpedo bombers did not shy away from the confrontation and quickly returned fire causing the destruction of three enemy planes: "Three Fulmars were lost, all of which force-landed in the sea, but all crews were picked up, uninjured by destroyers."[70] As the dogfight was taking place, the first to go into action against the British fleet were the Cant Z.1007bis bombers that flew over the ships at great speed and launched their bombs but from a high altitude that did not cause any damage. " While they (Fulmars) were away from the convoy, a second group of SM 79 torpedo bombers dived down over the convoy from out of the sun ...[71]

As the enemy destroyers opened fire the S.79s from 283ª *Squadriglia* split into two smaller squads in order to attack the merchantmen from both starboard and port. The first squad led by C*apitano* Giorgio Grossi with wingmen *Tenenti* Camillo Baroglio and Alberto Dolfus was not able to get into proper shooting distance being forced back by rapid anti-aircraft fire. The second squad was luckier. Comprised of the aircraft flown by T*enenti* Roberto Cipriani, Bruno Pandolfi and Francesco Di Bella it successfully carried out the launches from a south-east direction after finding a passage in the anti-aircraft screen. The first to drop his load was *Tenente* Roberto Cipriani which missed the target. Up next, the second pilot *Tenente* Bruno Pandolfi, quickly brought his plane down close to the water and dropped his torpedo at close distance striking the destroyer HMS *Fearless* at approximately 0940. The latter was a heavily armed, F-class destroyer of 1,375 tons. It suffered severe damage and stopped operating on its tracks. Twenty-five Royal Navy soldiers died as a result of the attack and several others were wounded. There was no way that the S.79 could have missed the target because it flew extremely close to the British destroyer. In fact it flew so close that the courageous Royal Navy personnel stood their ground even shortly after the torpedo struck their ship. They were able to open up considerable anti-aircraft fire from close range which shot down Pandolfi's plane immediately after the latter

70 James Somerville, "Mediterranean Convoy Operations", *Supplement to the London Gazette*, n. 38296, 10 August 1948, p.4477.

71 Major-General I.S.O. Playfair, *Mediterranean and Middle East, Volume 2: The Germans Come to the Help of Their Ally, 1941* (London: HMSO, 1954) <http://www.ibiblio.org/hyperwar/UN/UK/UK-Med-II/UK-Med-2-14.html#1> (Accessed 12 May 2021).

had dropped the torpedo. The crew was later recovered in the water by HMS *Avon Vale* and captured. Admiral Somerville recounted that:

> The torpedo bombers approaching low down from ahead were engaged with barrage fire by the destroyer screen. This fire appeared effective and on coming within range the enemy split into two groups of three, one group altering course to port, the other to starboard. One of the starboard group followed by one of the port group attacked FEARLESS who was stationed in the starboard bow position on the screen...... The two aircraft which attacked Fearless released their torpedoes from a height of 70 feet at a range of about 1,500 and 800 yards respectively. Avoiding action was taken and the first torpedo passed about 90 yards ahead. The torpedo from the second aircraft ran shallow. Course was shaped to comb the track but when abreast the stem on the port side at a distance of about 30 feet, the torpedo broke surface altered course to port, and hit the ship abreast the 3-inch gun. Both engines were put out of action, the rudder was jammed at hard-a-port, all electric power failed due to the switchboard being demolished and an extensive fuel fire was started aft. One officer and 24 ratings were killed outright or died later.[72]

The commander of HMS *Fearless* reported that the ship was entirely disabled. A large fire then developed on board. Given the grave conditions in which HMS *Fearless* found itself, Admiral Somerville after initially having considered the possibility of salvaging the ship ordered its destruction after the survivors were taken on board by HMS *Forester*. At 1050 a torpedo launched by HMS *Forester* scuttled HMS *Fearless*.

Meantime, the third plane still had to release the warhead. Piloted by *Tenente* Francesco Di Bella, the S.79 flew around the convoy in vain twice seeking a viable target. On the third attempt, the pilot focused his attention upon a cargo ship (Port Chalmers), got into a favorable position and released the warhead. The torpedo did not follow the track of the intended ship mainly because the latter's crew had taken evasive action. But given that the convoy was steaming in a very tight formation, the torpedo nonetheless managed to strike HMS *Manchester* of 9,400 tons badly splitting it open.

According to Admiral's Somerville report HMS *Manchester* took evasive maneuvers to avoid the torpedo but despite the quick action it was still struck by the torpedo:

> Meanwhile, MANCHESTER, who was to starboard of the convoy, sighted torpedoes approaching and turned to port to comb the tracks. Two torpedoes were seen to pass down the port side and another one passed astern from starboard. In order to avoid collision with Port Chalmers a turn to starboard was then commenced. At this time another aircraft released a torpedo from a position between the first and second M.T. ships of the port column. Wheel was immediately reversed in an endeavor to avoid this torpedo, but it struck MANCHESTER aft on the port side.[73]

72 James Somerville, "Mediterranean Convoy Operations", *Supplement to the London Gazette*, n. 38296, 10 August 1948, p.4476.
73 Ibid.

HMS *Manchester*, a Town-class light cruiser built for the Royal Navy in the late 1930s, and one of three ships in the Gloucester subclass, suffered immediate damage. The effects of the torpedo hit were: "to cause a list of 12° to port with large reduction of speed and steering gear out of action. Steering was changed over to the after position and a reasonable degree of control was, obtained. Subsequently the steering motors failed and hand steering had to be used. The explosion had travelled upwards through the decks to the upper deck, driving large quantities of oil fuel upwards into all the compartments affected. Water and oil fuel flooded the after engine room, after 4-inch magazine, main W/T office, ' X ' magazine and various other compartments between 179 and 209 bulkheads. Many ratings were overcome by fumes from the oil fuel but most of these recovered after treatment and were able to resume their duties. Only the starboard outer shaft remained serviceable. A speed of 8 knots was at first obtained which very gradually increased to 12 knots.[74]

The casualties on board were 3 naval officers, 5 military officers, 20 naval ratings and 7 other ranks killed, 3 naval ratings missing, and 1 military officer, 1 naval officer and 40 other naval ratings wounded. HMS *Manchester's* commanding officer initially signaled that the ship could steam 8 knots so he was ordered to return to Gibraltar escorted by HMS *Avon Vale*. The ship was put out of service for eight months. For his action *Tenente* Di Bella was mentioned in bulletin n. 415 of *Comando Supremo* and was awarded a second silver medal of military honor.[75]

As the remaining working aircraft of the first *Squadriglia* returned to base, a second wave of *Sparvieri* took flight and drowned toward the enemy convoy attempting to inflict further damage. But this second group, coming on the heels of a successful attack, encountered an alarmed and alert foe. The first attack was made at 1620 by three S.79s from 280ª *Squadriglia* led by *Capitano* Mojoli, and with *Tenenti* Ugo Rivoli and Alessandro Setti. Despite a stoic effort to get close to the convoy by the pilots which continued to advance in the face of concentrated enemy fire, the *Sparvieri* were met by one volley after the other and all missed their targets which were HMS *Avon Dale* and the crippled HMS *Manchester*. According to Admiral Somerville the attack to destroy HMS *Manchester* were fought off successfully by its escort HMS *Avon Vale* that "anticipating an attack from out of the sun, moved in that direction to a distance of about two miles from *Manchester*. The aircraft then approached low down on the starboard bow and were subjected to a heavy flanking fire from Avon Vale and to a barrage from ' A ' and ' B ' turrets backed up by the starboard 4-inch battery in Manchester."[76] The skillful maneuver by HMS *Avon Vale* together with the 152mm and 100mm guns on board HMS *Manchester* effectively kept the planes at bay and prevented them from launching at a favorable position. One torpedo was dropped at HMS *Avon Vale* and the other two were dropped at such long range that the crippled HMS *Manchester* had no difficulty in taking maneuvering out of the track of the torpedoes, one of which was seen to surface prematurely at the end of its run and detonated shortly afterwards.

Soon after, at 1640 a second attack was mounted by 283ª *Squadriglia* with four S.79s aircraft led by *Capitano* Grossi. This unit was even less fortunate as they were chased almost immediately

74 Ibid

75 Ufficio Storico: Italiani in Guerra <https://italianiinguerra.com/2019/07/25/i-bollettini-di-guerra-del-25-luglio-1940-41-42-43/> (accessed on 2 May 2021).

76 James Somerville, "Mediterranean Convoy Operations", *Supplement to the London Gazette*, n. 38296, 10 August 1948, p.4477.

by three Fulmars, one of which shot down one S.79. The crew, including its pilot *Tenente* Dolfus, were captured at sea by a British destroyer. Two S.79s of the same unit were shriveled with bullets. The one (flown by *Capitano* Grossi) made it back to base although several crew members had been wounded including the *Capitano*, while the other (flown by *Tenente* Cipriani) had to be ditched near Cape Carbonara and the crew was later recovered by an Italian seaplane. Finally at 1900 four S.79s of 280ª *Squadriglia* escorted by nine CR.42 fighters of 23° *Gruppo* made their last determined attack of the day on the convoy. The attack was pressed forward with determination, but equally determined were the crews of the attacked ships which not only heavily engaged the enemy as it approached from the starboard bow, but also took avoiding action which led to two torpedoes passing close to HMS *Edinburgh* and HMS *Hermione*. Meanwhile, as the torpedo attack was developing, FAA fighters took flight to intercept the attackers but the CR.42s properly screened the torpedo bombers and shot down one Beaufighter belonging to No. 272 Squadron. The last threat to the convoy on the 23 July was posed by a high level bombing attack at 1945 when S.79 standard bombers dropped a number of bombs on the convoy and inflicting damage to HMS *Firedrake* which included holes in Nos. 1 and 2 boiler rooms and its steering gear knocked out. This action was facilitated by the fact that Beaufighters, that had been dispatched from Malta to protect the convoy failed to intercept the bombers, and initially were fired on by the fleet that did not recognize them and forced them away.

This is how the British Official History summarized the action on 23 July: "The first air attack did not come until the morning of the 23rd, when the ships were south of Sardinia. This was a well-synchronized attack by nine high-level bombers and six torpedo-bombers. Fulmars from the Ark Royal intercepted the high-level bombers, whose attack failed, but the torpedo-bombers scored a hit on the cruiser Manchester and another on the destroyer Fearless. The Manchester, because her speed was greatly reduced, was ordered back to Gibraltar escorted by a destroyer. The Fearless had to be sunk."[77]

During the night between 23/24 July while Force H returned to the west toward Gibraltar, Force X and the convoy continued through the Skerki Channel towards Malta. The next day the RA again challenged the enemy convoy this time using the deceptive and hard to spot tactic of a lone S.79 piloted by *Capitano* Mario Spezzaferri of 278ª *Squadriglia* which nearly missed at 0937 an enemy steamer, the Sidney Star,[78] which had received a torpedo hit launched from Italian torpedo boats Mas 532 and Mas 533 the night before and was steaming at a reduced speed versus the rest of the convoy. After dropping the torpedo the pilot was chased by enemy fighters but was nonetheless able to get away. At 1000, some of the first ships of Operation Substance (Sydney Star, Hermione, and Nestor) were attacked by eight Ju.87 dive bombers and two high level bombers. The attacks did not yield any results. At 1130 the first set of transports entered Grand Harbour and a great reception was accorded them by the people of Malta. As the Malta bound convoy arrived in port the focus of the Axis units became Convoy MG 1 which was bound to Gibraltar with three merchantmen: America, Thermopylae and Hoegh Hood. A few hours later three torpedo bombers from 279° *Squadriglia* with *Tenenti* Mario Anselmi, Ugo Rivoli and

77 Major-General I.S.O. Playfair, *Mediterranean and Middle East, Volume 2: The Germans Come to the Help of Their Ally, 1941* (London: HMSO, 1954) <http://www.ibiblio.org/hyperwar/UN/UK/UK-Med-II/UK-Med-2-14.html#1> (accessed 2 June 2021).

78 Sydney Star had been torpedoed in No. 3 hold and took in 30 feet of water. Its 470 troops were transferred to HMS *Nestor.*

Alessandro Setti mounted an unsuccessful attack. All three torpedoes were launched but missed the target. At 1730 another attempt was made by two *Sparvieri* flown by *Capitano* Mojoli and *Tenente* Rivoli. This time they damaged the Norwegian tanker of 9,351-tons Hoegh Hood.

According to the Royal Navy post battle report Operation Substance was a success largely as a result of the Fulmar fighters on board HMS *Ark Royal* which on the 23rd multiple times intercepted the large deployment of Axis standard and torpedo bombers before they could attack the convoy.[79]

According to naval historian Francesco Mattesini Operation Substance was a tactical victory for the Allies because the majority of the transports made it into Malta but the Axis strikes on the British battlefleet had been considerable: "Up to that point, no large scale British convoy destined to reach Malta, even if attacked by Italian aircraft with the help of the Germans had sustained so much damage to its ships."[80] In addition, the Axis claimed 6 Fulmars downed from HMS *Ark Royal*, one Malta based RAF Beaufighter and 1 Blenheim bomber against the loss of eight aircraft (2 Cant.Z506, 4 S.79, and 2 *Macchi* M,200).

But despite the fact that considerable damage was made, once again even a debilitated convoy proved to be a lifeline for Malta. Most ships of Operation Substance made it through and hence Malta's position was ultimately strengthened. The Malta garrison in late July had had risen to 22,000 soldiers. The anti-aircraft defense could count upon 112 heavy and 118 light guns, while field guns were 104. Ammunition stocks were plenty allowing the island to have enough supply for at least a few months. The RAF on the island could count upon fifteen Hurricane Is and sixty Hurricane IIs.[81]

Malta had withstood heavy bombardments made by the Axis from the arrival of the *Luftwaffe* to July 1941. In April alone, for example, between 350 and 650 tons of bombs had been dropped by the Axis, but Malta had withstood the losses. On the other hand, the Axis loss of the air forces had not been slight. The *Luftwaffe* lost sixty aircraft while the RA sixteen during the seven month siege. During the period, the Axis lost an average of one aircraft every two days.

As Rommel's campaign in North Africa was unfolding with the siege of Tobruk and had taken central stage in the Axis strategy to succeed in North Africa, the convoy war in the Mediterranean and the neutralization of Malta became even more than ever before pressing tasks. The problem for the Axis was that as Operation Substance demonstrated their naval and air forces could inflict some pain upon the Royal Navy but they could not stop the convoys from reaching Malta or the shores of North Africa. Although the Axis bombing operations had somewhat subdued the fortress by July 1941 the Axis pressure upon Malta began to lessen due to the redeployment of X *Fliegerkorps* to North Africa. This meant that the RA was once again the main entity putting pressure on the British fortress but with a reduced force.

In August the *Sparvieri* units continued to score hits against British shipping. On 11 August *Capitano* Buscaglia together with *Tenente* Giulio Cesare Graziani and *Sottotenente* Aldo Forzinetti successfully targeted HMS *Protector*, a 2,900-tons net layer of the Protector class,

79 James Somerville, "Mediterranean Convoy Operations", *Supplement to the London Gazette*, n. 38296, 10 August 1948, p.4481.

80 Francesco Mattesini, *Luci ed ombre*, p.137.

81 Major-General I.S.O. Playfair, *Mediterranean and Middle East, Volume 2: The Germans Come to the Help of Their Ally, 1941* (London: HMSO, 1954) <http://www.ibiblio.org/hyperwar/UN/UK/UK-Med-II/UK-Med-2-14.html> (Accessed 12 May 2021).

40 miles to the north of Port Said. The latter was headed to Alexandria and was navigating without an escort. At 1630 the torpedo bombers pounced. HMS *Protector* was hit on its port-side by Buscaglia's crew. The explosion, which killed two and injured three naval personnel, took place in the boiler room and engine compartments causing the ship to almost immediately stop dead in its tracks. Then it began to take in water and had to be saved by HMS *Salvia* which managed to tow it back to Suez. It remained under repairs until 1947. The action was a perilous one has reported by *Sottotenente* Forzinetti: "Three Sparvieri swept in from the sea, to pounce upon enemy shipping convoys. The *Squadriglia* leader spotted a vessel bearing enemy markings. The three planes nosed down and lined up the target from a distance of 600 meters. As we made our descent toward the target enemy fire nearly crippled *Tenente* Graziani's plane. Then *Capitano* Buscaglia's crew released the deadly torpedo and the enemy ship absorbed the full impact of the warhead. Immediately a huge explosion rocked the ship and it started to stutter then it stopped."[82] The duo Graziani and Forzinetti were at it again nine days later flying unobstructed near the same location when they spotted the Turbo, a 4,782-tons tanker. The latter had no escort and the *Sparvieri* were able to pounce upon it at free will. According to *Sottotenente* Forzinetti: "unobstructed by the absence of any enemy fire, I brought down the aircraft to launching range and quickly released the warhead. In a matter of seconds it struck the tanker leading to huge explosions."[83] The vessel was in such a bad shape that it was later sunk by the British in 1942.

On 21 August *Capitano* Buscaglia, *Tenente* Graziani and *Sottotenente* Forzinetti flew over Alexandria and spotted three enemy destroyers at 1225. Upon sighting the enemy planes the crews on board the destroyers (HMS *Griffin,* HMS *Jackal* and HMS Kandahar) opened fire almost immediately. As a result of the heavy anti-aircraft fire, the *Sparvieri* pilots were not in a position to get within launch range and therefore aborted the mission. As they were making their way back to base, the S.79s were ambushed by two Blenheim fighters. The latter, however, were unable to score any hits as the S.79s put up very strong defensive fire while remaining in formation. All three returned to base safely. On 27 August a single aircraft from 279ª *Squadriglia* flown by *Capitano* Giulio Marini spotted HMS *Phoebe* at 2119, a 5,450-tons Dido class cruiser, off the coast of Libya in the vicinity of Bardia. The latter was in transit together with a vast naval formation including HMS *Naiad*, HMS *Galatea*, HMS *Abdiel,* HMS *Jackal*, HMS *Hasty* and HMS *Kandahar*. Unfazed by the great enemy deployment the pilot pursued the Royal Navy convoy with noticeable determination together with some degree of recklessness. The plane came down considerably in altitude and skimming the water approached perilously against its target. At 2145 and at 500 meters out the pilot proceeded to release the torpedo against HMS *Phoebe* which struck under the starboard side killing eight navy personnel and incapacitating the vessel for eight months. The cruiser managed to navigate at 12 knots to Alexandria, escorted by the destroyers HMS *Jervis*, HMS *Kandahar*, HMS *Kimberley* and HMS *Hasty*, from which it was dispatched to Brooklyn, New York for extensive repairs. On the same day 280ª *Squadriglia* targeted the 7,516-tons steamship Deucallion which was on its way to Gibraltar. It was spotted along the Algerian coast at 1315. *Capitano* Franco Melley and *Tenente* Mario Giacopinelli were ordered to pursue it. The ship was surrounded and attacked

82 Archivio Storico Aeronautica Militare: "L'azione contro il convoglio nemico", 24 August 1941.
83 Archivio Storico Aeronautica Militare: "L'azione contro il convoglio nemico", 24 August 1941.

by the two aircraft. The ship's crew, however, was able to avoid both torpedoes by zigzagging very swiftly and by the use of smokescreens. Determined not to let Deucalion go, the Italians dispatched two more S.79s at 1630. These were piloted by *Tenenti* Pietro Dona' delle Rose and *Tenente* Alessandro Setti of 283ª *Squadriglia* who had agreed beforehand that the former was to faint an attack against the ship, while the latter was to strike it from the flank. *Tenente* Dona' delle Rose carried out his assignment so flawlessly that he flew his plane so close to the enemy vessel that it attracted considerable enemy fire from Bofors guns allowing *Tenente* Setti to get a clear and unobstructed shot. The warhead struck the ship but failed to explode and produced only slight damage. Unfortunately, *Tenente* Dona' delle Rose's courage and suicidal action did not pay off as his companion's torpedo failed to damage the ship which would arrive in Gibraltar on the 29th.

Operation Halberd

Chief of Staff of the Armed Forces Cavallero on 21 August 1941 held a meeting with the service chiefs where he indicated that their common goal should be "to make impossible for the enemy ships to travel freely in the Mediterranean. Every weapon at our disposal such as destroyers, submarines and aircraft should be utilized to achieve such purpose."[84] New directives regarding how to conduct a combined arms operation against the British Navy in the Mediterranean were further refined as a result of this renewed focus on the anti-shipping campaign.

Between 22 and 25 August the RM and the RA coordinated a joint operation aimed at intercepting Force H, mainly HMS *Nelson* and HMS *Ark Royal*, who had conducted a diversionary action by sailing from Gibraltar to cover the movements of the minelayer Manxman. The IX *Divisione* (*Littorio* and *Vittorio Veneto*) escorted by fighter cover had been put to sea to intercept Force H. The anticipated naval engagement did not take place because Force H did not sail toward the Levant but *Supermarina* later expressed a positive assessment concerning the good cooperation achieved by both services during the operation. The new directive, however, placed an even greater burden on the RA, since a scant air force was tasked with performing multiple roles. The biggest concern for the Chief of Staff of the RA was providing adequate aerial protection of Axis convoys to North Africa since the force had too few fighters to fulfill this role. The RM required greater involvement by RA in support of its convoys, but the strength of the force remained a debilitating factor. The RM had also requested on multiple occasions that the RA guarantee at all times the readiness of a special torpedo bomber unit to pursue British light cruisers and destroyers that ambushed Axis cargo operations. Given the complexity of torpedo bomber operations the RA Chief of Staff had thus far resisted such a request. At any rate, Cavallero's directive would be put to the test with the massive convoy operation that the Royal Navy undertook in September. Moreover, the operation would also provide an opportunity for the new torpedo bomber tactics based on the deployment of a mass of aircraft to be put into effect.

At the end of September 1941, the Royal Navy led another major Malta bound convoy codenamed Operation Halberd. This was to the largest effort to date to supply Malta since the

84 Francesco Mattesini, *Luci ed Ombre*, p.133.

beginning of the war. The convoy was comprised of nine large freighters carrying over 81,000 tons of food supply and military equipment. The ships of convoy WS 11/X were the Ajax, Breconshire, City of Calcutta, City of Lincoln, Clan Ferguson, Clan MacDonald, Dunedin Star, Imperial Star, and Rowallan Castle. The Royal Navy split up the convoy escort fleet into two main groups to avoid detection: Force H which was comprised of HMS *Nelson,* HMS *Ark Royal,* and HMS *Hermione*, the 4th Destroyer Flotilla (*Cossack, Zulu, Foresight,* and *Forester*), and the 19th Destroyer Flotilla (*Laforey* and *Lightning*). While the other main battle group was Force X which was to include HMS *Prince of Wales*, HMS *Rodney*, cruisers HMS *Kenya,* HMS *Edinburgh*, HMS *Sheffield* and HMS *Euryalus* and the 13th Destroyer Flotilla. Force H would accompany the convoy during the first leg of the journey while Force X would escort it from the middle of the Mediterranean to Malta. Moreover, the plan guaranteed continuity with the air cover. When the aircraft carrier HMS *Ark Royal* had completed its task of escorting the convoy in the middle of the Mediterranean, the aircraft based in Malta were set to take control of the convoy from there and protect it from aerial Axis attacks (aircraft supplied were twenty-two Beaufighters and five Blenheim fighters). In addition, nine submarines were also deployed to obstruct the Italian surface fleet in case it attempted to ambush the convoy. Last but not least, the Royal Navy would also create a diversion in the Eastern Mediterranean so that Axis air forces were prevented from concentrating against the convoy. The presence of the extra-heavy escort including the 16 inch gun equipped Nelson and Rodney in addition to the new battleship Prince of Wales, which was the British counterpart to *Vittorio Veneto*, underscored the importance of this convoy. *Supermarina* was forewarned of Operation Halberd by a SIM operative based in Spain just a few miles from Gibraltar. A large number of ships was observed but the SIM could not determine what their objective was. After having determined that the available stocks of fuel oil were low, *Supermarina* issued the following directive which meant that the effort to counter the British ships' movements had to fall primarily on the shoulders of small naval crafts, torpedo bombers and the standard bomber units: "Recent intelligence reports indicate that a naval convoy will leave Gibraltar in order to reach Malta. Given the fleet's fuel oil situation, the enemy convoy shall be challenged by a combined force consisting of torpedo boats and submarines and a significant air force deployment heavily comprised by torpedo bombers."[85] The battlefleet could be deployed as a last resort but under very stringent conditions and *Supermarina* reiterated that it could do only be fielded if it possessed a clear superiority.

During the night of 24 September, the nine transport ships of the Halberd convoy, entered the Mediterranean. An Italian pilot of a reconnaissance aircraft located Force H at sea on the afternoon of 25 September, and assumed that the battleships, which were originally navigating at a distance from the main convoy, were on a bombardment raid against the Italian coast. This assumption was further strengthened the following day, when a CANT Z.506 seaplane observing Force H at 0932 on 26 September reported sighting a single battleship with an aircraft carrier incorrectly identified as HMS *Furious*. At this point, since SIM operatives had observed HMS *Ark Royal* depart from Gibraltar, the Italian intelligence services concluded that there were two aircraft carriers in the Mediterranean and that they likely had dual objectives: to shell the Italian coast in response to the X Mas attack against Gibraltar[86] and also to escort

85 Francesco Mattesini, *Luci ed ombre*, p.147.

86 On the morning of 20th September a human torpedo penetrated into the naval harbor at Gibraltar and was attached by its crew to the large tanker Denbydale. The tanker was seriously damaged by the

a convoy through the Mediterranean and/or to fly off planes to Malta. The incorrect reading of the enemy's movements initially caused the Italian fleet including the battleships *Vittorio Veneto* and *Littorio* to sail from Naples to take up a purely defensive position off northern Sardinia. From there it could be dispatched to Genoa in case the British aimed to bombard the Ligurian coast or it could be dispatch south to interdict the convoy in the Sicilian narrows. But overriding orders were not to engage the British fleet unless the Italians held a decisive superiority of forces and only in case the British warships were headed for a bombing foray against the Italian coast. At midday *Comando Supremo* received more intelligence from an Italian liaison officer that had received a report from a Vichy France aircraft that the convoy was comprised of more than twenty ships many of which were merchant vessels and were located 80 miles north of Algiers. Based on this latest information *Supermarina* became convinced that indeed the purpose of the enemy operation was to bring supplies to Malta. As a result orders were dispatched to the Italian battleships under *Ammiraglio* Iachino to chance course and head toward southern Sardinia and that they were given the green light to engage the convoy if the right conditions prevailed.

At the same time the *Capo di Stato Maggiore della Regia Aeronautica Generale* Pricolo on 26 September began to prepare his forces response to this major enemy passage through the Mediterranean. The tactic to be adopted was to engage the enemy force with a combination of bombers and torpedo bombers in a synchronized group attack. In short the plan reflected the Cavallero directive of August 1941 regarding how to properly conduct a combined arms naval/aerial battle against the Mediterranean Fleet. To this end, *Superaereo* ordered that Cant.Z.1007 from 51º *Gruppo* were tasked with conducting reconnaissance near the coast of Sardinia, while five torpedo bombers from 282ª *Squadriglia were* to be transferred from Sicily to Elmas in Sardinia to strengthen the torpedo bomber presence there and the immediate dispatch of five warheads from Guidonia to Elmas on two S.82. Also the transfer of the 52° *Stormo* comprised of thirty-two *Macchi* C.200 from Ciampino airport to Sardinia was also ordered to provide an escort for the bombing operations. The torpedo bomber units were given very specific orders: 280ª *Squadriglia/*130° *Gruppo Aerosiluranti* was to pursue the aircraft carriers; 283ª *Squadriglia/*130° *Gruppo Aerosiluranti* was to pursue the battleships; while 278ª *Squadriglia* and 282ª *Squadriglia* were to pursue the cruisers. The recently formed 36° *Stormo Aerosiluranti* with its 108° *Gruppo* was to pursue the aircraft carriers, while its 109° *Gruppo* was to pursue the battleships. All together the air force fielded a total of twenty-five torpedo bombers, of which fourteen belonged to the 130° *Gruppo* (two S.79 from 278ª *Squadriglia*, five from 283ª, four from 280ª, and three S.84s from 282ª *Squadriglia)* and eleven S.84s from 36° *Stormo* (five from 108° *Gruppo* and six from 109° *Gruppo*). At bases in Sardinia the 36° *Stormo* alone had almost forty torpedo bombers but many could not be deployed because the personnel had not yet been trained. Most were standard bomber crews which had recently been converted to the torpedo discipline and were reputed to be not combat ready. Some S.84 aircraft had yet to be converted to the torpedo bomber role, while some were out of service. Whereas the 130° *Gruppo* was newly formed, it was comprised of the more experienced personnel and all fourteen of its bombers were utilized in the operation. Therefore only 51% percent of the available torpedo bomber fleet available in Sardinia was utilized during Operation Halberd, a further indication of the overall

subsequent explosion. Two other merchant ships were attacked by human torpedoes; one was sunk and the other had to be beached.

modest efficiency of the fleet. The escort for the torpedo bombers was provided by 20 CR.42 belonging to the 24° *Gruppo Caccia* commanded by *Maggiore* Vincenzo Dequal (ex-commander of the 278ª *Squadriglia Aerosiluranti* in 1940). The operative plan reflected the new directives of *Superareo* which in order to counter a major enemy convoy was willing to commit a large force of torpedo bombers, bombers and fighters in synchronized attacks. Standard bombers and dive bombers were to make the first attack on the convoy, the purpose of which was to not only inflict damage but also to create a diversion for the torpedo bomber attacks which were to follow. A mass of torpedo bombers was then to attack in waves to inflict as much damage as possible by dropping twenty or more warheads. The overall objective was to degrade the enemy naval force ahead of the final confrontation with the Italian battlefleet.

The torpedo bombers scrambled from their airbases at 1145 on 27 September. Between 1300 and 1330 the twenty-five torpedo bombers attacked the convoy in three separate waves each attacking from a different direction. Radar forewarned the Royal Navy of the approach flight of the Italian formation and when the latter reached the convoy the artillery personnel were ready. As soon as the aircraft arrived the British naval formation reacted very strongly; the red hot naval guns began firing at an extended range, while the machine guns sent large columns of tracer in the sky. In addition, eight Fulmar and then seven more were dispatched from HMS *Ark Royal* to counter the enemy force. The first wave was comprised by five S.84s (108° *Gruppo* led by *Maggiore* Arduino Buri), quickly followed by three S.84s from 282ª *Squadriglia* (*Capitano* Marino Marini),which pressed forward the attack from the portside and were greeted with very strong anti-aircraft fire fed mostly by the 133 mm guns of the battleship HMS *Prince of Wales* and the cruisers Euryalus, and Hermione. At the same time, the Fulmar fighters of No. 808 Squadron managed to intercept one laggard S.84, flying out of formation and approaching ten miles from the convoy, and shot it down. Lieutenants E.D.G. Lewin and W.A. Metland, were credited with downing the aircraft of *Tenente* Vincenzo Morelli from 109° *Gruppo* who had remained isolated from the first wave of attackers. The second wave of this synchronized attack quickly followed suit comprised of six S.84s of the 109° *Gruppo* (*Maggiore* Goffredo Castaldi), led by *Colonnello* Riccardo Helmut Seidl. Meanwhile, the final wave was comprised of eleven S.79s from 130° *Gruppo* (*Capitano* Giorgio Grossi), which would follow.

Despite the furious barrage the first wave attacked the convoy with great determination with most of its planes managing to penetrate the anti-aircraft screen and release the torpedoes from advantageous positions. Their attack came from the portside of the enemy formation. As the attack was being carried out, *Capitano* Alfonso Rotolo, the commander of the 269ª *Squadriglia*/108° *Gruppo*, was the second victim of this operation when his plane was shot down by the fierce barrage. After the pilot lost control, his plane veered wildly to the right crashing into another S.84 flown by *Tenente* Danilo Barro, who also died when his plane due to the collision crashed into the sea. However, both *Maggiore* Buri and *Tenente* Remo Rossi, were able to launch their warheads at 1305 from a distance of 1,500 meters at HMS *Rodney* barely missing the British ship. The latter pilot, for example, dived down originally from 8,000 meters through a torrent of heavy fire to about 1,500 meters, released his warhead and then quickly pulled out. As the torpedo was approaching, HMS *Rodney* made an emergency turn of 60¼ to port and escaped unscathed the torpedo attack. The other pilot of the squad, *Tenente* Pier Carlo Amante also launched his minutes later against a destroyer but missed the target. The three S.84s of *Capitano* Marino Marini's squad with *Tenente* Ardito Cristiani and *Sottotenente* Saverio Meyer also failed to hit their targets which were the Lance, an L-class destroyer and the Isaac Sweers, a Dutch Gerard Callenburgh-class destroyer respectively. Both destroyers took evasive actions and managed to foil the torpedo strikes. The following is the British version of the events: "Three of the six attackers tried to approach over the port wing of the screen, but unable to face the barrage put up by the destroyers they dropped their torpedoes at the port wing ship, LANCE, who had considerable difficulty in avoiding them, two torpedoes passing very close. The torpedoes were released from about 300 feet height, and appeared to take up their depth very quickly, the tracks showing up plainly. ISAAC SWEERS, next in the screen to LANCE, reported one torpedo passed within 30 yards; RODNEY was swung 60° to port to avoid a torpedo which passed 100 yards to starboard."[87] During the attack of the first wave two Fulmars were lost to friendly fire. At 1310, a Fulmar which had been among the fighters sent to intercept this attack was returning damaged from combat with enemy planes when it was shot down by the barrage from HMS *Prince of Wales* and the crew were killed. Twenty minutes later another Fulmar was shot down by friendly fire.

The second wave of torpedo bombers, however, that struck at 1330 was successful. 109° *Gruppo* pressed forward its air assault after having conducted a diversionary flight to throw off the opponent. Many torpedo-bombers drove directly for the merchant ships which were in the middle of the convoy and drove headlong into a heavy anti-aircraft barrage – including the 16 inch guns on HMS *Nelson*. These projectiles were fired at low-trajectories so that the large columns of water thrown up would become a deterrent to torpedo bombers. All of a sudden its planes appeared on the starboard of the enemy naval formation managing to avoid any hits from the artillery barrage while coming within range. Then on the pilots dove further down into the inferno of tracer and guns. The first squad of three S.84s led by *Colonnello* Helmut Seidl launched the warheads which torpedoed HMS *Nelson*, which together with sister ship HMS *Rodney* comprised the Nelson-class 16 inch gun battleship of 33,950 tons, at a distance of only 411 meters. The battleship was struck by the torpedo causing a 40ft x 20ft hole in her hull. The strike immediately forced it to reduce speed to 18 knots and subsequently to 15 knots, but she remained temporarily with the convoy. An eyewitness on board the Royal Navy ship recounted that: "The Italians passed so close that I could see the crew plainly, bent over their instruments as if urging their machine to a greater speed. They must have sensed that they had only seconds to live. Prince of Wales' pom-poms were roaring away, and close range armament, which could have done better, appeared to chip bits off the aircraft's rear as she went past."[88]

With regards to HMS *Nelson,* Admiral James Somerville wrote:

> Three of the aircraft pressed on through the barrage of the starboard wing destroyers and carried out a most determined attack on the Nelson, who was swinging to starboard to comb the tracks. One aircraft dropped its torpedo about 450 yards on Nelsons starboard bow, passing over the ship at about 200 feet of height and track of the torpedo was not seen until about 150 yards dead ahead of the ship, which had been steadied on the course which proved to be the exact reciprocal of the torpedo. No avoiding action was possible and a second or two after the bubbles disappeared from sight there was a large crump, the ship whipped considerably and a column of water rose approximately 15 to 20 feet high

87 James Somerville, "Mediterranean Convoy Operations – Operation Halberd", *Supplement to the London Gazette*, n. 38296, 10 August 1948, p.4485.

88 Jack Greene and Alessandro Massignani, *The Naval War*, p.188.

> above the first to forecastle deck portside. The torpedo had hit on the port bow abreast 60 station, 10 feet below the water-line. Nelson's speed was reduced to 15 knots, pending a report on the damage sustained. A few seconds later another torpedo bomber of this formation dropped a torpedo from about 500 feet 1,000 yards to starboard bow of Nelson. This torpedo passed about 100 yards to starboard. The third of this enemy formation was shot down by destroyers just ahead of the screen at 1333. This aircraft was claimed by Laforey. Forester picked up the W/T operator, the only member of the crew alive. He had a broken leg.[89]

As the S.84s attempted to disengage they flew over HMS *Prince of Wales* and HMS *Sheffield* that from a very favorable position quickly shot down *Colonnello* Siedl's plane. Subsequently his wingman *Capitano* Tomasino suffered the same fate as he flew over HMS *Laforey*. The only survivor of Tomasino's crew was the radio operator/machine gunner *1° Aviere* Guerrino Soravia, who was rescued by the British destroyer HMS *Forester*. Despite the demise of the two S.84s the torpedo bombers had achieved an important success because even though HMS *Nelson* initially stayed with the convoy, she could not be deployed in combat against the Italian fleet if the latter decided to interdict the convoy. Later, she slowed down to 12 knots and was escorted back to Gibraltar by a number of destroyers and corvettes which were detached from the convoy. She would undergo repairs for almost a year.

Meanwhile, the second squad belonging to the second wave, also comprised of three S.84s of 259ª *Squadriglia* led by the commander of the 109° *Gruppo*, *Maggiore* Goffredo Gastaldi attacked the battleship that was trailing behind HMS *Nelson* and HMS *Hermione*. During the operation the aircraft of *Capitano* Giusellino Verna, who was part of Gastaldi's unit, was shot down by a Fulmar of No. 808 Squadron as he was about to launch the warhead. All torpedoes fired against HMS *Hermione* failed to hit the target. Lastly a Fulmar was unfortunately shot down by HMS *Rodney's* pom-pom.

The operation came to an end with the final attack mounted by the third wave comprised of eleven slower *Sparvieri* (nine from *130° Gruppo Autonomo* and two from 278ª *Squadriglia*) and it took place at 1345. By this time all the ships were in a state of full alert and they opened fire immediately against the S.79s. The fire was so fierce and intense, especially coming from HMS *Ark Royal*, that it shot down a 280ª *Squadriglia's* S.79 piloted by *Tenente* Carlo Deslex in the opening stages of the fighting. The plane crashed into the sea killing all onboard. The Ark Royal's Fulmars then took off to chase the remaining *Sparvieri* away. In the fierce fighting that took place over HMS *Ark Royal* two S.79 were slightly damaged by Fulmars, while two Fulmars were shot down by friendly fire. The fire from the British ships was so fierce that five S.79 from the 279ª *Squadriglia* were unable to penetrate the barrage and chose to turn back and make their return to Elmas base without firing one torpedo. Some aircraft of 130° *Gruppo* nonetheless persisted in the attack by spreading out to pursue the convoy from multiple directions: 280ª and 282ª *Squadriglie* attacked from the north, 278ª *Squadriglia* dove down from south, while 283ª *Squadriglia* attacked the western flank. Their targets were specifically HMS *Ark Royal* and the destroyer HMS *Cossack* which effectively fought off the torpedo bomber threat. Their

89 James Somerville, "Mediterranean Convoy Operations – Operation Halberd", *Supplement to the London Gazette*, n. 38296, 10 August 1948.

blistering fire prevented most *Sparvieri* from getting a good shot from a favorable position at the ships. The final attack was pressed forward again against HMS *Ark Royal* and HMS *Cossack* by two S.79s from 278ª *Squadriglia* piloted by *Tenenti* Arduino Venturini and Gaetano Buccesi. While dipping and weaving to avoid the hailstorm of fire both aircraft received, and despite their evasive actions, plenty of gusts of tracer fire. The anti-aircraft fire however, did not cripple them. Suddenly HMS *Cossack* came in sight and the pilots dove down skimming the water and released the warheads at 750 meters away. Both pilots then flew over the ship, rose the aircraft and quickly pulled away. In their post battle report affirmed to have hit a destroyer, but the torpedoes were avoided by the evasive actions taken by the crew of HMS *Cossack*. The British version of events states that only one pilot flew decisively in the direction of HMS *Cossack* and narrowly missed it while the other did not represent a threat: "At 1358 one aircraft, seen right ahead of NELSON, dropped a torpedo outside the screen. COSSACK was able to avoid this torpedo by the warning given by hydrophone effect on her A/S set."[90]

The RM meanwhile based on faulty intelligence that overestimated the number of battleships deployed by the British failed to engage the enemy even though it would have done so under more favorable circumstances as the air forces had torpedoed the battleship HMS *Nelson*. At 1400 the *Littorio* and *Vittorio Veneto* battleships, along with *Trieste*, *Trento*, *Bolzano*, *Duca Degli'Abruzzi*, and *Duca d'Aosta incrociatori* supported by fourteen other smaller ships were ordered "to be ready for combat."[91] by *Ammiraglio* Iachino. At the time the Italian battlefleet was south of Sardinia and within a reasonable distance to be able to engage the British fleet. Meanwhile, the latter had detached HMS *Rodney*, HMS *Prince of Wales* and six destroyers under the command of Vice Admiral Curteis at 0330 to close in and engage the enemy. A number of aircraft were also launched from the aircraft carrier to try to find the Italian fleet but they were not successful. At 1534, and 1627 *Ammiraglio* Iachino was informed of substantial damage to the British fleet but due to a lack of air coverage and other factors the decision was made not to engage. At 1700 *Supermarina* informed again the battlefleet commander that there was only one battleship and the fleet was once more turned around to purse the Royal Navy but by then the Italian ships were too far away from the enemy to have any changes of engaging him. Thus, as historian John Gooch asserts: "The Italian surface fleet missed another opportunity to engage the enemy …"[92]

The Italian post-battle report initially credited the torpedoing of HMS *Nelson* to the commander of the 108° *Gruppo Maggiore* Buri, who led the first attack wave at 1305 launching the torpedo from the portside of the convoy at a distance of 1,500 meters from the target. But Admiral Somerville's report clearly indicated that HMS *Nelson* was torpedoed by an aircraft that inched very closely to the ship and released the warhead at approximately 411 meters away at 1330 hours and which struck the starboard. As Francesco Mattessini's exhaustive research indicates, *Colonnello* Seidl and the other aircraft from 109° *Gruppo* were the ones that had attacked the convoy's starboard and were later reputed to be the ones responsible for torpedoing HMS *Nelson*. This version of events is also described in the post-battle report issued by the 109° *Gruppo* and specifically by *Maggiore* Goffredo Gastaldi:

90 Ibid. p.4486.
91 Francesco Mattesini, *Luci ed ombre*, p.122.
92 John Gooch, *Mussolini's War*, p.208.

> The attack was carried out against the middle and the rear of the naval formation. The two aircraft of the first squad, after starting their approach to the target were no longer visible. Of the aircraft participating in the attack, only two returned to the base at 1420 and 1435 respectively. Both had launched their torpedoes at a cruiser from the right flank. The loss of the two aircraft from the first wave, the one led by Colonnello Seidl, did not allow me to clearly establish how the attack developed. Thus I cannot assert with 100 percent certainty which aircraft from the first wave was responsible for the hit on the British battleship, but I can reasonably assume that the hit was achieved by the comandante of 36° *Stormo*, in consideration of the fact that he was leading the attack and that HMS Nelson was hit by the first torpedo dropped against it from a distance of about 411 meters.[93]

Colonnello Seidl and his wingman *Capitano* Bartolomeo Tomasino were conclusively credited with the kill also by the post battle report issued by the *Comando Aeronautica della Sardegna* which in reference to the action of 109° *Gruppo* wrote: "A column of smoke about three hundred meters high was observed rising from a warship against which the two torpedoes were launched. This column remained visible at a distance of about 40 km."[94]

For the most determined close quarters combat action and ultimate sacrifice, both *Colonnello* Seidl and *Capitano* Tomasino were awarded posthumously the gold medal of military valor along with *Capitano* Alfonso Rotolo commander of the 257ª *Squadriglia*, and *Capitano* Giuseppe Verna, commander of 259ª *Squadriglia*.

The casualties associated with this first attack against Halberd were high. Seven aircraft were lost, two S.84s from 108° *Gruppo* (Rotolo and Barro), four S.84 from 109° *Gruppo* (Seidl, Tomasino, Verna and Morelli) and one S.79 from 130° *Gruppo* (Deslex). An eight aviator, a fighter pilot of a CR.42 from the 354ª *Squadriglia*/24° *Gruppo*, (*Sergente* Luigi Valotti) was also shot down as he made a generous wide ranging maneuver to attract enemy fire while the attack by the third wave of torpedo bombers was being carried out. Royal Navy sailor George Gilroy, on board HMS *Lightning* wrote with regards to Valotti's actions: "I remember at one stage during an attack a Fiat fighter performing stunts over the convoy; some said that it was trying to divert attention from the incoming torpedo bombers. However, we shot him down."[95] Thirty-seven torpedo crew members died and few were the survivors from downed aircraft. *Aviere marconista* Guerrino Soravia, a crew member of *Capitano* Tomasino's aircraft was one of them as he was rescued at sea by the British HMS *Forester*. A few others were recovered by the Italian Navy.

An indication that the cooperation between the RM and the RA had still not fully improved was evidenced when the torpedo bomber crews returned to base. The latter upon their return were reprimanded for not having immediately communicated via radio that HMS *Nelson* had been struck. According to *Supermarina* this piece of intelligence would have been useful for the RM battle fleet which would have likely pursued a debilitated enemy force. Instead *Supermarina* only learned of the hit on HMS *Nelson* at 1500 on 27 September by a communication from the commander of *Aeronautica della Sardegna*, well after the torpedo bombers had returned to base.

93 Archivio Storico Aeronautica Militare: Comando Aeronautica della Sardegna, "Operazione Halberd", 29 September 1941.
94 Ibid.
95 Gianni Rocca, *I disperati*, p.131.

Admiral's Iachino's actions with *Littorio* and *Vittorio Veneto* were nevertheless indecisive and the RM failed to engage the convoy also because of its faulty intelligence. The RM's actions which failed to aggressively pursue the convoy showed the difficulties of fully implementing Cavallero's directives in a combined arms fashion especially because of the RM's overly cautious tactics. Another matter that plagued the operation was faulty, or delayed, air and naval intelligence reporting that either reported the information late (air) or overestimated the strength of the enemy fleet (naval).

Another torpedo bomber attack was made in the afternoon of the 27th but it was also opposed by enemy anti-aircraft fire. Two *Sparvieri* managed to drop their load but they did not strike any ship. But the convoy, despite fighting back vigorously was given no respite. 283ª *Squadriglia* pressed forward another attack at 2000 when three torpedo bombers led by *Capitano* Grossi launched their warheads but without any accuracy given the great enemy anti-aircraft fire. All three aircraft made it safely back to base at Decimomannu in Sardinia, although Barioglio's plane had taken some damage from machine gun fire when he flew over the convoy. At 2030 two S.79s from 278ª *Squadriglia* flown by *Capitano* Dante Magagnoli and *Tenente* Lelio Silva sallied again against the convoy. They had taken off from Elmas airbase with the objective of targeting either a large capital battleship or the largest transport ship. In a daring close range operation *Capitano* Magagnoli launched his torpedo almost at a stone throw from the 12,427-tons merchant ship Imperial Star. "At 2032 in position 37° 31' N0 10° 46' E, Imperial Star was struck port side aft by a torpedo"[96] which due to extensive damage sustained was later scuttled by one of the destroyers. In fact Imperial Star due to the explosion had its propellers and her rudder blown away; in addition No. 6 hold and the after engine room were both flooded.[97] With regard to the downed merchant ship the British Official History states that: "Admiral Somerville then turned back, leaving Admiral Burrough to escort the convoy on to Malta with Force X. Course was altered to haul over to the Sicilian side of the channel. As it grew dark torpedo-bombers in ones, twos, and threes made numerous attacks and one of the convoy, the Imperial Star, was hit. After repeated attempts to tow her had failed, she was sunk with depth charges."[98] Meanwhile, his companion *Tenente* Silva barely missed HMS *Sheffield* from a very favorable distance. Thanks to the evasive maneuvers taken by the latter the torpedo failed to inflict damage: "A torpedo was dropped on SHEFFIELD'S port bow at 2029, and five minutes later she had to turn to starboard under full rudder to avoid another dropped on her port beam."[99]

The last attack of the day against the convoy was conducted by *Tenente* Francesco Di Bella and *Tenente* Guido Focacci at 2250. The first pilot burst through the anti-aircraft screen and from an advantageous position attempted to release the torpedo twice but a fault in the release mechanism prevented him from firing. Focacci on the other hand, could not locate the convoy during the flight and had to return to base.

The Halberd convoy entered Malta with 50,000 tons of supply on 28 September. This operation had been a successful endeavor for the Royal Navy which achieved the stated aim of

96 James Somerville, "Mediterranean Convoy Operations – Operation Halberd", *Supplement to the London Gazette*, n. 38296, 10 August 1948, p.4489.

97 Ibid.

98 Ibid.

99 Ibid.

reinforcing the island fortress. The RA and specifically the *Comando Aeronautica della Sardegna* considered Operation Halberd as a missed opportunity. The latter considered the successful torpedoing of the two British ships as a success, but it also stated that the heavy losses sustained by the torpedo bomber crews was an "unjustified sacrifice of the air force"[100] while the RM had failed to exploit the situation by acting more aggressively. It also challenged the notion that increased cooperation between the two services could lead to success given the inability of the RM to go after the enemy ships even after the quasi-suicidal daytime actions of the torpedo bombers. The RM had adopted a playing for time strategy during the operation that in the RA's view had been too indecisive. "That is to show the fleet and to draw the British into the air force and submarine ambushes near the Italian coast."[101] Greater cooperation between the two services, mainly the timely exchange of information between the services, and a more decisive attitude by the RM might had improved the chances of halting the majority of Operation Halberd's transport ships. In the immediate post war period the Italian official naval historian, Bragadin, echoed this critique of the RM's handling of operation Halberd. He remarked that the torpedo bombers had attacked with skill and determination and regarded the breakdown of coordination as disappointing especially in light of the previous sortie of the Italian battlefleet in late August had been marked by good co-operation.[102]

The post-operation observations by the Royal Navy are very interesting. They underscore how the Italian Navy, especially its surface fleet, throughout the journey of the convoy in the Mediterranean failed to represent a threat. "On the other hand enemy air forces remained a potential and serious threat throughout the day and well after moonset."[103] Moreover, the report also underlined a weakness of the enemy, especially the Italian RA which was mainly its inability to fight effectively at night. The torpedo bombers especially lacking suitable instrumentation were not trained to fight after dusk. "It cannot be emphasized," the report stated, "too strongly that if operations of this character are carried out during moonlight the hazards are increased to a very considerable extent. Had the enemy concentrated his torpedo bomber aircraft in attacking from dusk onwards he might well have succeeded in torpedoing a large proportion of the convoy."[104]

At nighttime naval convoys typically advanced in a tighter formation increasing the likelihood of a torpedo hit. In addition, such tight formations often led to accidents when a ship took evasive actions from a torpedo attack and wound striking another ship.

A consequence of Operation Halberd was that the large number of torpedoes employed during the two days of intensive action had depleted a large part of the available stock to the point that *Generale* Cavallero was forced to broker a deal with the RM so that the latter reassigned twenty SI torpedoes to the torpedo bomber units. As historian Vincent P. O' Hara correctly argues " torpedoes were another necessary item in naval warfare that the Italians needed to husband and expend only with care."[105]

100 Greene and Massignani, *The Naval War*, p.191.
101 Ibid.
102 Marcantonio Bragadin, *Che ha fatto la Marina?* (Milan: Garzanti, 1947), p.225.
103 James Somerville, "Mediterranean Convoy Operations – Operation Halberd", *Supplement to the London Gazette,* n. 38296, 10 August 1948, p.4494.
104 Ibid.
105 Vincent P. O' Hara, *Six Victories*, p.170.

A positive consequence of the operation was the that the RA was looked upon more positively by the *Luftwaffe* head Hermann Goering. The latter at a meeting with *Generale* Pricolo in Berlin complimented the Italian air forces for the damaged inflicted on HMS *Nelson* and admitted that the *Luftwaffe* had made a mistake when it failed to build an adequate torpedo bomber fleet. Pricolo would write that the meeting revealed that: "From a political perspective I gained the impression that lately the Germans have grown to admire our air force units. Their views on our force are more positive and they have a better understanding of the difficulties we face and there is a greater recognition of our effort toward the common Axis objectives."[106]

One of the things that German *Luftwaffe* took away after the Italians had torpedoed HMS *Nelson* was a greater appreciation for aerial torpedoes as anti-shipping weapons. As Price argues: "A further deficiency in the Luftwaffe at the outbreak of the war was the lack of both an effective aerial torpedo and a modern aircraft that could carry it. Not until the early part of 1942 were these shortcomings made good, when the First Gruppe of KG 26 became operational with He.111s modified to carry the F5B torpedo; only then did the German torpedo bomber became a force to be reckoned with in the Allied calculations."[107]

The *Kriegsmarine* had become involved with naval torpedoes when it purchased Horton naval torpedo patents from Norway in 1933 and the Whitehead Fiume patent from Italy in 1938. But air-launched torpedo development was slow. In 1939 Germany held preliminary trials with Heinkel He.59 and Heinkel He.115 which were not successful given the almost fifty percent failure rate during the launches. In the first months of 1941 the *Luftwaffe* took an active interest in torpedo aerial development, but the *Kriegsmarine*, like the RM, resisted *Luftwaffe* involvement and collaboration. When the *Luftwaffe* began its heavier involvement in both the Atlantic and the Mediterranean anti-shipping campaigns, its crews needed effective weapons to interdict enemy shipping. In December 1941 the *Luftwaffe* was granted the lead in torpedo development. This lead the *Luftwaffe* to set up a number of schools dedicated to torpedo attack at Gossenbrode, (Germany) Grosseto, (Italy) and in Athens. The aircraft used by the Germans was the Heinkel He.111 which was highly suited to such operations. Trials at Gossenbrode enabled the He.111 to carry two torpedoes, while the Ju.88 was also used extensively. KG 26, the *Luftwaffe's* torpedo bomber unit, was equipped with both the He.111 and Ju.88.

On the Italian side one result of Operation Halberd was the request by *Generale* Cavallero of a further refinement for aerial-naval combined arms operations in the Mediterranean. With regards to the torpedo bomber units the newly updated plan titled "Norme Generali per la Cooperazione Aeronavale nel Mediterraneo"[108] assigned the specialty one of the main or primary roles during a combined arms operation aimed at interfering with enemy shipping operations. "A mass of aircraft shall be concentrated in a few bases of interest. The combat action shall be carried out by the torpedo bombers in close collaboration with the standard bomber unit and the fighters."[109] Now more than ever a combined arms operation aimed at neutralizing the Royal Navy at sea and the island fortress of Malta had become an imperative. Italian cargo

106 Francesco Pricolo, *La Regia Aeronautica nella seconda guerra mondiale. Novembre 1939-novembre 1941* (Milan: Mondadori, 1971), p.171.

107 Alfred Price, *Luftwaffe Handbook* (New York: Charles Scribner's Sons, 1977), p.47.

108 Ufficio Storico, Comando Supremo, "Norme Generali per la Cooperazione Aeronavale nel Mediterraneo", 10 October 1941.

109 Ibid.

losses in the latter half of 1941 were beginning to mount at the expense of the British aerial and naval forces based in Malta. On the night of 8/9 November, for example, the Royal Navy Force K, thanks to Enigma intercepts ambushed the Duisburg convoy headed for North Africa and carrying 34,473 tons of ammunition and 18,000 tons of fuel which represented a major loss for the Axis. In addition with Operation Crusader, which commenced on 18 November, the British Eight Army was able to capture the advanced air fields in Cyrenaica. RAF units began to operate from Cyrenaica bases and gained more advanced platforms from which to attack the Axis supply route to North Africa. As a result, Axis convoy losses for November were almost 75 per cent of the total bound for Libya, Only 8,400 tons of supplies arrived in Libya during the month, the lowest delivery of the Mediterranean war.[110] Something had to be done to neutralize Malta. This had become the number one priority for the Axis Mediterranean strategy.

On the heels of the Royal Navy attack upon the Duisburg convoy, *Superaereo* ordered *Comando dell 'Aeronautica della Sicilia* to deploy all operational torpedo bombers to pursue the British vessels before they returned to Malta. This was in fulfillment of a longstanding request by *Supermarina* to make the life miserable for those Royal Navy ships that attacked Axis cargo convoys in the Mediterranean. Since early on the RM had requested that the RA guarantee at all times the availability of a dedicated, special torpedo bomber unit to be fully staffed and armed and fully operational to effectively pursue those ships that had just ambushed a convoy. Given the complexity of torpedo bomber operations and the modest size of the torpedo bomber fleet, RA was never in a position to fully fulfill such a request. On 9 November, for example, on the day following the ambush of the Duisburg convoy there were only four operational aircraft (two S.79 from 278ª *Squadriglia* and two S.84 from 284ª *Squadriglia*) which could be deployed from Sicily. Two of the latter promptly took off in the early hours of 9 November. At 0900 the latter flown by *Tenenti* Antonio Cristiani and Mario Venturi spotted the Royal Navy Force K at sea and headed in the direction of La Valletta. Suddenly two Hurricanes from No. 185 Squadron, which had arrived from Malta to escort the convoy in its final passage, challenged the two Italian pilots. The S.84s opened fire and *Tenente* Cristanti's machine gunner promptly launched a hailstorm of bullets against Captain Graham Bailey's aircraft which caught fire and plunged into the sea. After having dealt with the Hurricanes, the S.84 pilots attacked the convoy. *Tenente* Cristanti released the warhead at 1,200 meters aiming at a destroyer, while moments later *Tenente* Venturi launched his warhead at a cruiser but to no avail. Both aircraft released their warheads from very favorable conditions but soon after had to climb higher and get away by flying over the enemy formation. During those perilous moments the planes were plastered by tracer but managed to escape the enemy fire. At approximately 0920 the other two aircraft from 278ª *Squadriglia* (*Tenenti* Giorgio Sacchetti and Emilio Juzzolino) flew over the British Force K but were greeted by a firestorm from an alert foe. Only the first pilot was able to get into a favorable position and launch his warhead at a position roughly 45 miles from La Valletta. He too missed the target even though in the post battle report the pilot asserted that a hit had been most likely made on a cruiser. The other pilot was met with intense anti-aircraft fire, which prevented him from attaining a dropping position. The last attempt on Force K was made by three German He.111 but they could not locate it. Thus at 1305 Force K sailed into the harbor at La Valletta cheerfully greeted by sailors and harbor workers.

110 Andrew Browne Cunningham, *A Sailor's Odyssey* (London: Hutchinson and Co. Ltd., 1951), p.420.

Operations, Fall 1941

On 13 October a bold attack was carried out by three S.79 against the battleships HMS *Queen Elisabeth* and HMS *Barham*. It was undertook by *Tenenti* Graziani, Faggioni and Cimicchi twenty miles northwest of Alexandria. While Graziani's crew machine gunned the deck of HMS *Barnham* by flying so low that the plane almost crashed against one of the towers, Cimicchi recalls that he pursued a cruiser: "I dove down against the concentrated fire of the anti-aircraft defense and managed to launch the warhead at almost a stone throw away from the cruiser."[111] All three S.79 received ack fire. Graziani, for example, was forced to limp back to base at Rhodes in his heavily damaged aircraft which barely made it back. On 17 October two S.79s from 280ª and 283ª *Squadriglie/130° Gruppo* flown by *Capitano* Giorgio Grossi and *Tenente* Giancarlo Borgazzi pursued the Clan McDonald transport ship near Galite Islands. The torpedo bombers misfired and the ship was able to arrive safe and sound to Gibraltar on 19 October. On 20 October *Superaereo* issued an important directive titled "Direttive d'impiego aerosiluranti" (directives for the deployment of torpedo bombers) in which it asserted that "experienced torpedo bomber crews could voluntarily attack enemy naval formations including aircraft carriers in the area of the Balearic Islands in nighttime operations."[112] Experienced pilots were reputed as the most capable in testing the endurance of the torpedo bombers as well as fighting in areas that had previously been considered to be outside the operational theatre of the S.79s. The first test of this new volunteer based tactic took place on 23 October when a lone S.79 from 278ª *Squadriglia* flown by *Tenente* Lelio Silva took off from Pantelleria at 0730 to pursue Royal Navy ships operating near Sicily. As the pilot approached the enemy formation his plane was greeted by the naval gunners. Its torpedo run was put off by this heavy fire. The plane received a hit which debilitated the engine forcing the pilot to crash land it near Kelibia in Algeria. The S.79 then overturned during landing operations and quickly began to burn. Burned and bloodied, the crew members ended up in a military hospital in Tunis. This attack was followed up by four S.84s from 36° *Stormo* (two from 256ª and two from 258ª *Squadriglie*) based in Decimomannu in Sardinia which began their operation at 1210. In rapid succession *Colonnello* Marcello Diaz, and *Tenenti* Arnaldo Casalotti, Eros Casali, and Fausto Jus Ian closed in and launched the warheads but the evasive action taken by the ships ensured that no torpedo hit the intended target. The failed combat action was the subject of an investigation by *Colonnello* Antonino Serra, the overall commander of the *aerosiluranti*, who asserted that the pilots of the *Stormo* had shown an inability to carry out attacks against enemy ships that were led by experienced seamen in taking swift evasive actions and that "the pilots had not reached the point where they could succeed in such situations."[113] The report concluded that more training was required especially for the newly transformed *Gruppi*. For such elite units, fully trained pilots and co-pilots were essential to the success of the discipline in the future. In a follow up report *Colonnello* Serra made some general considerations on torpedo bomber operations. Since the start of the war 222 combat actions had been carried out with the deployment

111 Giuseppe Cimicchi, *I siluri vengono dal cielo*, p.99.

112 Archivio Storico Aeronautica Militare: Superaereo "Direttive d'impiego aerosiluranti", 1B/18184, 20 October 1941.

113 Archivio Storico Aeronautica Militare: Ufficio Aerosiluranti, Colonnello Antonino Serra, "Visite ai reparti siluranti della Sardegna", 13 November 1941.

of 480 aircraft, of which twenty (or 4.16 percent of the total) aircraft had failed to return to base. Most casualties had taken place during twenty-seven daylight operations carried out against large enemy formations. These operations had been carried out by eighty-three aircraft with the loss of thirteen aircraft or 15.66 percent of the total aircraft deployed. In turn attacks made against single battleships or transport ships had seen the deployment of forty-four aircraft with a loss of only two planes or 4.76 percent of the total number of aircraft. The most egregious losses had taken place against largescale enemy operations such as Tiger, Substance and Halberd. *Colonnello* Serra concluded his report by stating that: "These great losses against large scale enemy operations dictate that we must consider what can be done to improve the success rate of operations. Such high losses have had an impact upon morale especially of some of the co-pilots (the *sottotenenti* class in particular), which have demonstrated hypersensitivity toward these risky operations. Combat tactics deployed especially during daylight operations against aircraft carriers must be improved by training pilots on the optimum distance and altitude to release warheads. Since German aircraft have superior cockpit instrumentation tools such as Siemens altimeters and distance meters to aid the pilots, we should request these instruments from Germany which should be able to furnish them in return for our supply of Whitehead torpedoes to the Luftwaffe."[114] It appears that despite this report, by 1943 S.79 aircraft were still assembled with Italian made instrumentation panels. It is not clear whether this was the result of pushback from Italian industry or from *Luftwaffe* reluctance to do away with diminishing inventory of aircraft components.

In some instances, the Royal Navy used disguise to achieve success in the convoy war. One example of this tactic is the merchant ship of 5,720-tons Empire Guillemot which was used to ferry supplies to Malta. It arrived on 19th September at Malta after sailing alone in the Western Mediterranean. The Royal Navy used Spanish, French, and Italian colors while the ship was passing along the North African coast to throw off their opponents. Nevertheless, Axis aircraft did spot the ship on several occasions but refrained from attacking it. On her return passage to Gibraltar, however, she was torpedoed and sunk by Italian torpedo bombers on 24 October 1941. The attack was made by three S.79s approximately 30 miles from Las Rosas. The first one was piloted by *Tenente* Guido Focacci of 283ª *Squadriglia*, while the other two were flown by *Capitano* Melley and *Sottotenente* Manlio Caresio both from 280ª *Squadriglia*. Eleven enemy soldiers were killed during the operation while the remaining crew members (thirty-one) were interned in Tunisia. The attack on the Empire Guillemot was made by *Tenente* Focacci who launched his torpedo at 1400 at a distance of only approximately 600 meters, while the other two S.79s provided air coverage. The ship sank forty minutes after receiving the torpedo hit. On the same day the cargo ship Clan Ferguson was unsuccessfully attacked by two S.84s from 282ª *Squadriglia* flown by *Capitano* Marino Marini and *Tenente* Saverio Mayer. The latter took off from Sicily at 1605 but were challenged by Hurricanes that were escorting the ship. This resulted in only one S.84 being able to launch the torpedo which misfired from an unfavorable position over 2,000 meters out. The other S.84 was met by intense anti-aircraft fire which prevented it from attaining a dropping position.

On 11 November 1941 a S.79 torpedo bomber was lost at sea. Two S.79 from 279ª *Squadriglia* flown by *Tenenti* Graziani and Giuseppe Cipelletti where returning back to base

114 Francesco Mattesini, *Luci ed ombre*, p.150.

at Rhodes after having completed a reconnaissance mission over the Aegean Sea. While Cipelletti's plane landed safely at 2100, *Tenente* Graziani's plane due to the heavy fog failed to land and plunged one mile from the base into the sea. The plane could not be recovered but the crew was saved by motorboat. Regarding this incident *Generale* Longo wrote that: "This incident that occurred to the aircraft of *Tenente* Graziani during landing operations was caused by the bad weather and the heavy fog on the runway. The loss of the plane should not be attributed to this great pilot who has numerous times demonstrated a great drive, high morale and considerable expertise."[115]

A similar attack to the one made against Empire Guillemot took place on 14 November, when the same unit 130° *Gruppo* targeted another merchant ship the 6,463-tons Empire Pellican traveling from Barry via Gibraltar to Malta alone. It was pursued by two S. 79s flown by *Tenenti* Camillo Baroglio and Francesco Cossu of 283ª *Squadriglia.* The ship was 10 miles southwest of Galite Islands when it was challenged by the torpedo bombers. In this instance, *Tenente* Camillo Baroglio swooped down and released the deadly torpedo which struck the steamship in the engine room and later sank off the coast east of Galite Islands. In the same area on 15 November the commander of 108° *Gruppo/36° Stormo Aerosiluranti*, *Maggiore* Arduino Buri, flying on his S. 84 of the 256ª *Squadriglia* along with *Capitano* Casali as wingman pursued the British vessel Empire Defender which was steaming from Gibraltar toward Malta. The 5,649-tons vessel was carrying important stocks of ammunition destined to the besieged island. It appears that the vessel was doomed from the start as the Italian SIM had pre-warned the air force once it sailed from Gibraltar alone. The first to pounce was *Capitano* Casali who missed the target. Then pilot *Maggiore* Buri at 1810 facing no opposition brought the aircraft within launching range and released the torpedo which struck the ship. On impact four sailors died. Empire Defender was set on fire and her crew abandoned her. They had only just done this when she blew up and sank 18 nautical miles (33 km) south of the Galite Islands, Tunisia. The survivors were recovered by an Italian ship and became prisoners of war.

On 17 November two *Sparvieri* flown by *Capitano* Buscaglia and *Tenente* Rovelli of 281ª *Squadriglia* pounced upon the 9,871-tons troopship HMS *Glenroy* off the coast of Egypt near Mersa Matruh. The latter was escorted by the cruiser HMS *Carlisle* and two smaller Hunt-class destroyers (Avon Vale, and Eridge) as well as fighters patrolling over the convoy which was transporting sixteen landing vehicles, two motor launches and 80 soldiers destined to reinforce the Tobruk garrison. The two pilots took off at 1440 from Rhodes airport and headed south toward the coast of North Africa. The attack took place at 1620. Buscaglia was the first to act striking the ship at 600 meters out. His wingmen *Tenente* Rovelli was up next and carried out an even more audacious close combat action than his superior officer. Diving from 4,000 meters and jinking the aircraft from side to side to keep the enemy gunners guessing as to which flank he would press forward his attack, Rovelli quickly got into striking range. He then levelled off his plane at 60 meters from above the water and then closed in on the target. He released the torpedo at 400 meters away and was assured a hit at such a favorable distance. The strike torpedoed *Glenroy* in Hold n.5 which flooded the ship's engine room. Such a close combat action allowed the aircraft's photographer (*Primo Aviere* Ricci) to take a number of photos that captured the damage made to HMS *Glenroy.* Then Rovelli's S.79 evaded most of the gun fire

115 Orazio Giuffrida, *Buscaglia e gli aerosiluranti* (Rome: Ufficio Storico, 1998), p.310.

by climbing wildly to 2,000 meters in just a few minutes. Although the crew was able to get away unscathed, the plane did receive some slight damage to its wings. Meanwhile, the ship stopped operating all of a sudden and HMS *Carlisle* began towing her east as the engine room soon began to take in water. The ship was so badly damaged that it was later run aground on 24 November so it did not sink west of Mersa Matruh. Emergency repairs had to be made prior to the ship being towed to Alexandria and then brought to Cardiff where it underwent extensive repairs which lasted until November 1942. The units post battle report indicated that the ship had been hit by two torpedoes and that both pilots shared the success.[116] According to historian O'Hara: "The S.79 achieved this success against a vulnerable target protected by fighters and three aircraft escorts."[117] With this action *Capitano* Buscaglia and Rovelli had obtained an important tactical victory that slowed down the British buildup at Tobruk aimed at increasing cargo capacity at a key phase in the conflict thus aiding Rommel's land based units. The Glenroy and her sister ships, the Glengyle and Glenearn, were the first Royal Navy ships to be used as large infantry landing ships. They were each able to carry three landing craft mechanized and fourteen infantry landing craft and could hold up to 1,087 assault troops. Each ship was armed with three twin 4-inch guns and numerous short-range anti-aircraft weapons.

Below are the recollections of Shipwright John Priscott who was on HMS *Glenroy* on 23 November. His recollections point to one of the tactics used by the torpedo bomber pilots when the enemy ships were traveling near the North African coast to avoid U-boats. The torpedo bombers would attack not directly by sea but by surprise from the south by sweeping in undetected over the coastal hills and then launch their deadly warhead.

Accordingly Glenroy was dispatched with the AA c Class cruiser Carlisle as escort. At approximately

> 1600 hrs. just as we were about to have Sunday tea our guns opened up, then there was an almighty explosion. The ship, which is really a living thing with the movement and the noise of fans etc., was dark, silent and still. The Tannoy announces "abandon ship", there was no "Action stations" and it all happened so fast, the ship was like a log in the water. I think we were caught on the hop because for the first time in the war, we had a fighter airplane flying over us. Fighter escort unbelievable! the Grumman Martlet had gone by the time I got on deck. There seems confusion as to whether the torpedo was from a U boat or from an Italian torpedo bomber which had suddenly popped up over the coastline. The U boats had recently appeared and claimed Battleship HMS Barham the day before, (22/11/41). The different temperatures of the sea due to the waters of the Nile with fresh and saltwater layers made ASDIC detection difficult. We had hugged the coast where it was shallow to avoid the U boats but this also gave the torpedo bombers an element of surprise just sweeping in over the coastal hills before they were detected. We mustered at our boat stations, mine was a carley float which was dropped into the water, just a few feet, as the ship was only six inches from sinking, The majority of the crew and army personnel went aft to be taken off by destroyer. I got into the float but then the Captain must have thought the ship might be saved and about 20 of us scrambled back aboard as a skeleton

116 Ibid. p.334.
117 Vincent P. O'Hara, *Six Victories*, p.65.

> crew. A stern line was passed to the Carlisle and we were towed stern first on to a sandbar where the ship settled.[118]

On 29 November two pilots from 281ª *Squadriglia, Capitano* Buscaglia and *Tenente* Giuseppe Cipelletti took off after two enemy destroyers had been spotted by a reconnaissance plane steaming at high speed near Mersa Matruh and headed to Alexandria. At 1650 the two pilots spotted the two cruisers (HMS *Naiad* and HMS *Euryalus*) escorted by two destroyers (HMS *Griffin* and HMS *Hotspur*) of Force C. *Tenente* Cipelletti was the first to strike from a distance of 500 meters and at an altitude of 30 meters above the water, but despite the favorable position the torpedo travelled a few meters away from one of the cruisers. *Capitano* Buscaglia first attempted to press home the attack but receiving a flurry of concentrated enemy fire emanating from ten 133 mm guns ultimately decided to turn back. His decision was based on two considerations: 1. on the impossibility of getting a clear shot due to the anti-aircraft fire and 2. the necessity to preserve a modicum of torpedoes for future, more favorable operations.[119] Force C was thus unarmed by the torpedo bombers. The former was part of a broader operation to escort Force B to strengthen the Malta garrison. Force B was comprised of four cruisers and four destroyers which in the next few days would contribute to sinking two Italian cargo ships (*Adriatico* and *Iridio Montanari*) further eroding the strength of Italian resupply operations headed to North Africa.

On the same day two S.84s from 282ª *Squadriglia* flown by *Capitano* Marino Marini and *Tenente* Saverio Mayer took off from Sicily to pursue a Royal Navy formation comprised of two cruisers and two destroyers that was spotted approximately 150 miles south east of Malta. Flying close to the coast of Cyrenaica it took the pilots almost two hours to locate their target because of the bad weather with heavy rains. At 1719 the two S.84s finally pressed home their attack. They headed in the direction of the largest cruiser and attacked flying northeast dropping their warheads in rapid succession from 1,000 and 1,200 meters out. In their post battle report the crews asserted that "one torpedo hit a 10,000 cruiser which moments later began to take in water and later sank."[120] As they flew over the enemy naval formation the enemy guns gave them a massive send-off that luckily for the crews made no hole in either plane.

On 1 December 1941 several enemy destroyers such as HMS *Jackal*, HMS *Jaguar* and HMS *Kipling* were spotted near the coast north of Tobruk while returning from a coastal operation to blockade Derna and Bardia when they were targeted by S.79s at 1218. These were piloted by *Capitano* Giulio Marini, S*ottotenente* Giuseppe Coci and *Sottotenente* Aligi Strani of 279ª *Squadriglia.* All three aircraft got within range and released their torpedoes from a very good position. Two of them did not hit the intended targets, while the third one did by damaging the 1,690-tons HMS *Jackal*, a J-class destroyer, to the point that she could not be utilized for five months. "A torpedo slammed into Jackal on the port side, opening the steering compartment to the sea and jamming the rudder port. She made Tobruk at 14 knots, steering by her

118 HMS Glenroy, Some Personal Experiences of CPO John Priscott-Shipwright Glenroy 1940-1942 <http://web.archive.org/web/20070630030940/glenroy.freeservers.com/custom2.html> (accessed 23 April 2021).

119 Francesco Mattesini, *Luci ed ombre*, p.142.

120 Ibid. p.152.

engines, and was five months under repair."[121] After the attack has the three aircraft flew over the enemy ships in order to disengage they were themselves targeted by strong anti-aircraft fire which damaged two of them. During their getaway there were further incidents dictated by the state of confusion caused by the torpedo attack. "After the action Jackal fired a shell to clear a 4.7-inch barrel, with Jaguar in the line of fire. The shell hit Jaguar's bridge and killed three men, including her captain, Lieutenant Commander J.F.W. Hines."[122] Despite the fact that *Capitano's* Marini aircraft was badly damaged with the loss of one fuel tank and one wheel, the pilot managed to desperately steer the plane back to base. While sustaining damage to two S.79s, all three landed safely back to base.

On 5 December three *Sparvieri* flown by *Capitano* Massimiliano Erasi of 284ª *Squadriglia,* who had assumed command of this newly formed unit on 7 November 1941, and *Tenente* Guglielmo Ranieri and *Sottotenente* Alfredo Pulzetti of 279ª *Squadriglia* during a reconnaissance sweep spotted a British naval convoy (TA 1) that had just sailed at 1800 from Tobruk and was bound to Alexandria. It comprised of the transport ships Chakdina and Kirkland escorted by two destroyers HMS *Farndale* and HMS *Eridge.* All three aircraft at first circled around the ships then swooped down and got within launching range of the convoy targeting the large transport ship which was carrying 600 men including 380 stretcher cases and 100 prisoners of war. *Capitano* Erasi released his torpedo ahead of the other two pilots. The British transport ship Chakdina was initially able to avoid getting hit by the first torpedo by zigzagging but was subsequently struck in the after hold by the second warhead launched by *Tenente* Ranieri at 2115. The 3,033-tons ship began to sink precipitously and took down with it two-thirds of the troops on board (370 British servicemen and 33 Italian prisoners of war). "The only surviving stretcher case recalled that the ship rolled after the torpedo exploded and the engine room crew rushed past him, trampling his fingers. He reached the deck just as the ship sank, hearing behind him a cry in an agony of terror from the trapped men below."[123] The surviving soldiers were rescued by the Royal Navy destroyer HMS *Ferndale. Tenente* Pulzetti, who still had his torpedo, observed the Chakdina sinking and decided to focus his attention on another target. A few minutes later he released his warhead against HMS *Ferndale* but missed it. Five German torpedo bombers from X *Fliegerkorps* also participated to the attack against the TA 1 convoy, but they all failed to hit a target.

Capitano Erasi on 10 December targeted HMS *Naiad* as the vessel had just shelled Italian positions near Derna. The operation was undertaken by the former along with another S.79 pilot from 278ª *Squadriglia Capitano* Mario Frongia. The combat action took place 35 miles north off Derna while HMS *Naiad* was steaming together with two destroyers: HMS *Griffin* and HMS *Hotspur* toward Alexandria. Both pilots were able to finally carry out the operation after flying over the enemy ships multiple times due to the extremely bad weather conditions which gravely limited their ability to locate their target. Despite receiving considerable enemy fire, the S.79s pressed on, attacking from the port bow. At 0920 *Capitano* Erasi's released the torpedo 1,000 meters out and barely missed the enemy ship. Meanwhile his flight companion *Capitano* Frongia failed to release his warhead due to the poor visibility. In the post battle report *Capitano* Erasi asserted that he did strike a cruiser but his optimistic assessment contradicted

121 Vincent P. O'Hara, *Six Victories*, p.84.
122 Ibid.
123 Vincent P. O'Hara, *Six Victories*, p.86.

the Royal Navy version of events that told a different story. That the evasive actions took by the ships caused the torpedo warhead to ultimately plunge into the sea.

First Battle of Sirte: Operations M41/M42

On the night between 13/14 December the Royal Navy dispatched elements of the Mediterranean Fleet (15th Division with three cruisers: HMS *Euryalus*, HMS *Naiad*, HMS *Galatea* and nine destroyers: HMS *Jervis*, HMS *Kimberley*, HMS *Kingston*, HMS *Napier*, HMS *Nizam*, HMS *Kipling*, HMS *Griffin*, HMS *Havock* and HMS *Hotspur*) to sea to pursue the Italian convoy M41. This was a critical convoy organized with haste and fury to aid the Italian and German troops under Rommel's command in North Africa involved in parrying the blow from the British armored attack of Operation Crusader. Rommel's troops were in desperate need of supplies after the heavy fighting that had raged for almost a month during the British counteroffensive. The Royal Navy thanks to Ultra intercept had been prewarned that the Italians aimed to launch a major convoy operation of eight transport ships escorted by battleships, and it aimed to engage it at sea. Once SIM reported that two large enemy formations were at sea, the RM, after suffering the loss of two merchantmen and the *Vittorio Veneto* torpedoed, ordered the convoy back to base. As a result on the afternoon of 14 December the 15th Division and four destroyers were ordered back to base in Alexandria and Gibraltar respectively. Meanwhile these Royal Navy ships had been shadowed throughout the day by both German and Italian reconnaissance planes which continued to report to *Superaereo* their position. Based on the intelligence provided several torpedo bomber formations were alerted and later dispatched in order to attack them. The first to be deployed on 14 December 1941 were the *Sparvieri* of *281ª Squadriglia/*41° *Gruppo* which took off from Gadurra airport at 1130. The aircraft flown by *Capitano* Cimicchi and *Tenenti* Luigi Rovelli and Giuseppe Cipelletti located an enemy naval force comprised of three cruisers (HMS *Naiad*, HMS *Galatea* and HMS *Euryalus*) and a number of smaller vessels such as corvettes as they were steaming just south of Crete. The three S.79s made several attempts to close in against the enemy formation but were prevented from doing so by the accurate fire of the British naval gunners which beat off all their attacks. As a result, the operation had to be aborted. In the post battle report the crews affirmed that they had been prevented from pressing forward with their attack because "of the deft and evasive maneuvers and the smokescreens put out by the cruisers."[124] In the afternoon eleven German dive bombers and torpedo bombers dispatched from Crete attacked the same enemy formation but due to the poor visibility were unable to inflict any damage. At midnight as the British Royal Navy ships were approaching Alexandria they were ambushed by a German submarine (U-577) which sank HMS *Galatea*.

On 16 December, the RM desperate to bring supplies to the *Panzerarmee Afrika* as soon as possible launched Operation M42 with the main convoy leaving Taranto and heading for Libya. The convoy was split into two sections: the first comprised the fast transport *Ankara* and two destroyers, while the second of the transport ships *Napoli*, *Monginevro* and *Pisani* escorted by six destroyers. The *Duilio* battleship and the cruisers *Montecuccoli*, *Muzio Attendolo* and *Duca d'Aosta*

124 Ibid., p.156

and three destroyers provided the main escort for the convoy. The latter was further supported by the battleship *Littorio* (Iachino's flagship), *Andrea Doria*, *Giulio Cesare*, the cruisers *Trento* and *Gorizia* and ten destroyers. According to *Comando Supremo* it was imperative that the RM by deploying its entire battlefleet to break the naval blockade imposed by Force K and the RAF based at Malta and the Mediterranean Fleet based at Alexandria as Rommel's army had to be reinforced at all costs. To achieve this end prior to the start of Operation M42 a large scale redeployment of aircraft was ordered by *Superaereo* that also involved the torpedo bomber units. *Comando Aeronautica dell'Egeo* took the precautionary measure to move to Benina airbase in Cyrenaica three S.79 from *Capitano* Buscaglia's 281ª *Squadriglia*/41° *Gruppo*, that stiffened the fleet along with the 279ª *Squadriglia* based near Tobruk and 284ª *Squadriglia* based in Derna. *Comando Aeronautica della Sicilia* readied its 278ª *Squadriglia* with five aerial torpedoes, while the Sicilian airbases were also strengthened by the arrival from Sardinia of the 130° *Gruppo* with five S.79s and by six S.84 from 36° *Stormo*. The Italian units were further reinforced by several units from the *Luftwaffe's II Fliegerkorps* which were transferred to Italian airbases. The latter in addition to X *Fliegerkorps* based in Greece and with *Fliegerfuhrer Afrika* would also be deployed in this largescale Axis operation whose overall objective was to take back control of the Central Mediterranean and ensure that the *Panzerarmee Afrika* could once again go on the offensive on the heels of the British Operation Crusader. In addition, on 28 November 1941, *Feldmarschall* Albert Kesselring was appointed *Wehrmacht* Commander-in-Chief South (Oberbefehlshaber Sud) and was transferred to Italy along with his *Luftflotte 2* staff, further reinforcing Germany's commitment to the Mediterranean theatre. The Fuehrer ordered *Fliegerkorps* II, commanded by General Bruno Loerzer, to withdraw from the Eastern front and combined with *Fliegerkorps* X to form the *Luftflotte 2*. The reorganized *Luftwaffe* force in the Mediterranean comprised three bomber squadrons, two dive bomber groups, three fighter groups, plus reconnaissance aircraft and anti-aircraft units. Kesselring's main objective was the elimination of Malta by air attack. Neutralization of the island meant the securing of the Sicilian region for Axis convoys and heavy interference with British east-west maritime traffic. The *Luftwaffe* main force was mainly comprised of two aircraft: Junker 88 (Ju.88) bombers that were conventional glide bombers, twin engine monoplanes with a maximum speed of 295 mph and a bombload of 2,200 lbs. The Stukas, Ju.87 were dive bombers. They were single engine monoplanes with a top speed of 245 mph, and a bombload of 1,100 lbs.

The Italian convoy sailed from Taranto at 1400 on 16 December and it deployed the vast majority of the Italian battlefleet as its escort to ensure its safe passage. Meanwhile the Italians were totally unaware that the evening before, the Royal Navy had dispatched the tanker Breconshire from Alexandria to Malta, escorted by two cruisers (HMS *Naiad* and HMS *Euryalus*, the smaller cruiser HMS *Carlisle* and eight destroyers from the 14th Flotilla (HMS *Jervis*, HMS *Kimberley*, HMS *Kingston*, HMS *Kipling*, HMS *Havock*, HMS *Hasty*, HMS *Decoy* and HMS *Nizan*). On 17 December this force was joined by two light cruisers from Force K (HMS *Aurora* and HMS *Penelope*) along with six destroyers (HMS *Lance*, HMS *Lively*, HMS *Sikh*, HMS *Maori* and HMS *Legion)* and the Isaac Sweers. This part of a British attempt to reinforce Malta. However, these large scale movements were soon detected by Axis reconnaissance aircraft and bomber and torpedo bomber attacks soon followed. This was in accordance with the directives of *Comando Supremo* for major aerial/naval engagements which required the air forces to degrade the strength of the enemy battlefleet prior to the head to head showdown with the fleet.

Accordingly, on 17 December at 1300 three S.79s from 281ª *Squadriglia* took flight from Benina airbase to press home an attack against the Breconshire. The aircraft were flown by *Capitano* Buscaglia, *Tenente* Faggioni and *Sottotenente* Forzinetti. Approximately an hour and a half later the three pilots spotted the enemy formation 150 miles north of Benghazi. The weather was clear and the visibility was excellent to the point that *Capitano* Buscaglia initially held back to await a more opportune time to attack the enemy. Meanwhile, the enemy's anti-aircraft fire opened up a thunderous barrage. In contrast *Sottotenente* Forzinetti did not hold back and decided to conduct a lone wolf attack against the convoy. He quickly brought down his plane, skimmed the waters and headed decisively in the direction of the Breconshire, which had been initially mistakenly identified by the pilots as an aircraft carrier. He was able to barely pass through the gun screen provided by the destroyers when his plane was shot to pieces and reduced to a ball of smoke and fire which quickly fell into the water. The other two aircraft soon followed up Forzinetti's action and lined up against a cruiser. But once again the defensive fire was so accurate and consistent that one torpedo bomber misfired by barely missing HMS *Penelope*, while the other did not even get to release his warhead. In their post battle report the two pilots asserted that one of their warhead had sunk the intended cruiser, but their optimistic view did not reflect the reality on the ground. The Royal Navy post battle report correctly indicated that its ships had sustained no damage. *Sottotenente* Aldo Forzinetti[125] was posthumously awarded a gold medal of military honor with the following motivation: "An outstanding torpedo bomber pilot who had already completed a number of glorious actions, in an action of supreme dedication to his Fatherland, he attacked head on and in broad daylight an enemy naval unit. With the precise intent to penetrate the naval barrage in order to strike at the largest cruiser he maneuvered the plane so he could hurl the warhead at the target. Despite the fact that his aircraft had already been hit, he pressed home the attack firing his weapon. Shortly thereafter his plane turned into a ball of fire and crashed into the sea ..."[126]

Up next were fourteen standard German bombers Ju.88/1./LG.1 which had taken off from Crete but could not harm the enemy formation which had been by then spotted 120 miles north of Benghazi. They were followed by six He.111 torpedo bombers of which four dropped the warheads but none of them struck the intended targets. These were part of a newly trained German unit headquartered in Grosseto, Italy (II/KSG.26). Most of them were 'green' pilots that had just arrived in Sicily overnight. At 1700 the air attacks against the Royal Navy continued. This time they were brought forward by seventeen Ju.88 bombers of the I./L.G.1 and three S.79s from 279ª *Squadriglia* (*Capitano* Giulio Marini, *Tenenti* Guglielmo Ranieri and Mario Fronza), while two more had to turn back due to engine trouble. The first formation to pounce was the German one. All the aircraft dove down and dropped their load but no

125 Aldo Forzinetti was born in Milan on 8 December 1914, but resided in Varese. He earned a law degree and a military pilot license in 1937 as sottotenente. In 1940 he was enlisted and opted to join the aerosiluranti units. During his active service he fought primarily in the Aegean Sea. After his death he was promoted to Tenente and the University of Pavia awarded him a degree ad honorem in political science. After the Second World War his hometown dedicated a Piazza in his name where a small tombstone still stands today which reads: "In questo luogo donato per il bene culturale da Virginia Masserizzi Forzinetti mi ricordo dei figli caduti per la patria ten. pilota Aldo Forzinetti 8-12-14- 17-12-1941 med. d'oro ten. di vascello Luigi Forzinetti 7-12-1909, 4-4-1940 i cittadini a perenne memoria."

126 Medaglie D'oro <https://www.quirinale.it/onorificenze/insigniti/13248> (accessed on 1 March 2021).

hits were made. Meanwhile one German bomber was shot down by the anti-aircraft gunners. At 1755 the torpedo bombers went into action barely missing HMS *Naiad* and HMS *Sikh*. The torpedo bomber intervention caused considerable disarray as some of the enemy ships to avoid the torpedoes had to maneuver wildly. This attack happened at the same time that a naval confrontation between the two sides was about to unfold. In fact, Admiral Philip Vian was aware since 16 December of the Italian convoy, thanks to the information coming from Ultra, and his plan all along was to attack it. Approximately at 1740 *Littorio* spotted the enemy cruisers and destroyers approaching from the east. Based on this sighting, which confirmed what the reconnaissance aircraft had reported in the morning, *Ammiraglio* Iachino gave the order to meet the enemy formation, to then close distances and open fire. After the Italian ships were at a distance of 32,000 meters from the enemy, *Littorio* was the first to open fire with its 15 inch guns followed by the *Andrea Doria*, *Trento* and *Gorizia*. Since the Royal Navy cruisers and destroyers were outranged and outgunned by the larger Italian battleships they attempted a diversionary action by steaming north and laying smoke screens. This did enough to ensure that no enemy naval fire landed on the ships. The only harm sustained was when fragments of a 203 mm shell damaged the destroyer HMS *Kipling*. A few minutes later both formations withdrew. The next day the Italian convoy successfully arrived at Tripoli "despite the best British attempts to intercept them"[127], while a group of light cruisers and destroyers from Force K ran into a minefield. A light cruiser and one destroyer sank. On 18 December there were further torpedo bomber attacks on the British fleet after an Italian reconnaissance plane spotted Force K 65 miles to the south of Malta. *Comando Aeronautica della Sicilia* soon alerted Castelvetrano and Comiso airbases that dispatched two S.79s from 278ª *Squadriglia* and three S.84s from 259ª *Squadriglia* to pursue the convoy. Immediately, a S.79 flown by *Sottotenente* Vittorio Moretti was forced to turn back given the grave weather conditions with torrential like rainfalls. Meanwhile, the other S.79 of pilot *Tenente* Gaetano Bucceri, who had departed twenty minutes earlier, was able to locate and attack the target at 1115 by launching his warhead at a distance of 800 meters against a destroyer. The torpedo narrowly missed. The plane, attracting considerable enemy fire, was damaged as it made its escape. Meanwhile, the attacks continued. The S.84s of 259ª *Squadriglia* with *Maggiore* Goffredo Gastaldi, and *Tenenti* Mario Paccarie and Bernardo Braghieri spotted the convoy at 1120. But they were intercepted 12 miles out from the Royal Navy ships by Hurricanes from No. 185 Squadron that had taken off from Malta to protect the convoy. Both S.84s were dispatched. *Maggiore* Gastaldi's plane was hit several times and it was downed. The *Maggiore* would be awarded a gold medal of military valor posthumously. Meanwhile, *Tenente* Paccarie's plane was also subjected to heavy fire but it ultimately made it safely back to base despite carrying on board a dead crew member and a severely wounded one. Operation M42, conducted according to the new all arms guidelines issued by *Comando Supremo*, achieved its stated purpose of bringing supplies to North Africa. As far as the torpedo bombers were concerned, they had carried out their prescribed combat mission although the near misses had precluded any large-scale success against Force K. Indeed, the latter, was still free to roam the Mediterranean in search of enemy convoys. Meanwhile the torpedo bomber units had been drained of precious resources losing two planes and several warheads.

127 Mark E Stille, *Italian Battleships of World War Two*, p.39.

On 28 December 1941 the torpedo bomber *Squadriglie* would gain another gold medal to their name when *Tenente* Luigi's Rovelli's[128] S.79 clashed with a British Martlet flown by Lt. Royston Griffin. The dogfight that took place over a British convoy south of Crete was deadly for both contenders. A sharp flurry of machine gun fire damaged the *Sparviero* which began to lose altitude and then crashed down into the sea killing all crew members. But seconds just before being downed, the S.79's machine gunner had returned fire in a last ditch attempt and killed the RAF pilot whose plane also crashed into the water. Tenente Rovelli's plane was part of a squad of four S.79s from 281ª *Squadriglia* that had taken off after an Italian reconnaissance plane had spotted British convoy ME8 which had sailed from Malta and was heading to Alexandria. It comprised two cruisers: HMS *Ajax*, HMS *Dido* and six destroyers escorting four merchant ships (*Clan Ferguson, Sidney Star, Ajax* and *City of Calcutta*). It was spotted south of Crete by the torpedo bombers which soon swooped in to press forward their attack. The pilots involved were *Capitano* Buscaglia and *Tenenti* Cimilli, Rovelli and Cipolletti. Three out of four fired their torpedoes but none hit a target mainly due to the strong barrage of fire by the Royal Navy. This was the last operation of note of the torpedo bomber units in 1941

The second year of the conflict was one were the *Sparvieri* units achieved considerable results such as torpedoing HMS *Nelson*. In turn losses had been fairly high and even the newer S.84s had suffered a high number of lost and heavily damaged aircraft.[129] The record of the torpedo bombers was impressive especially compared to the achievements of the standard bomber units of the RA or to the number of damaged ships by the RM. The S.79s however, together with the combined force of the RM and RA and even with the deployments of significant elements of the *Luftwaffe*, had not been able to stop the vital enemy convoys headed to Malta or Alexandria. Malta despite the almost daily bombing operations and the attempts to starve it of supplies by interfering with its convoys had not been subdued. Similarly, the Axis forces had not been able to significantly slow down the buildup of Commonwealth forces in North Africa. Operation Crusader, launched on the tail end of 1941, achieved a significant British victory against Rommel's forces in North Africa pushing them back significantly. Part of the success was the Royal Navy's relevant buildup of tanks and supplies prior to the start of the land based operation. On 15 November 1941 *Cavallero* forced Pricolo to resign and accusing the RA Chief of Staff of not providing enough fighter escort support to Italian convoys headed to North Africa and of not being able to further influence an increase of torpedo production and the monthly output of S.79s. With regards to shipping in October 1941 a total of 64,954-tons of supply were lost at sea due to enemy attacks, while in November 33,471-tons were lost. The average monthly tonnage sunk by the British during the second half of 1941 was much greater that what it had been over the first six months of the year, a result attributable to many causes, one of which was the deployment of a larger air striking force. Moreover, there had been a lull in

128 Luigi Rovelli was born in Rodi Garganico (Foggia) on 25 April 1915. In 1936 he enrolled in Regia Aeronautica where he pursued a pilot license and entered the service academy in Caserta. He graduated from the Sparviero course as a sottotenente. In September 1940 he was assigned to the 14º Stormo Bombardamento Terrestre where he saw active service in North Africa and Greece as a standard bomber pilot. In August 1941 he volunteered to the aerosiluranti specialty and received a gold medal of military valor after his death. In Rodi Garganico, the town of his birth, a public school was named after him along with a piazza. To this day the towns of Foggia, Manfredonia, and San Nicandro Garganico have streets named after Tenente Luigi Rovelli.

129 Gianni Rocca, *I disperati*, p.134.

the Axis air attacks on Malta which had allowed greater freedom of action for the RAF. Pricolo had privileged bombing operations over Malta rather than increasing the cooperation with the RM. As Brian Sullivan asserts "In particular, the air chief neglected the aerial escort of convoys to Libya, which were particularly hard pressed by British attacks in the fall of 1941."[130] The real issue, however, was that the force was not large enough for the many tasks that it was called out to do. Here there was not much Pricolo could do given the modest output of the Italian aviation industry and the delays experienced with the introduction of Macchi C.202 *Folgore*. Between 1940 and '41 there was an uptick in aircraft production which likely was the result of some of Pricolo's reforms. But the slight uptick was not enough to replenish out of service, retired or lost aircraft. As Sullivan asserts: "Total production from Italy's entry in the war through March 1941 totaled some 3,100 planes. Adding the results of accidents suffered in training or non-combat operations to the numbers cited earlier, the *Regia Aeronautica* lost about 3,500 aircraft during the same period."[131] With regard to the torpedo bombers *Generale* Pricolo's initiatives had left their mark and his record was nevertheless impressive. He was the first air force chief that had taken the bull by the horn by placing an order for warheads from Whitehead and also by constituting the first torpedo bomber unit. Therefore, in contrast to his predecessors he was an innovator being the first Chief of Staff to establish torpedo bomber units within the RA. Under his watch the torpedo bomber units had performed well, much better than the standard bombing units. The challenge going forward was to update the aircraft technology by bringing into service a torpedo bomber that could carry one heavier or smaller multiple loads while improving upon the speed of the S.79. Another was the introduction of an improved medium bomber and of a heavy bomber.

Generale Rino Corso Fougier was nominated as Pricolo's replacement. One of the reasons why he was selected was because he had previously worked closely with Kesselring during the Battle of Britain. His immediate concern was how to balance the limited resources of the air force corps in relation to its numerous theatres of operation. Possibly the most important priority was to influence the production of the *Macchi* fighter aircraft with the German DB-601A-1 engine so that output could be significantly increased. Under Pricolo new *Reggiane* Re.2001 and *Macchi* C.202 fighters had made their debut, but only in very limited numbers. His successor's role was to guarantee a steady output of these new fighter aircraft in the coming months. Second, he was to seek a solution to the failure of the S.84 torpedo bomber. Third he was to continue his predecessor's work of reducing the overall number of standard bomber units and transforming some of them into torpedo bomber units. On 24 November 1941 *Generale* Fougier at a meeting of the *Commissione per l'aeronautica* (aviation committee), which comprised all technical personnel of RA and had been set up in 1940 to select new aircraft production, argued that lacking a state of the art standard bomber, the service should reduce the sixteen standard bomber *Stormi* to nine and with the personnel of the seven to be disbanded he ordered the creation of three torpedo bomber *Stormi*, two *Stormi* 'da combattimento" and two for nighttime operations. This move would have allowed the constitution of at least seven new *Squadriglie* for torpedo bomber operations, three of which equipped with S.84 aircraft, three with S.79 aircraft which was nonetheless defined as an "obsolete model" and possibly one equipped with

130 Brian Sullivan, "Downfall of the Regia Aeronautica", in Robin Higham (ed.), *Why Air Forces Fail* (Lexington, Kentucky: University Press of Kentucky, 2006), p.164.
131 Ibid., p.165.

Caproni C.314 aircraft. The latter was an "aircraft that was a stop gap solution because while it had limited endurance/autonomy it nevertheless had the advantage of being highly maneuverable." Lastly, Fougier pointed out that the need for "a new torpedo bomber aircraft was keenly felt. One that was designed specifically for torpedo bomber operations, with great speed, high maneuverability, and great endurance."[132] Meanwhile, with regards to the S.84 it was stated that "compared to the S.79, the S.84 had poorer autonomy and reduced maneuverability and does not represent a sensible improvement."[133]

Summary and Conclusions

1. The second year of Italy's war (1941) was a banner year for the torpedo bomber units. In his book on the S.79 Sparviero aviation historian Marco Mattioli states that 1941 was when the torpedo bombers came of age by conducting a record number of operations by mostly experienced crews. Despite their successes the RA was faced with multiple challenges stemming from being tasked to operate in too many theatres with modest resources. Despite suffering huge losses during Operation Compass and the Greek campaign, the air service slowly replenished some of the losses during the course of the year. The torpedo bomber units, due to their effectiveness over standard bombing units, were significantly expanded with the constitution of fourteen additional *Squadriglie.*
2. Another positive aspect of the torpedo bomber campaign in 1941 was the adoption of more refined tactics such as the group attack method which was allowed by the expansion of the force with newly dedicated crews and aircraft. This tactic mirrored what the RAF had done at Taranto in 1940 and what the Japanese would do at Pearl Harbor in December 1941. These coordinated attacks were more lethal due to a combination of striking platforms (bombers, torpedo bombers, fighters and special weapons) as well as the execution of synchronized strikes hitting an enemy convoy at once from multiple directions.
3. Despite the positive changes that occurred in 1941 there were two main issues that continued to plague the torpedo bombers units. First, the slow production of aerial warheads meant that during some of the attacks the pilots had to be extra cautious and only release the torpedo when the changes of a strike were very high. This strategy likely led to some missed opportunities. Second, overall torpedo bomber units effectiveness remained low. For example during Operation Halberd only 51% of the Sardinian force could be deployed against the enemy while the lack of warheads, untrained crews and a few aircraft out of service grounded more than half of the force.
4. The other major issue was that the introduction of the S.84 had not solved the problem of replacing the S.79 with an improved torpedo bomber. Innovation of torpedo bomber technology stalled. This would be keenly felt in 1942 when the combination of up gunned Royal Navy defenses together with the introduction of improved fighters by the RAF would represent more than a match for the S.79s.

132 Cited in: Andrea Curami, "Piani e progetti dell'aeronautica italiana 1939-1943 Stato maggiore e industrie", *Italia Contemporanea*, No. 187, June 1992.
133 Ibid.

5. In the early part of the year Malta had been subdued thanks also to the intervention of the *Luftwaffe*. In the second half of 1941, with elements of the *Luftwaffe* redeployed to the Eastern Mediterranean Malta regained strength and its impact on the convoy war increased.
6. Despite the loss of Crete, Britain's influence on the Mediterranean convoy war was growing through both the deployment of destroyers and submarines to attack Axis convoy ships and the increasing effectiveness of the Royal Navy anti-aircraft defense against Italian fighters and bombers. Between June and November 1941, for example, ships, submarines, and aircraft from Malta were responsible for damaging or sinking 197,500 tons of Italian shipping headed to North Africa. In November alone the Italians had lost 77 percent of their cargo destined to North Africa.[134]
7. The great losses at sea suffered by Axis convoy operations in the autumn of 1941 compelled the *Luftwaffe* to once again transfer some of its forces to Sicily between the end of 1941 and early 1942. The German units would significantly contribute in the turning of the tide in 1942.
8. Together with reinforcements from the Germans in December 1941 a series of events late in the year began to shift the balance of power in the Mediterranean toward the Axis. A major Axis convoy (M42) got through to North Africa. Then the Royal Navy suffered a number of losses to its Mediterranean Fleet. These events would open a new scenario in the convoy war in the Mediterranean.

134 John Gooch, *Mussolini's War*, p.297.

Sparrohawk. The Savoia-Marchetti S.79 Sparviero (Italian for "Sparrowhawk") was a three-engined Italian medium bomber or torpedo bomber with a wood-and-metal structure. (Ufficio Storico)

HMS *Malines* listing after torpedo strike. (Ufficio Storico)

S.79 in action. US intelligence reports on Axis torpedo squadrons, for example, singled out the S.79 as one of the most powerful aircraft deployed by the Regia Aeronautica and noted that its pilots had the highest morale of any unit in the Italian military. Their effectiveness against enemy ships was recognized even by the better-equipped Luftwaffe, which in 1941 had dispatched bomber pilots to Italy for instructions in torpedo tactics. (Ufficio Storico)

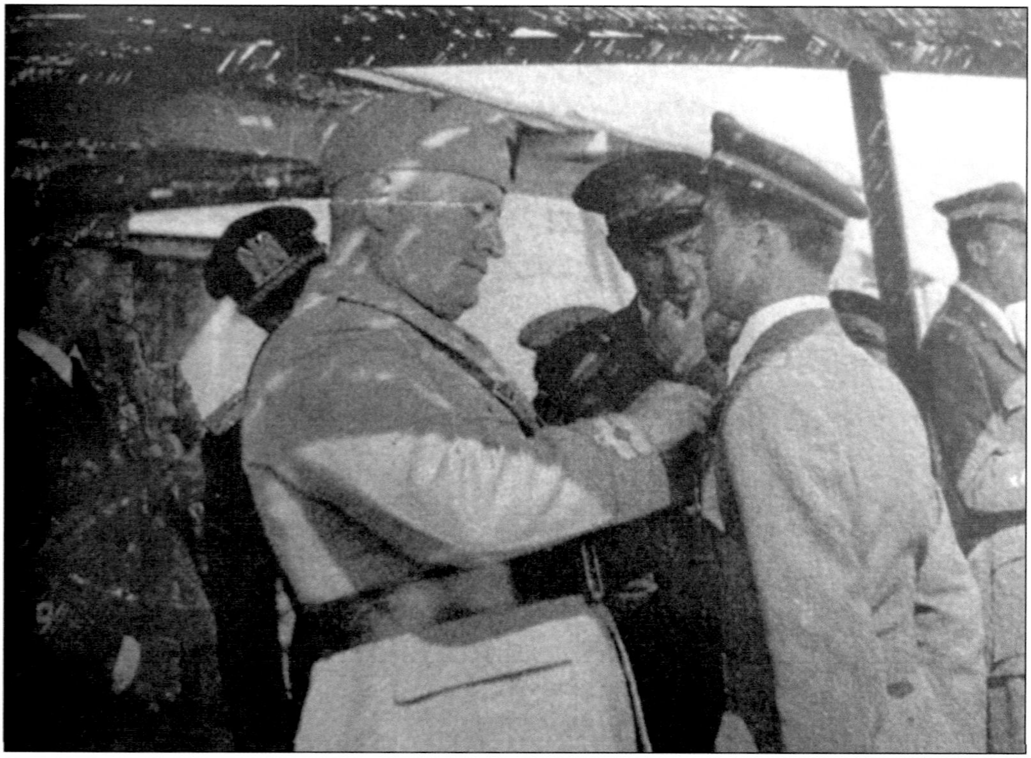

Mussolini awards a medal to *Tenente* Martino Aichner after the S.79 pilot torpedoed HMS Bedouin. (Ufficio Storico)

Party secretary speaks to S.79 pilots with Buscaglia on the right. (Ufficio Storico)

Torpedo wooden fins used to improve torpedo trajectory upon plunging into the water. (Ufficio Storico)

Rear view of S.79. (Ufficio Storico)

Front view of torpedo bomber. The S.79 was an outstanding aircraft and was certainly the best-known Italian aircraft of World War II. It was easily recognizable due to its distinctive fuselage dorsal "hump", and was well liked by its crews who nicknamed it Gobbo Maledetto ("damned hunchback"). (Ufficio Storico)

Torpedo service specialist making last minute preparations before the flight. Originally developed as a commercial airliner, the S.79 Sparviero (Sparrowhawk) became one of the most formidable weapons of Italy's air force, the Regia Aeronautica, during World War II. The original 1936 prototype was based on three 610-hp Piaggio radial engines and could accommodate eight passengers. With war clouds looming, the airplane was converted into a medium bomber. (Ufficio Storico)

Maggiore Carlo Emanuele Buscaglia at his desk. (Ufficio Storico)

Torpedo bomber training exercise. (Ufficio Storico)

Ettore Muti, one of Italy's most decorated pilots. (Ufficio Storico)

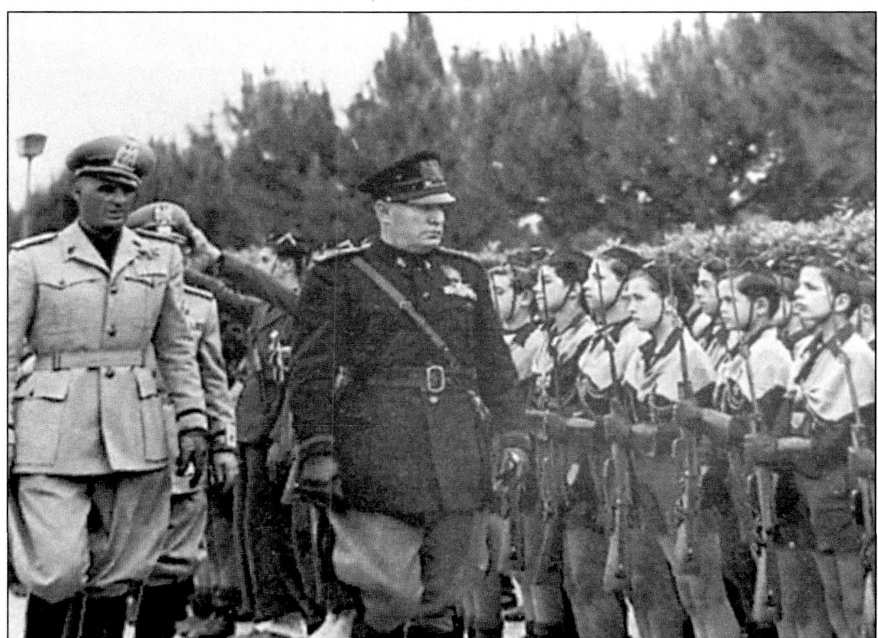

Il Duce and Ettore Muti at a party parade. (Ufficio Storico)

Ettore Muti and Galeazzo Ciano. Muti was one of Italy's most decorated pilots boasting several silver medals, one Iron Cross Second Class and one gold medal of Military Valor obtained during the Spanish Civil War. (Ufficio Storico)

S.79 torpedo bomber. (Ufficio Storico)

HMS *Indomitable* torpedoed by S.79 during Operation Husky. (Ufficio Storico)

28 March 1943 the 20th anniversary of the founding of Regia Aeronautica is being celebrated with a visit by King Vittorio Emanuele III to the airport of Furbara near Rome. (Ufficio Storico)

Torpedo bomber pilots.

Torpedo bomber pilots greeted at Pisa airport after Operation Pedestal. (Ufficio storico)

He.111 Torpedo bomber armed with two LT F5b torpedoes. (Ufficio Storico)

Torpedo bomber pilots. (Ufficio Storico)

HMS *Liverpool*. (Ufficio Storico)

S.79 in action.

Torpedo bombers readied for action. (Ufficio Storico)

Torpedo bombers readied for action. (Ufficio storico)

Mussolini at an air force awards ceremony. (Ufficio Storico)

HMS *Aircrest* explodes after the torpedo strike. (Ufficio Storico)

Torpedo bomber in action. (Ufficio Storico)

Torpedo bomber squads. (Ufficio Storico)

Torpedo bomber. (Ufficio Storico)

S.79 of Capitano Marino Marini heavily damaged after the combat action of 1 December 1941. (Ufficio Storico)

HMS *Glenroy* which on 23 November 1941 was torpedoed by S.79 Tenente Rovelli. (Ufficio Storico)

The 36 Stormo personnel present the unit's battleflag. (Ufficio Storico)

S.79 burning in the water during a combat action. (Ufficio Storico)

Photo 35: Helmut Seidl the commander of 36 Stormo who would die along with his crew after torpedoing HMS *Nelson*. (Ufficio Storico)

Close up view of S.79. (Ufficio Storico)

Close up view torpedo. The S.79 plane was retrofitted with an offset rack under the fuselage so that it could carry a 450mm Whitehead torpedo. S.79 ready for takeoff with the torpedo clearly visible. The SI torpedo differed from the Whitehead in length only, being 5.25 m (17.22 ft) long (Ufficio Storico)

Buscaglia and his crew. (Ufficio Storico)

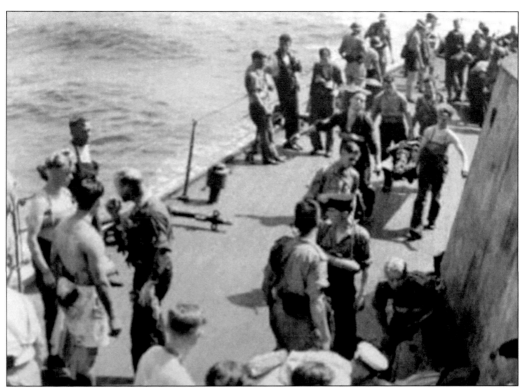

HMS *Liverpool* sailors being treated after torpedo strike. (Ufficio Storico)

British ship after receiving torpedo hit. (Ufficio storico)

Torpedo Bomber pilots. Cimicchi second to right, Buscaglia on the left. (Ufficio Storico)

Buscaglia and his crew. (Ufficio Storico)

Capitano Massimiliano Erasi. (Ufficio Storico)

Close up view of S.79. (Ufficio storico)

Mussolini's plane lands in Bologna airport. (Ufficio Storico)

Mussolini tours the newly built airbase of 36 Stormo Borgo Panigale in 1936 (Bologna). (Ufficio Storico)

Mussolini tours the newly built airbase of 36 Stormo Borgo Panigale in 1936 (Bologna). (Ufficio Storico)

Mussolini tours the newly built airbase of 36 Stormo Borgo Panigale in 1936 (Bologna). (Ufficio Storico)

Mussolini tours the newly built airbase of 36 Stormo Borgo Panigale in 1936 (Bologna). (Ufficio Storico)

Mussolini tours the newly built airbase of 36 Stormo Borgo Panigale in 1936 (Bologna). (Ufficio Storico)

S.79 pilots award ceremony. (Ufficio Storico)

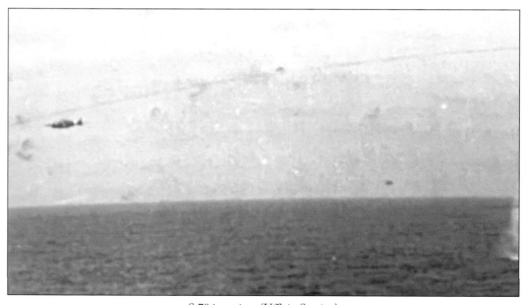

S.79 in action. (Ufficio Storico)

Francesco Baracca in front of his fighter plane. (Ufficio Storico)

HMS *Glasgow*. (Ufficio Storico)

Gabriele D'Annunzio delivers the funeral oration for Francesco Baracca. (Ufficio Storico)

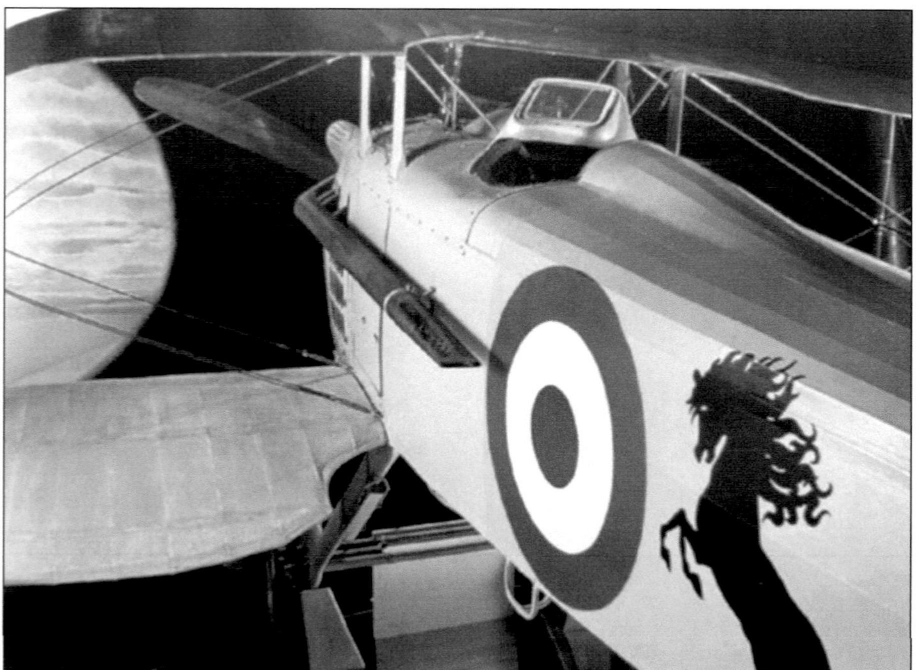

Restored Francesco Baracca plane with his personal emblem. (Author Photo)

Italian ace Francesco Baracca. (Ufficio Storico)

Corriere della Sera illustration of torpedo bomber attack. (Ufficio Storico)

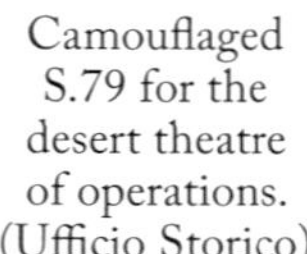

Camouflaged S.79 for the desert theatre of operations. (Ufficio Storico)

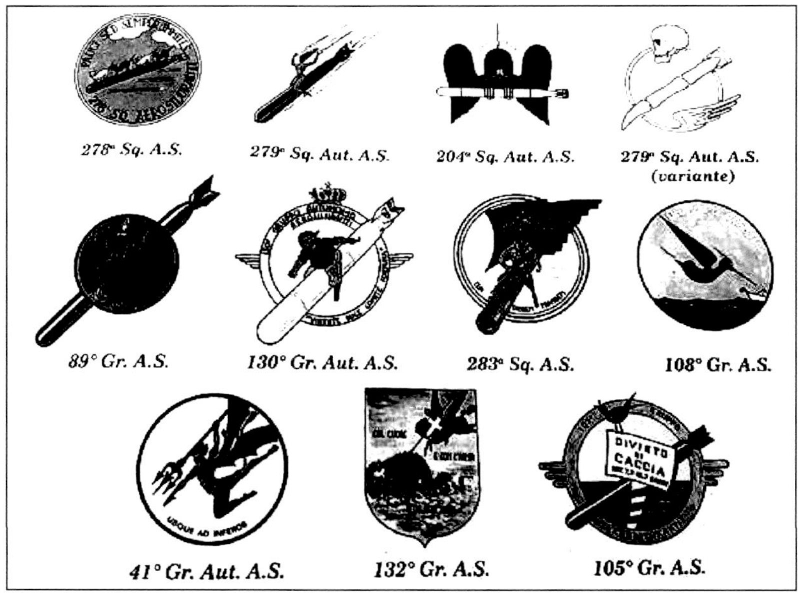

Torpedo bomber unit symbols and emblems. (Ufficio Storico)

British naval base Suda Bay. (Ufficio Storico)

HMS *Kent*. (Ufficio Storico)

Downed S.79. (Ufficio Storico)

6

1942 – The Pendulum Swings Twice

Overall Military Situation

At the beginning of 1942 the situation in the Mediterranean became more favorable for the Axis, although the potential for a future American intervention in the theatre did not bode well for both Germany and Italy in the long run. The Mediterranean Fleet, which already no longer had aircraft carriers, was now also without battleships, due to the losses sustained in the last months of 1941. Force K ran into a mine barrage on 17 December after which it sustained losses. Moreover, the attack suffered in port on 19 December 1941 in Alexandria, by three Italian assault vehicles (slow-running torpedoes or SLC; also known as "pigs"), had deprived the Mediterranean Fleet of both battleships (HMS *Queen Elizabeth* and HMS *Valiant)* after the other (HMS *Barham*) had been sunk the previous month by a German submarine.

Mainly because of these losses, the Axis was ascendant in the Central Mediterranean. Thanks to the combined effort of the *Luftwaffe* and the RA the island of Malta would be kept under a continuous siege until mid-1942 with almost weekly if not daily bombing missions which hampered the island's naval and aerial bases to the point that some of the Royal Navy small crafts and motorboats had to be relocated to more secure bases.

These factors combined so that the RM had achieved a greater control of the central-eastern Mediterranean with positive repercussions on maritime transport and operations in North Africa. Between January and May 1942 the RM brought to North Africa 409,551 tons of supplies losing only 4.3 percent.[1] This enabled Rommel to launch two successive offensives (January-February and May-July) and arrive at the gates of Alexandria threatening the position of the British army in the Middle East and placing the much depleted Mediterranean Fleet in serious danger.

But once Tobruk had been seized in June 1942 by the *Panzerarmee Afrika* the logical conclusion would have been to capture Malta as had been previously agreed by the Axis powers under the plan of Operation Venezia. The plan envisioned the capture of Tobruk by Rommel's army, followed by the invasion of Malta and finally, the continuation of the offensive in Egypt by the forces under the command of General Rommel with the ultimate objective being the capture of Alexandria and the Suez Canal. The most favorable moment for the invasion of Malta was

1 Ibid., p.299.

probably after the seizure of Tobruk in late June or July 1942. The command of Operation Hercules had been left to the Italian *Comando Supremo*, who was also in charge of training and arming the troops that were to take part in the airborne and seaborne invasion of the island.[2] The German High Command had hesitations about the plan, although Kesselring and Kurt Student, the head of the German paratroopers and the bulk of the *Kriegsmarine* considered the takeover of Malta as the key to turn the tide of the Mediterranean campaign toward the Axis side. Rommel finally brought the debate to an end by killing Operation Hercules arguing that the conquest of Tobruk had enabled him to reach the Nile in a single offensive. The stalemate that ensued in North Africa in September after Rommel's troops could not break the British/Commonwealth defenses would give the advantage to the British army, meanwhile the pressure on Malta lessened and once again the *Panzerarmee Afrika* was in trouble because of a lack of fuel and tanks and also because of its position at El Alamein which was quite distant from Axis logistic bases and ports. Cairo was never reached and Malta recovered its strength. The decisive battle of October/November 1942 in North Africa gave the Allies the opportunity to re-take the lead.

The RA in 1942

The RA under the new Chief of Staff had a number of priorities in 1942 dictated by *Comando Supremo*'s desire to curtail British shipping operations in the Mediterranean, starve Malta into submission and provide an advanced fighter and bomber force to aid Rommel's advance in North Africa. British shipping operations were to be interfered with the introduction of a new line of fighters and with improved torpedo bomber tactics. Beginning in late 1941 the *Macchi* C.202 fighter was introduced into service slowly to replace obsolete fighters. In 1942 approximately 40 fighters were coming out of the production line per month. In addition, in 1942 the RA counted on the introduction of the *Macchi* C.205 *Veltro* which along with the *Reggiane* Re.2005 and Fiat G.55, which comprised the Serie 5 of Italian fighters built around the powerful Daimler-Benz DB 605 engine. Indeed the *Veltro* would prove to be extremely effective, destroying a large number of Allied fighters and bombers. Fighter ace Adriano Visconti, for example, achieved 11 of his 26 credited victories with the *Veltro*, while *Maggiore* Luigi Gorrini managed to shoot down 14 enemy aircraft with his C.205. Unfortunately for the RA the production of the *Serie 5* aircraft proved to be excruciatingly slow, but these aircraft would breathe new life into an air force service that faced the air forces of the world's most advanced industrialized national states. With regards to the torpedo bombers *Generale* Fougier oversaw the largest fleet since Italy had entered the war and this force now made possible the new advanced tactics as practiced by the Japanese and the British Fleet Air Arm. Large deployments of torpedo bombers were to press forward an 'anvil and hammer attack,' or an attack from dual flanks of an enemy convoy to ensure one or more hits on the target. Improved fighter performance together with enhanced

2 A number of different plans were considered by Comando Supremo, including one submitted by the Japanese, who had experience at amphibious operations. An interesting question is whether there were any exchanges by the Imperial Japanese Navy and the *Regia Aeronautica* on the latest Japanese torpedo bomber tactics or technology. An interesting question to which the research for this book in Italian archives found no evidence.

torpedo bomber tactics were considered the two main elements to achieve a greater effectiveness in the anti-shipping war.

In order to purse the second objective, to starve Malta into submission, the RA counted on two factors. First an enhanced collaboration with the Germans and second the introduction of more powerful bombers such as the Cant.Z.1018 *Leone* II which after several modifications was to make its combat debut in 1942. The RA relied heavily on this medium bomber with a bomb load capacity of 3,306 lbs. (1,500 kg), although production difficulties would slow its introduction.

The third objective, aiding Rommel's advance in North Africa, was to be met by the introduction of large quantities of *Macchi* C.202 and the *Serie 5* fighters which were considered to offer more than a match to the most advanced British fighters such as the Submarine Spitfire Mk IX. Specifically with regards to the torpedo since the RA had not been able to introduce a suitable, new aircraft for the combat units, its planners sought to introduce improvements at the margins. The S.79bis, for example, was introduced in mid-1942 offering a system that improved temporarily the speed of the aircraft by 50 km/h and new Alfa Romeo 128 engines. The first system was useful when the pilot disengaged from a combat action and had to fly at maximum speed above the enemy battleships, while the new engines made the bis version faster than the standard S.79. With the S.84 being almost dead on arrival as a torpedo bomber, RA planners also evaluated the Cant Z.1007bis *Alcione* for the torpedo bomber units. The plane had a few good features mainly a top speed of 290 mph (reduced by almost 50 miles per hour while carrying torpedoes or bombs) and it could carry two Whitehead torpedoes without an excessive loss of speed as the S.79. In addition, it had a more effective rate of climb with respect to the S.79 making it a potentially good torpedo bomber as one of the necessities of the job was to get out quickly of the combat zone after the launch had been made. Despite these positive features the plane also had drawbacks such as the same defensive armament of the S.79 and its part wood construction which made it vulnerable to enemy fire. It appears one Cant Z.1007bis was converted to the torpedo bomber role but RA planners ultimately did not purse the constitution of a *Squadriglia* or *Gruppo* entirely made up by this type of aircraft. As naval historian Francesco Mattesini asserts: "Since our modest aeronautical industry was not able to build a new aircraft from scratch, the transformation into a torpedo bomber of the Cant Z. 1007, which combined the qualities of speed and good handling with the ability to carry two torpedoes, was a great missed opportunity since the aircraft did not transition beyond the prototype status."[3]

Cant.Z1007bis Specifications
Engine: Three 1,000 hp Piaggio P.XI R2C.40 14-cylinder radials.
Wingspan: 81 feet 4 1/3 inches
Length: 60 feet 2 ½ inches
Height: 17 feet 5 inches
Weight: 20,715 lbs. (empty); 30, 029 lbs. (maximum takeoff)
Maximum Speed: 290 mph at 13,150 feet (without the torpedo).
Climb Rate: 13,125 feet in 10 minutes and 30 seconds.

3 Francesco Mattesini, "I successi degli Aerosiluranti Italiani e Tedeschi in Mediterraneo nella 2 Guerra Mondiale", *Bollettino d'Archivio dell'Ufficio Storico della Marina Militare*, March 2002, p.2.

Ceiling: 24, 606 feet.
Range: 1,155 miles.
Crew: 5
Armament: one 12.7mm Breda-SAFAT machine gun in the dorsal turret, one 12.7mm Breda-SAFAT rearward firing machine gun, two 7.7mm Breda-SAFAT lateral machine guns.
Two torpedoes 1,800 lbs.
Source: Angelucci (1988)

Torpedo Bomber Units Organization

The torpedo bomber discipline reached its highest peak since by mid-year there were a total of 147 operational torpedo bombers subdivided into twelve *Gruppi* each based on two *Squadriglie.* A much larger number of support personnel was now part of these units including mechanics, cooks, torpedo warhead technicians and specialized armorers. The organization remained unchanged until the end of the year when some units equipped with S.84 aircraft were disbanded due to the unsuitability of the plane as a torpedo bomber. By early 1942 both 36° *Stormo*, and the 89° *Gruppo*/32° *Stormo*, were equipped exclusively with the older but more reliable S.79. *41° Gruppo Autonomo Aerosiluranti* was transformed by *Superaereo* on 1 January 1942 from a S.84 into a S.79 based torpedo bomber unit with its 204ª and 205ª *Squadriglie.* Equipped initially in 1941 with S.84 aircraft the unit received S.79 when the 281ª *Squadriglia* was disbanded and its crews merged into the *41° Gruppo. Tenente Colonnello* Ettore Muti maintained command of the unit which remained very active during the first half of the year participating to countless operations. Given this extensive activity which brought about large losses, on 29 June *Comando Aeronautica dell'Egeo* outlined to *Comando Supremo* that the 41° *Gruppo* had been reduced to only three working aircraft and four crews and that its diminished force could not even guarantee the basic service requirements of the Levantine Sea area. These encompassed that at a minimum three aircraft covered at least 1,500 kilometers to conduct standard reconnaissance on a daily basis. In addition, the loss of the Libyan air bases had limited the possibilities of harming enemy convoys giving the enemy a tremendous advantage because it could field hundreds of fighters and an intricate radar systems along the coast of North Africa to anticipate attacks. This nullified daytime attacks and relegated the torpedo bombers to nighttime operations which were costly and time consuming since many reconnaissance actions yielded no results.[4] Given this precarious situation, *Comando Aeronautica dell'Egeo* requested that the 104° *Gruppo* be transferred to Rhodes to take the place of the 41° *Gruppo.* The former was transferred to Gadurra airport in Rhodes on 30 June 1942. On 2 August 1942 the 41° *Gruppo* was brought back to Pisa airport with eight S.79. In late November 1942 the unit received brand new S.79bis made by the *Officine Reggiane* and equipped with radio controlled torpedoes. It was the first torpedo bomber unit to be equipped with such weapons, but it appears that they were not used in combat. Plans were drafted whereby the latter was tasked with attacking an enemy convoy during a daylight operation with these new weapons. But since the convoy was well escorted by enemy fighters

4 Archivio Storico Aeronautica Militare: Ufficio Operazioni Superaereo, folgio, n. 1B/7257, 17 April, 1942.

and by several cruisers and destroyers with radar, there was a sudden, last minute counterorder. *Superaereo* determined that attacking such a well defended convoy during the daytime deploying the few new torpedo bombers available was too much of a risk. Therefore the operation was cancelled. It is not clear whether the unit's new planes were deployed in other operations. It appears that the new weapon was used very sparingly, if not at all, until the armistice in mid-1943.[5] Even the top brass of RA were hesitant to deploy the new weapon out of fear of losing the few units industry had been able to produce.

In February a former bomber unit, 46° *Stormo Autonomo Aerosiluranti*, was converted into a torpedo bomber unit with the 104° and 105° *Gruppo*. It was based in Decimomannu, Sardinia for several months until it was later transferred to Gadurra with the 104° *Gruppo* replacing the 41° *Stormo* and it took part to the summer of 1942 major aerial-naval battles in the Mediterranean including Operation Pedestal.

In March 1942 the *Ufficio Aerosiluranti* issued a memorandum which outlined the plan to convert more units to the torpedo bomber discipline and it also set goals for the organization. Each of the three *Nuclei di Addestramento* based in Gorizia, Pisa and Capodichino were training one *Stormo* at the time which was to be readied after a period of training lasting three months. According to its assessment, the torpedo bomber units required eighty-eight new aircraft, of which eighty-six S.79 and two S.84. By June 1942 based on the production output of the aircraft factories and the available fleet of torpedo bombers it was estimated that there would be a total of 174 operational torpedo bombers and 164 warheads. Further expansion plans envisioned that in addition to the *Stormi* being trained and readied for combat, the *Ufficio Aerosiluranti* proposed the formation of three additional *Stormi*. One was to be assigned to the defense of the Ligurian Sea, one to the Naples region and one for the Tyrrhenian Sea.[6]

On 25 March 1942 the 131° *Gruppo Autonomo Aerosiluranti* was formed in Benghazi with the former autonomous 279ª and 284ª *Squadriglie* and it operated for the first half of the year out of North African bases, mainly Derna and Mersa Matruh. The 132° *Gruppo Autonomo Aerosiluranti* led by *Capitano* (then later in the year promoted to *Maggiore*) Carlo Buscaglia and originally based in Littoria, was constituted on 1 April 1942 with the 278ª *Squadriglia* and some elements of the former 281ª *Squadriglia*. Its main operative base for most of 1942 was Gerbini in Sicily. It's strength was of 12 officers, 10 nco, 16 machinists, 9 technicians, 8 radio operators, 11 machine gunners/armorers and 2 photographers. Buscaglia and Carlo Faggioni were its two most experienced pilots. Buscaglia's unit was reputed to be one of the most experienced torpedo bomber units with crews that had the highest morale of all units of the RA. Similarly, *Generale* Urbani, the commander of all Sardinian airfields, stated in an operational document that the pilots of the 130° *Gruppo* had also very high morale. The unit was comprised of many newly minted pilots that "strived to be involved in risky operations because of their youthful enthusiasm and their desire to be involved in large scale operations." On the other hand, Urbani argued, the co-pilots had low morale because they desired to be more involved in the decision-making process during the planning of operations and did not want to "play a secondary role during combat operations."[7] Regarding his other torpedo bomber unit, the 105°

5 Carlo Unia, *Storia degli aerosiluranti italiani*, p.211.
6 Francesco Mattesini, *Luci ed ombre,* p.173.
7 Archivio Storico Aeronautica Militare: Generale Urbani, "Reparto operazioni dell'Aeronautica della Sardegna", n. 27831, 30 September 1942.

Gruppo, *Generale* Urbani stated that the unit "was highly reliable for its audacity and for its aggressiveness." The recent turnover with newly minted pilots leading to the retirement of older pilots made the 105° *Gruppo* 'a well drilled unit." These considerations led *Generale* Urbani to argue that the Sardinian torpedo bomber units had further room for improvement if only "more fuel for training purposes was available."[8] Fuel was an overriding concern for both aircraft crews and the industry. In 1941, for example, 338 industrial plants manufacturing military equipment were idled for a time because of a lack of fuel, while 729 were idled in 1942 for the same reason.[9]

Later in the month of April the 133° *Gruppo Autonomo Aerosiluranti* was constituted in Benghazi with its 174ª and 175ª *Squadriglie*. Together with the 131° *Gruppo* it was set to take part in large scale torpedo bomber operations against Royal Navy convoys. Unfortunately due to the losses sustained by the 131° *Gruppo* during 1942, the 133° *Gruppo* was scrapped on 17 October as a torpedo bomber unit. Most of its personnel was merged into the 131° *Gruppo* to bring the latter back to full rank. Meanwhile, a scaled back 133° *Gruppo* would mainly carry out reconnaissance duties.[10] Finally on 1 May 1942 a former standard bomber unit, 32° *Stormo Autonomo Aerosiluranti*, was partly converted into a torpedo bomber unit. Its 89° *Gruppo* flew S.84 aircraft in the torpedo bomber role, while 38° *Gruppo* continued to carry out standard bomber operations. Its torpedo bomber unit operated mainly out of Sardinia. Regarding this unit *Generale* Ferruccio Ranza, commander of the 4ª *Squadra Aerea* stated that while the 89° *Gruppo* was comprised mainly of volunteers and many of its pilots were full of enthusiasm, the 38° *Gruppo*, was mainly comprised by crews and pilots that had seen a lot of service was far less enthusiastic. Its morale was low especially because it was comprised of many married, older soldiers that disliked being part of a standard bomber unit.[11]

The successes reaped by the Italian torpedo bombers in 1941-42 also brought about a reconsideration of the tactics adopted by the *Luftwaffe* which up until then had been lukewarm regarding the adoption of torpedo bomber units. "…The squadrons of I/KG 26 had in the spring of 1942 undergone a course at the torpedo school of Grosseto in Central Italy, as the Luftwaffe general staff had been impressed by the success of Italian, and still more, of Japanese, torpedo planes. In Germany the development of such a weapon had virtually lapsed owning to the futile competition between *Luftwaffe* and *Kriegsmarine* as to which service should control the maritime air arm."[12] The head of the *Luftwaffe* Hermann Goering himself prevailed against the *Kriegsmarine* and followed the Italian example.[13] As a result, several He.111, and later Ju.88 and some Do.217 were modified to carry torpedoes. At the beginning of 1942 tactical exercises were held at the torpedo school in Grosseto by *Kampfschulgeschwader* 2 under the leadership of Lieutenant Colonel Stockmann against the target ship Citta' di Genova and these drills showed promise.[14] Then on 5 July 1942 the German torpedo bomber units showed their worth

8 Ibid.
9 Maurizio Simoncelli, "L'Industria militare italiana nella seconda guerra mondiale", *Disarmo*, No. 1-2, January 1996, p.8.
10 Archivio Storico Aeronautica Militare: 3ª Squadra Aerea, "Lettera al Capo di Stato Maggiore", N. 9/4678. 26 September, 1942.
11 Archivio Storico Aeronautica Militare: Generale Ranza, "Lettera al Capo di Stato Maggiore", N. Op/00402, 1 October 1942.
12 Cajus Bekker, *The Luftwaffe War Diaries* (New York: Doubleday, 1968), p.265.
13 Ibid.
14 Ibid, p.266.

in the coordinated attack on the Royal Navy convoy PQ 17 as it streamed from Iceland towards Archangel.[15]

Another consequence of the successes reaped by the torpedo bombers units was a tighter coordination with II *Fliegerkorps* and the development of an ambitious joint plan to launch an unexpected attack on the Royal Navy near its own base of Gibraltar. This necessitated not only the prior retrofit of the 130° *Gruppo* S.79s aircraft with an additional fuel tank to increase their endurance, but also the completion of several drills with the *Luftwaffe* to instruct the units to fight cohesively together. The plan was to attack the British Fleet as it exited the port of Gibraltar on its way to Malta, or to attack the aircraft carriers in the same location when they were tasked with flying off fighter planes to Malta. Upon learning that the Royal Navy was to launch a large scale convoy out of Gibraltar, the most experienced pilots of 132° *Gruppo* and German reconnaissance aircraft were to head to Decimomannu in Sardinia. They were then to go out and find the convoy, to shadow it and to continue to feed intelligence information to headquarters. This was to pave the way for a sudden and unexpected attack that was to take place very near Gibraltar, in an area of the Mediterranean that the standard torpedo bombers had not been active in given their limited endurance. One German reconnaissance Ju.88D plane was to continue shadowing the enemy fleet, while a second one was to guide the 130° *Gruppo* to attack the convoy. The attack was to be made suddenly either at dusk or at night.[16] The plan, however, was delayed in definitively because of the slow pace of the conversion of a large number of S.79s to a greater fuel autonomy.

Another form of collaboration that was envisioned by *Feldmarschall* Kesselring was the creation of a dual Italian and German torpedo bomber squad based in Crete to be deployed primarily against "small enemy convoys in the eastern Mediterranean in nighttime operations."[17] The plan was unfortunately later scrapped since 104° *Gruppo* S.79 torpedo bombers were not suited to take off from Crete's airport when the strong winds from the south prevailed. Despite the fact that these two plans could not be made operational, during the course of 1942 German and Italian aircraft units would achieve a higher level of coordination during large scale aerial/naval engagements against the Royal Navy.

Combat Actions in 1942

The first operation of note of 1942 was conducted by the 41° *Gruppo* on 15 January when at 1516 an enemy convoy comprised of four transport ships and two destroyers was spotted at sea near the coast of Cyrenaica. This prompted the intervention of two S.79 but they could not approach the ships due to the strong anti-aircraft fire and the deployment of five enemy fighters which prevented the *Sparvieri* from getting close to the ships. On 18 January as four S.84s of 284ª *Squadriglia*/131° *Gruppo* were returning to base after having conducted a sweep over the central Mediterranean, three of them unexpectedly landed outside of the base because of very poor weather conditions. One plane crashed on landing which not only destroyed the aircraft but also killed all crew members. The other two planes suffered only slight damage on landing.

15 Francesco Mattesini, *Luci ed ombre*, p.251.
16 Ibid.,
17 Francesco Mattesini, *Luci ed ombre*, p.252.

The next day has Operation MF3 was being carried out by the Royal Navy which consisted of four transport ships being escorted by cruisers HMS *Ajax*, HMS *Naiad*, HMS *Dido,* HMS *Euryalus*, HMS *Penelope* and HMS *Carlisle* plus seventeen destroyers, several torpedo bombers were deployed to interfere with it. The S.79s from 278ª *Squadriglia* took off from Gerbini base in Sicily, while three S.79s from *41° Gruppo* took flight from Gadurra. The former was unable to locate the enemy ships, while the latter did locate the convoy but refrained from taking any action because of the small size of the transport ships and also in light of the necessity to safeguard the limited stock of warheads. One of the pilots of the second group, *Tenente* Carlo Faggioni continued on to Alexandria and wound up attacking a lone transport ship. The pilot affirmed in the after-action report that he had hit and sunk a 5,000 tons ship. The *41° Gruppo* based in Rhodes, on 5 February 1942 pursued a fuel tanker headed to Tobruk and escorted by several destroyers. As soon as the aircraft were within shooting range of the enemy ships they were mercilessly targeted by naval gunfire and machine guns. The heavy and highly concentrated defensive fire was responsible for rendering severe damage to both *Tenente* Giulio Cesare Graziani and *Tenente* Cimicchi's aircraft and killing photographer Tommaso Di Paolo while wounding three other members of Graziani's crew. With one dead and three other crew members wounded on board, *Tenente* Graziani was still able to bring the plane back to safety in Rhodes. In his memoirs Graziani recalls an eerie return leg to base with the blood from Di Paolo's head splattered on the cockpit and with the remaining crew members under shock as a result of the deadly enemy fire.[18]

On 9 February two S.79s from the *205ª Squadriglia/41° Gruppo* took off from Rhodes at 1340 and an hour later struck and damaged a 6,000-tons auxiliary cruiser near Mersa Matruth. As the two planes flew over the British ship escorted by two destroyers they were targeted by a flurry of machine gun fire that damaged both planes but did not prevent them from landing safely to base at 1750.

Operation MF5

Operation MF5 was a large-scale attempt to reinforce Malta with Convoy MW9. It was comprised of three transport ships (*Clan Chattan*, *Clan Campbell*, and *Rowallan Castle*) escorted by HMS *Carlisle* and eight destroyers. Moreover, Force B also supported the convoy with its 15th Division of Rear-Admiral Vian (HMS *Naiad*, HMS *Dido* and HMS *Euryalus*). At the same time the operation also entailed escorting back to Alexandria Convoy ME10 which was comprised of four empty transport ships that had already unloaded their cargo at La Valletta. These were the *Breconshire, Ajax, City of Calcutta* and *Clan Ferguson*. Its escort was to be provided by HMS *Penelope* and six destroyers of Force K. Finally, the plan entailed that ME10 and MW9 would swap escorts in the middle of the Mediterranean.

Convoy MW9 sailed from Alexandria on 12 February navigating in the heavily trafficked route alongside the African coast and Crete. The latter was called 'Bomb Alley' by the Royal Navy personnel since it was patrolled extensively by Axis aircraft. German dive bombers in particular harassed the convoy from the beginning to the point that the transport ships had to be

18 Giulio Cesare Graziani, *Con Bombe e Siluri fra le Cannonate* (Rome: Edizioni Graziani, 1982), p.145.

diverted. Clan Campbell, for instance, was rerouted to Tobruk after receiving several hits from German aircraft on the 13th. It would be the only transport ship of the convoy that after undergoing emergency repairs steamed to Malta. Meanwhile, *Clan Chattan* was sent to the bottom on the 14th. Ju.88/II *Fliegerkorps* heavily damaged the third transport ship Rowallan Castle also on the 14th. The destruction of the convoy was the result primarily of the work of the German *Luftwaffe*, but also by the deployment of Italian cruisers. The RM had attempted an interception but failed to find the British convoys and their escorting warships. *Ammiraglio di Squadra* Carlo Bergamini's force sailing from Taranto comprised the battleship *Caio Duilio*, the light cruisers *Emanuele Filiberto Duca d'Aosta* and *Raimondo Montecuccoli*, and the destroyers *Folgore, Fulmine, Saetta, Alpino, Carabiniere, Fusiliere* and *Bersagliere*, while *Ammiraglio di Divisione* Angelo Parona's force from Messina comprised the heavy cruisers *Gorizia* and *Trento*, and the destroyers *Aviere, Geniere, Camicia Nera* and *Ascari*. As she returned to port, *Carabiniere* was torpedoed and damaged by the British submarine P 36. But by deploying the fleet, the RM had been a contributing factor forcing the convoy toward Tobruk and giving the bombers more time to harass it. The action of the torpedo bombers was secondary to that of the German *Luftwaffe* bombers during this operation as the Italians scored no hits. On the 14th *Generale* Fougier, *Capo di Stato Maggiore dell'Aeronautica* transmitted to local commands that a large convoy had been sighted and ordered "the immediate transfer of torpedo bombers, if possible twelve aircraft, to Catania airport. The combat action of the torpedo bombers must be synchronized with the attack carried out by German bombers."[19] This resulted in several unsuccessful attempts throughout the 14th by the torpedo bombers. At 0700 the convoy MW9 escorted by Admiral Vian's battlefleet was spotted near Tobruk. At 1015 five S.79s from 41° *Gruppo* took off to pursue it. But once the torpedo bombers spotted the convoy and began to circle around it, the commander of the unit ordered his aircraft from refraining to attack the ships which were mistakenly deemed to be of small tonnage and "therefore an objective of scant importance."[20] It is not clear why the commander came up with this incorrect assessment which obliged the unit to not press forward with the attack. The post battle report indicates that the British HMS *Carlisle* light cruiser engaged the S.79s at 10,000 yards with a heavy barrage forcing the pilots to circle away. The report also indicated that the convoy did not have aerial protection hence the torpedo bombers most likely had missed a favorable opportunity to do some damage.[21] A second group of S.79s from 205ª *Squadriglia*/41° *Gruppo* spotted another convoy approximately two hours later 20 miles north of Mersa Matruh. At 1115 they pressed home the attack but they did not score any hits. It is not clear from the post battle report whether these ships were part of Operation MF 5 or were some of the British transport ships that readily supplied Tobruk. The second attack was carried out at 1522. This time by two S.79s from 284ª *Squadriglia* led by *Capitano* Oscar Pegna. The latter launched the warhead at a distance of 1,200 meters and affirmed, in the post battle report, to have struck a cruiser. His wingmen, *Tenente* Paolo Lombardi also released the torpedo against a 10,000 tons transport ship and incorrectly reputed to have made a hit. Instead, "The British reported that planes dropped torpedoes at long range and that tracks were sighted at a distance."[22]

19 Francesco Mattesini, *Luci ed ombre*, p.168.
20 Vincent P. O'Hara, *Six Victories*, p.170.
21 Ibid and also see: Archivio Storico Aeronautica Militare: Superaereo, "Azioni aeree dei giorni 13-14 Febbraio contro forze navali nemiche in navigazione fra Malta ed Alessandria", 20 February 1942.
22 Vincent P. O'Hara, *Six Victories*, pp.173-74.

Force B was sighted on 15 February north of Cyrenaica by the Italian submarine *Platino*. This prompted *Comando dell'Aeronautica dell'Egeo* to launch a combined attack by three Cant. Z. 1007 bombers/47° *Stormo* and five S.79s torpedo bombers from 205ª *Squadriglia/41° Stormo*. The attack took place in two separate waves with the standard bombers and three S.79s attacking first and then followed by two more S.79s. The first strike took place at 1505 and it did not yield any results since the aircraft were intercepted and bounced by Beaufighters from No. 252 Squadron. The latter prevented the S.79s to launch warheads as the planes with their vigorous and prompt intervention halted the torpedo bombers. The second attempt was made by the remaining two S.79s from the same unit (*Capitano* Marino Marini and *Sottotenente* Saverio Mayer) when they encountered the convoy north of Mersa Matruh. But after having launched the warheads against HMS *Coventry* they too were engaged in heavy fighting with the Beaufighters. During the heated dogfight that ensued *Capitano*'s Marini's plane was shot down and the pilot had to make an emergency landing on the water thirty miles north of Mersa Matruh. The crew survived for several hours on a raft and were later rescued by a German U Boat with the exception of one crew member (*Aviere Motorista* Giuseppe Colucci) who had been killed earlier during the confrontation with the enemy fighter aircraft. The RAF suffered one aircraft heavily damaged and one slightly damaged by enemy fire.

On 10 March two S.79s attacked elements of Force B which was comprised by 15th Division cruisers (HMS *Naiad*, HMS *Dido* and HMS *Euryalus*) and nine destroyers that had sailed from Alexandria and were bound for an area north of Cyrenaica where the RAF had spotted a large Italian battleship. The attack was pressed forward by two S.79s (205ª *Squadriglia*/ 41° *Gruppo*) and by Ju.88 bombers from X *Fliegerkorps* after the convoy was spotted by German reconnaissance planes. The enemy ships put out a deadly curtain of anti-aircraft fire procuring damage to the two low flying Italian planes to the point that they could not drop the torpedoes. At 1815 the convoy was targeted again by *Tenente Colonnello* Muti and *Sottotenente* Cionni of the same unit. Forceful enemy fire was concentrated against the two pilots which nevertheless pressed on though the hail of fire in a low level attack but could not release the torpedoes. The two pilots made a second deliberate pass over the enemy cruisers and destroyers despite being hit once more. Ultimately they were prevented again from approaching the ships to launch the torpedoes. Muti was lucky to escape unharmed from the close combat confrontation as anti-aircraft fire badly damaged his plane to the point that he barely landed at Rhodes. For his courageous action, Muti was awarded a silver medal of military valor.[23] On the 11th five S.79s from 279ª *Squadriglia* took flight to search for the convoy but they were unable to locate it. Finally, HMS *Naiad* was torpedoed by a German U-boat (U-565). On 13 March two more *Sparvieri* from Muti's unit 205ª *Squadriglia*/41° *Gruppo* flown by *Capitano* Ettore Sondalini and *Tenente* Ardito Cristiani at 1240 were intercepted and attacked by fighters from No. 274 Squadron before they could attack a convoy off the Egyptian coast. This time an enemy Beaufighter was shot down while the Italian planes, although badly damaged, made it back to base with their warheads.[24]

23 Marco Mattioli, *Savoia-Marchetti S.79 Sparviero*, p.30.
24 Ibid.

Second Battle of the Sirte

In March 1942 Malta was in a precarious situation as a result of the naval blockade imposed by the RM and German U-boats, the daily Axis aerial bombings and the failure of the prior Operation MF 5. The population and the military garrison, which totaled over 250,000 individuals, lacked food. On the island, both the Royal Navy and the RAF possessed low stocks of nafta and fuel. Particularly challenging was the spare parts inventories for both services which were at an all-time low. This worrisome situation prompted the British government to plan Operation MG 1, which was meant to bring much needed supplies to Malta. It was comprised of four ships (tanker Breconshire and three transport ships) transporting 26,000 tons of supplies. The escort was provided by Rear-Admiral Philip Vian of the 15th Division with three light cruisers (HMS *Cleopatra,* HMS *Euryalus* and HMS *Dido*), the anti-aircraft cruiser Carlisle, the 14th Destroyer Flotilla (Captain Albert Lawrence Poland) with four destroyers, the 22nd Destroyer Flotilla (Captain St. John Aldrich Micklethwait) with the six destroyers and finally the 5th Destroyer Flotilla with eight Hunt-class destroyers. It was envisioned that after the first day of sailing the convoy would be further reinforced by elements of Force K coming from Malta, mainly the cruiser Penelope and the destroyer Legion. The operation began on the morning of 20 March when the ships sailed out of Alexandria since "supplying Malta from the west was deemed impossible with the retreat to the Gazala line before Tobruk by the Allies and the loss of the advanced air bases in Libya between Derna and Benghazi"[25]. On that day the convoy was first spotted by *Luftwaffe* reconnaissance aircraft but Axis intelligence services were not certain at that point whether the convoy was headed for Malta or Tobruk. The next day it was spotted 48 miles southwest of Crete at 1610 by the submarine *Platino*, which by then based on its location convinced the Axis command that the convoy was indeed headed to Malta. Two *Sparvieri* were the first to pursue it on the evening of the 21st. These were piloted by *Capitano* Ettore Sandalini and *Sottotenente* Normanno White of 205ª *Squadriglia*/41° *Gruppo*. According to the Royal Navy post battle report the attacks were unsuccessful because conducted from too far away in the face of heavy barrages.

On the night of the 21st *Comando Supremo* alerted the two services and mobilized the battlefleet. The goal was to destroy the convoy or force it back to Alexandria. As a result, *Ammiraglio* Iachino departed on the same night onboard battleship *Littorio*, while *Ammiraglio* Parona left Messina with the heavy cruisers *Gorizia, Trento*, and the light cruiser *Giovanni delle Bande Nere*. Ten destroyers were also deployed. The RA also made a significant contribution to try to stop the convoy. *Capo di Stato Maggiore Regia Aeronautica Generale* Fougier ordered the immediate transfer of twenty-two torpedo bombers from Sardinia to Sicily, of which ten S.79 from 130° *Gruppo* were to fly from Elmas to Pantelleria Island, while twelve S.84 from 36° *Stormo* were to fly from Decimomannu to Sciacca. These were to join the seven operational S.79s from 278ª *Squadriglia* based in Caltanissetta and German bombers based in Catania, Gelmini, and Comiso. In a second instance all torpedo bombers were subsequently transferred to the three bases were the German bombers were stationed to enhance cooperation amongst the two services and better prepare synchronized attacks. Eleven serviceable aircraft from 279ª and 284ª *Squadriglie* were also alerted in Cyrenaica, while nine S.79 from 205ª *Squadriglia*/41°

25 Jack Greene and Alessandro Massignani, *The Naval War*, p.216.

Gruppo were transferred from Rhodes to Heraklion. This large torpedo bomber deployment was instructed to primarily go after transport ships to further aid the naval blockade of Malta.

At 0935 on 22 March five S.79s from 279ª *Squadriglia* took flight from Benghazi airport. The weather was terrible and visibility poor. One pilot recalls that: "we were really worried because we feared the mission would turn into a disaster due to the stormy seas. The High Command did not share our point of view, insisting we had to attack. Immediately after take-off, under the rain, we closed up our formation. Flying at a height of just 50 meters. We felt we were like on a roller coaster."[26] The unit led by *Capitano* Giulio Marini then ambushed the convoy but none of the warheads struck a target. Under heavy enemy fire one S.79 piloted by *Tenente* Guglielmo Ranieri was shot to pieces by naval gunfire. Its crew perished. A second torpedo bomber flown by *Tenente* Andrea Dell'Anna was badly damaged by enemy fire but managed to return to base.[27] A second attack was attempted at 1107 by four torpedo bombers from 284ª *Squadriglia*. Commanded by *Capitano* Oscar Pegna the attack was not successful even though the pilots in the post battle report stated that a likely hit had been made against a transport ship: "A large fire at once broke out …and dense smoke was seen."[28] The German bombers also attacked the convoy without scoring any hits and suffering the loss of one plane while forty Ju.88 were not able to take flight due to the worsening of the weather conditions. Three S.79s were not able to take off from Catania airfield due to technical difficulties, while nine S.84s from 36º *Stormo* due to the worsening weather conditions with wind gusts topping 90 km/h could not take off in the evening.

The naval action was also inconclusive. At 1443 HMS *Cleopatra* and HMS *Euryalus* engaged *Ammiraglio* Parona cruisers and the former was hit by the *Bande Nere* at a range of 20,000 yards. The shell knocked out Cleopatra's radio system and killed fifteen sailors. Shortly thereafter the battleship *Littorio*, through an opening in the smoke, struck HMS *Euryalus*. Whilst the 14th Flotilla provided close escort to the convoy, the 22nd Flotilla was dispatched by Admiral Vian to engage the Italian ships. At 1700 *Littorio* was again engaged in the action when it fired on HMS *Havock* which was hit by splinters of 15 inch shells that killed seven and flooded one boiler room. At 1740 HMS *Sikh*, the flagship of the 22nd Flotilla, came forward firing against *Littorio* but came itself under fire. The climax of the naval battle took place in the evening. "When Poland was about 5000 yards from the enemy, he turned and launched torpedoes. A total of twenty-three would be launched at the Italian fleet. The only hit on an Italian ship took place 1851, a 4 inch shell on the Littorio, doing little damage. The Kingston was then hit by a 15 inch shell that passed right though the ship, starting a small fire and wrecking some of the light anti-aircraft guns, killing fourteen and wounding twenty. She would be temporarily stopped by damage to her engine room. Micklethwait also launched some torpedoes from his division but at a longer range. The Lively was hit by a 15 inch splinters and suffered some minor flooding. The Italian fleet, ordered by *Supermarin* avoid night combat, turned away and headed north in the rising sea. The last shot was fired at 1856."[29] The combat action was inconclusive being fought under a storm. The main protagonist had been the battleship *Littorio* which fired 181 rounds of 15 inch shells halting an attack by enemy destroyers.[30] But blinded by the smoke-

26 Vincent P. O' Hara, *Six Victories*, p.212.
27 Marco Mattioli, *Savoia-Marchetti, S.79 Sparviero*, p.30
28 Ibid.
29 Jack Greene and Alessandro Massignani, *The Naval War*, p.220.
30 Mark E. Stille, *The Italian Battleships of World War II* (Oxford: Osprey, 2001), p.39.

screen and the bad weather the Italian formation had few chances to hit the British warships or the convoy. As Mark E. Stille asserts: "Most importantly, the aggressive attempts to engage the convoy forced it to move to the south and eventually to scatter in an attempt to reach Malta singly. This meant the ships were still at sea and exposed to air attack the next day."[31]

Further air attacks were made at 1805 on the evening of the 22nd when six S.79s from 278ª *Squadriglia* and six from 130º *Gruppo* (three from 280ª and three from 283ª *Squadriglie*) came within sights of the convoy. This large deployment of torpedo bombers, however, was not able to inflict any damage and lost three aircraft to naval gunfire flown by *Tenente* Emilio Iuzzolino, *Sottotenenti* Giovanni Scalia and Gaetano Marletta. Their dramatic fate was reported by Capitano Ugo Rivoli of 278ª *Squadriglia:*

> While I aimed for the merchant ship, Scalia directed his aircraft against the warships, facing an internal fire. Then we learned that, struck by anti-aircraft fire, he had managed to ditch in the vicinity of the Eolian Islands. The five crewmen settled the raft which shortly afterwards was overwhelmed by a wave. Four died, but flight engineer Vito Bonfiglio saved himself as he returned to the aircraft to retrieve a compass. He was picked up the next day by a seaplane. A similar thing occurred with Marletta's crew Forced to ditch off Cape Passero, having run out fuel, Marletta, WO Albino Csalabrin, and flight engineer Adriano Rossi disappeared forever after taking to the raft. Specialists Francesco Malara and Angelo Barba saved themselves because they remained aboard the aircraft, being picked up at 1000 hours on 23 March by the torpedo boat Stocco. Iuzzolino met a dramatic end. Returning from the mission after attacking a merchantman, he crashed into a mountain in the locality of Roccella Jonica. None of the crew aboard was saved.[32]

The British convoy finally reached Malta at dawn on the 23rd. Regarding this voyage Admiral Cunningham wrote that even if the German and Italian pilots had attacked with resoluteness, their actions had achieved no result. The only consequence of their actions was that many British ships had spent most of their stocks of anti-aircraft ammunition.[33] In fact the greatest damage to the convoy would derive from German bombers during unloading operations. The Breconshire, for example, was disabled by the bombers eight miles outside the harbor. This action ensured that only 5,000 of the 26,000 tons of cargo originally loaded for Operation MG1 ultimately reached Malta, along with a limited amount of fuel oil that was saved from the Breconshire. It can be argued that the RM's intervention to engage the convoy forced the latter to scatter and be subjected for an elongated period of time to Axis air attacks which successfully reduced the amount of supplies that arrived in Malta.[34]

On 23 March Force B, having completed its task, sailed from Malta to return to Alexandria. This prompted renewed attacks by both German bombers and Italian torpedo bombers. The attack took place at 1600 and was made by three S.79s of 205ª *Squadriglia*//41° *Gruppo* that had departed from Heraklion. This small unit, led by *Tenente Colonnello* Ettore Muti, fired all three warheads but none hit a target. The aircraft flew over the enemy ships when making

31 Ibid., p.40.

32 Marco Mattioli, *Savoia-Marchetti S.79 Sparviero*, p.31.

33 Supplement to the London Gazzette n. 38073, 18 September 1947.

34 Mark E. Stille, *The Italian Battleships of World War II*, p.39.

their escape and they were targeted by strong anti-aircraft fire which procured some damage to Muti's plane.[35] Ultimately, the three damaged aircraft made it back safely to their base. A second attempt to harm the convoy was made at 0735 on 24 March by two S.79s from 41° *Gruppo* (*Tenente* Giorgio Tourn from 205ª *Squadriglia* and *Sottotenente* Antonio Monterumici from 204ª *Squadriglia*) who had taken off from Rhodes. Both planes were greeted from the onset by intensive defensive fire. Nevertheless the two pilots continued to press forward with the attack by flying low and then releasing the torpedoes which misfired. The aircraft of *Sottotenente* Giorgio Tourn was shot down by the anti-aircraft defense. It caught fire and crashed into the sea. The second aircraft flown by *Sottotenente* Monterumici also received enemy fire but was able to escape. The latter observed the crew members of Tourn's plane getting into a small dinghy which prompted other S.79s from the same *Squadriglia* to head out and search for survivors. Unfortunately they were never found. Meanwhile, Force B steamed safely into Alexandria at 1230 on 24 March.

On 21-24 March 1942 the *aerosiluranti* units were unable to score any hits despite a large deployment of aircraft and a great expenditure of warheads. This prompted *Generale* Fougier to issue a strong worded communique titled "Azioni offensive degli aerosiluranti" that was critical of the *Sparvieri* tactics that had been adopted:

> During the recent combat actions in the Mediterranean against enemy ships, I have noted that the aircraft deployed were split up in small groups to target multiple ships. Despite some limited success, the large force deployed in piecemeal attacks did not yield a major result. In such circumstances it is more important to sink a battleship rather than slightly damage a few of them. Therefore it is imperative to concentrate on one or few objectives so that tangible results can be attained. Naturally, one can deviate from these guidelines when faced by a strong reaction from enemy fighters or from concentrated fire of the anti-aircraft defense. In such circumstances it will be more advantageous to disperse the Sparvieri in different directions for the purpose of dispersing the enemy force.
>
> I also want to reiterate that the post battle assessment regarding the results of combat actions are of extreme importance in detailing the results as well as furnishing information and intelligence on the enemy's position.
>
> Vague reports that do not capture the actual results of operations will not be tolerated.
>
> Post battle assessments must be documented, when possible, by photos of the damage inflicted to enemy ships. This type of intelligence is of vital importance toward assessing the effectiveness of the torpedo bomber specialty.[36]

In the document it was stressed once again that when facing a large convoy the attacks had to be synchronized with a mass of torpedo bombers lunging at one large battleship all at once instead of the piecemeal attacks by small squads of two or three aircraft at the time that had characterized the Second Battle of the Sirte. In addition, *Generale* Fougier requested more detailed assessments of the results of combat actions which were many times difficult to ascertain given the fluid nature of operations. At the end of every mission it was an established practice that

35 Domizia Carafoli and Gustavo Bocchini Padiglione, *Ettore Muti* (Milan: Mursia, 1993).
36 Alberto Santoni and Francesco Mattesini, *La partecipazione tedesca alla guerra aeronavale nel Mediterraneo 1940-1945* (Rome: Edizioni dell'Ateneo, 1980), p.334.

the aircraft crews would have a debriefing meeting with their commander. In these post battle meetings, crews would collectively discuss the results of the mission, for instance they would exchange opinions on what the various members of the crews observed and catalog the images their cameras had collected on film. While they were sometimes able to determine whether any hits on enemy ships had been made, in many instances it was impossible for them to say with certainty whether the ship had sunk. Some crews overestimated the results of their operations reporting more hits than had actually occurred. Given the dangers that the crews encountered right after they had dropped their torpedoes, few pilots were inclined to fly over repeatedly around the attack site to take pictures or to further assess the damage they had inflicted, as the threat of being taken down by enemy fighters, that circled the attack sites repeatedly like crows, was very high.

With regards to Operation MG 1 the Italian historian Alberto Santoni argued that the post battle reports of the *Sparvieri* units deployed were rife with inaccuracies and were way too optimistic in light of the actual poor results attained where no enemy battle or transport ship had been severely damaged.[37] This is the reason that likely prompted the head of the Air Force, *Generale* Fougier, to issue his sharp worded communique.

On 30 March there was another missed opportunity by the torpedo bomber units when they unsuccessfully pursued the British cruiser HMS *Aurora*, which was escorted by the destroyer HMS *Avon Vale* steaming from Malta to Gibraltar. They were pursued by fourteen S.84s of 36° *Stormo*, and three S.79s from 130° *Gruppo (*two from 280ª and one from 283ª *Squadriglie)* at 1430. All seventeen torpedoes were fired against HMS *Aurora* which was navigating at reduced speed given the prior damage it had sustained. But lamentably no hits were scored. *Sottotenente* Manlio Caresio's S.79 of 280ª *Squadriglia* was damaged by naval gunfire once the pilot attempted to disengage. Despite the heavy damage sustained to the plane's tail, Caresio was able to return to base. This failure prompted again the Chief of Staff of RA to complain bitterly against another lost opportunity: "The torpedo action of 30 March was very disappointing. My hope is that the 36° Stormo crews will in the future be worthy of the highest honor and of their glorious battle flag. Generale Fougier."[38]

This warning was followed up by a more detailed communication on 5 April which attempted to set out a refined attacking tactic for the *Sparvieri* units:

> Recently, a large torpedo unit launched a series of attacks against an isolated enemy cruiser navigating at low speed. Such unit achieved no success despite pressing forward their attacks with great courage and determination. The reason for the failure, apart from the conditions of poor visibility in the area, was due to the lack of coordination amongst the pilots as the attacks were made piecemeal. This gave the enemy the ability to maneuver the vessel and avoid the warheads by zigzagging. I want to reiterate the tactic of the coordinated and simultaneous attacks. Each pilot of the attacking formation must press forward the attack by maneuvering individually but at the same time each pilot is tactically linked to the others by targeting one main objective. This fundamental concept of well executed torpedo attack tactics must be shared by both commanders and wingmen. The commander of a

37 Alberto Santoni, *La seconda battaglia della Sirte* (Rome: Edizioni dell'Ateneo, 1982), pp.63-70.
38 Archivio Storico Aeronautica Militare: 1B/4400 – Superaereo, Punto Comando 36° Stormo , "Azione siluramento giorno 30", 2 April, 1942.

> torpedo bomber unit not only leads his squad into battle but also must adopt an attacking tactic that strives to achieve maximum results. All the commanders of torpedo units must adhere to these principles."[39]

The document reiterated the need for synchronized attacks targeting a battleship or an aircraft carrier. It reiterated the concept that if a large mass of torpedo bombers launched their warheads all at once the chances were that at least one hit be made by giving the enemy ship little or no chance to avoid the torpedo with evasive maneuvers. The latter were more likely to succeed than piecemeal attacks. This tactical directive was partially contradicted by another communication by *Generale* Fougier which on 2 April urged the commanders of 5ª *Squadra Aerea* (Libya), *Aeronautica della Sardegna, Aeronautica della Sicilia* and *Aeronautica dell'Egeo* to be parsimonious due to low stocks of torpedoes: "Please give your crews clear instructions so that torpedoes are launched against suitable targets and are released only if the weather and the launch conditions offer a good chance of success."[40]

Not only were the warheads valuable assets which were to be preserved if the pilot thought that he be unable to hit the target, but also the attack in waves tactic did not always guarantee success. The first torpedo unit in 1940, for instance, was comprised of highly skilled pilots which often attacked individually or in very small groups so that they could use stealth and the element of surprise to achieve their objectives. Often the synchronized attack in waves offered some degree of success because many warheads were launched against the target but on the other hand it negated the element of surprise which was vital to Buscaglia's unit early successes. Some of the most recent operations were led by recently newly formed *Gruppi* which contained a larger number of relatively inexperienced pilots.

On 8 April the run of bad form of the torpedo units continued when they failed to score a hit against the British cruiser HMS *Penelope*, that had set sail from Malta on the evening of 8th and was headed to Gibraltar. After passing the south of Sicily in the night, HMS *Penelope* was sighted on the morning of the 9th by a reconnaissance seaplane. The torpedo attacks followed but were all frustrated by the bravery of the crew that adopted evasive tactics as well as opened up a very lively fire to avoid all the warheads launched in its direction. The attacks were made in three waves by six torpedo bombers and six standard bombers (all S.84s) of 36° *Stormo*, five torpedo bombers S.79 of 130° *Gruppo*, and fourteen German Ju 88 bombers. The attacks took place along the coast of Algeria, but the crew of HMS P*enelope* bravely avoided all threats. On the morning of 10 April the cruiser entered Gibraltar and the crew was cheered on by the harbor personnel because of how well it had conducted itself under extreme pressure from the Axis forces. The operation resulted in yet another high expenditure of torpedoes which created a crisis for the service. The latter, having almost depleted its stock of torpedoes, was forced to request the rerouting of twenty SI torpedoes originally slated for RM torpedo boats. The latter agreed to the request in part by ceding 15 torpedoes to RA.

In April and May one of the primary torpedo bomber units deployed was the 41° *Gruppo* that since the beginning of the year had begun to phase out the S.84 in favor of the S.79 as the

39 Archivio Storico Aeronautica Militare: Superareo, "l'azione del 30 Marzo contro convoglio nemico", 5 April 1942.

40 Archivio Storico Aeronautica Militare: 1B/4580 Superaereo "Punto sulla situazione siluri", 2 April 1942.

torpedo bomber of choice. The latter were considered by its commander *Tenente Colonnello* Muti as more reliable. In April 1942 this unit was comprised of the 204ª and 205ª *Squadriglie* and it was headquartered at Gadurra on Rhodes Island. It had eighteen torpedo bombers in service.[41] Its 205ª *Squadriglia* on 6 April during a reconnaissance to the north of Port Said by one of its S.79 flown by *Tenente* Saverio Mayer experienced technical difficulties in flight to the point that the pilot was forced to down the plane. The crew did not suffer any injuries during the emergency landing but was later captured by the British. On 20 April two S.79s from the same unit attacked an enemy convoy but scored no hits even though the pilots indicated afterwards that they had successfully downed a transport ship. On 27 April two more S.79s attacked the transport ship Reliant at Port Said at 1300, but the ship escaped the attack.

At 0815 on 8 May two more S.79s pursued an enemy convoy in the same area and released two torpedoes in its direction. One torpedo barely passed under a transport ship. In a separate attack on the same day two S.79s from 205ª *Squadriglia* with pilots Emilio Pucci and Giuseppe Briatore attacked a freighter north of Kas Barum. According to Pucci's post battle report the freighter was reported in the aftermath of the strike to be engulfed in flames. 9 May was one of the most tragic days for the torpedo bomber crews as two S. 79s were destroyed. On that day five S.79s from 280ª *Squadriglia* had took flight from Pantelleria to search for Force H. They flew all the way to Algiers but could not spot the Royal Navy formation at sea. On the return flight two planes due to the bad weather and the poor visibility at night crashed into the small hill that abutted the airport of Pantelleria. The plane flown by *Tenente* Angelo Caponetti, was the first to collide with the rock and two crew members were injured during the crash while the rest of the crew was unscathed, while the plane of *Tenente* Renzo Sommadossi caught fire after the crash and the crew perished.

On 11 May two S.79s from 204ª *Squadriglia*/41° *Gruppo* pursued another convoy. *Capitano* Gian Battista De Stefano launched his torpedo at a steamer but he misfired, while his wingman *Tenente* Normanno White S.79 was attacked and shot down by a Beaufighter from No. 89 Squadron. After having downed the plane, the RAF pilot set his sights on Di Stefano's plane killing with his machine gun *marconista* Nicola Favero and injuring two other crew members. Despite the loss of Favero, the pilot was able to bring the plane back to base. Another action against Force H took place on 18 May. The latter was subjected to several attacks along the coast north of Algiers for most of the day without success by both German and Italian bombers. At 1905 *Comando Aeronautica della Sardegna* ordered that three S.79s from 130° *Gruppo* to take off to pursue Force H. The small unit was led by *Capitano* Franco Melley who had as wingmen *Tenenti* Manlio Caresi and Camillo Baroglio. The trio spotted a ship at 2115 when it was approximately 30 miles north of Cape Bengut and it was steaming at 18 knots. "At 2140 under very favorable weather conditions, the attack was pressed forward. It was a simultaneous attack made against an aircraft carrier. The bombers released their warheads at a distance of 700 to 1,000 meters in the face of heavy anti-aircraft fire."[42] During the combat action *Tenente* Baroglio faced extremely heavy fire to the point that even before he pressed forward with the attack his plane was struck at great distance (6,000 meters from the ships). As the plane received more hits, Baroglio positioned his S.79 at a distance of 700 meters and launched the torpedo

41 Archivio Storico Aeronautica Militare: Allegato numero 3 alla lettera di Superaereo, 18 April 1942.
42 Francesco Mattesini, *Luci ed Ombre*, p.183.

which travelled under the ship. During his getaway a machine gun round struck one of the engines. His slow and lame S.79 became an easy prey for enemy fighters which downed it. The plane crashed into the sea and the crew that were all injured took to a small boat. They were latter spotted at sea by a Cant. Z.506 and rescued. For the determination showed by the crew in the face of very heavy enemy fire the commander of *Aeronautica della Sardegna* Generale Aldo Urbani stated that: "The crew showed great determination during the combat action."[43]

On 27 May two S.79 from the 204ª *Squadriglia*/41° *Gruppo* were finally able to down a small transport ship navigating in the vicinity of Malta thus breaking the spell of bad luck that had befallen upon the *Sparvieri* crews. A day later 204ª *Squadriglia*/41° *Gruppo* pilot *Tenente* Salvatore Annona launched a torpedo against another small cargo ship, but the torpedo dropped precipitously into the seabed. 205ª *Squadriglia*/41° *Gruppo* based in the Aegean was able to finally overcome its unit period dry spell when *Sottotenente* Emilio Pucci's S.84 torpedoed on 9 June south of Cyprus the Stureborg transport ship of 1,661 tons. His attack was preceded by that of *Tenente* Luigi Vicariotto who misfired. Vicariotto attacked the transport ship at a distance of 1,000 meters while Pucci at 500 meters. The ship received the second warhead and sank very precipitously.

7: TORPEDO BOMBER PILOT EMILIO PUCCI

Born 20 November 1914 (Naples) – Died 29 November 1992.
The scion of an ancient Florentine family, Pucci was educated in the United States. He studied agriculture at the University of Georgia and then Political Science at Reed University where he received an M.A. in 1937. Pucci returned to Italy in 1937 but his hopes of joining the Italian diplomatic service were frustrated by the Second World War. He joined *Regia Aeronautica* in 1938 where he served for more than a decade and was awarded a medal of military valor. In 1941 Pucci began operating as a torpedo bomber pilot flying both the S.79 and the S.84. In 1944 when Galeazzo Ciano, ex foreign minister, was put to trial by the Repubblica Sociale, Pucci, whose loyalty to Ciano and his family remained undiminished while everyone else abandoned them, attempted to save his life in exchange for his diaries in a deal with the German SS. Despite his best effort, Pucci was unable to save Ciano's life, although he helped his wife and family escape to Switzerland. For his actions he was arrested by the SS and was forced to sustain several harsh interrogations.

In the post war period, Pucci became a world renowned fashion designer.

Operation Harpoon

In the summer of 1942 the Axis situation in the Mediterranean had improved largely has a result of the constant pressure against Malta. In May, for example, 86,439 out of 93,188 tons arrived safely in North Africa thus allowing General Rommel to resume the offensive. In contrast the Allied situation had deteriorated considerably due to the Axis neutralization of Malta and the

43 Ibid. p.189.

drain of resources represented by the Pacific theatre where Japan's offensives where checked also by drawing resources from the Middle East. In May Prime Minister Churchill urged General Claude Auchinleck, the commander of the Eighth Army, to initiate a major offensive in Egypt, but the latter had requested more time to build up his forces. In June 1942 Malta was again in a desperate need for supplies as the last major convoy had taken place in March and only a reduced amount of cargo had gotten through due to Axis disruptive attacks. Its garrison needed ammunition and weapons, while the population was in desperate need of food being in near starvation. Meanwhile, in April alone the Axis had conducted a record number of bombing raids against Malta to the point that most activities on the ground had been paralyzed. The major contribution on the part of these Axis air operations had been carried out by II *Fliegerkorps* comprised of seven bomber groups and five of fighters.[44] Malta's most critical needs at the time where fuel reserves for its aircraft which were at all time low, a minesweeper to make the harbor of La Valetta fully operational once again and more fighter aircraft to be able to properly challenge the Axis bombing forays. Given that the retention of Malta was at the heart of British strategy in the Mediterranean, the British government was determined to come to its aid with a new large scale supply operation. As result, the Royal Navy decided to run two convoys, Operation Harpoon from the west and Vigorous from the east, so as to encourage the Axis to disperse its naval and air forces.

Plans for the two convoys differed only in matters of detail from the previous ones such as Operation Substance and Halberd. While the massive escort of the convoy was central to the operation, the sailing of the convoy was to be preceded by the preventive bombing of enemy ports and airfields in mainland Italy, Sicily, Sardinia, North Africa and Crete, and over Cyrenaica. These attacks were to be continued during the passage of the ships in the Mediterranean to degrade the Axis air forces and reduce the number of aircraft that could be deployed in attacks against the convoy. The plan also envisioned targeted raids by commando units against select Axis air bases. Moreover, in anticipation of this major operation fifty Spitfires were flown off HMS *Eagle* and arrived at Malta in the first week of June bringing the total number of aircraft on the island to over 200. This force together with aircraft units based in Egypt had a dual role: to provide air coverage to the convoy and to counter any movements by the Italian battlefleet aimed at countering the convoy.

The Harpoon convoy included six transport ships: Troilus 7,500 tons, Burdwan, 6,000 tons, the 5,500 tons American Chant, Orari 10,500 tons, Tanimbar 8,619 tons and the Kentucky 9,300 tons.

The transports were covered first by Force W under the command of Admiral A.B.T. Curteis. This was comprised by the battleship HMS *Malaya*; the carriers HMS *Argus* and HMS *Eagle* that combined could field twenty-two fighters; the cruisers HMS *Kenya*, HMS *Liverpool* and HMS *Charybdis*; and the *destroyers Antelope, Escapade, Icarus, Onslow, Westcott, Wishart, Wrestler* and *Vidette*.

For the second leg of the journey from Bizerte to Malta, Force X under the command of Captain C.C. Hardy, in the light cruiser HMS *Cairo* (converted before the war into an anti-aircraft ship of eight single 4-inch guns), was to take control of the convoy. Force X was comprised by five fleet destroyers: HMS *Bedouin*, HMS *Marne*, HMS *Matchless*, HMS *Ithuriel*,

44 Cajus Bekker, *The Luftwaffe War Diaries* (Garden City: Doubleday, 1968), p.183.

and HMS *Partridge*. Four Hunt class destroyers: *Blankney*, *Middleton*, *Badsworth* and *Kujawiak*; and four fast mine-sweepers of the 17th Flotilla. The minelayer HMS *Welshman* was also to accompany the convoy. In addition, thirteen Allied submarines were to provide a screen against Axis naval attacks on the convoy.

Through the interception of the communication between the American foreign affairs office in Cairo and Washington DC, the Italian SIM agents had learned well in advance of the plans of Operation Harpoon and had given the services the opportunity to prepare a response. This was based on the deployment primarily of two light cruisers and several destroyers of the VII *Divisione*, ten Italian torpedo boats, six German U-boats, twenty-one Italian and three German submarines and aircraft (both bombers and torpedo bombers). VII *Divisione* units, for instance, were to await for the convoy south of Pantelleria island and strike it in the narrow waters of the channel. Meanwhile the RM estimated that the eastern convoy (Vigorous) would be the main effort of the operation and therefore directed the two battleships *Vittorio Veneto* and *Littorio* to attack it.[45] *Superaereo* ordered the commander of the Sardinian airbases *Generale di Divisione* Aldo Urbani, to take the initiative by launching preliminary spoiling attacks prior to the convoy reaching the island of Sardinia (expected to be the evening of the 13th or early dawn of the 14th) so that the next day the convoy was still in the flying range of the same Sardinian based bombers which were expected to mount a major strike sometime on the morning of 14th. On the afternoon of the 14th the aircraft based in Sicily would then get their chance to strike the convoy. The first set of attacks by the Sardinian based planes were to be the decisive ones as it was hoped that damaged enemy ships would be forced to navigate for as long as possible at reduced speed, in order to facilitate subsequent air attacks. According to historian Francesco Mattesini the plan of operation for the torpedo bombers was to be executed in synchronized waves by a mass of aircraft pressing forward simultaneous attacks on selected targets and based upon the tactical and strategic directive of *Generale* Fougier of April 1942.[46] In order to carry out such coordinated attacks the torpedo bombers throughout the approach flight to the convoy had to fly in a very tight formation so that each pilot could not lose sight of the other planes. They could then press forward and attack all at once. Moreover the RA was also deploying some of the first deliveries of its new fighters such as for example the *Reggiane* Re.2001 which equipped one *Stormo*. These new aircraft were believed by the RA top command to give its units an edge while fighting against the Hurricanes. It was believed that these aircraft could outmaneuver the RAF fighters and pave the way for the bombers to attack the warships with little or no interference from enemy aircraft.

The first Royal Navy ships that were part of the convoy entered the Mediterranean during the night between 11/12 June. They were immediately spotted by SIM agents based in Spain that communicated the intelligence information to Rome. The reports included a count of how many battleships and transports comprised the convoy. In addition, information was given on the presence of at least one aircraft carrier, possibly more, that was later to induce the RM to evaluate whether it was opportune to deploy its large battleships to counter the convoy especially in case the Axis air forces could not provide adequate fighter coverage. On the 12th the Axis launched reconnaissance operations undertaken by thirteen II *Fliegerkorps* and five long

45 Mark E. Stille, *Italian Battleships of World War II* (Oxford: Osprey, 2011), p.40.
46 Francesco Mattesini, "I successi degli Aerosiluranti Italiani e Tedeschi in Mediterraneo nella 2 Guerra Mondiale", *Bollettino d'Archivio dell'Ufficio Storico della Marina Militare*, March 2002, p.17.

range Cant.Z. 1007 bis from the 51° *Gruppo Ricognizione Strategica* based in Villacidro, Sardinia to shadow the convoy and further determine its strength. On 13 June the Axis intelligence gathering operations continued as two of these aircraft were shot down by the fighter escort launched from the aircraft carriers. Given the bad weather that prevailed on that day the Axis air forces were not deployed and therefore the convoy suffered no harm. Instead, the harm on that day was procured by a series of preemptive raids launched by the SAS against Axis air bases to create a diversion and to disrupt the planning of attacks against the convoy. The raid against Berka airfield, for example, led to three S.79s to be slightly damaged by Free French Special Forces, while the one raid by British Commandos against Maleme airfield on Crete yielded the damage and/or the destruction of sixteen Ju 88A. Another raid by Long Range Desert Patrols at Benina airport near Benghazi led to the damage to four German aircraft. Meanwhile on the 13th, the VII *Divisione* comprised of two cruisers and five destroyers was transferred from Cagliari to Palermo in order to interdict the convoy once it reached the Sicilian narrows.

14 June

By the morning of the 14th, the convoy was within 145 miles of Cagliari. With daylight, the convoy was reformed from its nighttime (anti-submarine) formation to its day-time formation which was designed to be both anti-aircraft and anti-submarine. HMS *Kenya* led the port column while HMS *Liverpool* the starboard, with the carriers providing close escort to the merchant ships inside the destroyer screen. The convoy was well defended by a powerful fighter escort that included: HMS *Eagle* which carried sixteen Hurricanes of No. 801 Squadron and four Fulmars of No. 801 Squadron but were subsequently transferred to HMS *Argus*. The latter carried eighteen Swordfish of No. 824 Squadron and two Fulmars of No. 813 Squadron. The escort functions assignments had been split with each aircraft carrier being responsible for low or high level attacks. Accordingly, HMS *Argus* was to carry out all the anti-submarine work and provided low cover with the Fulmars, while HMS *Eagle* took care of the high cover.

The convoy was first spotted by a Cant.Z.1007 of 51° *Gruppo* on the morning of the 14th at 0530 which reported back to base its estimated strength, the number of transports as well as its location. Shortly thereafter the interception operation was triggered. The Sardinian based squadrons were set to scramble at 0855 departing from Elmas airbase with two main formations: they were to deploy fourteen S. 84 from 108° e 109° *Gruppi/36° Stormo*; eight S.79 from 130° *Gruppo*, ten S.79bis from 104° *Gruppo*, a few S.79 planes from the 2° and 3° *Nucleo Addestramento Aerosiluranti*; eighteen Cant. Z. 1007bis from 29° and 33° *Gruppo*/9° *Stormo Bombardamento Terrestre*; nineteen CR.42 from 24° *Gruppo Caccia Terrestre*; twenty *Macchi* C.200 from 7° and 16° *Gruppi*/54° *Stormo Caccia Terrestre*. While *36° Stormo and 130° Gruppo* were considered to be comprised of experienced torpedo bomber crews, the *104° Gruppo,* who was recently trained to the new discipline, was to be deployed for the first time in its new role. The head of the torpedo bomber organization presumably considered the 104° *Gruppo* as combat ready. Harpoon was thus to witness the largest deployment to date of Italian aircraft to take off from Sardinian airbases since the beginning of the war with 103 planes of various kinds and thirty-three torpedo bombers. Despite the number of planes out of service and the torpedo bombers that were not yet ready for operations, the Sardinian based command had been able to deploy a considerable force.

Take off was at 0855. The flight to reach the convoy was made at a steady altitude of 700 meters with the S.79s flying in few formations of five aircraft each, while the S.84s in formations of three aircraft. The visibility was excellent so it allowed the aircraft to fly in very compact formations so not to lose sight of each other. The plan envisioned simultaneous attacks against the flanks of the convoy where 130° *Gruppo* (*Maggiore* Franco Melley) and 104° *Gruppo* (*Maggiore* Virginio Reinero) were to outflank it and then turn south to press forward the attack. Meanwhile the faster but less maneuverable S.84s of 36° *Gruppo* (*Colonnello* Giovanni Farina) were to go after the head of the convoy. CR.42 fighters of 24° *Gruppo* were tasked with escorting the torpedo bombers and were split into two units: one to protect the S.79s and the other the S.84s, while the *Macchi* C.200 fighters of 54° *Stormo* of *Colonnello* Francesco Beccaria were to clear the air of any enemy fighters that aimed to interdict the bombing attacks.

At 1000 the Axis air attacks began, approximately an hour after take-off. Some CR.42 armed with 100 kg bombs where the first to go into action as they attempted to release their load but were initially prevented from doing so by the prompt intervention of eight Hurricanes from No. 801 and No. 808 Squadrons. These British fighters also pursued the S.84s shooting down *Tenente* Alberto Leonardi's plane from 259ª *Squadriglia*, while a S.79 from 256ª *Squadriglia* (*Tenente* Isaia Rossi) was able to speed away, albeit with some damage to the plane after receiving machine gun fire from two Hurricanes. The CR.42s then reiterated their attack dropping their bombs and barely missing HMS *Charybdis*. As they sped to get away, however, two CR.42 were shot down by the prompt action of two Fulmars from No. 807 Squadron. The torpedo bombers had scrambled from their bases and had approached the convoy in tight formations, but their first attempt to harm the convoy was met by a violent British barrage especially by HMS *Malaya*, which by making full use of all its guns, including medium caliber 152 mm guns, forced most of the S.84s crews to launch their warheads from an unfavorable distance of 3,500 meters or more. As a result of this strong defensive tactic most torpedoes launched by 36° *Gruppo* did not score any hits. Only three S.84s pilots were bold enough to break through the curtain of enemy fire and close in on HMS *Malaya*. The first bomber barely misfired the ship, while one was shot down at close range and the other, due to a failure of the launching mechanism was unable to release the torpedo. After the three aircraft had carried out their attack closing in at point blank conditions, the precise anti-aircraft fire of the Royal Navy gunners continued to reap havoc on the S.84s. The formation had split up to perform the attack from various directions but despite diluting its force into smaller squads the torpedo bombers of 36° *Gruppo* continued to experience losses. The next two torpedo bombers to be shot down were from 109° *Gruppo*. *Colonnello* Farina's S.84 was hit by naval gun fire and his damaged aircraft fell in the sea in a ball of fire approximately 4,000 meters from the British ships, meanwhile the S.84 of *Capitano* Paolo Simeoni, commander of *259ª Squadriglia*, was engaged in a dogfight and then shot down by two Fulmars from the No. 807 Squadron piloted by Lieutenants Philip Hall and Peter Palmer. On board *Colonnello* Farina's plane was also *Maggiore* Mario Turba, who was the co-pilot and the commander of 109° *Gruppo*. Both would be posthumously awarded the gold medal of military valor. Then two more aircraft from 108° *Gruppo*, piloted by *Tenenti* Angelo Zanelli and Oreste Bedosti, were also downed by enemy naval fire. In addition, the crew of another plane from 109° *Gruppo*, with *Tenente* Angelo Abate as the pilot, also met the same fate shortly after. The pilot had vainly tried to disengage but to no avail as his aircraft was also taken down by naval fire. Finally, one S.84 from 108° *Gruppo* piloted by *Sottotenente* Oliviero Donati was shot to pieces losing one of its engines. It crashed into the sea but the crew survived on a dinghy and was later rescued after seven hours by a seaplane Cant.Z.506 from 613ª *Squadriglia Soccorso*, that had taken off in search of survivors. In the face of these S.84 losses, during the course of this first attack the RAF lost two Fulmars from No. 807 Squadron which were shot down by the combined fire of the *Sparvieri* and two CR.42 from *24° Gruppo*. The plane of Lieutenant Philip Hall was machine gunned and badly damaged by the combined fire of a S.79s and by the CR.42 fighters, but as the plane retreated it was also harmed by friendly fire and finally crashed into the sea. Meanwhile, the second Fulmar of Sub Lieutenant Peter Palmer was also shot down by enemy fire.

As the S.84s were being slaughtered, the slower S.79s also began their attack on the convoy. Led by *Maggiore* Melley, eight torpedo bombers from 130° *Gruppo* and ten from 104° *Gruppo* pressed forward from multiple directions. The planes were subdivided in various small groups each of four aircraft. They were escorted by twenty *Macchi* fighters. The torpedo bombers circled round the convoy and then came in from both ends flying 150 meters above the enemy destroyer screen. The attack on the port column was successfully dealt with by a combination of naval gunfire and by fighters, but that on the starboard column could not be stopped. One group of aircraft came in low through a gap in the destroyer screen and released their warheads at close range by dropping further down at a height of 60-100 meters and a range of 1,800 meters. At 1135, HMS *Liverpool,* steaming at 21 knots at the head of the convoy, and the Dutch ship *Tanimbar* were hit. Tanimbar (8,169 tons) was first struck by the torpedo launched by *Maggiore* Virginio Reinero, the commander of 235ª *Squadriglia*. Despite rapid anti-aircraft fire, *Maggiore* Reinero was able to approach the target and release the torpedo from a very advantageous position while receiving several hits that damaged his S.79. The badly damaged steamer was then finished off by 9° *Stormo* Z.1007 bis trimotors which bombed and sank it along with twenty onboard. Although successful the torpedo bomber attack on Tanimbar had been costly. *Maggiore* Reinero's plane was badly shot up and forced to raze the water to escape from the wrath of the enemy fighters. His wingman *Tenente* Mario Ingrellini courageously penetrated the anti-aircraft screen and got to within 400 meters of HMS *Eagle* when his plane ended its course and was finally downed by the enemy fire. At a perilously dangerous altitude of 40 meters his plane had already been badly damaged when Ingrellini, in a last ditch attempt, tried to crash it kamikaze style against HMS *Eagle,* but the plane fell prematurely into the water engulfed in fire. Meanwhile *Tenente* Giovanni Colonna's plane was shot down by No. 807 Squadron as he attempted to make his way toward the battleships. Both crews perished. *Tenente* Mario Ingrellini was later awarded a gold medal of military valor while *Tenente* Colonna a silver medal. Shortly thereafter, two more S.79 aircraft were slightly damaged by naval gunfire but nevertheless made it back to base. Meanwhile, HMS *Liverpool* was struck by one of four torpedoes launched by *Maggiore* Franco Melley's 280ª *Squadriglia* which was comprised of four planes and included Melley himself, *Tenente* Alessandro Setti, *Tenente* Angelo Caponetti, and *Sottotenente* Manlio Caresio. One of the attacking *Sparvieri* even managed to fly over the ship to courageously machine-gun the upper deck at close range killing seven sailors. The torpedo struck the starboard side abreast of the after engine room. A 24 feet by 19 feet rectangular hole was blown through the ship in engine room B on the ship's starboard side. HMS *Liverpool's* after boiler room and engine rooms, starboard oil fuel tanks and compartments up to the lower deck flooded immediately. Some sailors remained trapped in the flooded areas of the ship, while the torpedo strike killed fifteen and wounded twenty-one sailors. The ship's steering gear jammed and the flooding caused it to sink four feet down by the stern. Three other torpedoes were also launched in the direction of HMS *Liverpool* but all missed. One passed under the ship, while two others were dodged by the evasive action of the crew. The four S.79s under the command of *Capitano* Melley then safely returned to their base in Sardinia. HMS *Liverpool* was ultimately able to escape by being towed back at 3 knots by HMS *Antelope* and later by HMS *Salvonia* and screened by HMS *Wescott*. On the 17th it arrived at Gibraltar where it underwent extensive repairs. Then it was transferred to Scotland where it remained out of service for more than a year. During this second attack several Italian planes were damaged by gunfire, most of the aircraft damaged belonged to the less experienced 104º *Gruppo*. Losses from this second wave were represented by two *aerosiluranti* from 253ª *Squadriglia*/104° *Gruppo*, and two escort fighters: a *Macchi* C.200 from 16° *Gruppo*/ 54°*Stormo* and CR.42 from 24° *Gruppo* that was shot down by a Hurricane from HMS *Eagle*.

The Royal Navy post battle report with regards to the torpedo actions states that: "The port torpedo bomber attack was severely dealt with by gunfire and it is thought that not more than six aircraft got within 4,000 yards. A turn of 45° to port was made and no torpedo damage resulted. On the starboard side it was difficult to see what was happening as the wind was holding the cordite smoke on the line of sight. It appears that the three groups forced their attack well home from the bow, beam and quarter obtaining hits on Liverpool and Taninbar, setting on fire and sinking the latter."[47]

The surviving S.79 fled the area as fast as they could after having launched the warheads. The S.79 flown by *Maggiore* Reinero, for instance, who had been chased by enemy fighters, managed to escape by flying very close to the water. The pilot managed to return to base despite the heavy damage to his plane and was forced to land at the nearest base Elmas, rather than Decimomannu since *primo armiere* Pietro Chessa was gravely wounded and needed urgent medical attention. A second S.79, flown by *Sottotenente* Giovanni Babini, whose plane was also heavily damaged was forced to make an emergency landing at Elmas as well. Finally, a third S.79 flown by *Tenente* Enrico Marescalchi, that had been hit in the fuel tanks section and was spilling fuel throughout the return flight was ultimately forced to make an emergency crash landing on a small (of approximately four kilometers in length) and narrow runway near Capo Teulada. The landing was successful thanks to the pilot's adroit maneuvers which managed to save the crew and the plane. A final, third wave, comprised of ten Cant.Z.1007bis bombers of the 33° *Gruppo* then attacked the convoy but failed to achieve any hits.[48]

The offensive actions by *Aeronautica della Sardegna* were initially considered to be hugely successful because they relied exclusively on the post battle reports of the pilots which tended to be overly optimistic. In reality the operation had only been moderately successful while the losses to RA were severe. Against the damage inflicted upon HMS *Liverpool* and the sinking of the Tanimbar transport ship, the Italian air forces lost sixteen aircraft: nine *aerosiluranti* (six of which were S.84s of 36° *Stormo* including the one flown by its commander C*olonnello pilota* Giovanni Farina), two bombers: one Cant. Z. 1007 and one S.79, and five fighters: four CR. 42 and one *Macchi* C. 200. The attack on the Harpoon convoy demonstrated once gain how vulnerable the torpedo bombers were to anti-aircraft fire due to the nature of their low altitude

47 James Somerville, "Mediterranean Convoy Operations", *Supplement to the London Gazette*, n. 38296, 10 August 1948, p.4496.

48 Carlo Unia, *Storia degli aerosiluranti italiani* (Edizioni Bizzarri, Rome, 1974), p.197.

attacking tactics. Facing well drilled and experienced gunners, the Italian torpedo bombers were very vulnerable during daytime attacks.

On the afternoon of the 14th the initiative passed to the air forces based in Sicily as the enemy convoy had passed beyond Sardinia. Its commander *Generale* Silvio Scaroni had taken the preemptive action of moving the torpedo bombers ahead of time closer to the action by transferring them from Gerbini to Castelvetrano airbase. This move allowed "all aircraft, including the fighters with the least endurance, to pounce on the convoy when it was steaming past the Bizerte meridian."[49] It would also allow for attacks to take place the following day after the convoy was expected to have passed behind Sicily. Moreover, the vast deployment of Italian fighters "was to lead to air superiority over the enemy aircraft on the carriers."[50] The *Macchi* C. 202 and the *Reggiane* Re.2001, in particular, which were to be deployed for the first time with their more powerful German engines. There was much anticipation with regard to the combat performance of these two new aircrafts. *Superaereo* held them in high esteem and believed that they could more than hold their own against the enemy's carrier borne aircraft. In particular they were considered to be superior in both speed and maneuverability while operating at low altitude against Fulmars and Hurricanes. The first hard fought action, however, was conducted by German Ju.88 bombers of II *Fliegerkorps* that at 1755 pounced against HMS *Argus* but were not able to score any hits. The second attack was put forth by Buscaglia's new unit, the 132° *Gruppo* (otherwise known as *Gruppo Buscaglia*) that had been established on 1 April 1942 and had Buscaglia as its Commanding Officer supported by two experienced torpedo bomber pilots such as *Capitano* Graziani of 281ª *Squadriglia* and *Capitano* Rivoli of 278ª *Squadriglia*. The *Gruppo* at the time could field fourteen *Sparvieri* (seven from 278ª *Squadriglia* and seven from 281ª *Squadriglia*) escorted by a powerful fighter force comprised of seventeen *Reggiane* Re.2001 from 2° *Gruppo* and seven *Macchi* C.200 from 54° *Stormo*. The torpedo bombers were to act in conjunction with seventeen Ju.87 dive bombers of 102° *Gruppo* and eighteen standard bombers from the 5° *Nucleo Bombardieri*. The two torpedo squadrons took off from their Sicilian airbase at 1745 and 1800 respectively, followed by the standard bombers, but during their flight they were boldly attacked by two Sea Hurricanes from No. 801 Squadron which pursued the laggards, flying out of formation. Targeting isolate aircraft, they managed to down one plane (*Sottotenente* Giannino Negri of 278ª *Squadriglia*) and shoot up another S.79 (*Tenente* Vittorio Moretti) so badly wounding three crew members and forcing the pilot to crash land at the nearest Sicilian base of Castelvetrano. This attack, however, did not deter the synchronized operation by standard and torpedo bombers. The standard bombers and dive bombers attacked first. Their strike at the battleships terminated at 1920, but by this time they had absorbed the full attention of the enemy's anti-aircraft screen to the point that when the torpedo bombers arrived they enjoyed great freedom of maneuver. The torpedo attack took place in the vicinity of Cape Blanc, while the fighter escort, based on their numerical superiority, swept aside the enemy's Fulmar and Hurricane force. Despite enjoying a clear path toward the battleships and the transport ships, the torpedo bombers, as they inched closer to the enemy, were struck by murderous gunfire as the remaining twelve bombers all received hits of various kinds from the anti-aircraft defense. Four S.79s out of the twelve nevertheless were able to get within striking

49 Archivio Storico Aeronautica Militare, Comando Aeronautica della Sicilia, "Operazioni contro forze navali H provenienti da Gibilterra", 15 July 1942.

50 Ibid.

distance of the convoy and subsequently released their torpedoes from advantageous distances but all missed their targets including the most coveted one, HMS *Argus*. The latter was able to take evasive action by making a quick left turn, even though the torpedoes had been launched 300 meters out. One Fulmar from the No. 807 Squadron was shot down by friendly fire from HMS *Hebe*, while a Hurricane from No. 213 Squadron was downed by a *Reggiane* Re.2001. Finally, two Hurricanes were badly shot up by enemy fighters and forced to crash land on HMS *Eagl*e. While two *Reggiane* Re.2001 did not return to base forced into emergency landings at sea and in Tunisia respectively. The combat action of the torpedo bombers was particularly disappointing to the *Comando Aeronautica della Sicilia* because the fighters had paved the way for them chasing the Fulmars and Hurricanes away and creating the conditions for a favorable strike. Despite having a clearer shot at the targets, all torpedoes fired from close range missed. The last action of the day was conducted by another unit of Italian standard bombers which were also unable to inflict any damage.

The Royal Navy after-action report states that a tactical surprise was achieved by the Axis air forces with the deployment of the new fighters but that the prompt response by the Navy's guns did much to scatter and then repel the attack:

> About 17 torpedo bombers, 14 high level bombers and 20 single-engined fighters in addition to dive bombers were involved in attacks which began at 2006. During this period no less than four of the screen were out of position either investigating or attacking submarine contacts. During the attacks our fighters met considerable fighter opposition and were therefore unable to assist in breaking up the attacks. However, in spite of a number of near misses, the attacks were unsuccessful. The majority of the bombs from high level bombers and some of those from dive bombers fell round destroyers on the screen, ICARUS being particularly lucky to escape. A well-delivered attack was made by about 9 of the torpedo bombers who circled round astern out of range and then tried to come in from the starboard beam. Three emergency turns away were made to port to keep the sterns of the convoy towards the enemy, and the aircraft were forced to release their torpedoes at a very poor track angle, though from very close range, and failed to achieve any success. The gunnery of the force failed to obtain any known kills but did much in breaking up attacks.[51]

15 June

At dawn on 15 June 1942 the commander of Force X was alerted to the presence of the Italian VII *Divisione* (commanded by *Ammiraglio di divisione* Alberto Da Zara), with two light cruisers (*Raimondo Montecuccoli*, and *Eugenio di Savoia*) and five destroyers: *Ascari, Alfredo Oriani, Lanzerotto Malocello, Premuda* and *Ugolino Vivaldi*, by a Beaufighter. At 0530 in turn the Royal Navy convoy was spotted by the Sicilian reconnaissance units just south of Pantelleria island heading for Malta and a distance of approximately 22 miles from the forces of VII *Divisione*.

51 James Somerville, "Mediterranean Convoy Operations", *Supplement to the London Gazette*, n. 38296, 10 August 1948, p.4496.

The commander of Force X (Captain Hardy) onboard HMS *Cairo* had the convoy steaming closer to the coast of Tunisia and shielded by several smokescreens, while it dispatched five destroyers (Bedouin, Partridge, Ithuriel, Marne, and Matchless) to engage the Italian ships. His intent was to engage the enemy ships while HMS *Cairo* and the four Hunt class escorts defended the convoy. The naval engagement soon followed with HMS *Bedouin* and HMS *Partridge* in the lead which closed on to 15,000 feet of the Italian ships and quickly fired their warheads forcing the latter to take evasive action. The Italians struck first when they straddled with six inch shells HMS *Cairo* at a range of 20,000 yards. By then the Italian force had been split into two: the oldest and slowest moving destroyers were dispatched to counter the five fleet destroyers, while the rest of the battlefleet was interposed between Malta and the convoy. The Royal Navy destroyers hit back at the Italian ships who in turn fired at the destroyers concentrating their fire against HMS *Bedouin* and HMS *Partridge*. Both ships, facing longer range guns, came up worse off during the confrontation as they were hit repeatedly. The former received twelve strikes mostly by six inch shells, while the latter three times. HMS *Bedouin* was temporarily immobilized with its boiler and engine room sustaining some damage, while a fire developed on board HMS *Partridge*. The Italian post battle report asserted that the destroyers *Vivaldi* and *Malocello* were in the lead in the fighting as they closed at one point to within 6,000 yards of the enemy convoy and repeatedly fired at the enemy transport ships as well as the destroyers. This caused a strong reaction by the Royal Navy formation who quickly counter fired. The ship in the forefront of the action (*Vivaldi*) in turn took a direct hit from the British destroyers and caught fire. Both forces broke off the engagement at about 0800 showing once again the Italian Navy's hesitancy to engage the Royal Navy in a more protracted battle. The British post battle report tells a similar story: "By 0700 BEDOUIN's division was hotly engaged with the enemy cruisers and destroyers and about this time BEDOUIN and PARTRIDGE in the van were observed to have been hit and to have had their speed reduced. MARNE, MATCHLESS and ITHURIEL pressed on the attack past these two disabled destroyers engaging the enemy cruisers and destroyers. The Commanding Officer, MARNE reports that fire from MARNE and MATCHLESS was observed to take effect on two enemy destroyers who turned away under smoke."[52] The naval clash had been inconclusive but two British destroyers had been damaged.

At 0730 *Superaereo* received a communication by radio issued by VII *Divisione* which gave the location of the enemy convoy and also requested the intervention of the bombers under the command of the Sicilian airbases. This communication triggered the intervention of numerous units, amongst which was Capitano Buscaglia's unit which left Gerbini airport at 0900 with three S.79 (*Capitano* Buscaglia, and *Tenenti* Martino Aichner and Umberto Camera). In the meantime thirty Ju.88 from II *Fliegerkorps* spotted the convoy and dropped numerous bombs one of which struck the cargo ship American Chant while another one struck the tanker Kentucky.

After the German attack the convoy was in considerable disarray. Two ships of the convoy such as Troilus and Orari were intact. Kentucky was in tow making 6 knots while Burdwan was also steaming at a reduced speed. Bedouin was being towed by Partridge making about 8 knots and approaching the convoy from the east. The convoy was about 150 miles from Malta and the commander of the operation had to make a hard decision: Whether to continue at a speed of about 6 knots so to salvage the damaged ships, or whether to accept the losses by torpedoing the

52 Ibid.

slow ships and pick up speed to 14 knots or more with the intent of getting into Malta what was left of the convoy. It was in this context that *Capitano*'s Buscaglia's small squadron attempted to interfere with the convoy. But upon spotting the enemy transport and battleships at 1100 the three pilots were suddenly attacked by numerous Beaufighters from the No. 235 Squadron which swept in from above. The swift maneuver by the RAF squadron led to the S.79s receiving so much enemy fire that they had no other choice but to force land on Pantelleria airbase to nurse their damaged aircraft. "On Monday morning", recalls *Tenente* Umberto Camera, "torpedoes loaded, we set off again in search of ships. After an hour a Beaufighter attacked us. I was as usual, the right wingman of Capitano Buscaglia. The British fighter pilot attacked from the right, hitting my aircraft with his first burst. Three crew members were wounded and a fire started aboard. Nevertheless my gunners continued shooting as nothing had happened. The wireless operator was at the upper machine gun and the photographer and the gunner manned the waist ones, while the flight engineer, unable to use the damaged extinguisher, didn't hesitate to extinguish the fire, which had spread to the auxiliary tank (luckily empty!) with the flying suit he wore."[53] At Pantelleria *Tenente* Camera's plane was taken in for extensive repairs, while the other two S.79s were readily repaired and refit for action. As a result Buscaglia and Aichner after having refueled at Pantelleria airport resumed the hunt by droning again towards the enemy convoy. By 1300 they were again in its vicinity. At the time the two damaged Royal Navy ships HMS *Bedouin* and HMS *Partridge* were trailing the main convoy with the latter, the least damaged of the two, tasked with protecting HMS Bedouin. The plan was for HMS *Partridge* to tow HMS *Bedouin* but the plan was disrupted by the arrival of two Italian destroyers and two cruisers *Eugenio di Savoia* and *Montecuccoli*. HMS *Partridge* laid smoke around HMS *Bedouin* to shield it from the enemy ships that were about to close in. But this did not prevent HMS *Partridge* from being straddled at long range at 1310 by Da Zara's cruisers. At 1320 the two torpedo bombers of Buscaglia and Aichner began to circle around the convoy looking for a prey. Buscaglia was the first to strike at the enemy when he pounced upon an already damaged steamer (Burdwan 6,069 tons) which shortly after being torpedoed sunk. The 132° *Gruppo*'s war diary indicates that Buscaglia likely hit his target but does not specify whether his action was decisive as the vessel had been previously damaged either by German bombers or the RM. Meanwhile, *Sottotenente* Aichner was more successful than his *Gruppo* leader as he narrowed in on an enemy destroyer. His initial target was the merchant ship Kentucky but as the plane inched closer to it, Aichner observed that the ship had already been hit (German aircraft had already damaged it). He therefore abruptly changed course saving his torpedo for a more valuable target and by successfully targeting HMS *Bedouin* at 1325:

> Our orders are clear we must focus upon troop or supply carrying ships rather than battleships.
>
> We spot a large merchant ship that is barely visible behind great clouds of black smoke. Once again we go through our usual preparation to attack the target. The ship is within our reach but suddenly our pilot vigorously changes course and has we pass over the ship I can understand why. Why waste a torpedo when the ship has already been hit? There's fires on the ship and many sailors are bailing out by jumping into the sea.

53 Marco Mattioli, *Savoia Marchetti S.79 Sparviero*, p.50.

> Our pilot (Aichner) patrols the sea first by moving east then by moving north. A few minutes later we spot the silhouettes of several battleships. We identify them as our Marina ships of the VII Division that are traveling at great speed in a south west direction. Aichner instructs Del Bianco to focus his attention upon two enemy battleships in the vicinity of Pantelleria Island. The enemy ships under attack are firing in all directions to the point that the shots from the vessel's guns are getting dangerously closer but our job is to get within shooting range. As our aircraft swoops even lower its hit by strong gun fire. Suddenly it begins to rattle. A few seconds later the propeller stops working but our mission must continue. Then the engine catches fire and hot oil squirts all over the windshield. Aichner instructs Del Bianco to start using the fire prevention instruments on board but meanwhile he continues to get even closer to the enemy. Finally at a very close distance Aichner pats the torpedo switch and shortly thereafter at a distance of 600 meters releases the warhead. There is no more room to maneuver and the enemy machine gun fire continues to riddle the aircraft. One wing has more than one hundred holes. At first the plane responds to the pilots commands but all of a sudden begins to lose altitude.[54]

According to Sherard Manners who served on HMS *Bedouin*, a Tribal-Class destroyer, as Gunnery Control Officer: "Suddenly, at about 1400 a Savoia 79 aeroplane came out of the smoke on our starboard beam at a range of about 700yds. It turned towards us at a height of about 50ft. All guns that could, opened fire. I found the stripped Lewis gun which we kept on the bridge and opened fire also. Between the lot of us we managed to score some hits and later heard that they had ditched some 8-10 miles away. He dropped a torpedo at about 400yds and flew on straight over the ship. The captain and I watched the torpedo approaching and I remember saying "I wonder what it will be like when it hits." Unfortunately it struck the bulkhead between the engine room and gearing room – the two biggest compartments in the ship. It felt just as if a giant had kicked the ship."[55] The strike killed twenty-eight Royal Navy sailors, while the remaining 230 crew members were rescued by an Italian hospital ship and became prisoner of war. The S.79 struck the ship at such a short distance that the British naval guns were able to perforate the aircraft and eventually down it as it fled past the area. Luckily, *Sottotenente* Aichner and his crew survived the close combat action and were later rescued at sea by an Italian seaplane. Meanwhile in the late afternoon the British destroyer sank. Just before being struck HMS *Bedouin* could still be salvaged because even though it had received twelve hits and it was traveling at only reduced speed, it was being escorted to safety by HMS *Partridge*. But the torpedo hit presumably was the killer blow. Finally after being struck by the torpedo the commander of HMS *Partridge* stated that: " It is deeply regretted that even if the ship could not be saved, the Bedouin's commanding officer and her ship's company could not be rescued by a British warship."[56] After the sinking of its companion ship, HMS *Partridge* limped back slowly to Gibraltar as the RM failed to aggressively pursue a vessel that had already been struck several times and thus represented an easy target.

54 Ibid p.51 and Martino Aichner, *Il gruppo Buscaglia*, p.77.
55 WW2 Cruisers, HMS Bedouin 1942 <https://www.world-war.co.uk/bedouin.php> (accessed on 25 January 2022).
56 Malcolm Llewellyn-Jones, *The Royal Navy and the Mediterranean Convoys: A Naval Staff History* (New York: Routledge, 2007), p.66.

With regard to the sinking of HMS *Bedouin* and the merchant Burdwan the Royal Navy post battle report states that both ships were on their last leg and would have likely been torpedoed by the Royal Navy if it the enemy forces had not intervened:

> I have since learned that about this time enemy torpedo bombers most conveniently attacked and sank BURDWAN and KENTUCKY, a task which HEBE and BADSWORTH had been striving to accomplish for some time. I understand that both BURDWAN and KENTUCKY were fitted with scuttling charges but I do not at present know why these charges were not used. At 1430 PARTRIDGE reported that BEDOUIN had been torpedoed and sunk by enemy aircraft in position 36° 12' N., 11° 37' E., and at 1515 that enemy destroyers appeared to be picking up BEDOUIN's survivors. From this time until 1645, although unable to steam more than 8 knots, PARTRIDGE with great gallantry continued to shadow the enemy and report this greatly superior force.[57]

The Royal Navy dispatch appears to be more on point with regards to the merchantman Burdwan since at the time of the aerial torpedo hit it was already in bad shape. But with regards to HMS *Bedouin* it appears the destroyer could have been salvaged and repaired to be fit for action again if HMS *Partridge* had successfully towed it back to Gibraltar. Regarding HMS *Bedouin* there was a post war controversy between the RM and the torpedo bomber units as to who really was responsible for sinking the British destroyer. Most British accounts however, state that the torpedo bomber not naval fire was finally responsible for downing HMS *Bedouin*: "At 1245 an Italian aircraft torpedoed the Bedouin which sank within minutes, after managing first to shoot down the assailant. Italian torpedo aircraft also sank the derelict Kentucky and Burdwan at the same time."[58]

HMS *Bedouin's* Commander Scurfield finally put the controversy to rest when he commented in a letter in 1945 that it was: "A well-executed strike through smoke and against heavy anti-aircraft fire. All the guns were operational and were used against the torpedo bomber. The torpedo hit the bulkhead between the engine room and the gearing room on the starboard side. These two compartments were the biggest in the ship and they flooded immediately and we sank in about five minutes, stern first."[59]

One question that arises while describing the operations of the Sicilian based torpedo bomber units is why only three aircraft were fielded on the morning/early afternoon of 15 June given that many enemy ships had been already damaged and were reputedly considered to be easy targets? The answer lies in the low stock of torpedoes in the Sicilian airfields. In fact at dawn on the 15th *Aeronautica della Sicilia* was reduced to only four torpedoes, while 132° *Gruppo* had ten torpedo bombers in service.[60] Furthermore, several torpedo bombers that had been damaged on the 14th by enemy fire could not be hastily deployed due to a lack of specialized personnel. The

57 James Somerville, "Mediterranean Convoy Operations", *Supplement to the London Gazette*, n. 38296, 10 August 1948, p.4501.

58 Ibid.

59 Cited in Martino Aichner, *Il gruppo Buscaglia*, p.161.

60 Francesco Mattesini, "La battaglia aeronavale di mezzo giugno, 2017" <https://www.academia.edu/34682676/LA_BATTAGLIA_AERONAVALE_DI_MEZZO_GIUGNO > (accessed on 12 April 2021).

force also had difficulty fielding an adequate number of reconnaissance planes to keep track of the movements of the convoy as on the morning of 15 June just four S. 79 reconnaissance planes belonging to the 10° *Stormo Bombardieri* could be deployed. Of these only one, which took off at 0505 following a first sighting reported by a Cant Z. 506 reconnaissance seaplane made a relevant contribution to the operation by maintaining contact with enemy ships until 1300 when Buscaglia's team arrived on the scene. The latter's post battle report stated that: "Encouraging results were achieved by the combat action carried out by the crew of the aircraft that was forced to crash land on the water. This action is worthy of particular praise resulting in the sinking of an enemy destroyer."[61]

On the afternoon of 15 June 1942 further attacks were made by the RM and by the torpedo bomber squads based in North Africa. These were preceded by attacks made by X *Fliegerkorps* based in the Aegean. The target was the British convoy Vigorous which was sailing from the eastern Mediterranean and headed toward Malta. Indeed, the Italian Navy was in a good position to strike holding a numerical advantage over the escort of Vigorous, especially after during the night the *Kriegsmarine* had torpedoed HMS *Newcastle* and HMS *Hasty*. The battleships *Vittorio Veneto* and *Littorio* began to pursue the enemy convoy that morning but both came under heavy air attacks while en route to the designated interception point. The Allies attempted to interdict the warships by air. The major result of the Allied bombings were achieved by a bomb dropped by an American B-24 which fell on *Littorio*'s forward turret but did not damage significantly. Later in the evening a British torpedo bomber succeeded in striking *Littorio* and causing over 1,500 tons of water entering the ship. But with *Vittorio Veneto* still fully operational "the British convoy was forced to return to Alexandria since the Italian battlefleet out gunned the convoy escort. The mere threat of an Italian battleship had gained a major victory for the Axis."[62]

During the day the Axis air forces also attempted to pursue the Vigorous Convoy in an effort to reduce it. The fleet was spotted at 1440 by a Cant.Z.1007bis of 35° *Stormo*. The sighting triggered the intervention of the torpedo aircraft. The operation was conducted by ten torpedo bombers, six from the 279ª *Squadriglia/131° Gruppo* that took flight from Derna along with nine Cant.Z.1007bis bombers, and four from 204ª *Squadriglia/41° Gruppo* that took off from Gadurra in Rhodes. They were escorted by new state of the art twenty-eight *Macchi* C.202 of 4° *Stormo*. The former torpedo bomber unit led the attack at 1710 followed by the latter 15 minutes later in what became one of the most unsuccessful and costly operations ever conducted by the torpedo bombers. All ten aircraft released the torpedoes but the ships taking evasive actions managed to avoid the warheads. Shortly after releasing the warheads, one S.79, flown by *Tenente* Salvatore Annona of 41° *Gruppo*, was shot down by a Beaufighter and its crew perished. Another three S.79s were damaged severely by enemy anti-aircraft fire almost immediately after releasing their torpedoes. In turn three British fighters were shot down by the *Sparviero*'s defensive fire. The only success during the afternoon was the hit on the Australian destroyer Nestor which was damaged by the squad of Cant. Z. 1007 bis of *35° Stormo Bombardamento Terrestre*. Nestor had its boiler room flooded which immobilized the ship. On the 16th it sank north of Tobruk. HMS *Hermione* was torpedoed on the same day by U-Boat 205.

61 Archivio Storico Aeronautica Militare: 132° *Gruppo* Aerosiluranti Diario Storico, 18 June 1942.
62 Mark E. Stille, *Italian Battleships of World War II*, pp.40-41.

Thus it was the presence of a large battleship which stood in the way of the convoy rather than the ineffectual action of the torpedo bombers launched from the North African bases that caused the Vigorous convoy to give up its operation and to call back its ships to Alexandria. The Royal Navy managed to get supplies into Malta (two transports from Harpoon made it into the port of Malta for a total of 15,000-tons) that were enough to last the island for a few more weeks although it had lost the majority of the transports and its valuable cargo during the journey for both Vigorous and Harpoon. Out of seventeen transports six were sunk and nine of the Vigorous Operation were forced to turn back. Royal Navy escort forces suffered heavy losses as well. Cruisers of the Town class HMS *Liverpool,* HMS *Hasty* and HMS *Newcastle* were damaged requiring extensive repairs that kept them away from the Mediterranean for a long time. Destroyers HMS *Bedouin* and HMS *Nestor* were sunk, while HMS *Partridge* was damaged. In addition, thirty aircraft were lost as part of this operation. Eight from the aircraft carrier and the remaining from the RAF base at Malta. It can be argued that the *Luftwaffe* and the *Kriegsmarine* along with the Italian Navy played a key role in this operation but that the Italian air forces also contributed to the Axis success with the torpedoing of HMS *Liverpool*, the sinking of the two transports Taninbar and Burdwan and the sinking of two destroyers HMS *Nestor* and HMS *Bedouin*. In turn, the Italian Navy suffered the loss of the cruiser *Trento* and damage to the *Littorio* battleship and the *Vivaldi* destroyer. Moreover, the Axis lost 43 aircraft (28 Italian and 14 German). The after-action reports issued by the two sides specifically focused on the air attacks: "On the whole the Italians seem to have attacked gallantly. Captain Russell of Kenya, for instance, remarked on their outstanding bravery and Captain Armstrong of the Onslow called the attacks unexpectedly impressive though other officers were not so kind. On the other hand, had their timing been more exact and the two torpedo attacks delivered together instead of one after the other, they would probably have proved more successful."[63] The general opinion was that the Sicilian based pilots on the evening of 14 June had put forth more effective attacks using deception by coming on the heels of the standard bombers. Captain Armstrong of the Onslow remarked that the bombers "entirely took the screen's attention away from the torpedo bombers … The air attacks … were unexpectedly impressive. The high level bombers kept good and close formation and were undeterred from H.A. fire. The torpedo bombers also pressed their attacks well home."[64] The attacks put forward by Buscaglia's unit appeared to be "timed in better coordination and some officers considered the torpedo attack more vigorously carried out."[65] With regards to the Royal Navy's anti-aircraft fire Captain Waller of HMS *Malaya* remarked on the efficiency of the 6-inch barrage in inducing the Italians to drop their torpedoes prematurely."[66] Moreover, radar had worked well. "Radar warning of the enemy's approach gave time to increase the British air patrol from four to eight fighters."[67] Historian Malcolm Llewellyn-Jones has written that the effectiveness of radar combined with the defensive action of the anti-aircraft weapons and the RAF fighters achieved significant success against the Italian air forces. They were able to shoot

63 Malcolm Llewellyn-Jones, *The Royal Navy and the Mediterranean Convoys: A Naval Staff History* (New York: Routledge, 2007), p.59.
64 Ibid, p.60.
65 Ibid. , p.60.
66 Ibid., p.59.
67 Ibid., p.61.

down or damage a large number of aircraft.[68] The critical contribution of the German bombers and fighters was not overlooked by the post battle assessment made by the Royal Navy especially the several strikes made against British transports.

In contrast, the RA post battle report remarked on the effectiveness of its new fighter aircraft the *Reggiane* Re.2001 an the *Macchi* C.202: "The superiority of the Re.2001 and the MC.202 with respect to the British naval aircraft allowed our fighters to maintain supremacy of the skies during the entire action."[69] The work of these new fighters was credited with creating favorable attack conditions for the waves of bombers. This view was shared by the British commander of the operation. On the air action Admiral Curteis reported that "our fighters met considerable fighter opposition and were therefore unable to assist in breaking up the attacks."[70]

In conclusion it can be argued that Operation Harpoon was a success for the Italian naval and air forces. British historian, Stephen Roskill, for example, asserted that the Axis success was undeniable. Malta had been supplied with few resources and badly needed fuel for the ships and the airplanes had not arrived. Moreover, the Royal Navy had experienced heavy losses in tankers, cruisers and destroyers against comparable fewer losses suffered by the RM and some heavier losses by the Axis air force.[71] He also underscored the key role played by the German air and naval forces.

Historians Greene and Massignani assert that the Axis interference action against Harpoon and Vigorous was one of the few undisputed squadron-sized victories for the RM in the Mediterranean shipping war: "Clearly this was an Axis victory and a tactical victory for the RM. Part of the convoy did get through to Malta, but the British suffered far heavier losses than did the Italians…."[72] Moreover they argue that it was one of the few tactical victories achieved by the RM during the conflict. Both authors also remarked upon the impact exerted over the supply war by the torpedo bombers that managed to damage two transports, a light cruiser and a destroyer. Their success had been a low cost one especially in relation to the amount of fuel and ammunition spent by the RM which had achieved comparable results. Finally, historian Giorgio Giorgerini wrote that the *Battaglia di Mezzo Giugno* (battle of mid-June as it's called by Italian historians) was a tactical success for the RM as its warships fought aggressively and pursued their opponents. Moreover, they collaborated well with the air forces especially during the two pronged attack with the Sicilian based *Sparvieri* units. The trials by combat during 1940-42 had evidently enhanced the tactical acumen of both services. Both had made progress with respect to the start of the war.[73] The only drawback to the RM tactics used in Operation Harpoon was its hesitancy in destroying the whole convoy including the two transports that were still operating on 15 June and eventually made it into port at Malta. Given its superior forces, the RM on 15 July could have acted more aggressively.

68 Ibid., p.67.
69 Archivio Storico Aeronautica Militare, Superaereo, "La Battaglia di Mezzo Giugno", 19 June 1942.
70 Cited in Vincent O'Hara, *In Passage Perilous: Malta and the Convoy Battles of June 1942* (Bloomington, Indiana: Indiana University Press, 2013), p.178.
71 Stephen Roskill, *The Period of Balance. History of the Second World War: The War at Sea 1939–1945. II* (London: HMSO, 1962), pp.71-72.
72 Jack Greene and Alessandro Massignani, *The Naval War,* p.238.
73 Giorgio Giorgerini, *La guerra italiana sul mare. La marina tra vittoria e sconfitta 1940–1943* (Milan: Mondadori, 2004), p.201.

In the week following Operation Harpoon both the Navy and the Air Force insisted upon the neutralization of Malta at the expense of a further advance in Egypt after Rommel had captured Tobruk on 20 June. *Ammiraglio* Riccardi, for example argued that "We cannot guarantee a steady supply of Tobruk unless we take Malta." In turn *Generale* Santoro stated to *Comando Supremo* that the RA had only seven aerial torpedoes after the great expenditure represented by Operation Harpoon. Moreover, this low stock, reflective of the ebb and flow of torpedo bomber operations, would impede his units if they were called upon to halt any major enemy convoys in the next weeks.[74] Both Cavallero and Kesselring were also of the opinion that Malta ought to be taken prior to the end of the summer of 1942 to allow the resumption of the offensive in North Africa. But these calls were to no avail since Rommel, spurred on by his victories, would successfully induce both governments to allow him to advance even further beyond the Gazala line and to place the invasion of Malta on the backburner.

On the 17 June further attacks were made on the British fleet. Four *Sparvieri* from 130° *Gruppo* made their attack from afar because of heavy anti-aircraft fire. Only two torpedoes were released from very distant positions and missed their targets. Further losses were sustained on 26 June when two torpedo bombers from 41° *Gruppo* made a determined attack in the Easter Mediterranean against a British convoy. *Tenente* Luigi Vicariotto of 204ª *Squadriglia* and *Tenente* Giuseppe Briatore of 205ª *Squadriglia* spotted their target and then began their descent toward the freighter escorted by a destroyer. The former pilot attacked first but could not release the torpedo unable to attain a proper launching position, while *Tenente* Briatore fired his torpedo but missed. A few minutes later the plane was attacked from behind by two British fighters who managed to shoot it down and killing the crew.

On 30 June *Tenente* Pucci achieved another success when he sank the British Aircrest steamer which was navigating west of Jaffa. *Tenente* Emilio Pucci, *Sottotenente* Dorando Cionni of 205ª *Squadriglia/41° Gruppo* and *Tenente* Luigi Vicariotto of 204ª *Squadriglia/41° Gruppo* took off from Gadurra airbase in Rhodes with their S.79s to conduct a reconnaissance operation along the coast of Palestine. *Tenente* Pucci was the only pilot of this small unit to spot a convoy comprised of five transport ships escorted by two destroyers that was heading from Port Said to Haifa. The 5,237 tons Aircrest was steaming ahead when it was torpedoed at 0820 at approximately 20 miles to its destination. The ship then sank to be the bottom of the sea. The area of Port Said was targeted again by torpedo bombers on 3 July at 0755 when two S.79s of *41° Gruppo* led by *Capitano* Stelio Di Stefano attacked a small convoy comprised of four transport ships and two destroyers. The pilots affirmed in the post battle report that they had scored two strikes against the convoy, but the Royal Navy report stated otherwise. No damage was inflicted on the convoy.

On 22 July two *Sottotenenti* from the same unit (205ª *Squadriglia/41° Gruppo*) Dorando Cionni and Ferruccio Coloni flying on S.84s attacked a convoy near Port Said and managed to score a hit against the 2,969-tons convoy escort ship HMS *Malines*. "On 22 July Malines was approaching Port Said and was ordered to wait outside to allow HMS *Dido* and the destroyer screen to leave the harbor. While there at 1030 an aerial torpedo hit her on the starboard side, passed through her and exploded on the port side, killing seven crew members and injuring

74 *L'Italia in Guerra, Il Terzo Anno, Parte Seconda* (Rome: Ufficio Storico, 1993), p.320.

seven others."[75] At 1110 the ship was towed by HMS *Whitehaven* which brought it back to the harbor where it was inspected and then extensively repaired. The repairs took a year to complete. This was one of the last operations undertook by the *41° Gruppo* which in August of 1942 was transferred to Pisa airport in order to be rebuilt. Upon vacating the Aegean theatre the unit was just a shadow of its former self with few operational aircraft and less than five active crews. It was replaced at Gadurra airport in Rhodes by the *104° Gruppo*.

Operation Pedestal

Operation Pedestal was the largest Allied convoy, and probably the most important, operation to aid Malta and to attempt to ensure its survival as a base from which the British could launch further attacks against the Axis. Its importance in the Mediterranean shipping war and in the fate of the Axis armies in North Africa could not be underscored. On the heels of Operation Harpoon in June, which had not been successful, Malta was in a precarious situation. Its population was near starvation, the troops had low stocks of certain armaments and ammunition and fuel supplies were low to power aerial and naval submarine operations. Stocks of white oil and aviation fuel, for example, were sufficient only until about mid-August, while only about 920 tons of diesel fuel and two thousand tons of furnace oil for refueling warships were available. The island also was bereft of vital anti-aircraft ammunition since available supply was sufficient for only six weeks of fighting. The future of Malta as a base for submarine and destroyer attacks against Axis convoys was at stake since the latter could not operate out of a base with low or no stocks of fuel and under recurrent enemy bombardments. Moreover, it was not just Malta that was under threat of extinction, it was also the overall situation of the Allies in North Africa which in mid-1942 was precarious. In fact, Operation Pedestal took place at a time when the Allied fortunes in the Mediterranean were at their lowest ebb. In North Africa Rommel's forces had been forced into a standstill after the inconclusive first battle of El Alamein (1–27 July 1942). However, the Axis ground units were still threatening to launch a new offensive against the British with an ultimate push toward Alexandria and the Suez Canal and they were stockpiling fuel, ammunition, tanks, and other supplies. For the Allies, the priorities were to not only retain Malta, but also to halt any future Axis advance in Egypt. The two objectives were tightly intertwined given that Malta offered the first line of defense against a major Axis advance in North Africa. With the stakes so high it is no surprise that: "The operational decision to run a major resupply operation to Malta was made by the strategic leadership in London, not by the Admiralty or the fleet commanders in the theatre."[76] Under pressure from Prime Minister Winston Churchill, the Royal Navy was tasked with planning this large and most essential convoy destined for Malta. The latter, according to the Prime Minister, had to receive the much needed aid and the Royal Navy was to push through the convoy even if the operation was risky and presented many difficulties in its execution. The Prime Minister's determination would ensure that this transport operation would be escorted by the largest and most

75 John de S. Winser *Short Sea: Long War. Cross-Channel Ships' Naval & Military Service in World War II* (London: World Ship Society, 1997), p.63.

76 Milan Vego, "Major Convoy Operation to Malta, 10–15 August 1942 (Operation Pedestal)", *Naval War College Review*: Vol. 63: No. 1, 2010, p.8.

powerful force ever fielded by the Royal Navy. Sea Lord Admiral Dudley Pound, who agreed with Prime Minister Churchill that Malta had to be maintained at all costs, personally took control of the planning team behind Operation Pedestal. The overall objective as stated in the final draft of the plan was "to pass a convoy of 14 M.T. [motor tanker] ships through the western Mediterranean to Malta and to cover the passage of two merchant ships and two destroyers from Malta to Gibraltar."[77] In other words the plan was to ensure Malta's survival past September 1942 by delivering a sufficient amount of fuel, ammunition, and food supplies. The planning team worked under the premise that surprise would be difficult to achieve because of the Axis strong intelligence capabilities in the Gibraltar area. The next town over from Gibraltar, the Spanish town of Algeciras was a major base of Axis spies and intelligence agents. The X Mas, for example, operated agents out of a house that overlooked the waters. Since surprise could not be achieved, the plan was founded on the premise that for Operation Pedestal to succeed the Royal Navy had to deploy sufficient forces to counter diverse threats posed by the Axis air and naval forces based in Sardinia, Sicily, and Libya. Not only the Royal Navy was to deploy the largest naval force ever fielded for a convoy but also the largest escort fighter force ever deployed by the RAF and Fleet Air Arm that was to interdict the Axis bombers, dive bombers and torpedo bombers menacing the convoy.

Based on the lessons learned from the prior convoy operation organized in June 1942 as historian Milan Vego asserts: "….the Allies correctly assumed that the enemy would concentrate its heavy surface forces in the area south of Sardinia and then either attack the convoy or draw off Allied escorting forces, leaving the convoy open to attack by its light forces. They also expected synchronized attacks by enemy high-level bombers, torpedo bombers, and dive-bombers on the third and fourth days, and high-level bombing and torpedo bomber attacks on the second and fifth days of the operation. To minimize losses from enemy aircraft, the convoy would transit the Sicilian Narrows at night."[78]

Thus, the convoy codenamed WS 21/S was set to start from Britain on 2 August then head to Gibraltar, pass through the Mediterranean within the range of Axis air bases on Sardinia and Sicily and ultimately reach Malta on the 14th of August. It was heavily escorted not only by battleships and destroyers but also by a formidable fighter aircraft force based on three aircraft carriers and comprised primarily of Sea Hurricanes and Martlets and some Fulmar fighters. In total it would field seventy-two fighters and thirty-eight bombers.[79] Support for the convoy would also come from the RAF squadrons based in Malta, the strength of which on 3 August was 155 serviceable aircraft, including ninety-five Spitfire fighters and about fifty-five bombers. The latter forces were to not only attack in preemptive strikes the Italian and German air bases on Sicily, Sardinia, and Pantelleria but also protect the convoy after it had reached the middle of the Mediterranean. Moreover, seven submarines were also to be deployed in the escort of the convoy to tackle the enemy's small naval crafts and the battleships thus providing a screen against potential enemy attacks. The Mediterranean Fleet had also planned a diversionary action in the Eastern Mediterranean with some warships escorting a dummy convoy to deflect the attention of the Axis forces from the real action and split them up in different operations. The convoy,

77 Operation "Pedestal" (Main Convoy), W.H. Case 8269, Part I and II, 2–16 Aug 1942,ADM 199/1243, Public Records Office (London), p.1.

78 Ibid.

79 Ibid. p.10.

under the command of Acting Vice Admiral Edward Neville Syfret, was comprised of fourteen merchant vessels, the largest of which was the Ohio, with its 12,000 tons of oil. The other vessels included: Santa Elisa 8,379 tons, Almeria Lykes 7,773 tons, Rochester Castle 7,795 tons, Deucalion 7,516 tons, Clan Ferguson 7,347 tons, Empire Hope 12,688 tons, Wairangi 12,436 tons, Waimarama 12,843 tons, Port Chalmers 8,535 tons, Dorset 10,624 tons, Melbourne Star 12,806 tons, Brisbane Star 12,791 tons and Glenorchy 8,982 tons. "The total of 85,000 tons of supplies were loaded in such a way that every ship had a mixed cargo so that the loss of one ship would not mean that all of one particular item went down with her."[80] Moreover, in a separate but contingent operation, forty Spitfires transported on HMS *Furious* were to fly off in the proximity of Malta to augment its force. The carrier Furious was set to sail independently of the convoy from Gibraltar and after reaching a point south of Sardinia, approximately 550 miles from Malta, would launch its Spitfires. The convoy was to be protected by Force Z between Gibraltar and the middle of the Mediterranean with two battleships (HMS *Nelson* and HMS *Rodney*) and three large aircraft carriers (HMS *Eagle*, HMS *Indomitable* and HMS *Victorious*), three cruisers (HMS *Sirius*, HMS *Phoebe* and HMS *Charybdis*), and the 19th Destroyer Flotilla with fifteen destroyers. Force Z was to rendezvous in the Central Mediterranean with Force X who was in charge of escorting the convoy on its last leg from Sicily to Malta. Force X, under command of Rear Admiral H. M. Burrough, was comprised of three light cruisers (HMS *Nigeria*, HMS *Kenya* and HMS *Manchester*), one anti-aircraft ship (HMS *Cairo*) of the 10th Cruiser Flotilla, eleven destroyers of the 6th Destroyer Flotilla, and one ocean tug. An additional five destroyers were assigned to tackle potential Axis submarine attacks against the convoy during its transit from Britain to the Strait of Gibraltar. Force R (Refueling) was to provide the convoy; the fuel that was needed to continue the journey in the Mediterranean. It was composed of three fleet oilers and one ocean tug plus four corvettes for escort.

The Malta Escort Force (17th Minesweeping Flotilla) was also to be activated inclusive of four minesweepers and seven motor launches. The unit was to safeguard the convoy from falling prey to any minefields laid out by the Axis especially in the tight areas such as the one near Sicily. In order to leave nothing to chance, the Royal Navy extensively trained the personnel destined to take part in the operation by organizing several drills in the Atlantic (a three-day exercise west of the Strait of Gibraltar prior to the passage of the convoy through the strait code-named Operation Berserk) where the crews were taught such tactics as how to deploy evasive maneuvers in the face of naval and aerial torpedoes and how to fight off fighter and bomber attacks. Particular attention was given to the combination of evasive maneuvers and anti-aircraft fire: "The convoy was repeatedly exercised in anti-aircraft gunnery, in emergency turns and in changing from one cruising disposition to another, using both flags and short range W/T."[81]

Axis agents were the first to communicate that a large scale enemy operation was afoot. Reports from Abwehr agents, for example, concerning enemy movements in the western Mediterranean were received by Kesselring on 5 August, while the convoy was first spotted by Italian agents at Algeciras as it passed through the Straits of Gibraltar on 10 August. At first it was not clear to the Axis commanders what the intent of this enemy operation was, mostly because it was so sizeable. Some like head of *Comando Supremo* Cavallero believed that the

80 Jack Greene and Alessandro Massignani, *The Naval War*, p.244.
81 James Somerville, "Mediterranean Convoy Operations", *Supplement to the London Gazette*, n. 38296, 10 August 1948, p.4502.

Allies wanted to land troops and tanks somewhere in North Africa. As a result the Tobruk garrison was placed on high alert and troops were readied to counter a potential enemy landing. The RM expressed a different idea. *Ammiraglio* Luigi Sansonetti maintained that the convoy was organized to bring more Spitfires and Hurricanes to Malta. He argued that the operation had to be shadowed by aerial reconnaissance and that the RM was to deploy its small assault crafts to attack it. On the 11th *Ammiraglio* Ricciardi issued a report submitted by X Mas agents in Spain, that detailed the size of the enemy force put at sea. It stated that this operation was by far the largest ever undertaken by the Royal Navy and that given its size, it was not possible to determine its intent. A day later the Axis main commanders in the Mediterranean met again to debate how best to respond to counter the large convoy and which forces could be deployed. The meeting showed how the Axis, unlike the Allied coalition, was a looser and less coherent alliance where there were hugely divergent views and goals.[82] It epitomized the war effort in the Mediterranean where the Germans had more limited objectives whereas the Italians had altogether another set of priorities. The RM requested that a fighter escort be provided to its battleships so that it could counter the convoy. But Kesselring denied the request and argued that the bulk of the *Luftwaffe's* 235 fighter planes located in Southern Italy and the Aegean could not be deployed to escort the RM into battle since the force was already tasked with other actions focused primarily on the Eastern Mediterranean. He also argued that the best way to check the convoy was to ambush it by laying a new set of mines in the Mediterranean. Kesselring's position reflected the position of both air services, who felt they did not have enough fighter force to provide the escort to the Navy as well carry out other operations such as escort the bombers. As a result, it was decided that the RA and the *Luftwaffe* were to deploy the fighter force to escort torpedo and standard bombers to attack the convoy, while providing an escort to the Navy was not an objective of their operations. The rationale behind Kesselring and Fougier decision was that aerial attacks against the convoy were reputed by the two services to be more effective over providing air cover for the battleships. Kesserling, however, did mention that sizeable part of his aircraft fleet could be utilized to make aerial attacks on the convoy and that the transfer of German aircraft from Crete to Sicily was already underway.[83] Kesselring's decision to deny the RM the escort fighters for the fleet was also dictated by the earlier experience during the aerial/naval battle of 15 June where the Italian battlefleet had shown a degree of hesitancy despite favorable circumstances especially in challenging the remnants of Operation Harpoon during the last leg of its voyage. Meanwhile, the RM argued that given the size of the enemy convoy the main objectives of the Axis should be to intercept the force coming from Gibraltar while the RA through *Generale* Fougier was initially mistaken in reading the enemy's intentions by arguing that the main point of the British operation was to bring supplies to Malta from the Eastern Mediterranean.[84] The RM stated that it could deploy four battleships, three heavy and

82 Strategic decision between the two allies were often taken at infrequent sessions which were the only opportunity for a direct exchange of information on military matters. Within the Axis alliance no combined operational staff or Axis war planning board existed primarily because of the basic mistrust between the two allies.

83 Newly trained German torpedo-bombers moved from the Mediterranean to Norway in June 1942 and did not return in time for the operation. Twenty Ju-88s based in Crete moved to Sicily on 11 August, while an additional eight Ju-88s from Crete flew to Sicily on 12 August.

84 While the Allies through the Ultra intercept had a better overall estimate of the enemy's strength, the Axis command had to rely almost exclusively on intelligence coming from agents located in Spain

ten light cruisers, twenty-one destroyers, twenty-eight torpedo boats, and sixty-four submarines, but that its largest battle ships were hampered by the lack of fuel and inadequate air cover. As per the RM the fuel supply was the most precarious situation it faced since the 12,000 tons of fuel received at the beginning of June were enough to cover about one-fifth of that consumed by convoys to North Africa. At the conclusion of the meeting it was decided that the battleships were not to be deployed for the interdiction operation because of the shortage of fuel and the lack of a substantial escort force. Instead the Axis aimed to interfere with the convoy by deploying primarily aircraft, light vessels such as cruisers, destroyers, torpedo boats and submarines. Thus, *Supermarina* was able to field for the pending operation three eight-inch cruisers (*Gorizia, Bolzano, and Trieste*) and seven destroyers of the *III Divisione*, three six-inch cruisers (*Eugenio di Savoia, Raimondo Montecuccoli, and Muzio Attendolo*) and five destroyers of *VII Divisione* plus eighteen submarines, nineteen torpedo boats (six *Motoscafi Siluranti* and thirteen MAS (*Motoscafi Armati Siluranti*). The *Kriegsmarine* could deploy two U-boats and four S-boats (torpedo boats). These forces were to be deployed in a combined arms operation alongside the forces fielded by the RA and the *Luftwaffe* in coordinated attacks. The Axis plan resembled the one adopted against Operation Halberd and Harpoon. First, heavy air reconnaissance of the western Mediterranean by the Italian aviation units and the *Luftwaffe*. Second, attacks on the convoy by the Italian and German aircraft based on Sicily and Sardinia. The latter was to make the most potent attack, while the former was to deploy its dive bombers with specially selected new weapons. Third, Italian submarines and German U-boats together with Italian torpedo boats would then be unleashed to conduct surprise attacks at night while the convoy passed below southern Sicily. Finally, with the convoy degraded and dispersed, Italian cruisers and destroyers would then intervene to inflict major damage on the remaining enemy ships just prior to the end of their journey. Then based upon the degree of success of the RM strike, the Axis command also envisioned last minute strikes by dive bombers on the docks of La Valetta upon the arrival of the remnants of the convoy. According to the minutes of the meeting *Generale* Cavallero urged the aviation force to focus their efforts on sinking the merchant ships in both attacks mounted from Sardinia and Sicily. To this, *Generale* Fougier replied that it was difficult to damage the merchant ships because they were typically at the center of the convoy and well protected by the outer destroyer screen. But he also stated that the air force would mount three attacks: One major combat action from Sardinian airbases, followed by a less sizeable action out again of Sardinia but focused upon already damaged enemy ships. Finally, another major attack mounted from Sicilian air bases. Despite the difficulties presented in targeting the merchant ships, the Chief of Staff of the air service asserted that the planners at *Superaereo* had put in place an elaborate plan, perhaps their most detailed and articulate plan of the war, to attack the convoy. The overall objectives were first to destroy the enemy aircraft carriers to degrade the enemy's aerial escort and their launching pads and second to target the merchant ships.

RA Chief of Staff Fougier counted upon the deployment of new weapons such as the newly arrived *Macchi* C.202 fighters and a host of semi-experimental perforating bombs as well as upon established ones to achieve a tactical surprise. The new fighters were considered to offer a superior performance to those on the British aircraft carriers and hence could neutralize their interference on Axis bombers and torpedo bombers. The new weapons were to be used primarily to damage

and hence had fewer information prior to the battle engagement.

the aircraft carriers thus debilitating the escort fighters.[85] For the first time the RA would implement the deployment of a large number of *Motobombe FFF* (circular torpedoes) to be launched by ten S.84 bombers.[86] These air dropped torpedoes equipped with parachutes were meant to create artificial waves, unsettle the steady navigation of the ships and then on contact damage them.[87] Their role was to sow confusion and procure some damage to the ships and ultimately disperse them so to pave the way for the massive bomber and torpedo bomber attack which was to follow. With the enemy warships and destroyers out of formation, it was envisioned that the subsequent bomber attacks could be more successful against a decentralized and unsettled anti-aircraft defense. After the circling torpedoes had caused some damage, then the bombers and the torpedo bombers would be unleashed along with a radio controlled S.79 bomber carrying two 1,000 kg special torpedoes with a 650 kg warhead, that in a kamikaze like action, was to "crash on board the aircraft carrier."[88] The unmanned aircraft, which had been stripped of its steel mainframe and substituted by aluminum to make it lighter hence more controllable, was to be flown in the combat area by a lone pilot whom having reached the destination would jump out of the plane by parachute. At that point the S.79 would be radio controlled by the shadow pilot flying on a Cant.Z.1007 bis that was to release it against the carrier at the most opportune time. The two torpedoes were carried in the same position of the standard Whitehead warhead and upon contact with the enemy ship the plane would crash against the flank or the bow of the ship, while the torpedoes would be unleashed as well. This specially equipped S.79 was painted yellow and it was named the *canarino* (canary), so that it be more visible.

Lastly, to further damage the aircraft carriers, two *Reggiane* Re.2001 of RA Special Section/New Weapons unit were to drop 630 kg low altitude armor piercing bombs on the flight deck. The latter were expected to damage the deck of one of the aircraft carriers and inhibit its use by the aircraft. Each wave was to be supported by the new *Macchi* and *Reggiane* fighters available to the RA. Thus, new weapons alongside established ones were to be used in a detailed and what apparently appeared to be a very comprehensive response to the Royal Navy's massive attempt at a passage through the Mediterranean. The planners maintained that in order to work effectively the various weapons had to be deployed in sequential waves with intervals of between five or seven minutes between each wave.[89] The faster S.84s were to fly together with the S.79bis while the S.79s torpedo bombers were to fly in a separate group but taking a shorter route. To ensure success the "torpedo bomber and standard bomber squads were to be escorted by the most modern fighters available."[90] The operative document also furnished the number of aerial warheads available. On 10 August the units of RA could count on: 67 torpedoes in Sardinia, 36 in Sicily, 17 in Libya and 15 in the Aegean.[91] The modern fighters referred to in the operational

85 I verbali delle riunioni tenute dal capo di stato maggiore generale, Vol. 3 (Rome: Ufficio Storico, 1993), pp.746-47.

86 United States Intelligence Services, *Tactical and Technical Trends*, No. 11, 5 November, 1942.

87 Giuseppe Ciampaglia, "La sorprendente storia della motobomba FFF", *Rivista Italiana Difesa*, July 1999.

88 Ibid.

89 Archivio Storico Aeronautica Militare: Superaereo, "Ordine operativo contro convoglio scortato", GAM 6, 11 August, 1942.

90 Ibid.

91 During the operation between 12 and 15 August the manufacturers of torpedoes were able to supply three more aerial warheads which were transferred to the operative bases by S.82 aircraft.

document were the *Macchi* C.202 *Folgore* and the *Reggiane* Re. 2001, some units of which were beginning to be delivered to the RA by the domestic suppliers. Both the *Macchi* C.202 and the *Reggiane* Re.2001 were considered as superior in both speed and maneuverability to the British fighters on board the aircraft carriers. Thus, the Italian command held that the fighter cover was capable of creating a favorable space so that both high altitude bombs and torpedoes launches could be made from advantageous positions in order to achieve some kills. These plans, however, were hampered to some extent on the night of 11 August when the RAF conducted a number of preemptive air raids by hitting airfields in Sardinia (Decimomannu and Elmas). The low altitude bombings resulted in the destruction of one torpedo bomber with the warhead already attached and five damaged aircraft at Elmas. While at Decimomannu, four torpedo bombers with their warhead were set on fire and damaged beyond repair, one torpedo was destroyed, one CA.164 aircraft was destroyed while three *Macchi* C.202 and eight torpedo bombers were damaged. The operation caught the Italians by surprise as many planes were refueling and the bombers had already been fitted with the warhead so that given the scarce number of these weapons available the losses were even more considerable. Thus, the hardest hit unit, 36° *Gruppo* had been decimated prior to the big battle.

11 August

But let's return to the passage of the convoy through the Mediterranean. By the morning of 11 August, the Allied convoy was steaming ahead as it was located south of the Balearics and headed toward Cape Bon. At about 0620, a U-boat sighted the enemy convoy and its screen. A German aircraft reported at 0815 the enemy convoy approximately ninety-five miles northwest of Algiers. As soon as the long, snaking column of warships and merchantmen was spotted on the morning of the 11th by aerial reconnaissance it was shadowed by a powerful Axis naval and aerial force comprised of eighteen Italian and two German submarines and by seven reconnaissance planes. The report provided by the reconnaissance units at 1010 stated that: "Enemy naval formation comprised of three aircraft carriers, three battleships, twenty cruisers and destroyers and twenty transports observed navigating at unidentified speed, route 90 degrees, position latitude 38 08 long 01 56 East."[92] At noon, the convoy was spotted about seventy-five miles south of Majorca and sailing east. Between 1230 and 1515 the first British objective of the operation was met when thirty-eight Spitfires flew-off from HMS *Furious* and later reached Malta safely. On the same day the Axis first attack on the convoy was made by German submarine U-73 which penetrated the enemy's anti-submarine screen and launched four torpedoes at 1315 that sank the aircraft carrier HMS *Eagle* (27,230 tons). The ship was struck by torpedoes launched at a distance of 400 meters and it began to sink almost immediately together with sixteen fighter aircraft and 260 men which were lost. It took eight minutes for HMS *Eagle* to sink. Thus approximately twenty percent of the convoy's fighter cover had been eliminated with this first deadly strike. This was a major set-back which prompted a response from the commander of the convoy. The Royal Navy countered the threat of further submarine strikes by deploying

92 Sebastiano Licheri, "Le azioni di mezzo giugno ed agosto: L'aspetto aereo", *Italia in Guerra 1942*, Vol. 2, 1997, p.492.

the destroyer HMS *Wolverine* which thanks to its Type 271 radar detected the presence of underwater attacking units. After U-73 had fled to safety, the RM dispatched one of its own submarines to attempt to further degrade the convoy. But once the submarine Dagabur was at a range of 4,900 yards from the convoy, radar picked it up. HMS *Wolverine* then picked up speed and rammed the Dagabur and sunk it. In the collision the British destroyer was also damaged and had to return to Gibraltar, but it had foiled the second major submarine attack against the convoy.

The first attack from the air was made by a German squadron comprised mainly of thirty-seven Ju.88 and three He.111 torpedo bombers. As the *Luftwaffe* units pressed home their attack at dusk on 11 August they were met by heavy gunfire. Despite the German aircraft making a well-executed, synchronized attack whereby the torpedo bombers dropped in altitude to make the launch at close range and the bombers attacked with the dusk lights behind them, they were not able to inflict any damage. Two planes were shot down by the anti-aircraft fire while three more planes were destroyed when they dove down, received hits and crashed against the aircraft carriers and the battleships. The convoy was unscathed.

12 August

During the early morning hours Allied intelligence intercepted Axis secret communications. In one instance they learned that the Italian SIM had sighted part of the convoy that had left Gibraltar, while they also intercepted operational orders issued by the *Luftwaffe* to its units in Sardinia instructing them to be ready to attack the convoy. Moreover, the order stated that a largescale Axis operation was set to take place once the convoy reached the Sicilian Narrows. Thus, despite the preemptive strike by the RAF against Axis air bases in Southern Italy, it was clear to the Allied commands that the RA and the *Luftwaffe* were still able to deploy a considerable force to interfere with the British supply operation as the convoy passed through the area close to the Axis Sardinian air bases.

The first seaplane, a Cant. Z.1007bis, to spot the convoy on the 12th was piloted by *Tenente* Lamberto Pardini of 51° *Gruppo Ricognizione Strategica* which at 0620 communicated back to base the sighting, the location and the intelligence it had gathered. No sooner had the pilot ended his intelligence report that the plane was immediately attacked by five enemy fighters. The slow Italian reconnaissance trimotor plane at first put up a considerable defense downing two enemy planes. Then suddenly a hail of bullets invested it killing instantly *marconista* Franco Garzi. Moments later, two other crew members were wounded by more machine gun fire. The plane then caught fire and the pilot was forced to make an emergency landing on the water. The remaining survivors of the crew, the pilot and two others, would remain on a dinghy for three days and three nights before being rescued by a German submarine.

The sighting, however, prompted the second German aerial attack that was conducted at 0900 by nineteen Ju.88, but the operation was not successful in harming the convoy. Five German bombers were downed by the precise anti-aircraft fire and two by a friendly fire mistake by G.50 Italian fighters. The remaining aircraft then suddenly made their return to base.

The *Comando Aeronautica della Sardegna* on the 12th had a total of 189 aircraft available including seventy-eight torpedo bombers, twelve standard bombers, nine reconnaissance aircraft, and ninety fighters. Not all of them where operational, but according to estimates at least seventy percent of the force was deemed combat ready. The torpedo bomber squads began their operation between 1125 and 1135:

At 1125 twelve S.79 torpedo bombers from 109°*Gruppo*/36° *Stormo* (*Maggiore* Alfredo Zanardi), two from 3° *Nucleo Addestramento Aerosiluranti* (*Tenente Colonnello* Vittorio Cannaviello), and one S.79 from 2° *Nucleo Addestramento Aerosiluranti* (*Capitano* Carlo Putti) scrambled from Decimomannu airbase. At the same time from Elmas airbase nine S.79 from *130° Gruppo Aerosiluranti* (*Capitano* Mario Frongia) took flight.They were followed at 1130 by ten S.84 from 89° *Gruppo Aerosiluranti* (*Tenente Colonnello* Antonio Fadda) scrambled from Villacidro airbase. Finally, at 1135 nine S.79 of 105° *Gruppo Aerosiluranti* (*Tenente Colonnello* Remo Cadringher) took flight from Decimomannu.

Commencing at 1200 three waves of Italian aircraft from Sardinia attacked the convoy, which by then had reached near the shores of southern Sardinia. Expecting attacks, the convoy was well escorted by the fighters including four Martlet from No. 806 Squadron, six Hurricane from No. 800 Squadron, which had scrambled from HMS *Indomitable,* two Fulmar from No. 884 Squadron, four Fulmar from No. 809 Squadron and four Hurricane from No. 885 Squadron which had scrambled from HMS *Victorious.*

The first Italian assault wave was comprised of ten S.84 of 38° *Gruppo/ 32° Stormo Bombardieri-Siluranti* equipped with the *motobombe FFF*, or circular torpedoes, and fifteen CR.42 fighters, eight of which were to drop 100 kg bombs while the remaining seven were to machine gun the decks of the ships. Both were escorted by fourteen *Macchi* C.202 of 53° *Gruppo Caccia.* They attacked as the convoy was approximately 60-80 miles from Capo Spartivento. The former dropped the circling torpedoes, described by the British as "dropped parachute mines in the path of the fleet",[93] at 1220 at a distance of 2,000 yards from the convoy and a height of 10,000 feet on both portside and starboard while the fighters dove down to strafe and bomb the warships. Defensive fire opened up almost immediately, as the naval gunners fought back with ample anti-aircraft fire which downed *Tenente* Tullio Dessi's S.84 plane whose "smoke of which could be seen from the fleet."[94] as well as damaging two more S.84s forcing the pilots to crash land at Villacidro. Meanwhile, some of the British ships targeted by the circling torpedoes began to list violently but none of them took a direct hit as HMS *Nelson* led the convoy in several successful evasive maneuvers: "An emergency turn of 90 degrees to port was executed to avoid these. Several explosions some distance to the south-eastward, at about 1229 were probably these mines detonating…… No damage was sustained by any ships."[95] As soon as the circling torpedoes launches had taken place, the torpedo bombers, according to the plan, should have arrived to take advantage of a confused situation. Instead, "The torpedo bombers wave had been delayed for 15 minutes because of a shortage of maintenance personnel to prepare the Re.2001 fighters that were to accompany them."[96] A lack of synchronization between the first and second wave therefore upset the attacking plans. In fact, the second wave comprised of only forty-one torpedo bombers (two S.79s from 36° *Stormo* were forced to turn back due to engine trouble) arrived in proximity of the convoy at 1300, or forty minutes later from the first

93 James Somerville, "Mediterranean Convoy Operations – Operation Halberd", *Supplement to the London Gazette*, n. 38296, 10 August 1948, p.4508.

94 Ibid.

95 Ibid.

96 Jack Greene, and Alessandro Massignani, *The Naval War*, p.248.

strike wave, flying at an altitude of 400 meters. It then split into two main groups to perform an anvil attack on the convoy. The first group comprised of nine S.79s and ten S.84s (105ª and 89ª *Squadriglie*/36° *Stormo*) escorted by fourteen *Reggiane* Re.2001s (2° and 22° *Gruppo*) dove down in the direction of starboard while twenty-two S.79s (four from 280ª *Squadriglia* and five from 283ª *Squadriglia*/130° *Gruppo*, ten from 109° *Gruppo*/36° *Stormo*, and three from the 2° and 3° *Nuclei Addestramento)* escorted by twelve *Reggiane* 2001s (2° *Gruppo*) attacked in the direction of port side. The former group of aircraft was fitted with Alfa Romeo 128 engines that were more powerful than the 126 which powered the torpedo bombers of the second group. Thus, it was envisioned that the first group would attack the starboard of the convoy but after having conducted a longer and more difficult approach flight, while the second group would attack the portside of the convoy in a more conventional, straightforward maneuver. Given the different performance of the Alfa Romeo 126 versus the 128 engines it was envisioned that both groups having to conduct different approach routes to the convoy would arrive at the rendezvous point roughly at the same time. Radar played a big role in this encounter has it forewarned the naval crews of the arrival of the bombers. As a result both groups were met by heavy anti-aircraft barrages from the onset to the point that few were able to get close to the ships. Due to the lack of surprise, the torpedo launches were conducted in a very haphazard way with the bombers often pressing home their combat action in a scattered and unorganized fashion. Most importantly, most torpedoes were released at a great distance from their targets. Only a few very experienced pilots were able to bypass the curtain of fire and target the ships from more advantageous positions but they too failed to hit a target.

The Royal Navy description of the attack is as follows: "This attack was followed by a large number of torpedo bombers which came in formation of 5 or 6 on the port bow, port beam and finally on the starboard. None of these attacks were pressed home and no aircraft penetrated the destroyer screen. All dropped their torpedoes well outside the screen and outside range of the convoy. Several destroyers on the port side were near missed by torpedoes. One torpedo bomber was probably shot down by ships' gunfire."[97]

This impenetrable curtain of fire caused the loss of two aircraft and several others were damaged. One *Reggiane* 2001 of 2° *Gruppo Caccia* was shot down by a Hurricane while a S.79 was cut down just before the pilot was ready to launch the torpedo. The latter, flown by 109° *Gruppo Maggiore* Alfredo Zanardi, was attacked simultaneously by three enemy fighters and was given no chance to fight back. The pilot, a very experienced torpedo bomber, had just spotted HMS *Nelson* and was getting ready to attack it when several enemy fighters intercepted his plane and prevented him from launching the warhead. The plane after receiving machine gun rounds from three enemy fighters caught fire. The pilot, facing a very dire situation, was then forced to land it in the sea where the crew survived for more than 50 hours on a raft before being saved by a German submarine. Meanwhile, the fierce and concentrated naval barrage claimed two more aircraft when the S.79s of *Maggiore* Francesco Campello and that of *Sottotenente* Ernesto Borelli returned to base badly damaged by enemy Flak. The remaining *Sparvieri* teams would make their return to base at 1335 having scored no hits. According to their post battle report the anti-aircraft fire that they faced was the fiercest that they had experienced since the start of the war.

97 James Somerville, "Mediterranean Convoy Operations – Operation Halberd", *Supplement to the London Gazette*, n. 38296, 10 August 1948, p.4509.

In addition, even the more veteran pilots, asserted that the combination of heavy fire together with the interference of many enemy fighters was enough to unsettle even the most experienced torpedo bomber crews to the point that most of them misfired. Some pilots were forced to launch their torpedoes at 7,000 meters out due to the unabating enemy fire.[98] The effectiveness of the anti-aircraft defense was also singled out by the post battle report of the Royal Navy which stressed that: "This successful defense was partly due to the improved A.A. armament of the merchant ships, all of whom carried Oerlikons, whose tracer ammunition provides an excellent deterrent to close and accurate air attack. … Even so, the effect of the A.A. fire put up must make the German and Italian Air Forces begin to realize that air attack in daylight is becoming less and less profitable. Their "interest" in air attack by night will correspondingly increase and it is essential that the fleet should be equipped without delay to deal with night air attack."[99]

The only hit scored on the convoy was made against HMS *Victorious* by the third wave comprised by two *Reggiane* 2001s piloted by *Tenenti* Guido Robone and Riccardo Vaccari, each equipped with one 630 kg special perforating bomb. The two pilots were successful because of a case of mistaken identity. As the two *Reggiane* approached the battleship the aircraft were mistakenly identified by the Royal Navy personnel on board HMS *Victorious* as RAF fighters returning from their mission and that were about to land on the ships flight deck. For this reasons the machine guns and the large and medium caliber guns were stood down: "As VICTORIOUS was flying on at the time, these were taken for friendly fighters and they got away practically unfired at."[100] Facing no opposition, the pilots were thus able to fly over the convoy and drop the weapons from a very advantageous, low altitude position (20 meters above HMS *Victorious*). Both pilots then observed their weapons strike the enemy carrier, but without causing excessive damage. The first bomb killed six and injured several other Royal Navy personnel, while with the second strike the bomb initially made impact with the deck of the ship but then unexpectedly rolled into the sea without causing major damage. In fact, it exploded in the water and it injured three sailors in the lower decks. According to the Italian post battle report if the second special bomb had stayed on deck rather than rolling into the water, it could have provoked extensive damage to the carrier. But being experimental new weapons and the pilots were not particularly experienced in dropping them at low altitude, both bombs ultimately did not produce any long standing damage to the aircraft carrier despite the very good attacking circumstances in which they were released. As per the Royal Navy version of the attack it basically reiterates the version offered by RA but without mentioning the first successful strike: "Finally, at 1345 hours, the two *Reggiane* fighters approached *HMS Victorious* as if to land on. They looked like Hurricanes and *HMS Victorious* was at that time engaged in landing her own fighters. They managed to drop their bombs and one hit the flight deck amidships. Fortunately the bomb broke up without exploding. By the time *HMS Victorious* could open fire both fighters were out of range."[101] Similarly, the radio controlled S.79 plane with

98 Francesco Mattesini, *Luci ed ombre*, p.230.

99 Minute by Director of Gunnery and Anti-Aircraft Warfare [ADM 199/ 1242] 5 March 1943 Lessons learnt from Operation 'Pedestal.'

100 James Somerville, "Mediterranean Convoy Operations – Operation Halberd", *Supplement to the London Gazette,* n. 38296, 10 August 1948, p.4509.

101 Uboat.net, "Allied Warships HMS Foresight" <https://uboat.net/allies/warships/ship/4387.html> (accessed on 3 April 2021).

loaded 1,000 kg explosives would also fail its mission. Originally piloted by *Maresciallo* Mario Badij the aircraft scrambled from Villacidro until it reached the convoy after an hour flight. It is at this point, at approximately 1503, that the pilot ditched the plane by jumping by parachute. The S.79 was now radio controlled by *Brigadiere Generale* Ferdinando Raffaelli, who was on board a specially equipped Cant 1007 bis that was shadowing it. The objective was to hit a carrier in a kamikaze-like attack. Near Galite Islands the plane was set to strike at the convoy, but its control system ultimately malfunctioned and it could no longer be controlled by radio. It then crashed against a mountain in Algeria.[102]

The combat action of the Sardinian based forces was unsuccessful just like the submarine strikes on the convoy which took place randomly throughout the day. The only significant strike had been achieved by Ju.88 *Fliegerkorps* II bombers at 1314 when a 250 kg bomb blew a hole into the Deucalion transport ship. She reported that No. 1 hold was half flooded and No. 2 completely flooded, but it could steam at 10 knots. During the attack two Hurricane from the No. 884 Squadron were shot down by a Ju.88 bomber and a Bf.109 fighter respectively. The overall results of this combat action were very disappointing in relation to the host of new weapons employed and to the great aircraft force deployed. As historian Francesco Mattesini asserts: "This action was the greatest Axis air effort against Force F and also, as previously mentioned the largest ever deployment of aircraft by the two air forces of the Axis in the Mediterranean."[103]

In the late afternoon, the convoy was approximately twenty miles north of Galite Islands, a favorable position for the Sicilian based aircraft to launch their squadrons which now took the lead in the attacks. On the night of 11 August the *Comando Aeronautica della Sicilia* had notified *Comando Supremo* that it had approximately 200 aircraft at its disposal but only 154 aircraft were deemed combat ready: 20 torpedo bombers (of which 14 S.79 and 6 S.84), 40 standard bombers, 16 dive bombers, 11 reconnaissance aircraft, 63 fighters and 4 seaplanes.[104] Its plan was to continue to carry out standard bomber attacks upon Malta utilizing the BR.20 fleet, while the more efficient Cant.Z.1007 and the torpedo bombers were to be deployed against the convoy. At 1835 fourteen torpedo bombers from 132° *Gruppo* (278ª and 281ª *Squadriglie*), nine Stukas from 102° *Gruppo Tuffatori, and* twenty German piloted Stukas of 1st Group/III Stuka Wing, escorted by twenty-eight *Macchi C.202* fighters from 51º *Stormo* and fifteen Bf.109 German fighters struck at the convoy from a more favorable position. The torpedo bombers this time were led by the second in command *Capitano* Ugo Rivoli, since on that day the commander of the 132º *Gruppo*, *Capitano* Buscaglia, was in Rome to be promoted by the head of government to *Maggiore,* a feat that only a handful fighter pilots or bombers such as Francesco Baracca had managed to achieve in the air service. The operation got underway after numerous organizational delays. The torpedo bombers experienced a delay before take-off because the original intended escort fighter unit from Sardinia was unable to support the operation. The unit had took part in the earlier Sardinian based attacks and its service personnel was unable to ready the aircraft on time to escort the Sicilian based bombers. As a result, the torpedo bombers were transferred to Pantelleria so they could depart together with the available escort squadron of the

102 Archivio Storico Aeronautica Militare, "Studio critico sulla battaglia aeronavale dell'agosto 1942", 27 August 1942.
103 Francesco Mattesini, *Luci ed ombre*, p.237.
104 Ibid.

51° *Stormo* that was based there. Then during the loading of the torpedoes six S.84 aircraft were grounded because the warheads could not be attached. Finally, four Ju.87s from 102° *Gruppo Tuffatori* were also unable to depart because they lacked supplementary fuel tanks.

Despite the technical and timing problems experienced during the preparations for this combat action, the operation was well executed. According to the British version of events: "The first attack commenced at 1835 and comprised at least 13 torpedo bombers; simultaneously an unknown number of high level bombers, dive bombers and minelaying aircraft attacked. An emergency turn was made to avoid the mines and torpedoes which had been dropped outside the starboard screen."[105]

The first unit to press forward the attack was the mixed Italian/German Stukas unit (102° *Gruppo*) which 120 miles west of Sicily struck hard at the convoy at 1835 despite fierce enemy anti-aircraft fire and the interference of the enemy fighter escort comprised of three Martlets, twelve Hurricanes and six Fulmars. The Axis aircraft dropped a 500 kg bomb on HMS *Rodney* which rolled off and exploded at sea, while the German Stukas pilots of 1st Group/III Stuka Wing targeted the aircraft carrier HMS *Indomitable* from out of the sun and seriously damaged the ship's runway. A large fire developed on board the main deck and fifty were killed while fifty-nine were wounded. The carrier was forced to slow down making only 17 knots, but the damage was not large enough to force the ship from being separated from the convoy. Prior to the start of the attack, the German aircraft received orders that under no circumstances were they to attack damaged ships or ships out of formation that could not keep pace with the bulk of the convoy.[106] It stemmed from the failed attacks on crippled warships during Operation Harpoon as the Axis crews had spent considerable time pursuing the damaged battleships but achieved no kills. This order would influence the course of the fighting in a negative way for the Axis, as we shall see later. Like the Italian pilots who later claimed to have hit an aircraft carrier and two destroyers, the German pilots also over-estimated the losses inflicted on the convoy in the attacks during the day. German pilots, for instance, believed that they damaged one enemy aircraft carrier, a cruiser, and a destroyer, in addition to one twenty-thousand-ton merchant ship. The results of their operation however were relegated to the only strike on HMS *Indomitable*. The heavy anti-aircraft fire downed one Ju.87, while another one was shot down by a Hurricane.

The torpedo bomber unit was the last to be deployed. The attack was made according to the tactic of the mass, simultaneous strike by three groups of aircraft each going after a specific target. While the torpedo bombers were about to make their descent toward the targets, the fighters of 51° *Stormo* intervened to clear the way for them by challenging RAF fighter planes and bouncing them out of the way. Despite the favorable circumstance the torpedo releases were made at a distance of approximately 2,700 meters from the nearest ship because of the heavy anti-aircraft fire which continued unabated. Most torpedoes missed their targets since the pilots released them "too quickly."[107] Out of twelve torpedoes only one struck an enemy ship.

105 James Somerville, "Mediterranean Convoy Operations – Operation Halberd", *Supplement to the London Gazette*, n. 38296, 10 August 1948, p.4510.
106 Operation "Pedestal", Operations Intelligence Centre, Special Intelligence Summary, 14 August 1942, ADM 223/559, Public Records Office (London), p.3.
107 Operation "Pedestal", Operations Intelligence Centre, Special Intelligence Summary, 14 August 1942, ADM 223/559, Public Records Office (London), p.3.

At 1843 the plane piloted by *Capitano* Giulio Cesare Graziani released a torpedo that struck the 1,850 tons destroyer HMS *Foresight* just north of Bizerte. It was part of the outer, destroyer screen that was closer to the were the launches took place. HMS *Foresight*, one of nine F-class destroyers built for the Royal Navy during the 1930s, had its rudder blown away and the engine room flooded with water. According to its Commander, Captain Venables: "…The first torpedo passed underneath and the second passed close along the starboard side. Later starboard paravane wire commenced to vibrate violently; ship was stopped and on paravane being hoisted out of the water, the torpedo was found fixed firmly along paravane body, the fins of the torpedo having caught in the guard of the paravane tail. The clump chain forward was unshackled and let go and the derrick purchase holding paravane was then let go. The torpedo exploded on bottom in 400 fathoms but the uplift was tremendous though the ship was clear."[108] The ship was originally taken in tow with the intent to bring it back to base for repairs. But the next day given the extent of its damages it was scuttled at 0955 by the destroyer HMS *Tartar*.

The Royal Navy summary of the second torpedo attack:

> The enemy started attacking at 1835 hours, the bombers attacking from both ahead and astern which last was the direction of the sun. The torpedo aircraft came from ahead to attack on the starboard bow and beam of the convoy. The Italian SM-79's torpedo bombers dropped their torpedoes from ranges of about 3000 yards outside the destroyer screen, and once again the convoy turned away to avoid them. However the destroyer HMS Foresight was hit by a torpedo and disabled. The bombers chose HMS Indomitable as their main target. She was astern of HMS Rodney at the time on the port quarter of the convoy. Four Ju.88's and eight Ju.87's came suddenly out of the sun and dived steeply towards HMS Indomitable from astern. Some of the Ju.87 came down to 1000 feet and the carrier received three hits and her flight deck was put out of action. Her airborne fighters eventually had to land on HMS Victorious. HMS Rodney meanwhile had a narrow escape when a bomber attacked from ahead. One enemy aircraft was claimed to have been shot down by AA fire from the ships while the fighters claimed nine more although there were about twice as much enemy fighters in the air then British.[109]

All torpedo bombers returned safely to base, although seven had been damaged by enemy fire.

Further attacks that critical day were made by the *Axum* Italian submarine which launched four warheads at 1955 at HMS *Nigeria*, HMS *Ohio*, HMS *Pathfinder* and HMS *Cairo* which were all damaged to some degree. The latter, the hardest hit, had to be scuttled. HMS Nigeria was able to return to Gibraltar, while Ohio was crippled but it was towed and remained in the convoy. According to the post report of the Royal Navy: "At about 1956, as Cruising Disposition No. 21 was being taken up, H.M.S. NIGERIA leading the port column was hit, supposedly by a torpedo, and within a few minutes H.M.S. CAIRO, S.S. OHIO and another merchant transport ship (probably S.S. BRISBANE STAR) were also hit."[110] HMS *Cairo*, whose stern was

108 Malcolm Llewellyn-Jones, *The Royal Navy and the Mediterranean Convoys,* p.94.
109 Uboat.net, Allied Warships HMS Foresight <https://uboat.net/allies/warships/ship/4387.html > (accessed 12 June 2021).
110 James Somerville, "Mediterranean Convoy Operations", *Supplement to the London Gazette*, n. 38296, 10 August 1948, p.4510.

blown off and engines disabled, was not salvageable and was sunk by the Royal Navy personnel. This attack was followed by thirty German Ju.88 bombers which successfully damaged Clan Ferguson and Empire Hope between 2030 and 2130, inflicting more pain on the merchantmen. A short while later two German HE.111 also torpedoed the already damaged transport ship Deucalion. Finally during this last Axis attack the Italian submarine *Alagi* torpedoed non-fatally HMS *Kenya*. The latter given its robust constitution was still able to keep pace with the convoy and along with HMS *Manchester* remained the two most important cruisers of Force X to escort the convoy on its final leg. According to the Royal Navy post battle assessment this was the most perilous time for the convoy: "The effect of this series of disasters was to cause the convoy to become scattered, though they continued on their course for Cape Bon."[111]

In the Italian post battle report the air attacks put forward by the Sicilian based units were deemed more successful because they had a "strong fighter escort of high quality aircraft, MC202s and Me109s."[112] Meanwhile the key contribution of the Navy to the fighting was also highlighted.

The Italian after action report states that seven torpedo bombers from 132° *Gruppo* were damaged by the heavy anti-aircraft fire put out by the destroyers, cruisers and large battleships. In turn one strike was made on HMS *Foresight*. Altogether the aerial torpedo bombing aspect of the operation had been disappointing, but the successes achieved by the dive bombers had vindicated the new group attack method based on the simultaneous attack by both dive bombers and torpedo bombers: "The combat action of the torpedo bombers was coordinated with the dive bombers and with the fighters escort. The tactic used in the operation was based on the deployment of a large number of aircraft against a limited number of enemy ships. This tactic served us well as it allowed us to obtain concrete results."[113]

Further losses were sustained by the torpedo bomber units when three No. 248 Squadron Beaufighters gave chase to the Sicilian based S.79s near their base in Pantelleria. After the planes had landed the British fighters made their sudden and unexpected attack at 2045. At very close range and by way of a most daring surprise attack, the British aircraft opened machine gun fire that set ablaze one S.79 and damaged two more, one S.84 and one JU 52/3m. Twenty-eight fuel tanks were also set on fire. A S.79 pilot, *Sottotenente* Vittorio Moretti died while he was climbing down from his plane. He was struck by machine gun fire while *Aviere Scelto* Giuseppe Caringella was shot in the head but ultimately survived the attack. S.79 pilot Martino Aichner recalls that when he landed: "A vehicle passed by so I asked the driver if I could hop on to see what had happened to Moretti. I had just gotten on board the vehicle when I heard the crackle of the machine guns. In front of us there were several dust clouds raised by the enemy guns. We jumped off the vehicle at once and threw ourselves to the ground. Two Beaufighter had passed like meteors over our heads and had machine gunned several parked aircraft. They then escaped behind the hill …When we reached the hangar I saw lot of commotion, something had definitively happened because several pilots were gesticulating very wildly. 'What happened?' I asked to the first person that I encountered. 'Tenente Vittorio Monetti has died'. He had just

111 Ibid., p.4505.
112 Jack Greene and Alessandro Massignani. *The Naval War*, p.251. Me-109s were single-engined monoplane fighters with a maximum speed of 395 mph and a range of 650 miles.
113 Archivio Storico Aeronautica Militare: 132 ° *Gruppo* Aerosiluranti Diario Storico.

descended from his aircraft when he was hit by a round of machine gun fire. The latter pushed him forward and he wound up hitting the moving propeller of his plane."[114]

By nighttime the convoy was approximately 250 miles from Malta and although it had suffered some losses it had preserved the bulk of the transport ships and the oil tanker. The main problem of the convoy at this point was the damage procured to HMS *Indomitable* which was no longer able to transport aircraft since its flight deck had been bombed. Its aircraft landed on HMS *Victorious* and some planes which could not be accommodated had to be thrown overboard. The loss of HMS *Eagle* together with the damage to HMS *Indomitable* meant that the convoy no longer had full fighter escort coverage and that it thus had become more vulnerable to Axis air attacks. On the other hand, the convoy was inching closer to its final destination so it was a matter of pushing forward during the last leg of the journey. By this time, the convoy had been split into two columns. The first was led by HMS *Kenya* with HMS *Manchester* at the back while the second one was led by HMS *Nigeria* and shepherded at the rear by two destroyers. The ten cruisers of Force X surrounded the convoy providing the outer screen. Meanwhile during the night the cruisers and destroyers of the Italian Navy were alerted for a possible ambush on the convoy on the 13th. Accordingly, cruisers *Eugenio di Savoia* and *Raimondo Montecuccoli* with three destroyers received orders to proceed to Naples, while cruisers *Gorizia, Bolzano, Trieste,* and *Muzio Attendolo* and the remaining destroyers were tasked with reaching Messina.

13 August

The next day (13 August) 132° *Gruppo* mounted other strikes upon the convoy. They came after Axis torpedo motorboats had already pounced on the British ships. The main body of the convoy passed Cape Bon around midnight. Forty minutes later torpedo motorboats appeared and started to attack. At dawn on the 13th at 0102 Italian torpedo boats fired their deadly weapons against HMS *Manchester*, a Town-class light cruiser, which caused serious damage especially to its boiler room. She was later scuttled by its crew. Many of her ships company landed in Tunisia and were interned by the Vichy-French but about 300 were picked up by destroyers such as HMS Pathfinder, HMS Eskimo and HMS Somali. Italian torpedo boats also shot at the transport ship Glenorchy causing severe damage to the point that later she had to be abandoned. MAS 552 at 0330 fired torpedoes at HMS Kenya and at the Wairangi transport ship crippling the latter. The last success was achieved at 0340 when MAS 557 launched a naval torpedo that struck the Santa Elisa which was carrying fuel and the ship quickly was set on fire due to the triggering of large explosions. Greene and Massignani argue that at this stage: "The convoy could have probably been completely destroyed if the Italian fleet had decisively attacked the remaining ships."[115] Cruisers *Eugenio di Savoia* and *Raimondo Montecuccoli* with three destroyers were in the Tyrrhenian Sea near Naples, while cruisers *Gorizia, Bolzano, Trieste,* and *Muzio Attendolo*, and several destroyers were near Messina. All could have easily intervened to intercept the convoy if the order had been given. The reason why this decision, to not deploy the Italian surface force, was made has to do with a host of factors. First the decision

114 Martino Aichner, *Il Gruppo Buscaglia*, pp.114-15.
115 Jack Greene and Alessandro Massignani, *The Naval War*, p.255.

was dictated primarily by the overly cautious approach of the RM leadership which evaluated the situation by relying on inaccurate intelligence information. This information once again overestimated the enemy force and led to the decision not to pursue the convoy. But the erroneous decision by the RM not to intervene was influenced by several other factors such as lack of fighter coverage for the battleships, lack of fuel and the Royal Navy submarine Unbroken attack on the Italian fleet which heavily damaged two cruisers the *Bolzano* and the *Attendolo* on the early morning of 13 August. Most importantly, Kesselring's early decision, mainly the decision not to provide strong air cover for the Italian heavy surface forces had weighed heavily on the RM's decision to not deploy its big guns in the four day convoy battle.

Naval historian Mark Stille adds another factor which inhibited the RM cruiser attack on the convoy when he argues that: "The decisive moment of the entire battle might have been when the six RM cruisers attacked the decimated convoy. This was not to be. Only six hours before the moment of interception, the force was recalled by Mussolini. The decisive factor was a report that the convoy escort included a battleship which the RM cruisers could not have handled in a daylight action."[116] These factors ensured that at least a portion of the convoy would arrive at Malta.

At 0717 the convoy was shadowed by Axis reconnaissance planes which reported that the enemy force consisted of two cruisers (HMS Kenya and HMS Charybdis), twelve destroyers and four transport ships (Ohio, Melbourne Start, Rochester Castle and Waimarana). Navigating at lower speed and trailing the main convoy were two additional transport ships (*Dorset* and *Port Chalmers*) escorted by four destroyers (*Bramham, Penn, Eskimo* and *Somali*).

After the debilitating dawn naval assault, German Ju.88 and Ju.87 escorted by fighters attacked the convoy at 0915. Whilst two German aircraft were shot down, the bombers sunk the Waimarana transport ship and narrowly missed the Ohio, thus further reducing the amount of cargo to be brought into Malta. Then again at 0923 eight Ju.87 flown by Italian pilots of 102° *Gruppo Tuffatori* attacked out of the sun but did not achieve any hits while losing two aircraft. A few minutes later a German Ju.88 successfully struck the Dorset, while the Port Chalmers was also damaged by another Ju.88. Under constant attack at 1125 five S.79 from 132° *Gruppo* led by *Capitano* Ugo Rivoli escorted by fourteen *Macchi* C.202 from 155° *Gruppo* made a sudden strike upon the British ships. This time they were challenged from above by Spitfires from No. 126 Squadron which in a very timely manner came down to interfere with the torpedo launches. This more than the defensive fire from the ships was enough to unsettle the pilots and cause torpedoes to misfire as the enemy convoy had enough time to maneuver outside of the torpedo tracks. Only one torpedo did not misfire and struck the steamer Port Chalmers, but it did not explode and just procured limited damage to the paravane, while another missed by a few feet the same ship. When the planes disengaged they had to fly over the British naval deployment and were fired upon at close range from the anti-aircraft guns and cannons. According to Ted Gibbs, commanding HMS *Pathfinder*, a P-Class destroyer, the torpedo bomber attacks were carried out with determination on that day but they did not succeed in the face of the volume of fire produced collectively by Royal Navy cruisers and destroyers: "One can get tired of being attacked by aero planes, we had to alter course to avoid the torpedoes, so we decided to do the attacking ourselves. We increased speed to thirty knots and turned straight out to seaward to

116 Mark E. Stille, *Italian Cruisers of World War II* (Oxford: Osprey, 2018), p.21.

meet the Savoias. The noise was tremendous, and I personally remember this as the most exhilarating and enjoyable moment of the war. The nearest Savoia was almost within biscuit toss, and the whole formation was surrounded by shell bursts and streams of tracer bullets, though they dived, twisted and climbed, dropping their torpedoes in almost all directions, except that of the convoy."[117] During the return flight to base, the S.79s were again chased and attacked by British Spitfires from No. 126 Squadron and one torpedo bomber was shot down killing the crew (*Tenente* Guido Barani). The fighter cover provided by the Spitfires from Malta weighted heavily in this engagement preventing the Axis aircraft from further damaging the transports such as Port Chalmers, which were limping to their final destination.

At 1520 there were further attacks upon the British convoy. This time the target was the cruiser HMS *Nigeria* and four destroyers that were returning to Gibraltar. At 1300 five torpedo bombers (three from 130° *Gruppo* and two from 105° *Gruppo*) led by *Tenente Colonnello* Cannaviello scrambled from their airbase in Sicily as the British ship had been spotted by reconnaissance planes near Bougie, Algeria. The operation soon bogged down, however, as one plane had to return to base due to engine trouble. The other four S.79s pressed on. But to their surprise the British cruiser at 1540 responded with very heavy fire causing the first attacker to make an unexpected move causing it to misfire with the launch of the torpedo. The other three bombers released their torpedoes from very favorable positions (approximately 900 meters) but they all misfired although not by much. All had been unsettled at the moment they launched the warheads by the enemy persistent fire. Desperate for not being able to harm the convoy substantially, the torpedo bombers took another stab at it when two S.79s from 255ª *Squadriglia*/105° *Gruppo* flown by *Capitano* Giulio Ricciarini and *Tenente* Silvio Angelucci targeted the destroyer HMS *Ledbury* near Hammameth, Tunisia. At 1600 the S.79s descended from the sky and lined up close to the water to release the warheads. All of a sudden, just as they were about to unleash their torpedoes, the duo was fired upon by 20mm Oerlikon gunners aboard the destroyer. The latter had used a new tactic allowing the planes to approach the ship without making recourse to the large caliber guns. Once within range of the machine guns, the planes were plastered with heavy fire. Within minutes the planes caught fire and dropped into the sea. Ricciarini's plane was riddled with bullets one of which had hit the tank on the aircraft's right flank causing a large fire, forcing the pilot to down it on the water near HMS *Ledbury*. The crew led by *Tenente* Silvio Angelucci was even less fortunate. Unlike the other crew, it had the time to launch the torpedo. But once it tried to speed away it was targeted by heavy fire to the point that the plane was shot down and the crew perished enveloped in a ball of fire. Meanwhile, the crew of *Capitano* Ricciarini survived on a raft for 21 hours when it was finally saved by a Cant Z506B seaplane. The following are the pilots recollections of the aircraft being shot down:

> I started my attack and at about 800 meters range I dropped the torpedo just as a burst of 20mm cannon fire struck my aircraft. I initially thought that it had hit the right engine, but I soon saw that the right wing fuel tank was on fire. I ordered my copilot *Tenente* Nicola Titi to pull out the fire extinguisher as a precautionary measure, but the blaze soon grew in intensity and I decided to ditch at once. I was trusting in the support of the second aircraft while I looked for somewhere to ditch, *Tenente* Angelucci having positioned his S.79 about

117 Max Hastings, *Operational Pedestal*, pp.292-93.

> a kilometer away from me. As I turned away from the vessels and glided towards the water, I saw *Tenente* Angelucci's aircraft fly over the cruiser at low level, increasingly losing altitude. My aircraft was literally wrapped in flames and smoke. I saw my co-pilot, outlined in the cockpit's chocking greyness, abandon his seat after he had sustained severe burns to his left hand. Given that I had almost no visibility out of the cockpit, I ditched almost by instinct. As we hit the water I was thrown into the torpedo aiming sight, injuring my nose. At once the water flowed into the cockpit and, luckily, extinguished the fuel tank fire. Unable to open the cockpit roof, I then had to remove my parachute so that I could crawl inside the fuselage. Here, I saw a crewman lying on his back. I lifted him up and believing he was dead, decided to leave him there. The raft was still on board. Although I couldn't swim I reached the fuselage hatch and threw myself into the water. Then I saw the rest of the crew who had gathered on the port wing. I held onto the aircraft with one hand and used the other to try to remove the raft from its housing and put it into the sea. After several attempts, and with the crew's help, I managed to pull the dinghy out. The aircraft's fuselage fabric had been burnt away and just its skeleton was left, through which I saw a crewman who I hadn't previously spotted in the smoke. It was flight engineer Aviere Scelto Tedeschini, who showed signs of life despite his legs clearly being on fire. I threw water on him and managed to extinguish the flames. [118]

The other pilot, whose plane was observed by *Capitano* Ricciarini losing altitude, *Tenente* Angelucci was post humorously awarded a gold medal of military valor for his daring attack with the following motivation: "A pilot blessed with exceptional skills and experience having fought in several campaigns. During a torpedo action against a cruiser, despite a crippled plane that had been already hit several times, he pressed on impassively in the attack which ended with the holocaust of his flourishing youth."[119] Finally, after having deployed the entire combat ready torpedo bomber force, a last ditch attack was pressed forward by the trainees of 3° *Nucleo Addestramento Aerosiluranti* with two S.79s that took off from Chinisia airport at 1430. The attack led by *Capitano* Dante Magagnoli took place in Hammamet Gulf and their target was the already severely damaged Brisbane Star transport ship. Both S.79s failed to hit their target when they suddenly dropped to the bottom of the sea.

At approximately 1600, the Malta Escort Force took over the protection of the convoy and Force X turned westward toward Gibraltar. That same day (13 August) Aegean based *Sparvieri* mounted an attack in the Eastern Mediterranean against the dummy convoy MG 3 that was launched to disperse the Axis bomber force and relieve the pressure from the large convoy headed to Malta. As planned, the Allies had carried out Operation MG 3, with a convoy composed of three merchant ships, sailed out of Port Said after dusk on 10 August, accompanied by two cruisers, ten destroyers, and two escorts, while one merchant ship escorted by two cruisers and three destroyers left Haifa at 0300 on 11 August.

Three *Sparvieri* from 253ª *Squadriglia/104° Gruppo* dove down in the face of concentrated anti-aircraft fire to tackle the cruisers HMS *Cleopatra* and HMS *Arethusa* and four destroyers. The combat action was unsuccessful due to a combination of enemy fighters interfering with the

118 Marco Mattioli, *Savoia Marchetti S.79 Sparviero*, pp.56-57.
119 Medaglie D'oro <https://www.quirinale.it/onorificenze/insigniti/45315> (accessed 10 April 2021).

torpedo launches and the rapid fire coming from the cruisers. However, the decoy Operation MG 3 failed to deceive the Axis and attract the attention of the majority of the Axis air forces in the hope of reducing the number of attacks on the main convoy in the western Mediterranean.

14 August

The final combat action of the torpedo bombers during Operation Pedestal was conducted on 14 August when some of the battleships were making their return voyage to Gibraltar. Eight torpedo bombers S.79 from 132° *Gruppo* were tasked with splitting up into two groups: one was to attack a battleship, while the other a cruiser. The following is an extract of the article written in a daily newspaper describing the preparation of the last combat action mounted by the torpedo bombers during the massive operation: "We have come to the last day. Numerous aircraft have been damaged. They need to be nursed just like their wounded pilots and crews. But for the 132° Gruppo it's impossible to forgo this combat action. *Aviere scelto* Caringella, who has a headwound caused by a splinter, refuses to head to the hospital opting instead to take part in the operation. *Aviere scelto* Torello, with high fever, is determined to take flight at any cost. Two squads are dispatched against the enemy ships sailing west to Gibraltar. Each has an objective. The crews of Rivoli, Pfister, and Graziani target a cruiser, while those of Manfredi, Aichner, Coci, Marini, and Bargagna are set to attack a battleship. The action takes place north of Cape Buogaron and once again the war bulletin of 15 August mentions the great courage of our torpedo bombers."[120] But despite the dedication of the airmen to their cause, the operation did not yield any results. According to torpedo bomber pilot Martino Aichner, whose squad targeted HMS *Malaya*: "We launched all together from too great a height to have a chance of a hit before the ship takes evasive action. We see it make a high speed turn to port, churning up a great cascade of water."[121] HMS *Malaya* evaded all torpedoes and so did the other battleship of Force X.

The merchants Melbourne Star, Port Chalmers, Rochester Castle and Brisbane Star arrived at Malta on the 14 August, while the oil tanker Ohio made into Malta on 15 August. The arrival of about 32,000 tons of general cargo, together with 11,100 tons of petrol, oil fuel, kerosene and diesel fuel, was enough to give the island the capacity to wage war for another ten weeks, so a vital lifeline. It allowed the island "to live for another day and recommence attacking Axis traffic."[122] Coincidentally, these supplies allowed the Allied submarines and aircraft to intensify their attacks on the Axis transports headed to North Africa during the most decisive phase of the campaign. One data illustrates the effectiveness of Malta's resurgence as a result of Pedestal. During September 1942, for example, British submarines out of Malta sank more than 100,000 tons of Axis supplies destined for North Africa.[123] This came ahead of the major battle of El Alamein III in October 1942 which proved decisive for the campaign.

120 Mirko Giobbe, "Le vie dell'aria", *Il Corriere della Sera*, 15 August 1942.
121 Max Hastings, *Operation Pedestal* (New York: Harper Colins, 2021), p.157.
122 John Gooch, *Mussolini's War*, p.317.
123 Milan Vego, "Major Convoy Operation to Malta, 10–15 August 1942 (Operation PEDESTAL)", *Naval War College Review*: Vol. 63: No. 1, 2010, p.37.

Analysis of the Results

Although the interference by the Axis forces against the convoy had successfully weakened it causing large losses, Operation Pedestal was ultimately a strategic victory for the Royal Navy since it managed to get the Ohio, the big oil tanker, plus additional cargo to arrive safely and to fly off several Spitfires into Malta. Historian James Sadkovich wrote that Operation Pedestal was a tactical defeat for the British.[124] Meanwhile, historian Richard Woodman argued that Operation Pedestal was a strategic victory for the Royal Navy and for Malta as an operational base. It resulted in raising the spirits of the garrison of Malta and it averted its surrender due to famine and lack of ammunition.[125] Italian historian, Giorgio Giorgerini wrote that the operation was an Italian success; Italian submarines and torpedo boats, along with German U Boats and Axis aircraft had adopted very offensive minded tactics and achieved the following results:

- The German U-boats sank one aircraft carrier while the Italian submarines sank one cruiser (HMS *Cairo*) and two merchant ships.
- The Italian and German torpedo boats sank one cruiser (HMS *Manchester)* and three merchant ships.
- The Axis aircraft damaged one carrier (HMS *Indomitable*) and three merchant vessels and sunk HMS *Foresight*.
- An Italian submarine damaged one enemy cruiser (HMS *Nigeria*), and an Italian submarine damaged another cruiser (HMS *Kenya*).
- An Italian submarine and the German bombers heavily damaged the tanker Ohio.
- In contrast Royal Navy submarines damaged two Italian cruisers (*Bolzano* and *Muzio Attendolo*), while the Axis lost sixty-two aircraft (19 German and the balance Italian), including a significant number of S.79 and S.84 torpedo bombers. Allied destroyers sank two Italian submarines (Cobalto and Dagabur), while the Allied aircraft damaged one Italian submarine (Giada). British aircraft losses included 29 aircraft belonging to Fleet Air Arm and six from the RAF.[126]

Historians Greene and Massignani provide the most balanced analysis of Operation Pedestal calling the Axis efforts to disrupt the British operation the last Axis victory in the Mediterranean but that it was a tactical not a strategic success.[127] Similarly, historian Gianni Rocca argued that Operation Pedestal was an Axis tactical victory, but that in the long turn it revealed itself to be a strategic loss because Malta was ultimately reinforced and because the RA spent an abundance of its resources that ultimately depleted its strength.[128] The greatest disappointed had come from the torpedo bombers squadrons which had managed to inflict very light losses against the convoy while deploying a large aircraft fleet, launching over 100 torpedoes and losing several

124 James Sadkovich, *The Italian Navy in World War II* (Westport, Connecticut: Greenwood Press, 1994), p.297.
125 Richard Woodman, *Malta Convoys, 1940–1943* (London: John Murray, 2000).
126 Giorgio Giorgerini, *Uomini sul fondo: storia del sommergibilismo italiano dalle origini a oggi* (Milan: Mondadori, 2002).
127 Jack Greene and Alessandro Massignani, *The Naval War,* pp.260-61.
128 Gianni Rocca, *I Disperati*, p.237.

aircraft to enemy fire. The operation had been conducted according to the group attack method which was the most advanced torpedo bomber tactic that was adopted by both the Japanese and the British torpedo bomber units. "Aircraft attacking in groups from different directions would not only divide the anti-aircraft defenses but cancel out any maneuvering."[129] In addition the operation had been carried out in conjunction and in cooperation with standard bomber units, and new units deploying new weapons (radio controlled aircraft carrying explosives and bombers launching circling torpedoes). Despite the many novelty weapons and the execution of enhanced tactics, the air attacks had not been particularly successful and the bulk of the successes had been achieved by the Axis naval forces and the German *Luftwaffe*. From the British perspective the group attacks by air had been checked primarily through the combination of FAA and RAF fighter interference and the evasive tactics put in place by the Royal Navy. With regards to the evasive tactics the post battle report of the Royal Navy states: "That 27 emergency turns were made on passage to the Straits and 48 during day one, two and three, consequent on warnings given by the A/S screen, is an illustration of the value of their work. Besides this, their defense of the fleet against torpedo bomber attack was so successful that only one torpedo bomber aircraft managed to get past them."[130]

In contrast, according to the post battle report a lack of training had been responsible for the lackluster results since many crews were recently converted to the torpedo bomber discipline.[131] The report however, made no mention of how effective the Royal Navy had been in opening up a tremendous defensive anti-aircraft fire, an indication that its crews by mid-1942 were well trained in confronting the torpedo bomber threat. They no longer perceived the torpedo bomber to be an innovative, new threat and had developed tactics to properly confront it. Moreover, no mention was made to the fact that the torpedo attacks were not surprise attacks made by small but extremely well trained units but mass attacks deploying ten or more aircraft at any one time. It also failed to recognize that the S.79 and the S.84 were no longer as effective as in 1940-41 due to their lack of speed when facing more advanced enemy fighters and the requirements to effectuate the torpedo launch from low altitude in the face of well drilled, concentrated fire. This report prompted *Generale* Fougier to issue a strong reprimand to the torpedo bombers units: "The recent operation revealed that perhaps many crews did not press home their attacks against their targets with all their might and conviction."[132] It stated that the torpedo launches in most cases had been released from too far away due to the disruptive action of enemy fighters and the strong anti-aircraft fire.

Colonnello Carlo Unia of the torpedo training school with regards to Operation Pedestal argued that: "The training of the new crews left something to be desired as it was too brief and or unsatisfactory. We no longer had a large pool of pilots from which to draw from, preferably volunteers or highly experienced and capable airmen. On top of that there was a scarcity in 1942 of top notch instructors and of courageous and well equipped crews."[133] According to Unia two years of war and of heavy losses had taken their toll as the crews were thrown into combat much

129 Donald Nijboer, *Flak in World War Two* (Mechanicsburg: Stackpole, 2018), p.26.
130 James Somerville, "Mediterranean Convoy Operations", *Supplement to the London Gazette*, n. 38296, 10 August 1948, p.4505.
131 Archivio Storico Aeronautica Militare: Superaereo, Prot n.5 21774, "Aerosiliranti", 3 September 1942.
132 Ibid.
133 Carlo Unia, *Gli autosiluranti italiani* (Rome: Edizioni Stato Maggiore A.M.I., 1974), p.125.

earlier than before due to the high loss rate of experienced personnel and as a result the quality of the pilots was also in decline.

Italian Air Force historian Tulio Marcon has argued that there was a major difference between the effectiveness of the torpedo bombers during the first half of the campaign (1940-41) over the second half (1942-43). In the first half the attacks were made by the "usual four cats", that is experienced pilots who attacked their targets by stealth and surprise in quasi lone wolf attacks. This enabled the pilots to suddenly plunge upon an enemy ship often by taking the most unexpected routes to reach the enemy convoy. The lone wolf tactic was much harder for the enemy to anticipate and also because both radar and fighter escorts of the British fleet were not fully operational. After 1941 torpedo attacks were made by larger groups of aircraft. These, given their numbers, were easier to spot and track by the enemy. Moreover the latter had developed improved anti-aircraft fire techniques to keep them at bay.[134] Historian Sebastiano Licheri also listed several other factors to explain the lack of success or better yet their decreasing effectiveness of the *aerosiluranti* units as the war progressed. He argues that: "The risky but beneficial operations of the torpedo bombers necessitated a large pool of experienced pilots, a newer more modern aircraft, a large stock of warheads and of modern aiming devices and large stocks of fuel of different types. The lack of a tight coordination between Superaereo and Supermarina, and between the various attacking squadrons made up of fighters, bombers and torpedo bombers further reduced the efficacy of the attacks. The continuous pressure by the head of government and the head of Regia Aeronautica for the prompt formation of new torpedo bomber squadrons did not help matters either because it forced into battle many crews that were inexperienced due to a lack of extensive training. The increase in the number of torpedo squadrons did not lead to greater effectiveness. On the other hand, the greater efficiency of the Royal Navy in facing down torpedo bomber attacks with evasive maneuvers and improved anti-aircraft fire blunted the multiple attacks. Therefore, even if conducted with the usual determination, torpedo bomber attacks lost their effectiveness as the war progressed."[135] Overall, it can be argued that even though the torpedo bombers pilots of 1942 were generally less experienced than those from the early days, they did carry out their attacks with conviction which is attested by the high loss rate of aircraft during Operation Pedestal. Regarding the aerial attacks historian Milan Vego asserts that: "Both the German and Italian pilots showed a great deal of determination, skill, and courage in their repeated attacks against the convoy and its supporting forces."[136] The factors that hampered their effectiveness, especially of the torpedo bombers, were more structural. First, the attacks during Pedestal demonstrated that coordination with the other units, especially the units deploying the new weapons had been substandard as the delays between the deployment of the first wave of new weapons and the second wave of the torpedo bombers compromised the value of some of the new weapons. Second, warhead development had not kept up with the evasive and defensive tactics of the British Royal Navy. In essence, the Italian aviation industry had failed to refine warhead development introducing more effective and faster weapons that also could be launched at greater distances than before. This would have helped

134 Tulio Marcon, "Sul rendimento degli aerosiluranti italiani", *Storia Militare*, December 1997, p.54.

135 Sebastiano Licheri, "Le azioni di mezzo giugno ed agosto: L'aspetto aereo", *Italia in Guerra 1942*, Vol. 2, 1997, p.508.

136 Milan Vego, "Major Convoy Operation to Malta, 10–15 August 1942 (Operation PEDESTAL)", *Naval War College Review*: Vol. 63: No. 1, 2010, p.39.

safeguarding some of the most experienced crews as casualties would have diminished over time as pilots became proficient in launching the new weapons. The same can be said about the S.79 whose maximum speed was no longer adequate to fight against state of the art aircraft such as the Supermarine Spitfire Mk IX fighters, single engine monoplanes with a maximum speed of 408 mph (656 km/h) and a range of 434 miles. Nor with such speed could they evade the greater number of high caliber anti-aircraft weapons retrofitted to British Navy ships.

With Malta resurgent, thanks to the lifeline provided by Operation Pedestal, and the Battle of El Alamein in October 1942, which resulted in the defeat of Field Marshal Erwin Rommel's *Panzerarmee,* signaled a shift in the war in the Mediterranean as the Allies gained once again the upper hand. From November 1942 onward, Axis forces would only experience retreat and defeat. Meanwhile, Italian torpedo bombers continued to desperately fight on to stave off the final collapse. El Alamein was a very important land battle that turned the tide of the war in North Africa. But equally important was the aid to Malta provided by the convoy of Operation Pedestal and the convoys that followed, which enabled naval and air attacks against Axis convoys to North Africa to resume at a critical juncture in the campaign. During the months of October and November, for example, submarine attacks out of Malta focused upon crippling Rommel's Army with the pursuit and ambush of Italian transport vessels headed to North Africa. The deliberate British strategy of going after oil tankers, while letting other transports go, even those transporting ammunition, strongly debilitated the ability of Rommel's mechanized forces to maneuver on the El Alamein line. This together with the massive deployment of Allied aerial power and heavy artillery contributed to the Axis defeat.

8: "ITALIAN CIRCLING TORPEDO" FROM TACTICAL AND TECHNICAL TRENDS

The British Navy has recently made known the recovery of an Italian circling parachute torpedo, which has a number of characteristics that distinguish it from any other torpedo of its kind.

After the torpedo had been rendered inoperative and examined, it was found to have no depth-setting device and would therefore travel on the surface of the water with a probable wake. It is 19 inches in diameter, approximately 8 feet long, and weighs about 700 pounds, the weight of the explosive charge being nearly 200 pounds. The torpedo has a maximum speed of 6 knots, and a running time of about 30 minutes. It is equipped with a three-blade propeller and a 250-volt electric motor.

Features of the torpedo that differ externally from other Italian circling torpedoes are listed below:

a) The position of the impact fuses.
b) The use of a ring bolt for the carrying fitting.
c) The location of the switch on the underside, port quarter.
d) Propeller streamlined flush with the body of the torpedo.
e) 19-inch instead of 18-inch diameter.

Internal differences which characterize the torpedo include the following features:

a) 250-volt instead of 220-volt motor.
b) Motor speed of 3,700 rpm instead of 2,880 rpm (geared down to 750 rpm).
c) Mercury switch on the battery. (Hitherto not found.)
d) Spring-loaded tail switch operated by a spring-loaded rod inside the after-part of the propeller shaft.
e) Starboard helm setting. (Others are set for port helm only.)

The rudder of the circling torpedo is actuated by the arm bearing on the eccentric projection of the cog-wheel, which is driven by the worm on the propeller shaft. The torpedo moves to starboard in a series of increasing circles.

Of the three fitted switches, one is an external hand switch on the port quarter and one a mercury switch on the battery, cutting out when the torpedo head lies approximately 45 degrees depression to horizontal. The third switch, which is spring-loaded, is placed inside of the after-part and is held open by a roller bearing and a disc fitted around the propeller shaft. The disc is secured by a spring-loaded rod inside the propeller shaft and projecting inside the propeller boss, where it appears to be held by a parachute lug and a plug, which is soluble. When the plug dissolves, the spring-loaded rod ejects the parachute lug, and simultaneously brings the disc further aft, permitting the spring-loaded switch to close and the motor to start.

It is believed that the torpedo had been dropped about two months prior to its recovery, as it was heavily corroded. Since the corrosion prevented the unscrewing of the impact fuse, it was decided to remove the war head complete, and recover the propulsion machinery, etc. This was successfully accomplished and the war head rendered inoperative. Following the examination of the torpedo, the propulsion machinery and other parts of the mechanism were dispatched to London for further study.

It is believed that circling torpedoes have been used only experimentally up to the present time. When employed against convoys, the pilot would probably not have to maneuver his aircraft within close range of antiaircraft fire in order to score a hit but could drop the torpedo at a reasonably safe distance and immediately resort to evasive tactics. The average running time of the torpedo, which is from 30 to 40 minutes, would give an additional advantage. A weapon of this kind would, therefore, present a serious problem to a convoy.

This type of torpedo might also be used against large vessels lying at anchor. They could best be protected against such an attack either by being surrounded with lighters made fast to the ships or by being anchored in an area enclosed by a barrage net extending to a depth of 5 feet.

Source: Tactical and Technical Trends, No. 11, Nov. 5, 1942.

Operation Torch

Operation Torch was planned to follow the attack launched by the British Eighth Army against Rommel's *Panzerarmee* deployed at El Alamein. Dwight D. Eisenhower, supreme commander of the Allied forces in the Mediterranean theatre of operations, planned a three-pronged attack on Vichy French held Algeria with the targets being Casablanca (Western), Oran (Center) and Algiers (Eastern). After the Algerian territory had been secured and with Vichy France forces subdued, Eisenhower aimed to plan a rapid advance toward Tunisia. Torch was an American centered operation. It was to be supported by the Royal Navy and the RAF, but American forces would be deployed in the landings to sway French public opinion and push it toward the Allied side.

With the occupation of Algeria and later Tunisia the Allies could obtain multiple objectives: "For the Allies control of all the North African coast would mean the Eastern Mediterranean would be more secure and Malta could be supplied more easily. Furthermore, it would make it easier to run convoys through the Mediterranean thus avoiding the long route around the Cape. It would also open up Italy and her islands for possible invasion and potentially bolster the people of France and further depress Italian morale."[137]

A Western Task Force headed to Casablanca was led by Major General George S. Patton and it consisted of the United States 3rd and 9th Infantry Divisions, and two battalions from the United States 2nd Armored Division. It comprised a total of 35,000 troops in a convoy of over 100 ships. Meanwhile, the Center Task Force, commanded by Major General Lloyd Fredendall, was to land at Oran. It was comprised of the United States 2nd Battalion, 509th Parachute Infantry Regiment, the United States 1st Infantry Division, and the United States 1st Armored Division for a total of 18,500 troops. Finally, the Eastern Task Force was to land at Algiers and it was commanded by Lieutenant-General Kenneth Anderson and consisted of a brigade from the British 78th and the United States 34th Infantry Divisions, along with two British commando units (No. 1 and No. 6 Commandos).

The Italian SIM had already warned the military authorities in Rome during the last week of October that something big was afoot, although at first it was not clear whether the Allied forces were to land in North Africa or somewhere in Southern Europe. A major build up and increased traffic into the port of Gibraltar was observed by SIM. Originally, it was envisioned that another large scale resupply of Malta was on the table, but then the large scale deployment of troops and material for infantry of all kinds such as guns, jeeps, machine guns, etc.. led the intelligence services to believe that something different was being planned.

By early November SIM had concluded that seaborne landings were to take place in Africa, although it was not clear whether Tunisia or Algeria were the targets. Based on the intelligence received in early November *Superaereo* decided to reinforce the air bases in Sardinia in order to disrupt the operation. A few weeks prior to the start of the operation Sardinian airbases could count upon thirty bombers Cant. Z. 1007 bis, forty-two torpedo bombers S. 79 (from 105° and 132° *Gruppi*) , two reconnaissance planes and thirty-three fighters mainly G. 50 and CR.42. Between 6-7 November forty bombers (25 S. 84, 16 Cant. Z. 1007 bis and 6 P.108), twenty torpedo bombers S. 79 (15 from 36° *Stormo Aerosiluranti* and 5 from *3° Nucleo Addestramento*

137 Jack Greene and Alessandro Massignani, *The Naval War*, p.272.

Aerosiluranti), and eighty fighters (57 *Macchi* C.202 and 23 *Reggiane* Re.2001) were transferred into Sardinia between Elmas and Decimomannu to further reinforce the island's air fleet. The Sicilian airbases could count upon thirty bombers Cant. Z. 1007 bis, thirty-five torpedo bombers S.79, three reconnaissance planes, and fifty-five *Macchi* C.202 fighters. Additional support was provided by the *Luftwaffe* that added to its total in Southern Italy by dispatching additional aircraft to Sicily, while Sardinian airbases were used by the *Luftwaffe* only to refuel because they were already at full capacity and could not house any more aircraft. The RM also planned a large deployment of mainly small crafts such as submarines, torpedo motorboats, MAS etc… to disrupt the landings. Kesselring, who had direct command of all German armed forces in the theatre except for Rommel's German-Italian Panzer Army in North Africa, aimed to severely disrupt the invasion by relying primarily on the combined power of the Axis air forces. He had instructed *Generale* Fougier to throw everything that was combat ready in the fight "without sparing a single soldier or aircraft."[138] He also ensured that every German pilot that was combat ready was readily deployed by denying any leave request.

Buscaglia's unit was to be one of the air force's foremost units deployed against Operation Torch. In a meeting held on 7 November *Maggiore* Buscaglia told his subordinates of 132° *Gruppo Autonomo Aerosiluranti* not to be too overly impressed about what was happening in North Africa and especially with regards to the American intervention. "For us nothing has changed", argued Buscaglia, "We are soldiers and the war goes on. We are soldiers and must continue to fight. I will try to spare you from too risky operations or to sacrifice our crews, but everyone must be aware that the most difficult phase of the war is upon us. We officers are responsible for maintaining the highest morale of our soldiers. I believe you are all in agreement with me. Soon we will begin a new operation against the port of Algiers. We will arrive there at dawn so we should be able to avoid the enemy fighters. Each of us will launch the torpedo against enemy targets. Enemy transport vessels are the preferred targets even over navy warships."[139]

Sparviero units were first deployed against Operation Torch on the afternoon of 8 November when fourteen planes from 105° (five S.79) and 130° (nine S.79) *Gruppi* made a determined attack against American Navy ships near Algiers. The torpedo bombers did not score any hits and one of them from 105° *Gruppo* flown by *Tenente* Antonio Poggi Cavalletti was shot down by rapid anti-aircraft fire. In the afternoon three *Sparvieri* from 280ª and 283ª *Squadriglie* made another determined attack against enemy ships anchored at Algiers but were repelled by anti-aircraft fire. Two aircraft were so badly damaged that the pilots were forced to ditch them. *Tenente* Alessandro Setti's plane was ditched in the gulf of Cagliari and the crew was able to make its way back to the coast of Sardinia on a dingy. Meanwhile *Sottotenente* Antonio Vellere's plane was ditched also off the coast of Sardinia. Two members of the crew had been slightly injured during the landing but were all brought to safety by a motorboat dispatched by the air force service.

Tenente Francesco di Bella of 3° *Nucleo Addestramento Aerosiluranti* made a bold attack on 9 November without escort against American convoy vessels sailing near the Algerian coast but the effort was not successful. The next day five aircraft from 130° *Gruppo* led by *Maggiore* Massimiliano Erasi took off from Elmas at 1724 and targeted, amongst other, the 1,250 tons

138 Gianni Rocca, *I disperati*, p.245.
139 Martini Aichner, *Il Gruppo Buscaglia*, p.122.

British sloop HMS *Ibis*. Erasi and his small squad flew fifty miles into the coast of Algeria then turned back toward the sea. The five aircraft then circled over the port of Algiers and spotted several Royal Navy ships nearby. They then spread out approximately to 250 meters apart and began to descend upon the enemy ships. Suddenly a British ship (HMS *Ibis*) appeared in front of Erasi. Its gunners fired against the torpedo bomber until some of the crew members saw the splash of the warhead, leading some to dive into the water and begin to swim away. The torpedo struck at 1724 slamming into the bow of the ship and splitting it open. It began to take in water and its boiler room stopped operating. The ship sank three minutes later after being penetrated by the torpedo ten miles north of Algiers. Its crew suffered the loss of 98 ratings including its commander, Lt. Cdr. Henry Maxwell Darell-Brown, while 111 ratings were later recovered by HMS *Scylla*, and three by HMS *Ct. Clare*. The four other torpedo bombers part of Erasi's squad flew on. They saw two more ships. Alerted by Erasi's strike, they were already under full alert firing their guns at the torpedo bombers. Two bombers launched the torpedoes but missed their targets, while two more were unable to launch due to heavy fire. *Luftwaffe* units in the meantime procured damage to HMS *Argus*.

9: MASSIMILIANO ERASI

Born Bagni di Lusnizza, 12 July 1908. Died on 21 February 1945.
Originating from an Austrian family (last name Errath), Erasi gained a diploma at the Technical institute in Klagenfurt and in 1928 entered into *Regia Aeronautica*. In 1934 he was assigned to 9° *Stormo Bombardamento Terrestre* and took Italian citizenship changing his last name to Erasi. In 1936 he fought as a bomber pilot in the Spanish Civil War and gained a silver and a bronze medal of military valor. In September of 1940 *Capitano* Erasi took command of the first torpedo bomber unit, 278ª *Squadriglia Autonoma Aerosiluranti*, leading this famed unit to several successes including the torpedoing by Erasi himself of HMS *Liverpool* and HMS *Glasgow*. In November 1941 he was assigned to command the 284ª *Squadriglia Autonoma Aerosiluranti* initially based in Ciampino and later moved to Sicily and then to North Africa. In 1942 Erasi was promoted to *Maggiore* (Major) and in late 1942 was given command of 41° *Gruppo Aerosiluranti*, who had previously been commanded by Ettore Muti. Erasi held command of the unit until the armistice in September 1943. After the armistice he chose to fight on the side of the Allies joining the Italian Co-belligerent air force. While conducting a combat mission on 21 February 1945 on a Martin Baltimore bomber, Erasi's plane was struck by Flak and he died along with his crew. He was awarded a gold medal of military valor.

On 11 November *Sparvieri* units were deployed again after an Axis reconnaissance aircraft spotted several Allied ships in Bougie Bay. Four *Sparvieri* appeared suddenly over the bay and proceeded to launch the torpedoes but they failed to score any hits. These were flown by 132° *Gruppo Aerosiluranti with Maggiore* Buscaglia, *Capitano* Giulio Cesare Graziani, *Tenente* Carlo Faggioni and *Sottotenente* Ramiro Angelucci. Prior to the attack the S.79 were intercepted and attacked by seven Spitfires at 1450 who managed to wound *Aviere Scelto* Francesco Maiore's arm who was flying on board Buscaglia's plane as well as slightly damage two other planes.

Sottotenente Angelucci, the least experienced of the four, was the only one that after the attack did not make it back to base as his plane was intercepted and shot down by enemy fighters. It's crew perished. Graziani recorded the following recollection of the attack on Bougie Bay: "There were cruisers, destroyers, torpedo boats that were patrolling the harbor in search of any enemy submarines lurking. We had to attack the steamers docked at the quay. We flew over the cruisers at 50-60 meters. Then I saw hundreds of guns spitting fire at us. Our unit advanced in the midst of this deadly tangle of bullets. Loud bangs from shells and shrapnel could be heard hitting the propeller blades or the aircraft's sheet metal outer layer. The aircraft themselves bounced and skidded as a result of the explosions of anti-aircraft artillery grenades. It was also difficult to maintain a tight formation."[140]

On 12 November the attacks against Operation Torch continued. The target of the torpedo bombers was again the port of Bougie which was buzzing with Allied crafts of all kind. The attack was led by Buscaglia and five other torpedo bombers from the 132° *Gruppo* which took off from Castelvetrano in Sicily at 1050 with the intent to strike the ships of the Eastern Task Force. With Buscaglia were *Tenente* Francesco Bargagna, *Sottotenente* Carlo Pfister, *Sottotenente* Martino Aichner, *Sottotenente* Marino Marini and *Sottotenente* Giuseppe Coci. The operation presented many difficulties tied to the lay of the land and the heavy enemy defense. The Atlas Tellien, the mountains surrounding the bay, forced the pilots to fly around them on the way to the attack. The plan was to fly behind Bougie Bay by going much deeper into mainland Algeria. Then the planes were to suddenly turnaround and target the enemy unexpectedly from the rear. In order to disengage the S.79s had to dangerously fly over the fleet since the mountains in front blocked the way out of the attack area. The area was also well defended by guns and it was patrolled by Supermarine Spitfires Mk.Vb from No. 81 Squadron. Everything went according to the plan until the planes were in proximity of the Bay when they were intercepted by Spitfires from No. 81 Squadron. Buscaglia's plane was in the lead and began to attract considerable enemy fire. Two of its crew members died almost instantly (*1 Aviere Armiere* Walter Vecchiarelli and wireless operator *Maresciallo* Edmondo Balestri) while the plane came out of the confrontation looking like a slice of Swiss cheese. Despite facing tremendous fire and also forced it to be separated from the remaining aircraft of his team, Buscaglia's crew made a daunting attack releasing the torpedo and machine gunning enemy sailors on deck after flying low over the ship. The torpedo missed the target. Riddled in bullets the *Sparviero* had to be ditched at sea. Buscaglia barely managed to crash land his plane on the water and seconds later two other crew members died on impact (*1 Aviere Motorista* Vittorio Vercesi and co-pilot *Sergente Maggiore* Francesco Sogliuzzo). Buscaglia and photographer *Aviere* Francesco Maiore were the only survivors although both were badly burned.

The only hit by 132° *Gruppo* was made at 1445 when a torpedo struck the hull of the anti-aircraft ship HMS *Tynwald,* which had previously been hit by a torpedo from an Italian submarine (*Argo*). The ship was to provide escort to HMS *Roberts* and shield the latter from Axis aerial attacks. Despite the fact that she was heavily armed with six 4-inch anti-aircraft guns and eight 2-pounders anti-aircraft guns, its crew was unable to halt the torpedo bomber attack or to cause the enemy aircraft to launch the warhead from an unfavorable position. The torpedoed ship immediately sank into the sea. The remaining *Sparvieri* fought off the enemy Spitfires by

140 Giulio Cesare Graziani, *Con Bombe e Siluri fra le Cannonate*, p.171.

downing three of them before disengaging. One plane crash landed at Djidjelli while the other two crashed into Bougie Bay.

Buscaglia recollected as follows:

> At 1430 we arrived over the target. I launched the torpedo at the enemy vessel and strafed the decks of the other ships. I could not observe the result exactly. At the moment I found myself isolated. The other five aircraft, I don't know why had spread out. I saw them four or five kilometers away.
>
> A formation of spitfires I counted more than seven, jumped on to me and I had to engage them in combat. The tail gunner and the wireless operator were killed instantly while the rear machine gun no longer worked as the plane was on fire. Wrapped in flames it crashed into the sea from a height of 70-80 meters. I was unconscious and I am not sure how I didn't drown. Photographer Maiore was close to me but the others burned on the water. Two hours later Maiore and I were picked up by a British unit engaged in the action. We remained unattended all afternoon through the night and the next morning. Then we were transported to a French hospital in the Bougie area. My companion's condition was very bad and I had burns to my feet, legs, hands and face. I was not able to see for a month. On 15 November I was moved to an English military hospital near Bougie. On 27 November Maiore passed away after atrocious suffering.[141]

Aichner's recollections of the same combat action are as follows:

> In my earphones I could hear my commander's voice. "In a single line spaced to avoid slip-stream." Then a short while later he radioed: "Come into attack formation." Suddenly before us appeared the endless and bright sea, with a roof of identical white clouds. We were overlooking the bay from a balcony more than 1000 meters high and wide. We dropped down behind the commander but even at full speed we could not reach him. The first Spitfires single out the leader and struck him with their opening bursts. Fire immediately broke out in the aircraft. I was behind Buscaglia when his aircraft was hit. I was a little out of line because although I was at full throttle I had been unable to catch him. I gained a few tenths of meters but I lost altitude. I could see the underside of the aircraft and the carousel of Spitfires attaching him, ignoring us wingmen. They had realized Buscaglia's plane was the bigger target.[142]

The after-action report singled out the courageous nature of the attacks pressed forward by pilots and crews against overwhelming enemy fire. "The combat action was carried out with great audacity against a fierce response by enemy fighters. After having flown for over two hours in enemy territory the *Sparvieri* emerged out of the clouds in Bougie Bay and despite great enemy fire they got within launching range. The action was conducted in the face of extreme interference from enemy fighters that even before we could drop the warheads had already downed Buscaglia's aircraft."[143]

141 Marco Mattioli, *Savoia Marchetti S.79 Sparviero*, p.60.
142 Ibid, p.61.
143 Archivio Storico Aeronautica Militare: 132° *Gruppo* Aerosiluranti Diario Storico, "Operazioni 1942", 20 December 1942.

Upon their return to base, the remaining *Sparvieri* crews were convinced that Buscaglia and his crew had perished during the combat action. Two days later a communication by *Comando Supremo* informed the Italian people that: "Major Carlo Emanuele Buscaglia, who had led into battle his glorious aerosilurante unit which had inflicted severe damage upon the enemy's naval convoy, failed to return to base."[144] Both Buscaglia and his crew member Maiore, who were thought to not having survived, were awarded gold medals of military valor. Photographer Maiore, has Buscaglia's own recollections reported would die a few days later of his wounds, while Buscaglia, who had multiple burns and no eyesight for over a month, would survive and was later transferred to an American POW camp. Further losses were sustained by the *Sparvieri* crews during the continuation of Operation Torch.

Later in the afternoon on 12 November nine *Sparvieri* (four from 280ª *Squadriglia* and five from 283ª *Squadriglia*/ 130° *Gruppo)* pursued a convoy headed for Bougie Bay. The pilots pressed forward with a coordinated attack at 1800 but were met with continuous and sustained anti-aircraft fire. Only one *Sparviero*, the one flown by *Sottotenente* Nico Meschiari, was able to drop the warhead but has the pilot was flying over the enemy ships to quickly disengage it was shot down killing the crew. Then on 16 November another *Sparviero* was lost to enemy fighters when it attempted to strike again at convoys near Bougie Bay. It was shot down by Spitfires killing *Tenente* Nicola Titi and his crew of 255ª *Squadriglia*/105° *Gruppo*. A few minutes later another S.79 from the same unit piloted by *Tenente* Lorenzo Cangemi was also struck down by murderous machine gun fire from enemy Spitfires.

On 18 November three S.79 from 105° *Gruppo* took flight to interdict a British destroyer that had been spotted near Algiers, but after almost two hours of reconnaissance they were not able to locate it and were forced to turn back. Buscaglia's famed unit was back in action on 20 November and renamed *Gruppo Buscaglia* in honor of the fallen commander. It's command had been assumed on an interim basis by *Capitano* Giulio Cesare Graziani and the vice-captain was *Tenente* Martino Aichner. Upon taking the reins of the unit, the newly appointed commander was forced to alter the combat tactics of the unit due to the obsolescence of the S.79. According to *Tenente* Aichner, Graziani gathered his direct reports before the combat action and gave the following briefing: "Given that it is almost impossible to operate during daylight given the dangerous presence of enemy fighters escorting the convoys. And also given the almost suicidal attacks against well defended seaborne landings, I decided that we shall carry out a night raid taking advantage of the full moon forecasted for the next few days.[145] Since the days of the Spanish Civil War many S.79 pilots, especially the less experienced ones, had refrained, for the most part, from flying the plane at night as it was considered not suitable for a whole host of reasons. However, the changed situation called for a change in torpedo bomber tactics ensuring that the attacks would go forward only when the bombers were concealed by darkness.

The goal was to pursue a large convoy that was spotted in Philippeville Bay and to achieve this the top night pilots were selected such as Tenenti Faggioni, Pfister, Aichner, Martini, di Coci and di Mazzocca. Following takeoff at 1515 from Castelvetrano in Sicily on 20 November the formation comprised of seven S.79s arrived south of Algiers at 1745, but let's follow Aichner's recollections of this first mass nighttime torpedo bomber attack:

144 Gianni Rocca, *I disperati*, p.247.
145 Martino Aichner, *Il gruppo Buscaglia*, p.134.

> Daylight had almost disappeared and the moon was still covered by clouds so it was not easy to spot the targets. As soon as we turned on our lights so that we could avoid colliding against one another, the anti-aircraft guns and the machine guns opened fire further reducing our visibility. This was our first nighttime operation and the machine gun tracers were extremely intimidating. It felt like all the enemy fire was concentrated against the windshield. We saw the tracers flying up toward us at great speed and they appeared to be concentrated on the aircraft. It's the same feeling as driving at night during a snowstorm when all the flakes appear to be coming into the windshield. But unlike a snow flurry these were real bullets. We reacted to the enemy fire by zigzagging and by making quick moves flying right up and then quickly bringing the plane down. But with great speed I then brought the aircraft further down so that I was in a good position to launch the warhead against what appeared to be the long shadow of a steamer. The veins in my face and neck felt like they were about to burst. Immediately after releasing the torpedo I quickly disengaged and for a few minutes the aircraft without the torpedo load picked up speed almost 50 kilometers per hour faster than during standard flight.[146]

While making their return to base the aircraft were intercepted by Beaufighters from No. 46 Squadron which scored one hit downing *Sottotenente* Giuseppe Coci's plane near Cape Serrat. The enemy guns had also damaged the dinghy to the point that it was taking in water and could not be utilized by the downed crew members. They were forced to swim for over two hours to reach the shore. The next day they walked into Bizerte's fort where they received medical aid.

The post battle report described that a 10,000 steamer had been torpedoed while two other torpedoes struck two more ships. "This action was the first nighttime operation conducted by our crews. Seven aircraft took part in the operation subdivided into two smaller squads that fired their loads at close range against enemy ships. The enemy was taken by surprise by this daring operation conducted under the cover of darkness into the bay and with the grave danger of colliding against the mountains or into each other."[147]

That same day six S.79s aircraft from 105°, 108° *Gruppi* and 36° *Stormo* took off from Decimomannu to locate enemy targets but were not able to find any. Later in the day five S.79s from 130° *Gruppo* took off from Elmas to reach Algiers where they launched torpedoes against two merchantmen. Three additional S.79 from the same unit took off in the late afternoon to pursue the same targets at the port of Algiers but they were forced to turn back given the worsening weather conditions.

On 23 November three *Sparvieri* from the 130° *Gruppo* pounced upon enemy ships harboring at Algiers Bay. At 0300 the aircraft pressed ahead with their attack despite being met by extremely vivacious anti-aircraft fire and released torpedoes, two of which struck enemy ships while one misfired. The hits were made by *Sottotenente* Francesco Cossu and *Sottotenente* Antonio Vellere that damaged one ship, the 19,791 tons steamer Scythia and sunk a second unidentified freighter. The Royal Navy post battle report stated that the Scythia had been damaged by an aerial torpedo with the loss of five soldiers out of 4,300. The following are the recollections of a

146 Ibid, p.134.
147 *Capitano* Graziani, 132 ° *Gruppo* Aerosiluranti, "Azione del 20 Novembre," cited in Martino Aichner, *Il gruppo Buscaglia*, p.138.

British Tommy on board HMS *Scythia*, who provides however what appears to be an incorrect date for the torpedoing of the ship:

> We were bombed out twice while I was waiting to join the RAF. I had finished my engineering course and was hoping to get in as a pilot but no luck. At first I went into Motor Transport then I joined the 129 Spitfire Squadron and they immediately put me on re-fueling aircraft. I then did a commando course and was posted to 13 Squadron on Blenheims.
>
> In 1942 shortly afterward joining 13 Squadron we were told we were going away but we were not told where. We were taken to Liverpool, kitted out and boarded RMS Scythia. We had been afloat some days when on the night of 11th November 1942 we were torpedoed just a few miles from Algiers harbor, whilst I was asleep. We had been sleeping wherever we could and in the hold where we were there was a wooden hatch. The torpedo came just under where we were sleeping and the force of the explosion went through the hatch and so saved our lives – there were only two or three casualties, we were very lucky.
>
> We were then taken to Algiers without kit or anything – we had lost everything – and then to a transit camp for a couple of nights before being taken to Blida aerodrome, just outside Algiers, to be refitted and the squadron reformed, ready to join the North African Campaign.[148]

On 24 November another hit was scored by three torpedo bombers from 280ª *Squadriglia/*130° *Gruppo* at 1400 near Cape Bougaroun. *Tenenti* Alessandro Setti, Ferruccio Lo Prieno and Mario Tredici released two warheads in the midst of heavy defensive fire striking two 6,000 tons steamers that were later sunk. On the return flight to base a further hit was scored when a 5,000 steamer was struck and damaged south west of Cape Bougaroun. The hits are not confirmed by the Royal Navy war diary but it is also feasible that the steamers were American.[149] However, no mention of the strikes was found in the United States Navy accounts of the war. In a separate operation in the same area one aircraft from 257ª *Squadriglia*/108° *Gruppo* was downed by anti-aircraft fire and its crew perished.[150] Meanwhile on the same day four S.79s departed from Sardinia for a reconnaissance action along the Algerian coast. The four *Sparvieri* from 132° *Gruppo*, however, were forced to turn back to base due to adverse weather conditions.

On 25 November *Superaereo*, with a focus on interfering with the vast increase of enemy traffic along the coast of Algeria, ordered the 132° *Gruppo* to transfer from Sicily to Decimomannu in Sardinia, so that it be closer to the area of operations but also because the base was better equipped to handle the servicing of large numbers of S.79.

On the same day nine S.79s belonging to 108°, 105° and 130° *Gruppi* departed from Sardinia to attack various convoys that had been spotted navigating along the coast of Algeria. They were split up into four patrol units. The first three patrol units were not able to locate the enemy while the last one comprised of two S.79s from 255ª *Squadriglia*/105° *Gruppo* pursued a 6,000 tons merchant ship north east of Cape de Fer. *Tenente* Vincenzo Giannone attacked the ship by

148 BBC Southern Counties Radio "Torpedoed on the Scythia", <https://www.bbc.co.uk/history/ww2peopleswar/stories/36/a4445336.shtml > (accessed on 10 November, 2021).

149 Francesco Mattessini, *Luci ed Ombre*, p.274.

150 Marco Mattioli, *Savoia Marchetti S.79 Sparviero*, p.64.

launching his torpedo at 700 meters out. As he flew over the enemy convoy, his crew was not able to ascertain the conditions of the ship or take photos as a strong thunderstorm hampered their visibility.

On 27 November the commander of II *Fliegerkorps* in a note to *Superarereo* requested greater collaboration by the aircraft of *Aeronautica della Sardegna* in attacks against enemy transport ships that were unloading soldiers at Bone, and Philippeville. As a result on 28 November the Italians fielded a sizeable force for a daytime operation including four Cant.Z.1007bis of 88° *Gruppo*, and six S.79s. The latter belonged to 3° *Nucleo Addestramento Aerosiluranti* flown by *Capitano* Giulio Martini, *Tenente* Vazio Terzi and *Tenente* Francesco di Bella awhile the remaining three belonged to 132° *Gruppo* and were flown by *Capitano* Giulio Cesare Graziani, *Sottotenente* Carlo Pfister and *Tenente* Martino Aichner. The escort was provided by fifteen *Macchi* C.202 fighters of 6° *Gruppo*. The operation did not begin well because one the fighters, *Capitano* Dante Occorso, was shot down by Spitfires even before the squads had gone into action. Meanwhile, *Sparvieri* crews were busily scouring Allied convoys navigating near the coast of Algeria when they spotted a number of vessels between Algiers and Bougie carrying supplies, ammunition and weapons. All six attacked the convoy utilizing a new tactic that consisted in bringing the aircraft down suddenly from an altitude of 3,000 meters (or 1.8 miles) and then releasing the torpedoes a few feet above the water. This was a new tactic to avoid the anti-aircraft fire during daylight operations. Accordingly the S.79s dove down in a coordinated fashion and then launched several torpedoes, one of which struck and sunk the 1,774 tons steamer Selbo at 1320. This was a transport ship loaded with fuel that exploded immediately killing thirteen of its twenty-five member crew. The Allied ships then opened up a very fierce barrage against the S.79s flying over them and managed to inflict some damage upon *Sottotenente*'s Pfister's plane and injuring one of its crew members. As *Tenente* Aichner's recalled:

> When we were a few kilometers away from the convoy we spotted the silhouette of the enemy ships. We spotted several medium sized cargo ships navigating on a straight line. They were traveling at slow speed and without escort. With such an easy prey Graziani ordered us to spread out and to each identify a target. At a distance of 800 meters Graziani was the first to release the warhead against the nearest target. Pfister and I continued to get closer to the convoy in order to get in a favorable position just like in one of our training sessions in Gorizia. We then veered towards the ships and as we are flying over them we were subjected to the machine guns fire coming from the steamers. The squad led by Marini released the torpedoes almost at the same time. Terzi's aircraft was the only one that misfired during this combat action due to the malfunctioning of the release mechanism and his plane was damaged by enemy fire.…Looking at the convoy we observe a large column of black smoke that looks like a mushroom cloud.[151]

In the afternoon more *Sparvieri* were deployed to strike at the enemy convoy. At 1445 three S.79 from 283ª *Squadriglia/*130° *Gruppo* were engaged by a number of enemy Supermarine Spitfires IX before flying over the enemy ships. Subjected to rapid machine gun fire, one *Sparviero* flown by *Sottotenente* Michele Virdis was shot down and its crew perished. The leader of the squad,

151 Martino Aichner, *Il Gruppo Buscaglia*, p.211.

Tenente Cimicchi recalls that: "The sky over the area was controlled by enemy fighters. In order not to be seen, we went in at wavetop height and thus managed, incredibly, to exploit the element of surprise. Torpedoes were dropped and some struck home. In fact the explosions alerted the Spitfires, which jumped us, immersing us in a hail of bullets. *Sottotenente* Virdis' aircraft, which had straggled during the escape, was struck and set alight, crashing into the sea. Hit by an enemy bullet, the central engine of my aircraft stopped working, but I managed to return to base."[152]

By conducting a daylight operation, which exposed the slower *Sparvieri* to the fire of the much faster enemy Spitfires, the *Comando Aeronautica della Sardegna* had none the less fulfilled the *Luftwaffe's* request for greater collaboration in anti-shipping operations. In the same operation the latter deployed fifteen He.111, torpedo bombers three of which were downed by enemy fire.

The second combined largescale Axis operation was organized as a reprisal against Force Q that on 1 December had ambushed the *Aventino* convoy which had departed from Palermo and was on its way to Tunisia comprised of four large transport ships escorted by five destroyers. Force Q knowing the route plans of the convoy through the Ultra intercept was able to pounce on the transports downing all four and a destroyer (*Folgore*). The war diary of *Luftflotte* II asserts that: "As soon as the attack on the Italian/German convoy became known, II FK received the order to take off."[153] In response, the command center of II *Fliegerkorps* mobilized sixteen He.111 aircraft led by Colonel Karl Stockmann in addition to six Ju.88 bombers, while *Aeronautica della Sardegna* committed nine S.79s (five from 283ª and four from 280ª *Squadriglia*/130° *Gruppo* commanded respectively by *Capitano* Franco Melley and *Capitano* Giuseppe Cimicchi*)*. The goal was to seek Force Q and inflict damage. The *Luftwaffe* aircraft departed first and at 0640 on 2 December and two of its standard bombers sank HMS *Quentin*, a newly built Q-class destroyer. The Italians departed at 0730 from Elmas. After the first hour of flight *Capitano* Melley had to abort the mission when his plane experienced engine failure and he was forced to return to base leaving his four plane squad to fend for itself. Continuing on their mission the remaining *Sparvieri* of 130° *Gruppo* vectored for more than two hours but failed to find Force Q, which by 0940 had sailed into Bone harbor, but would up spotting another British convoy near Bizerte. Just as the *Sparvieri* were setting up for the attack they were in turn attacked by a number of Spitfires from No. 242 Squadron. The encounter in the skies over the Algerian coast was fierce and a small patch of airspace became a maze of aircraft zigzagging all over and with tracers flying everywhere. The *Sparvieri* put up a gallant fight against the much faster enemy planes and managed to down one Spitfire (pilot Hamblin) through the fire coming from *Tenente* Caresio aircraft. But soon after the Spitfires gained the upper hand by maneuvering around the five Italian aircraft and firing at will from the flanks. As a result four Italian planes were downed and the crews all perished. The planes were flown by *Sottotenente* Amorino Ingrosso, *Tenente* Ferruccio Lo Prieno, *Sottotenente* Antonio Vellere and *Tenente* Manlio Caresio. The latter and his crew, with the exception of *aviere marconista* Aldo Manca who died on board, were the only survivors and remained at sea seventy-two hours despite being tormented by hunger and thirst before being rescued by a German Do.24 seaplane. As *Capitano* Cimicchi later recalled:

152 Giuseppe Cimicchi, *I siluri vengono dal cielo* (Milan: Longanesi, 1964), p.167.

153 Uboat.net, "Allied Warships, HMS Quentin" <https://uboat.net/allies/warships/ship/4502.html> (accessed on 16 April 2021).

Here they are the fighters, they are 13 Spitfire IXs, the latest type, really new and bright. They jump on us from all sides, firing on us without giving us a break, one, two, three times. The first to be hit is Tenente Lo Prieno's aircraft. 'Lo Prieno is falling!' My co-pilot cries. I see the aircraft catch fire, explode, fall off on a wing and sink. The Spitfires resume their assaults. How long will this hell last, and how many of us will follow Lo Prieno? The enemy fighters are evidently trying to scatter our formation, isolating, encircling single torpedo bombers.

We are able to advance as a compact formation. But the terrible enemy fire continues. 13 Spitfires, with all their weapons, against us, against our four surviving aircraft. 'Vellere's aircraft is burning!' My co-pilot cries again. It's true, but it isn't enough, for I see flames spewing from Tenente Ingrosso's aircraft too. The two aircraft seem to struggle with the fire for some moments, pulling up, fighting their destiny, but in vain. One at a time, they are too exploding, falling and plunging into the sea, where they continue to burn. Thirteen Spitfires are now vomiting all their firepower at my aircraft and at Caresio's plane and we close in on each other as if seeking protection and go low zig zagging over the surface of the water to avoid the enemy's attacks. But the 13 Spitfires like a pack of dogs excited by the smell of blood, are more aggressive than ever. Are they invulnerable? No at last one of them, struck by gunfire, catches fire and plunges into the sea. Flying as we are a few meters above the sea's surface, we see the water seething with spray under the hailstorm of enemy fire. One Spitfire has threaded it's way between Caresio's and mine. Caresio is challenged to a duel. At the machine gun is wireless operator airman Aldo Manca, a good, brave boy, He has a good aim, for the British fighter is hit and breaks away, it's tail smoking. But Manca too, is fatally hit. He will be awarded a posthumous Silver Medal.[154]

The operation was a complete disaster for the *Sparvieri* which not only suffered the loss of several aircraft but also the few bombers that were able to release the warheads misfired. It highlighted how torpedo bomber technology had stalled and had not kept pace. Most likely, the faster *Reggiane* Re.2001 torpedo bomber prototypes that the RA was testing out at the time would have put up a better fight against the enemy fighters even while carrying a torpedo. Thanks to its maneuverability, speed and its improved armament it could dogfight even with the more powerful enemy aircraft like the Supermarine Spitfire Mk IX.[155] The operation in

154 Giuseppe Cimicchi, *I siluri vengono dal cielo* (Milan: Longanesi, 1964), p.167.

155 RAF fighter pilot Laddie Lucas recalled in his memoirs that the *Reggiane* could be a difficult and dangerous opponent for the Spitfire V: " On 13 July 1942, 249 Squadron was engaged high above Malta with a mixed force of German and Italian fighters. Jack Rae, then fast developing into one of New Zealand's outstanding pilots and his able No. 2, the Australian, Alan Yates, despite being low on ammunition, had finally set upon a lone Re.2001 as it was about to disengage and head for Sicily. What then followed gave Jack such a shock that the incident has stuck starkly in his mind for half a century. "To my amazement the Italian proved to be an extremely competent opponent. I had never before been involved in such a complex sequence of aerobatics as I pursued him. Twice I nearly 'spun off' as I stayed with him; I found it difficult to get any sort of worthwhile deflection shot at his aircraft. At times he got dangerously close to getting a bead on me. Eventually he started to smoke and we hit his tail, but we were halfway across the Strait of Sicily and our position was getting dangerous as we were now low in fuel and would be in real difficulty if we were attacked. But, as we turned back to base, the Italian, to my amazement, turned with us and made one final and defiant

essence grounded the 130° *Gruppo* for the month of December as it attempted to reorganize and replenish the ranks.

On 9 December at 1400, despite very adverse weather conditions, a small patrol unit comprised by three S.79s from 254ª *Squadriglia*/105° *Gruppo* piloted by *Capitano* Urbano Mancini, *Tenente* Ernesto Borelli, and *Sottotenente* Casanova were able to penetrate the anti-aircraft screen in the bay of Algiers in order to attack the MKS 31 convoy. At 1515 one torpedo struck HMS *Marigold,* a 940 tons Flower-class corvette of the Royal Navy. It obliterated the hull of the ship, with the destruction of the radar tower and the removal of its 102mm gun which plunged into the sea. The heavy damage and the flooding caused the ship to sink in less than ten minutes, while forty-nine crew members died. On their way back to base the torpedo bombers were ambushed by enemy fighters. Several *Sparvieri* were on the receiving end of enemy fire and suffered damage to their aircraft, while one P-40 was shot down.[156]

On 10 December the 132° *Gruppo* returned to Trapani in Sicily, after having completed its extended stay in Sardinia. On 13 and 17 December three Sardinian based S.79s from 130° *Gruppo* carried out a number of patrol actions that did not lead to any positive results.

On 12 December three S.79s (one from 280ª and two from 283ª *Squadriglie*/130° *Gruppo*) conducted a combat patrol action targeting a Royal Navy formation but were attacked by P-40s. In the heated confrontation, *Sottotenente* Salvatore Giarrizzo downed an enemy plane.[157] The 130° *Gruppo* carried out an anti-shipping patrol action on 27 December, which was unsuccessful despite the pilots' claim that they sank two merchantmen.

The third year of the war (1942) proved to be very difficult for the torpedo bomber units as many of their attacks were preempted by the new state of the art enemy fighters or by fierce anti-aircraft action. The courageous attacks pressed forward by the *Luftwaffe* and RA during Operation Torch had achieved some success against the Allied landings but had only disrupted the operation without halting the Allies in any way. Kesselring's aim to interdict such a massive operation as Torch primarily with the air forces had not succeeded. Between 8 November and 31 December 1942 the Axis lost 101 aircraft, 21 of which belonged to the RA while the Allies had gained another foothold in North Africa. The trap against Rommel's army could now be put into effect. Rommel himself by late 1942 had given up all hopes of holding on to Libya and had advised *Comando Supremo* and the Fuhrer about the proposal for the concentration of Axis forces in the Axis bastion of North Africa (Tunisia).

Summary and Conclusions

1. Very high losses amongst the Axis supply convoys to North Africa in the fall of 1941, forced the Axis to shift additional resources to Sicilian airbases in 1942 to subdue Malta. In 1942 the constant bombings of Malta led to an improvement of the supply situation in North Africa especially during the first half of the year when German bombers were fully engaged

attack upon our section – as if to show what he thought of a pair of Spitfires!" Laddie Lucas, *Malta The Thorn in Rommel's Side* (London: Penguin Books, 1993), pp.251-52.

156 Marco Mattioli, *Savoia Marchetti S.79 Sparviero*, p.66.

157 The Curtiss P-40 Warhawk was an American single-engine, all-metal monoplane fighter and ground-attack aircraft. The aircraft had a top speed of 354 mph (570 km/h).

in the reduction of Malta. The latter' submarine and small craft flotilla force, was also neutralized by a large deployment of forces by the Italian battlefleet which began escorting large convoy operations to North Africa in large numbers. As a result, Malta's forces had a more difficult time attempting to launch torpedo strikes or other forms of attack against such a large deployment of forces. The focus on Malta by Axis air forces allowed more supplies to come in and Rommel was finally able to start his offensive which led to the capture of Tobruk and the victory at Gazala. In July 1942, at the height of Axis pressure against Malta, 94 percent of the material shipped (97,332 tons) from Italy or Greece arrived in North Africa. In the second half of the year with a resurgence by Malta the percentage of material that arrived to North Africa began to fall each month.

2. Operation Harpoon on 15 June 1942 revealed that both the RM and air force were by then working in closer coordination as their joint operation scored several hits against the Royal Navy. This was in contrast to earlier operations where the air force had seriously degraded enemy convoys while the RM had failed to take advantage of the favorable situation by acting more decisively. Such successful operation was again achieved with Operation Pedestal, in August 1942 although the Royal Navy was able to get larger quantities of supplies into Malta at the cost of losing some steamers, aircraft carriers, cruisers and destroyers.
3. The planned invasion of Malta was much debated by the Axis commanders in 1942 while the troops (parachute, seaborne infantry and artillery) were trained and readied for the planned operation codenamed Operation Hercules or Operation C3 for the Italians. But the planned operation was eventually delayed and then scrapped altogether when Rommel captured Tobruk. By then Rommel was convinced that he could reach the Nile with a major offensive. Mid-1942 was the highpoint of the Axis war effort since victory appeared in site in North Africa.
4. Rommel's army was stalemated at El Alamein in the summer of 1942 and Malta, no longer the focus of Axis attacks mainly because German bombers had been moved, recovered and became again a launching pad for attacks on Axis shipping convoys. After the final battle of El Alamein in October 1942 the Axis position in the Mediterranean deteriorated considerably. Axis infantry was forced to retreat to Tripolitania first and then Tunisia. The fuel supply situation in North Africa was particularity precarious as the Royal Navy focused its interdiction efforts mainly against Axis transport ships carrying fuel. This made Axis North African tank operations as well as aerial operations particularly challenging forcing many aircraft, including the torpedo bombers, to operate less frequently.
5. The torpedo bombers continued to achieve success against British shipping in the Mediterranean but their attacking tactics were no longer a novelty as the Royal Navy and the RAF adopted very aggressive defensive tactics to blunt their attacks. The torpedo bomber command shifted the focus from lone wolf to simultaneous and synchronized mass attacks involving both standard and torpedo bombers and often involving dive bombers and new weapons. Although the tactic was sound, it lead to large losses of aircraft and to diminishing returns mainly because torpedo bomber development had stalled. Allied fighters in mid-1942, for example, were so much faster than the S.79 and also much better armed than their predecessors. The combination made flying a S.79 an even more dangerous proposition than before. Operation Pedestal, for instance, was a tactical success for the Axis forces but a great failure for the torpedo bomber units as they lost a high number of aircraft and a large wastage of warheads. Some were downed by fighters while others by concentrated anti-aircraft fire.

6. By late-1942 the RA was overstretched and running quickly out of resources. The gamble of winning a short war had been lost, aircraft production decreased and the rate of replacement did not keep up with the wastage of material in the battlefield. The failure of the S.84, for example, meant that the S.79 had to continue being produced. Soon this aircraft was no longer a match for the new American and British aircraft and weapons even in its improved S.79bis version. Even the latter was produced in very limited numbers. The S.79, due to its obsolescence, began to be operated primarily at dusk or dawn or at night thus limiting deployment hours during the day.

7

1943 – Defeat and Exit from the War

Overall Military Situation

By early 1943 the Axis forces were retreating in North Africa toward the Tunisian frontier. The city of Tripoli was encircled by the advancing British 7th Armored Division on the morning of 23 January 1943. Three months had passed since El Alamein, during which time Montgomery's Eighth Army had advanced over 1,400 miles to Tripoli, the Italian control of Tripolitania was lost. Cyrenaica had already been lost in late 1942. This defeat, amongst other, resulted in the abandonment of the air bases in Libya. The Axis troops then retreated from Tripolitania to the Tunisian bastion to maintain a foothold in North Africa. The Tunisian campaign began with an Allied amphibious landing near Sfax in eastern Tunisia on 5 January 1943. On February 4, 1943, Eighth Army crossed the Libya–Tunisia border.

Caught between British Commonwealth and United States armies and forced to receive his supply of fuel, armaments and food through the Mediterranean convoys, *Feldmarschall* Erwin Rommel attempted to halt the Allies by adoption of a defensive posture. German and Italian troops managed to rout the American Second Corps at the Kasserine Pass on 18 February, but the Axis forces were vastly outnumbered and outgunned and with this victory only bought more time. The Allies made slow but steady progress in forcing the Axis troops into a small piece of territory along the north central Tunisian coast. As the Axis troops slowly retreated, the naval convoy war intensified as it became much more precarious for the Axis even if the direct route between Southern Italy and Tunisia to ferry supplies took less time. Not only were both German and Italian forces of fighter escorts much reduced but the naval convoys also were challenged by the Royal Navy and the RAF but also by the deployment of American battleships and aircraft. According to *Comando Supremo* estimates, the Axis army in Tunisia necessitated 70,000 tons of supplies per month to keep the campaign alive. In January and February the troops received adequate supplies, but by March the cargo losses due to Allied attacks began to mount. By April and May further losses of supplies and ammunition were sustained to the point that it began to influence operations. Armored units, for example, could not launch several operations due to the concern to safeguard stocks of fuel.

On 7 May the British 7th Armored Division captured Tunis, while the American Second Army Corps captured Bizerte, the last remaining port in Axis hands. Six days later, on May 13, 1943, the Axis forces in North Africa, having sustained 40,000 casualties in Tunisia alone, surrendered; 267,000 German and Italian soldiers became prisoners of war.

The fall of the Axis position in Tunisia permitted the invasion of Sicily and of the Italian mainland in the summer of 1943 and it also removed the Axis threat to the oilfields of the Middle East and to British supply lines to Asia and Africa. Moreover, Malta was now safe as a British base in the Mediterranean. For the RA, defeat in Tunisia and then Sicily diminished dramatically its theatre of operations with the loss first of all Libyan air bases, followed by the loss of Tunisian and then Sicilian air bases. Especially during the Sicilian campaign the RA along with the *Luftwaffe* attempted to disrupt the Allied landings with the torpedo bomber units especially focused on pursuing the troop transport and the battleships taking part in the seaborne invasion of the island. Unfortunately, the massive, Allied deployments of ships, airplanes, guns and troops would nullify the courageous yet inconsequential activities of the Axis air forces. Italian estimates of Allied strength was that 747 Axis fighters faced 2,270 Allied fighters, while 1,116 Axis bombers and torpedo bombers were matched against 2,000 Allied bombers.[1] "The Axis was heavily outnumbered and as far as Italy was concerned there was no hope of reducing the imbalance."[2]

The RA in 1943

The RA in 1943 had two main objectives. First to maintain the Axis airbridge to Tunisia. Second, plan against a potential pre and post invasion defense of Italy. For both objectives, as mentioned above, the RA faced a desperate situation given its limited force. The imbalance was not about numbers alone, but it also involved technological development such as the lack of a more modern torpedo and of a heavy bomber or of better armed fighters. Let's take the S.79 torpedo bomber overall performance for example in relation to other non-Italian torpedo bombers. In each category such as armament, speed, quality of the aircraft, torpedo load and drop height and position, the S.79 by 1943 was inferior to other bombers. First, its standard armament was based on 3 x 12.7mm machine guns and one 7.7mm machine gun, while the German He.111, for example, had six or seven machine guns and a 20mm gun. Second, while the S.79's fuselage was made from steel tubing the wings and the rear components were still primarily made of wood. Most torpedo bombers, whether German, Japanese, British or American, in 1943 were made completely of steel. Third, the Grumman TBF-1 Avenger, used in the Battle of Midway, had a large bomb bay, allowing for one Bliss-Leavitt Mark 13 torpedo (569mm) with a range of 6,300 yards (5,761 meters) and a speed of 33,5 knots. In contrast, the S.79 for most of the war could only carry the Whitehead torpedo (450mm) with a range of 3,300 yards (3,000 meters) and a speed of 40 knots. The Avenger also had a top speed of 271 mph (436 km/h), while the S.79 top speed was 200 mph carrying the torpedo. Fourth, the Japanese Nakajima B5N and its successor the B6N torpedo bomber could carry warhead that could be launched at a higher launch speed and from greater altitude than the S.79.[3] The B6N, for example, could be launched from an altitude of 328 feet (100 m) and at a speed of 230 mph (370 km/h). In addition, Japan's industry was much more proficient being able to produce 1,149

1 John Gooch, *Mussolini's War*, p.354.
2 Ibid.
3 Mark R. Peattie, Sunburst: *The Rise of the Japanese Naval Air Power, 1909-1941*, p.77.

B5N and 1,268 B6N, while Italian industry could produce approximately 1,217 S.79 and 309 S.84 during the war.[4]

Another deficiency of the RA was the slow introduction of newer and more advanced medium and heavy bombers. The Cant.Z.1018 *Leone* II experienced a number of production difficulties in 1942 and it came out in very small numbers. Similarly, the heavy bomber was still under engineering review at the beginning of 1943. Finally, the RA's fighter force, in light of a potential invasion of Italy by the Allies, was to be overhauled with newer aircraft many of which had to be more strongly armed with 20mm cannons instead of machine guns. This was a necessity if the RA intended to seriously counter the flying fortresses bombing forays on Italian cities and infrastructure and the invasion force itself at sea. By mid-1943 very few fighters would be fitted with the 20mm cannon with industry encountering several delays due to lack of experienced personnel and slow factory output. Despite the difficulties one of the positive notes for Italy in 1943 was the introduction of state of the art fighters belonging to the new line of production even though few came off the assembly line equipped with the 20mm cannon. It was at this point that the Italians deployed in combat the *Macchi* C. 205 *Veltro* and the series manufacture of the Fiat G.55 and the *Reggiane* Re.2005 which were very effective aircraft and fully competitive against Allied planes, while fitted with German engines. Unfortunately for the RA they came out in too little numbers and too late. The *Veltro* was designed by Mario Castoldi and bore a strong resemblance to its predecessor the *Folgore*. "The *Veltro* was an all metal low wing monoplane with retractable landing gear, with elegant and aerodynamic lines. Its only external differences compared to the *Folgore* lay in the engine housing and the presence of two oil radiators on the side of the fuselage. However its performance differed greatly thanks to a more powerful power plant, the prototype proved capable of reaching 404 mph (650 km/h) in horizontal flight and of climbing 19,735 feet (6,000 m) in four minutes and 52 seconds."[5] The *Veltro* went into service in April 1943 and was used mainly in the Mediterranean and Sicily and was heavily deployed against the Allied landing in 1943. Similarly, the *Reggiane* Re.2005 represented another important innovation of the Italian aviation industry thanks to the design work of Roberto Longhi and Antonio Alessio. It too was fitted with the Daimler Benz DB 605A-1 engine obtaining a maximum speed of 390 mph (628 km/h). Its major downsides were that it was introduced relatively late into the conflict (December 1942) and only 48 aircraft were produced due to manufacturing delays and lack of engines. Its operational history before the armistice of 1943 was relegated to the Mediterranean theatre as it was assigned to the 6° *Stormo*. The *Reggiane* Re.2005 was also well armed with two Breda-SAFAT 12.7mm machine guns and three 20mm cannons. Thus, in the realm of fighter planes the Italian aviation industry was able to innovate considerably during the conflict improving the speed, reliability, and firepower of its fleet. Unfortunately, due to several factors innovation came about with considerable delay and some of the most effective aircraft saw limited service as Italy capitulated in September 1943. Moreover, the material scarcity brought about by the war economy ensured that industry could not maintain a particularly high pace of production.

The RA continued to struggle in 1943 due to its multiple operational/territorial commitments and the dwindling resources at its disposal. Facing a downturn in production due to

4 Enzo Angelucci, *Combat Aircraft of World War II.* p.18.
5 Ibid., p.224.

Allied bombings and a lack of raw materials, the government decided to investigate the causes behind the low production output (700 more aircraft were produced in 1941 versus 1942). It appointed vice secretary of the party Carlo Ravasio whose task was to find ways to streamline production and process more aircraft quickly from the production line and into combat. His investigation found several shortcomings in the process manufacturing of aircraft, components and engines. First, in 1942, despite a proposal by the head of *Regia Aeronautica Generale* Rino Corso Fougier to standardize production to only four aircraft, it was found that industry, mainly Fiat, still produced 500 obsolete CR.42, which were totally uncompetitive versus modern Allied fighters. It appears that the production of uncompetitive aircraft was the result of a combination of industry's resistance to change together with government policies that aimed to keep some factories afloat despite a lack of demand for their obsolete products. This was done principally to maintain social stability and to refrain from taking decisions that would antagonize labor. In 1942 Carlo Favagrossa, who was the plenipotentiary for the government's production board, had advocated the creation of joint government-aircraft industry committees aimed to steer aircraft production toward newer, more technologically advanced models. This was not to compete with the RA *Commissione per l'aeronautica* that had been set up by *Generale* Pricolo to oversee production issues, but was meant to integrate its work in collaboration with industry representatives. The goal was to standardize production by selecting two fighters and two bombers to focus the manufacturing effort. But these joint committees were set up with considerable delay only in March 1943 when the war effort was languishing and the regime was on its last leg. Thus, the committees were ineffectual since they did not have time to have any meaningful influence on aircraft production. Second, Ravasio also highlighted that with the exception of the factories of the *Macchi* fighters and *Breda* bombers, industry was unable to keep production and output constant. *Caproni*, for example, was singled out for not being able to supply reliable aircraft, while the S.79 production line of *Savoia Marchetti* was considered obsolete, and the S.84 a huge mistake.[6] In Ravasio's view, technological development during the conflict had lacked especially for torpedo bombers and standard bombers but not for fighters, while with few exceptions the aviation industry was still fragmented and lacking modern means of mass production. The only real bright spot was the introduction of the 5 Series fighters by *Macchi*, *Fiat* and *Reggiane* which held considerable promise. It can be argued that the 5 Series, although representing a leap forward for the domestic aviation industry, was still fairly representative of the industries original impediments. Whereas in Britain fighter production was centered upon the Spitfire, whose basic design was renewed each time, in Italy, whose aviation industry was less mechanized, there were still several different types of fighter aircraft being produced by different entities. A consolidation about one fighter aircraft would have better served the interests of the state and of the military as well as lowering production costs and by having a few larger; assembly line. In his report Ravasi wrote that: "The aviation industry has maintained its original artisan based nature. It is useless to search within it for a strong organization, mass production, or the standardization of production into a few viable aircraft models. The typical Italian aeronautical industrialist is not a great technician or engineer but owns his fortune to owning one of the first entities to enter this relatively new industry. Generally he has not taken care to improve himself, to keep up to date, to study, to fully staff research and development departments. Moreover,

6 Gianni Rocca, I *disperati*, p.257.

he does not innovate and designs with the latest discoveries in engineering science or manufacturing best practices in mind. In fact, industry does not innovate by updating its systems of production because industrialists are acutely aware that the state will 'buy anything from anyone at any price."[7]

The report also stated that the gap between Italian industry output versus that of Britain or the United States had not been narrowed during the war years. Ravasio's report concluded with three main recommendations. First, to further decentralize production so that industry was less vulnerable to Allied air attacks. Industry was highly concentrated in the northern industrial triangle (Milan, Turin, Genoa) with 62 percent of all production taking place there in 1941. Some provinces such as Milan (that was responsible for 16% of the nation's industrial output), Varese, Genoa and La Spezia were the recurring targets of multiple enemy bombing attacks because of their large industrial districts. Eighty-five percent of engines for aircraft, for example, were manufactured in the North. The situation could be rectified by continuing the relocation of plants (which began in 1941) to southern and central Italy as a way to disperse production. Two, to shift production to newly constructed underground plants less vulnerable to attacks. Third, to introduce a harsh 'war economy' based on strict governmental control of prices and labor. All appeared to be sound recommendations in wartime but a regime that was becoming highly politically unstable due to defeats in Russia and North Africa remained unable during 1943 to force these reforms through.

The RA throughout 1943 continued to study the feasibility of launching torpedoes from fighter aircraft and also from aircraft carrier as the effort to supersede the S.79 as a torpedo bomber was far from dead. Since the S.84 had been such a great disappointment, RA planners began to look at alternatives to the S.79 and after several meetings and debates the *Reggiane* Re.2001 was identified as the most viable fighter/bomber for torpedo launches. During the war a dedicated team led by *Colonnello* Antonino Serra worked for a long period of time on this project which entailed developing a prototype of a smaller aerial torpedo to match a suitable fighter aircraft.[8] The *Reggiane* Re.2001G was selected for this application because it held several advantages over other fighters. The aircraft was powered by one of the most advanced engines available in 1940, the Daimler Benz DB601, a liquid cooled inline engine allowing to improve the speed by nearly 20 percent compared to the engine used in the Re.2000 which was powered by an Italian radial engine. In official tests at the RA base at Guidonia the Re.2001 achieved a top speed of 337.4 mph (543 km) at 18,000 feet or 5,470 meters. Since the *Macchi* C.202 was also undergoing technical evaluations at the same time achieving a top speed that was slightly superior to the Re.2001, the latter was produced only in small numbers (approximately 250 units). The final design was a metal monoplane that offered several design improvements over the Re.2000 as it included improved, more robust wings and armored fuel tanks. Re.2001 standard firepower was provided by two 12.7mm Breda-SAFAT machine guns in the nose and one 7.7mm machine gun in each wing. A slightly modified version also included two 20mm cannons in gun pods under the wings. However, the most important difference versus the *Macchi* C.202 was its greater autonomy and the possibility to hook external loads under the fuselage. It could hold a 640 kg (1,410 lbs.) aerial torpedo or two bombs. The dedicated team then matched the aircraft to the

7 Fortunato Minniti, "La politica industriale del ministero dell'aeronautica", *Storia Contemporanea*, N. 1, 1981, pp.21-22.
8 Franco Pagliano, *Storia di 10.000 aeroplani*, p.84.

newly developed aerial torpedo, the team's major effort, the *silurotti*, or small torpedoes. Being highly maneuverable at low altitudes, the *Reggiane* Re.2001 was specifically attractive for the torpedo fighter/bomber role. During Operational Pedestal two *Reggiane.* Re.2001 had given a good account of themselves when they attacked HMS *Victorious* each carrying a special armor piercing weapon with a weight of 630 kg (1,389 lbs.) and an explosive charge of 120 kg (264.5 lbs.). The pilots had been able to skillfully maneuver the aircraft by bypassing the enemy's anti-aircraft screen in order to drop the bombs from an extremely close position. Although the British admiralty report fails to report that one bomb caused some damage to HMS *Victorious,* it highlights the aircraft adroitness and maneuverability in dangerous situations: "Of the many attacks which were delivered on the convoy and escort this day, only one, by two Re.2001 fighter bombers, was actually carried out on Victorious. These two aircraft flew in on the port side, end on at about 300 feet, swooping low over the ship and dropping two bombs, one of which bounced on the Flight Deck and went over the side, exploding under water. Unfortunately, these aircraft delivered their attack unfired at as they were mistaken for Hurricanes, a number of which were flying about in the vicinity."[9]

Those features such as the high maneuverability at low altitudes and its top speed made the *Reggiane* Re.2001 very attractive when carrying a torpedo or other external loads such as bombs. The plane was matched to the *silurotti* which were smaller sized torpedoes for aerial use which were 450mm in diameter and 2.8 meters in length. Their main characteristics included: the possibility of launches taking place at higher altitudes than 100 meters and at greater speeds.

Unfortunately for the Italians the smaller torpedo, which was designed to weigh considerably less than the standard Whitehead aerial torpedo, and was suited for a fighter aircraft, was only developed as a prototype in mid-1943. The modified *Reggiane* Re.2001G was delivered to the *aerosiluranti* base in Gorizia in February 1943 and the prototype of the *silurotto* arrived sometime after. In May and June 1943 several flight trials were conducted, but even if these were successful, the RA in the meantime had made no effort to requisition the twenty or thirty odd *Reggiane* Re.2001 still in operation from the fighter *Squadriglie.* In the summer another proposal was evaluated by both the RA and the RM which entailed using the available *Reggiane* Re.2001 in the torpedo launching role but from the refurbished aircraft carrier that the *Regia Marina* had commissioned.[10] This was another interesting project that never came to fruition given the armistice. Such a weapon when employed against convoys, would have allowed the pilot to not have to maneuver his aircraft within close range of antiaircraft fire in order to score a hit, but would have allowed him to drop the torpedo at a reasonably safe distance and immediately resort to evasive tactics. Thus, it can be argued that the delays in the introduction of the small torpedo meant that the new fighter/torpedo combination never saw active service since by September 1943 Italy signed an armistice with the Allies. It appears that after the 8 September surrender the only prototype of the *Reggiane* Re.2001G was lost or was destroyed in the hectic days following the armistice. An even more brutal fate was experienced by the two *Reggiane* Re.2001 carrying the special perforating bomb suitably designed to accommodate 120 kg of explosive. This special bomb was named 630 PD (Perforante-Dirompente). After the unsuccessful attacks against HMS *Victorious*, its inventor *Tenente* Guido Robone, of the torpedo

9 Commanding Officer, HMS Victorious letter No. 0190/3748, Appendix VIII "Attacks by Enemy Aircraft", 15 August 1942.

10 Chris Dunning, *Courage Alone: The Italian Air Force 1940–1943* (London: Hikoki Publications, 1989).

bomber units, was told by the head of the RA to desist from conducting any further experiments with this weapon, was transferred out of the Furbara Centro Sperimentale and sent back to his operational unit.[11]

Reggiane Re.2001 Specifications
Engine: One Daimler Benz 601A liquid cool inline engine.
Wingspan: 36 feet 1 inch
Wing Area: 220 sq ft
Length: 27 feet 5 inches
Height: 10 feet 2 inches
Weight: 5,265 lbs. (empty); 6,989 lbs.
Maximum Speed: 337 mph at 17,946 feet (without the torpedo).
Climb Rate: 26,247 feet in 12 minutes and 11 seconds
Ceiling: 36,089 feet.
Range: 684 miles.
Crew: 1
Armament: two 12.7mm Breda-SAFAT machine gun, , two 7.7mm Breda-SAFAT machine guns
Source: Angelucci (1988)

The other major new weapon developed in 1943, S.79 equipped with radio controlled torpedoes, advanced further than the *Reggiane* Re.2001, as a small *Squadriglia* was established in 1943 within the 41° *Gruppo* based in Pisa but was never deployed in combat. The project originated in the 1930s after Piero Crocchi, an RA engineer, had first considered such a weapon. According to Crocchi "the radio guided torpedo could be controlled from onboard a plane that flew at a relative low altitude that while observing the track of the torpedo could alter its course to ensure a strike on a warship and even if the latter took evasive maneuvers."[12] Despite the fact that it had been identified since the early 1930s, primarily due to the disinterest of the upper echelon of the RA, it made very little progress until 1940 when Italy entered the conflict. In 1941 tests were conducted using a S.79 torpedo bomber and a Piaggio P 108 with the torpedo launched with a parachute and a final report was issued recommending its use. The A/170 torpedo (170 kg or 375 lbs. warhead) could be launched at a distance of 5,000 meters (3.1 miles) from an enemy ship from an altitude of 100 meters (328 feet). The torpedo could travel about 6 km (3.7 miles) at the speed of 36 knots emitting a green, fluorescent trail which could be seen from above, while if launched with a parachute the warhead could be released from an altitude of 500 meters (1,640 feet) above an enemy ship. When operating at night the torpedo was equipped with a light that could be seen from far away by the pilots. Both options offered one big advantage over non-radio controlled torpedoes given that they could be launched at distances that were greater than the standard Whitehead aerial torpedo thus enabling the pilots to avoid the direct fire of the battleships.

11 Franco Pagliano, *Storia di 10.000 aeroplani*, p.84.
12 Daniele Lembo, *Prototipi e progetti della Regia Aeronautica* (Milan: IBN Editore, 2010), p.81.

In early 1942 a demonstration of the new weapon was held at Pola by the *aerosilurante* school personnel that was highly successful as all three torpedoes launched struck their target even when the ship took evasive maneuvers. This successful trial prompted the leader of the RA to place three S.79 aircraft into service on 13 November 1942 and they were put at the disposal of the 41° *Gruppo*. A month later the three aircraft were taken out of service and returned to Gorizia airport due to a malfunctioning of the release system. They were then returned to the combat unit but were never deployed in a combat operation. In July 1943 the *Luftwaffe* would place an order for ten aircraft endowed with the radio controlled torpedo proving once again that its planners and engineers had more foresight than their Italian counterparts. According to military aviation historian Franco Pagliano the radio controlled torpedoes "could have been a game changer in the naval war in the Mediterranean but they were introduced after long experiments and too late in the conflict to have an impact."[13]

In 1943 there were also three radio controlled and unmanned S.79 armed with two 1,000 kg torpedoes each that formed a small Kamikaze *Squadriglia* along with a *Macchi* C.202 which was flown by the pilot radio commanding the unmanned aircraft and that also functioned as the fighter escort. These were the same weapon used during Operation Pedestal. On that occasion the radio controls had malfunctioned and the plane had veered out of control and crashed on a mountain in Algeria. But according to those who witnessed the crash, the explosion had been tremendous pointing to the lethality of such a weapon. This weapon was the brainchild of *Generale* Ferdinando Raffaelli who after the failed attempt during Pedestal had doubled down to further improve the radio controls. With a limited budget, Radaelli was responsible for creating this new unit called *Aerei Radio Pilotati* (Radio Controlled Aircraft) comprised of three S.79 and one *Macchi* C.202 which was planned to be deployed against Allied battleships during Operation Husky near Augusta but at the last minute the attack was called back by *Comando Supremo*.

In 1943 the *Luftwaffe* would place an order for 10 of these new weapons as well as order 2,000 *Motobombe* FFF (the circular torpedoes), which were used very effectively by the German during 1943 and 1944 in several engagements. For example, on 22 March 1943 *Luftwaffe* units attacked the port of Tripoli targeting a number of moored battleships and transports. The attack weapons were a combination of standard bombs along with seventy-two circular torpedoes which damaged the destroyer HMS *Derwent* along with two merchant ships. The decisions to purchase these weapons were made by *Luftwaffe* engineers who obviously saw value in them. The same cannot be said by the top commanders and planners of the RA which were never fully behind these new weapons.[14] Various other factors have been listed as to the cause of the various delays in introducing these new weapons such as a rigid bureaucratic structure that was not friendly toward innovation and the lack of funds for these new initiatives. Hence their slow development and introduction. This rigid position toward new weapons probably had to do with limited budgets but also with the air service failure to technologically innovate during the conflict.

13 Franco Pagliano, *Storia di 10.000 aeroplani*, p.84.
14 Daniele Lembo, "Le armi segrete della Regia", *Aerei Nella Storia*, N. 15, 2015.

Torpedo Bomber Unit Organization

By early 1943 *RA* had lost 495 aircraft during combat operations and 864 due to Allied bombings of airfields and many hundreds more due to a multiplicity of reasons. The hard fighting conducted by the torpedo bomber units in the Mediterranean forced a reorganization of the discipline mainly due to the high level of losses of aircraft and pilots which could not be readily replaced. As a result, some units with few planes and pilots were disbanded and their personnel was consolidated into the remaining units. In January 1943 a report by RA listed the following torpedo bomber units:

2ª *Squadra Aerea*, *Generale* Porro.
 -41° *Gruppo Autonomo Aerosiluranti* based in Pisa.
3ª *Squadra Aerea*, *Generale* Mazzucco.
 - 36° *Stormo Aerosiluranti* led by *Colonnello* Milianti comprised of 108° (*Maggiore* Bianchi) and -109° *Gruppo* (*Maggiore* Zanardi) and,
 -131° *Gruppo Autonomo Aerosiluranti* (*Maggiore* Pernazza).
4ª *Squadra Aerea*, *Generale* Ranza
 -32° *Stormo Aerosiluranti* (*Tenente Colonnello* Mariani based on only the 38° *Gruppo* (*Tenente Colonnello* Bressan).
Aeronautica della Sardegna, *Generale* Urbani
 - 105° *Gruppo Autonomo Aerosiluranti* (*Tenente Colonnello* Cadrigher).
 - 130° *Gruppo Autonomo Aerosiluranti* (*Capitano* Melley).
 -89° *Gruppo Bombardamento/ 32° Stormo Aerosiluranti* (*Tenente Colonnello* Fadda).
Aeronautica della Sicilia, *Generale* Monti
 -132° *Gruppo Autonomo Aerosiluranti* (*Maggiore* Casini).
Aeronautica dell'Egeo, *Generale* Longo
 104° *Gruppo Autonomo Aerosiluranti (Tenente Colonnello* Asinari Di Bernazzo).

A few more *Squadriglie* were transferred to Sardinia in January 1943 because the priority became to counter the numerous enemy convoys in the western Mediterranean headed to Algiers. The 132° *Gruppo* was therefore brought back to Decimomannu airfield on 10 January, while the 89° *Gruppo* was also transferred there although at the time it was still in the process of being transformed into a torpedo bomber unit and its S.84 aircraft were being phased out in favor of the S.79. Meanwhile, 130° *Gruppo* was transferred out of Sardinia in January 1943 and into Forli's airport to undergo an overhaul due to the high losses experienced in late 1942. Meanwhile 36° *Stormo* was headquartered in Pisa were many of its newly formed crews were being trained to the torpedo bomber discipline. Finally, 104° *Gruppo* was transferred temporarily from Gadurra to Kalamaki in Greece where its pilots underwent night fighting training provided by *Capitani* Paolo Lombardi and Aurelio di Bella respectively of 1° and 3° *Nucleo Addestramento Aeosiluranti*.

By the time of Operation Husky the discipline was reorganized once again into the *Raggruppamento Aerosiluranti* (torpedo bomber grouping) with air bases in Siena and Pisa with a force of approximately only seventy S.79s in working order. This unit was formed on 2 June 1943 with the 89°, 41°, 131° and 108° *Gruppi*. Its purpose was to consolidate the torpedo bomber units into one major organization and allow the new *Raggruppamento* to quickly shift a mass of aircraft from one key aerial-naval battle to another. Other units remained autonomous such as the 104° *Gruppo* based in the Aegean with eleven aircraft, 132° *Gruppo* based in Gorizia with five aircraft, 130° *Gruppo* based in Littoria (modern day Latina) with nine aircraft, 1° *Nucleo Addestramento Aerosiluranti* based in Gorizia with twelve aircraft and the 3° *Nucleo Addestramento Aerosiluranti* at Salon, France with ten aircraft. Subsequently, 130° *Gruppo* had to be disbanded due to its losses of crews and pilots and its remaining pilots were merged into the 132° *Gruppo*. This remained the most experienced and probably the largest *Gruppo* of the RA and had the lion share of the torpedo hits in 1943. There were also two other units: 109° *Gruppo* based in Pisa and the *2° Nucleo Addestramento Aerosiluranti* based in Naples but they had no aircraft and remained mostly non-operational. A detailed report by *Superaereo* dated 9 June 1943 revealed that there were a total of 280 torpedo bombers (either S.79 or S.79bis), of which 180 were at bases near the front, while 100 were kept in reserve. However, approximately 150 of these planes had not been fully converted to the torpedo bomber discipline as they still lacked the launching mechanism for the torpedo. The plan was to complete retrofitting these planes by the end of November 1943. Therefore the report concluded that there were only approximately 110 torpedo bombers that were in essence combat ready, of which 30 had been loaned out to the pilot schools and were used exclusively for training. [15]

By 1943 attacks by torpedo bombers were usually made at dawn, dusk or at night by the more experienced pilots. Dusk was considered preferable since the aircraft could make a low, unobserved approach toward the target. Also, the pilots could see the targets and avoid collisions. The attacks were primarily made from the east since this was the direction of poorest visibility. Daylight attacks were no longer viable due to the speed, the heavier armament and the number of the enemy fighters which could more easily intercept the *Sparvieri*. Also the latter's speed made the S.79 attacks quasi suicidal especially when made against the Royal Navy's much improved anti-aircraft fire especially in relation to the beginning of the war. The lack of a new, faster torpedo bomber was a painful experience for the crews given the many losses in 1943 due to them flying on an obsolete plane and it also largely impeded daylight operations as the S.79 could be easily intercepted and outmaneuvered by state of the art fighters such as the Spitfire. As a result, by 1943 daylight *Sparvieri* operations were deemed quasi suicidal and were very seldom attempted. *Capitano* Graziani of 132° *Gruppo* would write regarding the last phase of the war for the *aerosiluranti* that: "Our last operations had gone well but it was mostly down to luck. In most cases operations had become almost impossible to carry out. Usually at a distance of 50 kilometers from the coast of North Africa our crews were intercepted by storms of Allied fighters which were constantly flying reconnaissance and escort operations day and night. They were guided by radar installed on the coast and reinforced by radar on ships."[16] As a result losses were extremely high for the Italians and the successes were being paid at a heavy price, much heavier than before. The units were therefore trained to fight at night, which for most pilots of the S.79 torpedo bombers was a complete novelty, even though the enemy had excelled at using torpedo bombers in night operations since the early strikes against the Italian fleet in 1940.

By 1943 the *Sparvieri* crews suffered several organizational problems due to the sagging war effort that limited their effectiveness:

15 Ufficio Storico Aeronautica Militare: "La situazione al 9 luglio 1943", 4° Reparto di Superaereo n. 7025077, 9 July 1943.

16 Martino Aichner, *Il gruppo Buscaglia*, p.134.

1. Crews were getting thinner given the huge casualties in the ranks. At the beginning of 1943, for example, the famed 132° *Gruppo* could count upon only seven crews as opposed to twelve in 1942.[17] Many new recruits were inexperienced and lacked extensive training. "Fuel shortages was becoming a major issue. It impacted primarily the young officers that were dispatched to the torpedo bomber units to replace pilots lost in combat. The former were particularly lacking in operating at night that given the strong challenges by enemy fighters had become a necessity."[18]
2. Many older, more experienced crews were exhausted morally and psychologically due to being deployed almost nonstop. According to a report issued by Ettore Muti pilots were kept active at least five months prior to receiving any day off or a rotation into non-combat duties. Most were combat weary.
3. Many pilots and crew members had low morale and confessed their fears in being deployed in quasi suicidal attacks with S.79 aircraft that now more than ever were vulnerable to Allied fighters.
4. The logistics situation was getting worse day by day and the crews had to scrounge for torpedoes by collecting the few available from other airbases.
5. Fighters for escort were fewer and fewer. "One time", according to *Capitano* Graziani, "we had to abort a mission because once we reached Tunis airbase to join up with our escort, we were told by the commander *Tenente Colonnello* Remondino that he could not spare any fighters and that we had to turn back to Castelvetrano."[19]
6. The crews were worn out due to lack of rest. Often there was no respite from combat actions. Often times the lack of qualified personnel meant that the crews had to attach the warhead to the bombers themselves or they had to refuel the aircraft due to the lack of support personnel. Graziani himself wrote that "often I had to help my crew to push the cart carrying the torpedo so that it could be affixed to the aircraft."[20]
7. Another major issue that plagued torpedo bomber efficiency especially in the last year of the war was the decreasing number of aircraft available for daily service. "In Sardinia", writes historian Mattesini, there were approximately sixty S.79 aircraft belonging to the 105°, and 130° *Gruppi* and 36° *Stormo* while some also belonged to the three training units. But the number of aircraft that could be counted upon on a daily basis for both training or operations was much more modest. On some days only five aircraft were available."[21]

1943 was also the year in which German torpedo bombers began to have an important role in the Mediterranean theatre. The German torpedo bomber tactics were somewhat different from those of the Italians reflecting the greater number of resources available to the *Luftwaffe*: "For a typical attack on a convoy, KG 26 would employ between twenty to forty bombers. They would approach the target in loose Vics of between six and ten aircraft, with two miles between Vics, flying at the He.111's most economical flying cruising speed of 165 mph and at an altitude of 150 feet.....The Blohm and Voss 138 flying boat was often used as a shadower; it would orbit the

17 Francesco Mattesini, *Luci ed ombre*, p.290
18 Ibid.
19 Ibid., p.142.
20 Ibid.
21 Francesco Mattesini, *Luci ed ombre*, p.270.

convoys just out of reach of their defending guns and, when the attacking force was near, radiate signals on which the formation leader would home."[22] The most favorable launch conditions for the F5B torpedo were from a He.111 flying at 170 mph and a height of 150 feet. The best range to release the torpedo was approximately 1,000 yards from the target. The torpedo had a water speed of 33 knots and carried a 440 lbs. warhead. Needless to say one of the keys to German torpedo bomber efficiency was that the He.111 had a decent top speed of 252 mph (405 km/h) with a reliable power plant enabling the pilots to get in quicker and then make their escape.[23]

10: PLANS TO SUBDUE MALTA

Throughout the Mediterranean campaign Kesselring consistently advised the German High Command that the final solution of the supply problem to Libya required the capture of Malta. Cavallero and *Commando Supremo* began to study the possibilities of an invasion of Malta soon after the arrival of the German air forces in 1941. In January 1942 the Italian General Staff actually began training its forces for a combined sea end air invasion of the island, Cavallero believed that Italian troops alone could capture it, with the support of the *Luftwaffe*. But C*omando Supremo* did not plan for an immediate assault because of a lack of certain special troops and equipment. Special landing craft had to be made available to cope with the island's rocky coast, and airborne units (mainly the *Folgore* Division) necessitated special training. Cavallero expected that the assault force would be ready by about the first of half of June 1942. Meanwhile, the *Luftwaffe* and *Regia Aeronautica* must complete its neutralization of Malta's defenses. In the spring of 1942 Operation Venezia was brokered between the Italians and the Germans which entailed the seizure of Tobruk and then the launch of the seaborne and airborne invasion of Malta. But Rommel's huge victory at Gazala and Tobruk altered such a plan. In the summer of 1942 the plan to invade Malta was put on hold by the German High Command in order to allow Rommel's army to make a further advance in North Africa and beyond the El Alamein line. This decision was heavily opposed by Cavallero and Kesselring who argued that Rommel's seizure of Tobruk "had such a rapid and smashing effect that General Rommel requested and received, against my objection, permission for the continuation of the North African campaign."[24] General Cavallero in vain argued that the Axis should undertake Operation Herkules before the *Afrika Korps* launched any major desert offensive.

Undaunted by the changed circumstances, Kesserling and the Italian *Comando Supremo* aimed at gaining permission to raid the island the next year but their plan was again put on hold by the German High Command to accommodate the African and most importantly the Russian campaign. Together with General Bruno Loerzer of II *Fliegerkorps*, Kesselring devised a three pronged plan to soften Malta prior to the seaborne and airborne invasion.

22 Alfred Price, *Luftwaffe Handbook*, p.47.
23 Ron Mackay, *Heinkel He 111* (Wiltshire, UK: Crowood Press, 2003).
24 Albert Kesselring, *A Soldier's Record* (New York: William Morrow and Company, 1954), p.116.

This called for a first aerial attack to neutralize the enemy's anti-aircraft guns. It was to be followed by a concentrated aerial offensive against Malta's airport to cripple RAF fighters. Third, a massive bombing attack was envisioned against Malta's naval and artillery installations. Kesselring's plan did not give the Italian *Regia Aeronautica* a central role, perhaps due to the fact that the Italians lacked the numbers and types of aircraft to support a sustained bombing offensive. He argued that the S.79 standard bomber was too slow during daylight operations and that its crews were not fully trained for nighttime operations, while the S.84 was a failure. Thus, the Italians were given two more narrow, support type, specific tasks, which were to contribute to *Luftwaffe* bombings of infrastructure and artillery weapons and to torpedo bomb the harbor. Cant.Z.1007 bis and BR 20 bombers were to undertake nighttime bombing attacks alongside the *Luftwaffe* bombers, while S.79 torpedo bombers were to conduct repeated assaults against harbor installations. German bombers were to take the lead in attacking enemy bases. A larger role was to be played by Italian fighter planes whose task was to engage enemy fighters in protracted duels and clear the skies thus paving the way for the bombing forays. Kesserling ultimately delayed the Malta plan because he lacked aircraft: "In view of necessary replacements and weather conditions, a new operation in Malta was out of the question before spring 1943. By that time, the forces meant for Malta were in part used up and in part tied down by this offensive."[25]

Combat Actions 1943

The first *Sparvieri* operation of 1943 was conducted on 3 January when at 1345 three S.79s from 105° *Gruppo* took flight from Sardinia to conduct a patrol action along the coast of Algeria. Their objective was to seek out enemy shipping. Two planes returned home without firing their warheads, while *Tenente* Alessandro Senni's S.79 attacked a destroyer but the warhead passed under the enemy ship. During the disengagement the S.79 was challenged by a Beaufighter which was repulsed by strong machine gun fire to the point that it was forced to crash land.

An air patrol over the coast of Algeria led three S.79s from 130° *Gruppo* to attack a sixteen ship strong enemy formation on 19 January. At 1530 the *Sparvieri* pressed forward with the attack but they were met with strong anti-aircraft fire and also with the interference of three Beaufighters which attempted to separate one of the S.79 from the other two by surrounding it and firing at it. As a result of this strong concentrated fire, one *Sparviero* was forced to turn back when machine gun fire damaged the gear of the plane. *Capitano* Giuseppe Cimicchi and *Sottotenente* Mario Galletti continued with the operation and at 1835 they launched the torpedoes. Both barely missed their targets. During the disengagement the S.79 of Mario Galletti was shot down by enemy fighters. "After this loss, in Sardinia there were only twenty S.79s that were deemed combat ready."[26] The next day at 1050 three S.79s of 105° *Gruppo* took flight from Decimomannu to conduct a reconnaissance mission along the Algerian coast. After forty minutes of flight one S.79 had to abort the mission because the pilot could not

25 Ibid.
26 Francesco Mattessini, *Luci ed ombre*, p.292.

continue. The other two pilots (*Capitano* Giulio Ricciarini and *Tenente* Alessandro Serri) pressed on and flew down toward the bay of Algiers were they were greeted by very strong enemy fire. At 1905 they made a determined descent and launched the torpedoes against two transport ships of 10,000 tons moored at the harbor. According to the pilots both ships were damaged, although they could only briefly observe during the flyover the results of their action as the enemy fire and the glare of the lights prevented further observations or the taking of photographs.

Between 19-21 January the Axis crews were busy attacking the KMS 6 convoy comprised of forty-nine merchantmen and the escort which had left Clyde on 26 December and was headed toward Algiers transporting stocks of ammunition. The first attack was made by German torpedo bombers on the night of the 19th but no hits were made. The next day seven He.111 and fourteen Ju.88 bombers targeted the convoy again, this time damaging the 7,176 tons Walt Whitman transport ship. Further attacks were made by the Germans in the afternoon which yielded the sinking of the Hampton Lodge British ship (3,645 tons) against the loss of three German torpedo bombers. At dawn (0230) ten S.79s (three from 105° *Gruppo*, three from 132° *Gruppo* and four of 130 ° *Gruppo*) took off from their airbase in Sardinia to attack an even larger convoy (sixty-three ships), codenamed KMS 7 that had left Clyde and was also headed to Algiers. The convoy was targeted at 0520 near Cape Tenes. The pilots reported that they released warheads from very favorable distances against three transport ships "which were most likely damaged."[27] But the Royal Navy reports indicate that only the Ocean Rider ship (7,178 tons) was damaged by German He.111 torpedo bombers. Meanwhile the Italians threw at the convoy two successive waves of standard bombers on the afternoon of the 21st but none achieved any results.

On 22 January six S.79s from the 105° and 132° *Gruppi* together with seven Cant.1007 bis of 50° and 88° *Gruppo* made a very dangerous foray against enemy ships moored at Bone harbor. Defensive installations included several medium caliber guns which began firing even before the planes were spotted flying low over the harbor. The standard bombers attacked first releasing seventy-four 100 kg bombs between 1925 and 2020 but achieved only limited results. The torpedo attacks took place between 2055 and 2117 when four warheads were released in rapid succession from favorable positions. The post battle report states: "During the attack a merchant ship was hit. Extremely violent and precise response from the anti-aircraft fire. Reiterated attacks by enemy fighters throughout the night."[28]

During the disengagement from the harbor one S.79 flown by *Maggiore* Gabriele Casini of 132° *Gruppo* with *Tenente* Martino Aichner as co-pilot was severely damaged and had its fuel tanks rattled by enemy fire. The pilot of the stricken aircraft was forced to retreat flying very low close to the water in case the plane ran out of fuel. An hour later it was struck again from guns from an enemy ship and the pilot was forced to ditch the plane at sea near Cape Spartivento. The crew survived, although all members had been wounded, on a raft for several hours until they were rescued by an Italian ship. The following are the recollections of the co-pilot which recount the dramatic events leading to the second strike against the S.79:

27 Ibid. p.295.
28 Martino Aichner, *Il Gruppo Buscaglia*, p.146.

> We are able to get away from the harbor by flying very low almost on the water. No longer under enemy fire we regain altitude and the aircraft, despite having received several hits, responds well to the pilot's commands. We are flying for about an hour when all of a sudden on our way back to base and flying at an altitude of 600-500 meters we are met by a fountain-like barrage. We realize that we are flying over a well escorted enemy convoy that due to the darkness of the night we had not spotted. The aircraft flying so low in altitude is hit several times by enemy fire. The barrage follows us for several kilometers and when we are almost certain that the worst of the enemy reaction is behind us the three engines suddenly stop working. There is no time to think. The pilot sends out the SOS, while I prepare the plane for an emergency landing. This time, however, I can't see anything because its pitch dark. Having no reference point, I keep an eye on the speedometer. The plane makes impact on the water while still traveling at a speed of 200 kilometers per hour and the impact is so fierce that I violently hit my head against the cockpit instrument panel. I am bleeding profusely and can't see anything from my right eye and my right hand is crushed by the impact. Even commander Casini has crashed his head against the damned aiming device that no one uses to release the warhead but has been responsible for injuring so many pilots during emergency landings. The S.79 begins to sink, but then after a few seconds reemerges. In the darkness and with the roughness of the sea the waves crash violently against the wings and the frame of the plane……After a few seconds the Maggiore and the crew members exit the plane. We are all wounded and the sea salt burns us increasing the pain but it also keeps us wide awake. A crew member is able to get the dinghy into the water and we all get in it."[29]

Another offensive action was conducted on 27 January when five S.79s belonging to 105° and 130° *Gruppi* flew off the coast of Algiers. They were met again by very heavy fire from the harbor defenses of Algiers, but one plane (*Tenente* Gian Battista Murra) managed to penetrate beyond the curtain of fire and torpedo a large steamer. During the return flight they were intercepted by enemy fighters which managed to down one aircraft from 105° *Gruppo* flown by *Tenente* Alessandro Senni. The crew perished.

On 29 January *Comando dell'Aeronautica della Sardegna* and II *Fliegerkorps* hammered out a plan to attack a large convoy TF 14 near the coast of Algeria that was comprised of twenty-three large transport ships that had been spotted by an Axis reconnaissance plane at 1230. The plan was for a mass torpedo attack to be undertaken in waves deploying twelve German and eight Italian torpedo bombers.

At 1630 the large torpedo squad comprised of eight S.79 from 105°, 130°, and 132° *Gruppi* took off from Elmas and queued up behind the *Luftwaffe* formation of He.111 and Ju.88 of the I and III/KG.26. As they met up with the convoy just as it was pulling out of Algiers and heading into Bone harbor, one *Sparviero* was immediately hit by heavy fire coming from a squadron of Hurricanes (No. 32 Squadron) and was forced to disengage and return to base with its torpedo. The others continued the mission and upon spotting the convoy dove down to attack against the concentrated fire of the enemy ships. One bomber swept even further down and made a steep right turn through a flurry of tracer fire. Undeterred, the pilot flew at an altitude of 80 meters

29 Ibid, p.147.

above the water and came at the British formation from the starboard. The pilot then dropped his torpedo 800 meters out from the target at 1837 which struck at the stern of the auxiliary ship HMS *Pozarica* of 1,893 tons. This was an anti-aircraft ship equipped with eight 4 inch guns and eight 2pdr guns. It was taken to Bogue harbor for repairs but a few weeks later it capsized. The pilot then pulled up to avoid the machine gun fire and got away over heavy gun fire from the destroyers.

The pilots reported having struck three transport ships and one destroyer at a distance of 800, 900 meters out. The destroyer was identified as a Jervis class destroyer. Subsequently, the Germans attacked after flying over the convoy several times to confuse the enemy gunners. As they were pressing forward their attack one He.111 was struck down by a Hurricane, while the other eleven remaining aircraft completed the operation which led to a strike against HMS *Avon Vale,* an escort destroyer of the Hunt Type II class. It sustained major damage in the air attack as the whole of the bow structure was destroyed. It had to be towed to Gibraltar by the escort destroyer HMS *Bicester.* It is not clear whether the vessel received one or two hits, since the Royal Navy war diary reports that she was hit by an Italian torpedo bomber.

After the torpedo attack the TF 14 convoy was pursued by Italian submarines. At 0017 on 31 January the submarine *Platino* launched four torpedoes in rapid succession and one of them fired at a distance of 1,000 meters out struck and damaged HMS Samphire, a corvette, The ship sank within minutes and the forty-five men crew perished including its commander Captain Fredrick Thomas Renny. At 0554 there was a further submarine attack. This time by the *Mocenigo* which torpedoed a transport ship. Finally on 1 February *Comando Aeronautica della Sardegna* ordered another torpedo bomber foray to further damage the convoy. This time by five S.79s from 105° *Gruppo* and five German torpedo bombers. The mission, however, had to be cancelled when the convoy was sighted entering the port of Algiers.

Nevertheless, the joint combat action was noteworthy. The RA after-action report stated: "The joint German Italian torpedo bomber action was successful. According to the Italian pilots involved it could have been even more successful if the torpedo bombers had set upon the convoy five minutes earlier in order to fully exploit the conditions of good visibility."[30] It appears from the report that the German bombers had more accurate on board instruments for night attacks, while the Italian pilots preferred attacking at dusk when good visibility of the convoy was still possible since they had poorer instrumentation.

On 6 February three S.79s from 253ª *Squadriglia*/104° *Gruppo Aerosiluranti*, piloted by *Capitano* Enrico Marescalchi, and wingmen *Tenente* Mario Dattrino and S*ottotenente* Giovanni Del Ponte launched their torpedoes against a 75 tons sailing vessel (Al Ameriaah) which sunk almost immediately. The next day a preemptive action by US Air Force B-17 aircraft bombed the airport at Elmas in Sardinia between 1500 and 1550 which resulted in the destruction of three S.79s and six German torpedo bombers and severe damage to four He.100. On the 8th it was the RAF bombers (eight Wellington) turn to attack the airfield which led to further destruction of one German torpedo bomber and damage to several others. Both bombing operations were a response to the joint successful German-Italian torpedo bomber forays during the month of January 1943. The aim of the preemptive strikes was to destroy as many torpedo bombers as possible thus preventing future operations.

30 Francesco Mattesini, *Luci ed ombre*, p.312.

On 9 February another *Sparviero* attack by four S.79s from 105° *Gruppo* and three from 3° and 1° *Nucleo Addestramento Aerosiluranti* was carried out against enemy vessels near Algiers. The S.79s took off from Elmas at 1620. *Maggiore* Erasi claimed a steamer, while *Colonnello* Carlo Unia dove down at 1900 into the concentrated anti-aircraft fire and dangerously approached a freighter disregarding the blistering enemy fire. At 1,000 meters he launched the torpedo which most likely, the pilot and crew could not linger to observe the results of their action due to the anti-aircraft fire, hit the freighter.

A failed attack was carried out on 18 February when nine S.79s from 1° *Nucleo Addestramento Aerosiluranti* and five from the 132° *Gruppo* took off from Decimomannu airbase at 0155. Unfortunately due to the bad weather conditions only five S.79s reached the objective at 0402. Thirteen minutes later the remaining aircraft pressed the attack but all pilots misfired as none of the torpedoes found a mark. On 28 February one of the most experienced pilots of 132° *Gruppo* lost his life when he flew a S.79 that had just gone through extensive repairs. The plane, flying in very poor weather conditions, took down with it *Sottotenente* Carlo Pfister and his crew. The former was awarded posthumously a gold medal. Born in New York City on 5 June 1916, when Italy entered the war in 1940 Pfister came back to Italy to join the RA as a volunteer. Initially he was assigned to a standard bomber unit and then subsequently was transferred into the torpedo units.

89° *Gruppo*/36° *Stormo* fielded six S.79s which took off at 0415 on 1 March. Their objective was to attack a British convoy sited between Cape der Fer and Bougie. The attack, however, was halted prematurely by several enemy fighters which intercepted two of the six S.79s which were forced back. Meanwhile the four remaining aircraft released their warheads from favorable positions at 0600 but were unable to score any hits. One of the pilots streaked across Bougie Bay losing altitude all the time. After having made out the shape of a large transport ship, he turned to starboard bringing her into the line of sight of the torpedo. It dropped near the ship but it grounded short and exploded harmlessly. Nine days later six S.79s from 105° *Gruppo* attacked an enemy convoy at 0600 but despite the pilots optimism expressed in the post battle report, they were not able to score any hits. They dove down to about 60 meters above the water under an intense barrage. The leader of the squad in close collaboration with the other pilots went for the largest transport ship but the torpedo passed under it.

On 27 March, during a major operation, twelve S. 79s from 89° and 105° *Gruppi* (three of which were S.79bis) and ten German bombers He. 111 of the III./KG.26 and two Ju.88 from the same unit were able to hit and sink the 9,545 tons freighter Empire Rowan and several other small craft ships in the Gulf of Philippeville. Between 1010 and 1020 the planes took off from Decimomannu aiming to attack British convoy Untrue which had been spotted at 0625 and was comprised of twenty transport ships and several escort freighters. The convoy was also heavily escorted by the RAF with Hurricanes of the No. 87 Squadron and Spitfires from No. 43 and No. 242 Squadrons. Due to very poor weather conditions and the poor visibility, the *aerosiluranti* and the German torpedo bombers had to split up in small groups. The first casualties of this operation were two German He. 111 which were downed near Cape Takauch. Soon after No. 242 Squadron intercepted and fired at a lone Ju. 88 which disengaged but later crash landed in Sicily killing the crew. Meanwhile two Spitfires piloted by No. 43 Squadron Lieutenants Torrance and Turkington attempted to intercept the remaining He. 111, but they were not able to inflict any damage nor halt their attack. These remaining German aircraft pressed forward at 1150 targeting six transport ships. The pilots post battle report stated that four out of the six targeted ships were set on fire. They also stated that two torpedo bombers were prevented from launching their attacks given the strong anti-aircraft fire. Intense fire was observed from battleships and cruisers. The German attack preceded the ones put forth by the Italians has their pilots arrived on the scene ahead of the S.79s. The same RAF unit which had interfered with the German attack was able to intercept and then chase away three S. 79s of the 105° *Gruppo*, led by *Capitano* Giulio Ricciarini who had managed to reach the African coast near Capo de Fer. Due to the heavy fire, the S.79s were forced to make a hasty retreat without the chance of launching their warheads.

A second group of S.79s (those flying the faster S.79bis) then made its way against the convoy. At 1220 two S.79s of 105° *Gruppo*, flown by *Capitano* Urbano Mancini and *Tenenti* Ernesto Borrelli dove down, almost razed the water and rapidly hit and broke the back of the 9,545 tons motorship Empire Rowan. The torpedo struck the ship on the starboard side. The latter transporting coal and military ammunition of all kinds exploded killing three men of the crew. The motorship was beached northwest of Bone and declared a total loss. As the S.79s disengaged they were challenged by Spitfires of No. 43 Squadron 25 miles north of Cape de Fer and downed. *Capitano* Mancini, who seconds before being downed had communicated "mission accomplished we are returning to base",[31] would later be awarded posthumously a gold medal. Soon after more S. 79s from 89° *Gruppo* led by *Tenenti* Mura Gian Battista and Irnerio Bertuzzi spotted the convoy. The crews observed a large freighter on fire that was slowly sinking and a capsized S. 79 and three of its crew members on a dingy. The six *Sparvieri* flying in three groups pressed forward their attack at 1550 against three large transport ships. According to their records two of them were struck by torpedoes. In turn, two 89° *Gruppo* S.79s were downed. One was shot down by two No. 43 Squadron Spitfires flown by Lieutenants Torrance and Turkington, while the other by anti-aircraft fire. During the late afternoon of 27 March seven S. 79s from 105° *Gruppo* and a Cant Z. 506 from 613ª *Squadriglia Soccorso* were dispatched to locate any survivors. Despite the heavy rains they were able to spot a raft at sea with the survivors but given the poor visibility they later lost contact and returned to base without having saved them. The fierce action over the skies of North Africa was praised by the commander of *Aeronautica della Sardegna, Generale* Aldo Urbani: "I want to recognize the great action of the torpedo units of Sardinia which, despite huge losses strove without respite and with audacity to inflict high losses upon the enemy." [32] Despite the success against the Empire Rowan and other small craft ships, the operation had been very costly demonstrating once again that experienced pilots could obtain results but at the expense of heavy losses. The Italian torpedo bomber, even in its improved S.79bis form was not fast enough to avoid deadly confrontations with state of the art enemy fighters or experienced and well drilled anti-aircraft defenses.

As historian Marco Mattioli asserts: "These heavy losses marred the last large scale daylight attack flown by the Italian torpedo bombers, which had already begun to operate under the cover of darkness."[33] This was the last large daylight wave after wave attack conducted by the torpedo bomber crews.

31 Francesco Mattesini, *Luci ed ombre*, p.311.

32 Ufficio Storico Aeronautica Militare: Comandante dell'Aeronautica della Sardegna, Generale Aldo Urbani, "Relazione n. 1775/O a Superaereo", 4 March 1943.

33 Marco Mattioli, *Savoia Marchetti S.79 Sparviero*, p.69.

11: GERMAN TORPEDO BOMBER SCHOOL GROSSETO, ITALY

Kampfschulgeswader 2 was established in mid-1941 by Colonel Karl Stockmann to train German pilots and crews in the torpedo bomber discipline. In January 1942 the school was transferred from Germany to Grosseto, Italy. The pilots received a training program that lasted approximately four weeks. It was based on the practice launch of the Whitehead torpedoes against an Italian ship (Magnaghi) moored near the harbor. The instructors were Italians and the training program followed the standard one received by Italian torpedo bomber pilots. The planes utilized were He. 111 and Ju.88 both converted from standard bombers to torpedo bombers. In some cases German pilots flew the Sparvieri as well. In 1942 Colonel Martin Harlinghausen was nominated as the new commander of the school. The school remained active until mid-1943. It was later in the year transferred to Riga after the Italian surrender. It is one of those rare examples where the Italians instructed the Germans on an effective combat tactic.

As a reprisal against the Axis torpedo bomber attack on the Untrue convoy, the Allies launched a major bombing operation against Decimomannu and Villacidro airfields on 31 March. The two pronged attack was first made by sixteen Wellington bombers from the 330th Wing which pounced upon Villacidro. They were followed by a massive attack against Decimomannu by ninety B.17 US Air Force bombers (12th Air Force Unit) that damaged three S.79s and several Cant.Z.1007bis. One He.111 was also destroyed, while several more were damaged. To make matters worse for the Italians on 5 April four S.79s from 41° *Gruppo* took off from Elmas in Sardinia at 1800 to conduct a night raid upon an enemy convoy but never returned back to base. *Capitano* Ernesto Brambilla, his crew and the other three crews were never found. Nor were the remains of their planes ever found. Their objective was a convoy spotted at 1600 near Bougie Bay but they did not score any hits and therefore the most likely hypothesis is that they were shot down by an enemy squadron while on their mission to torpedo bomb enemy ships steaming along the coast of Algeria. These losses crippled the Sardinian airbases which were left with only sixteen working S.79s. 41º *Gruppo*, for instance, was the hardest hit being almost totally obliterated with only two remaining S.79s. Due to the heavy losses in Sardinia, the initiative passed to the Sicilian based torpedo bombers. On 10 April three S.79s from 279ª *Squadriglia* led by *Capitano* Vito Di Mola departed Castelvetrano at 2100 to attack a convoy spotted near Bone Bay. The convoy was put under pressure by the first torpedo bomber which pressed forward the attack but as the pilot was just about ready to release the torpedo his plane was struck by enemy guns that forced him to turn back. A second S.79 piloted by *Tenente* Romeo Mutti was also hit prior to releasing the torpedo and was later forced to make an emergency landing near Mazzara del Vallo. The crew was subsequently rescued. Finally, the third plane flown by *Capitano* Di Mola was shot down by enemy fire. As a result, the already severely tested 279ª *Squadriglia* was left with only few working aircraft. Only on 23 April it was able to field two S.79s for a nighttime sweep near Tripoli which did not yield any results. On the same day Sardinia based 89º *Gruppo* committed two small aircraft squads to conduct a search for enemy shipping near Bougie. Both operations failed to identify any targets and returned empty handed to base. Four days later three S.79s from the same unit attacked near Philippeville a small merchantmen that the crews affirmed to have struck with one torpedo. During the disengagement one of the S.79s flown by *Sottotenente* Ernesto Catalano was shot down by anti-aircraft fire. The decimation of the Italian crews paved the way for a larger role by the German torpedo bombers that on 1 May torpedoed and bombed two British vessels, the Erinpura merchantman and the Trust oil tanker. In May after the total collapse of Axis forces in North Africa, the *Sparvieri* crews were tasked to interrupt major convoys in the Mediterranean as the Italians feared the potential Allied invasion of Sicily or Sardinia. Despite the many missions undertaken there were few hits on enemy shipping. 89° *Gruppo* conducted a nighttime patrol over the skies of Bougie on 18 May. Three S.79s launched torpedoes against a merchantman and a destroyer but they failed to hit their targets. Similarly, another action conducted on 19 May by five S.79s from 89° and 105° *Gruppi* achieved no results. The attacks were made at 0240 and 0410 in an area between Bougie and Algiers and both crews of *Tenente* Vasco Pagliarusco and *Capitano* Bruno Pannoncini optimistically reported to have hit their targets. The Royal Navy reports, however, do not indicate that significant damage was made to its convoy. On the night of 20 May four S.79s from 279ª *Squadriglia* took off from Gerbini airbase to reach the coast of Tunisia near Bizerte were a large enemy convoy had been spotted. In a daring direct attack made at close range from the convoy, the four pilots released the warheads in rapid succession but did not achieve any hits. One of the escort ships, an aircraft carrier, rapidly targeted *Tenente* Giovanni Tresta's plane which forced the pilot to make an emergency landing in the sea while his plane was engulfed in flames. The crew members, all badly burned, were later recovered by a British ship and taken into captivity. On 23 May another bold operation was undertaken by seven S.79s by 89° *Gruppo* which between 0243 and 0335 scoured the coast of North Africa to locate a large enemy convoy. The operation had mixed results. Two S.79s returned to base without having the opportunity to fire the warheads, while one S.79 torpedoed a 5,000 merchantman near Bougie Bay, which was later observed by the crew engulfed in fire. The four remaining S.79s failed to return to base when they were shot down by enemy fighters. On 25 May four S.79s of 36° *Stormo* pursued a convoy north of Cape Sigli. Three warheads were launched by *Capitani* Carlo Putti, Giuseppe Zucconi and Pietro Greco and a small merchantman was torpedoed and sunk. A fourth S.79 did not return to base. Finally on 28 May *Tenente* Dorando Cionni, a decorated pilot, lost his life when his plane malfunctioned and the pilot lost control.

In June both Kesserling and *Generale* Fougier made the important decision to transfer torpedo bomber units based in Sardinia and Sicily to Pisa, Siena and Grosseto. The decision was made necessary by the almost daily carpet bombings made by the American Air Force against the Sicilian and Sardinian airbases. These were well known to the enemy, who took advantage of the debilitated Axis anti-aircraft defenses to target repeatedly bombers and torpedo bombers on the ground and their hangars and runways. At the meeting Kesserling asserted that "presently I cannot commit forces to target enemy shipping. These can be targeted by Generale Fougier."[34] Thus the decision was made to leave in Sardinia only the aircraft from 108° *Gruppo* and 41° *Gruppo* which continued throughout the month of June to conduct reconnaissance action against enemy shipping. On 2 June *Generale* Fougier ordered the constitution of the *Raggruppamento Aerosiluranti* based in Pisa. This unit was to consolidate several *Gruppi* with the purpose of defending Sicily and Sardinia from a potential seaborne invasion by the Allies.

34 Francesco Mattesini, *Luci ed ombre*, p.311.

The order envisioned the "assembly of a special force comprised of experienced pilots and crews in both daylight and nighttime operations." Moreover, this special force was to be further augmented by the "newly made pilots and less experienced crews."[35] The purpose of this unit was to deploy a mass of torpedo bombers were they were most needed and to shift them swiftly from one to another area of operations. Another task envisioned for this unit was to carry out the most strategically important operations such as the planned raid against Gibraltar. It was placed under the command of the 3ª *Squadra Aerea* which was based in Rome. If the need was to concentrate the unit in Sardinia the order envisioned the torpedo bombers to be based at Decimomannu, while if they were needed in Sicily they were to be headquartered in Lecce. The unit was to be deployed where it was most urgently needed while shielding the aircraft has much as possible from Allied carpet bombings by shifting them from numerous bases or by splitting them up into different bases.

Operation Scoglio

Operazione Scoglio (Operation Rock as Gibraltar was called by the Italians) was primarily a morale boosting operation planned by the RA to harm the British naval base. The war for Italy had taken a negative turn after defeat at El Alamein and the retreat against the armored and infantry forces of the Soviet Union after the crushing defeat at the Don River and as a consequence the morale of the home front was sagging. The regime and the armed forces aimed to boost morale with a couple of exemplary actions. One was to torpedo bomb Alexandria or Gibraltar and another was to launch naval torpedoes against ships moored in New York harbor. *Scoglio* was the first operation conducted by the newly formed *Raggruppamento Aerosiluranti*, the so-called special brigade of the torpedo bomber units destined to carry out the most dangerous large scale operations of the discipline. Since the beginning, the operation was planned at the highest level by *Comando Aerosiluranti di Superaereo* led by *Colonnello* Antonino Serra. The plan had begun to be drafted in February 1943 and it relied heavily on several reconnaissance flights that had photographed the base and its main installations. Moreover, key intelligence on its strength and its defenses was provided by SIM operatives based in Spain. *Superaereo* had built a small scale model of the base which was used to instruct the crews of the location of the main targets. The enhanced S.79, the S.79bis, was to be deployed for the operation. "Led by the redoundable Colonnello Carlo Unia, the new unit was equipped with the latest Sparviero variant, the S.79bis, which was faster and better armed than previous versions. To improve speed and range the S.79bis was fitted with the new Alfa Romeo 128 engines and had its ventral gondola removed."[36] The new version of the S.79 was also equipped with an enhanced compass and the warhead for the first time was fitted with a magnetic flintlock. Moreover, a new device allowed the power plant to improve temporarily the aircraft's speed. In 1942-43 efforts were made to improve the effectiveness of the S.79 by installing a system that injects ethyl into the carburetor, otherwise known as +100. This device allowed the S.79 to increase its speed for a few minutes by 50 km/h. It came specially handy when the S.79s crews had launched the

35 Ufficio Storico Aeronautica Militare: Comando Superaereo, "Costituzione Raggruppamento Aerosiluranti", 2 June 1943.

36 Marco Mattioli, *Savoia Marchetti S.79 Sparviero*, p.71.

warhead and were ready to disengage. The plan was for ten *Sparvieri* to conduct a nighttime flight on three small formations of three aircraft each and led by *Colonnello* Unia to make a pre-dawn attack on Gibraltar. Each had a specific target and the plan was fairly simple; a mass attack to do as much damage as possible. The ten pilots selected were handpicked by *Superaereo* so that the most able and experienced could take part in the operation. These were: *Capitani* Giuseppe Amoruso, Giuseppe Cimicchi, Francesco Di Bella, Carlo Faggioni, Giulio Cesare Graziani, Dante Magagnoli, Marino Marini, Vittorio Pini and, *Maggiori*: Gabriele Casini and Franco Melley. Four were from 130° *Gruppo*, three from 132° *Gruppo*, two from 1° *Nucleo Addestramento Aerosiluranti* and one form 3° *Nucleo Addestramento Aerosiluranti*. A few days prior to the start of the operation the planes had been transferred to Istres in southern France, the launching pad for the operation. During the landing on Istres on the 14th one S.79bis was damaged, leaving the team with only nine operational aircraft. For several days the operation could not begin because of bad weather and poor visibility. Finally, the nine remaining torpedo bombers departed from Istres on June 20th headed for the long flight to Gibraltar. During take-off *Maggiore* Melley's plane experienced technical difficulties forcing him to abort the mission, while *Capitano* Marini was forced to turn back having lost sight of his comrades during the first 15 minutes of flight. *Colonnello* Unia and the remaining six aircraft reached the coast of Spain but due to extreme bad weather and poor visibility the former issued an order to bring back all the planes. The aircraft of Faggioni and that of Giuseppe Cimicchi, which had flown ahead of the main group, continued their flight having failed to receive Unia's order. As they arrived at Gibraltar they found a British anti-aircraft defense that was totally unaware and unprepared to fight off the S.79bis. Searchlights illuminated the sky trying to spot the planes, but there was only a feeble reaction from guns and machine guns. The two pilots, (Cimicchi going in first) proceeded to launch their torpedoes from favorable positions at 0510 and 0533. Cimicchi launched at an altitude of 200 meters while Faggioni at 170 meters. Both failed to explode and Faggioni's torpedo could only be released at the second attempt due to an initial failure of the release mechanism. The fact that these warheads did not produce any damage led the crews to believe that sabotage was again at play, but a subsequent inquest did not find any proof of malfeasance. The torpedoes landed in the shallow waters of the harbor, much the same way things had gone during the first torpedo operation of the war against Alexandria. Both aircraft were able to disengage without any significant damage. "Despite its unsuccessful outcome, the Gibraltar raid was a remarkable action."[37] Full surprise on a heavily defended enemy naval base had been achieved and the pilots had had considerable time to launch their torpedoes without the usual interference from the enemy guns. The operation, however, paid the price of a lag in industrial and technological development since the domestic industry had been unable to build a successor to the S.79. The S.84 had failed due to its lack of maneuverability, while the S.79bis had represented only a marginal improvement (Alfa 128 engine versus the 126 and a device that allowed the power plant to improve temporarily the speed by 50 km/h during the launch of the torpedo). Unfortunately these were not the much anticipated structural changes leading to an enhanced and faster torpedo bomber that could launch multiple smaller warheads from longer distances, hence giving the crews enhanced protection during operations. The domestic industry was too busy trying to replace losses with the existing models of aircraft and was not able to

37 Ibid.

dedicate any large scale production efforts toward the mass construction of the various enhanced prototypes being developed in 1943. Of this combat action, *Generale* Fougier wrote that: "Some planes had to abort the mission due to technical difficulties. This forced the leader of the formation to cancel the operation after four hours of flight and call back the few remaining planes that were approximately 30 minutes from reaching the objective. Given that the element of surprise and the mass attack are the two factors that enhance the success of such operations, I concur with the decision taken by the unit leader."[38]

On 24 June the same experienced pilots utilized their stay at Istres air base in France to carry out another ambitious operation against British shipping along the coast of Algeria. Between 0200 and 0220 eight S.79s took flight at the command of *Tenente Colonnello* Unia. At 0415 the S.79s attacked a convoy near Cape Bengut comprised of seven transport ships. The first attack was pressed forward by the three lead S.79bis of *Tenente Colonnello* Unia and *Capitani* Di Bella and Amoruso. All three pilots missed their targets. The second strike was made by *Capitano* Graziani and *Maggiore* Melley, but the worsening weather conditions ensured that the warheads did not hit any targets. Lastly, *Capitani* Cimicchi, Pini and Vinciguerra, who had pushed much further than their predecessors, would up attacking another convoy. The latter escorted by several battleships opened up a tremendous fire stifling the torpedo launches which were made from too far away. During the attack *Capitano* Pini's aircraft was downed by fierce enemy fire. On 26 June, based on previous agreement with the Germans, the elite unit, had to vacate Istres airport and on the 27th its crews landed in Littoria. During the return flight one aircraft was lost due to poor visibility when *Tenente* Pasquale Vinciguerra's S.79bis crashed in the Romagna region. All crew members died in the crash. The regime's propaganda machine hailed the deeds of this special unit, but the concrete, non-propaganda related results of their combat actions had been poor.

Operation Husky

After defeating the Axis forces in the North African campaign the Allies began planning their next moves considering whether to move against Italy or France first. The Allies decided to move first against Italy, hoping that an invasion of the peninsula would not only remove Mussolini's regime from the war but also force Germany to divert divisions from France where the Allies subsequently planned to attack. The Allies' Italian campaign began with the invasion of Sicily on the night of 9-10 July 1943. The plan for Operation Husky, under the overall command of General Harold Alexander, called for the airborne and amphibious assault by two Allied armies, one landing on the south-eastern and one on the central southern coast of Sicily. An Eastern Task Force was led by General Bernard Montgomery and consisted of the British Eighth Army (which also included the 1st Canadian Infantry Division) that was to land on eastern Sicily and with the main objective being the capture of Syracuse. Once ashore and after having captured Syracuse, the Eighth Army would thrust northward toward Augusta and Catania and make the final leap toward Messina.

38 Francesco Mattesini, *Luci ed ombre*, p.328.

The Western Task Force was commanded by Lieutenant General George S. Patton and consisted of the American Seventh Army (three divisions supported by parachutists from the 505th Parachute Infantry Regimental Combat Team and the 3d Battalion, 504th Parachute Infantry) was charged with taking south-central Sicily by effectuating main seaborne landings in Gela, and Licata, to then capture a number of airfields located between Licata and Comiso. The amphibious landings were to be supported by powerful naval gunfire barrages as well as preemptive aerial bombings by Allied fighter and bomber squadrons. Ahead of the main attack, paratroopers were to land in Sicily and carry out disruptive missions against enemy gun positions and fuel depots. The Allies could deploy a total of 181,000 soldiers, 14,000 vehicles, and 600 tanks. Moreover, they also planned to deploy 3,445 aircraft and 2,590 ships of all kinds escorted by the mighty Force H of the Royal Navy.

In contrast, Axis forces consisted of 250,000 Italian and about 30,000 Wehrmacht troops under the overall command of *Generale* Alfredo Guzzoni's VI Army. The Italians were organized into six coastal divisions, four infantry divisions, and a variety of local defense forces. The strongest unit was the 16,000 strong *Livorno* Division while the weakest were the coastal units comprised of older soldiers many of which belonged to the party militia which for the most part were woefully deficient in equipment, training, and morale. The German troops were divided into two divisions, the *15th Panzer Grenadier* and the *Hermann Goering* Panzer Division. They formed with their Tiger tanks alongside the *Livorno* Division the most valuable component of Sicily's defenses. The *15th Panzer Grenadier Division* was essentially combat ready, but the *Hermann Goering Division* was significantly understrength and contained some inexperienced personnel. The Axis air forces could count upon the following assets: 932 aircraft of *Luftflotte* II (50 reconnaissance, 356 bombers, 32 torpedo bombers, 279 fighters, and 213 various other aircraft) and 930 Italian planes (3 reconnaissance, 192 bombers, 100 torpedo bombers, 28 dive bombers, 514 fighters and 103 other various aircraft). This strength changed slightly on a daily basis but by the start of Operation Husky the numbers of serviceable and available aircraft decreased significantly due to the massive Allied preparatory bombings which preceded and accompanied the operation. "The combined German and Italian air forces in the Mediterranean early in 1943 consisted of some 2,000 planes, one-half of them fighters. By May 1943 the number had dropped more than fifty percent, and of these many were obsolescent. Hundreds of planes had been destroyed on the ground because of failure to camouflage and disperse them and because antiaircraft defenses proved ineffective."[39] Between 10 and 22 July, for example, the almost daily attacks against Axis airfields yielded the loss of 118 German and 50 Italian aircraft. The preemptive aerial strikes by the Allies also concentrated upon destroying the airfields to make them inoperable by the Axis aircraft. To this end Sardinian and Sicilian bases were targeted very fiercely causing many of them to be inoperable and forcing the Axis aircraft to depart for operations from other southern Italian bases in Puglia, Calabria and Campania. According to historian Giuseppe Santoro the Allied bombings of the most southern Italian airfields reduced the flying endurance of certain aircraft such as the *Sparviero* which had to take flight from airfields further north to then operate in Sicily and to consume more fuel as a result.[40] Another key characteristic of the Sicilian campaign for the RA was the deployment of every possible serviceable aircraft to counter the Allied invasion. Given

39 Albert N. Garland and Howard McGaw Smyth, *Sicily and the Surrender of Italy* (Washington, DC: US Army Publications, 1965), pp.46-47.

40 Giuseppe Santoro, *L'aeronautica Italiana nella Seconda Guerra Mondiale*, Vol. 1, p.211.

the dire situation of the Italian air force service in 1943 pitted against the massive air forces of the Allies, every available aircraft was deployed. Even Fiat G.50 fighters, which by 1943 standards were totally obsolete, were deployed. There were forty of these aircraft on the start of the Allied operation, while two days later there were only ten as the other thirty had been all shot down by the enemy. In a planning meeting in June 1943 *Generale* Mario Roatta, who had been put in charge of preparing the defenses of Southern Italy from an enemy attack, had stated that any Allied bridgeheads that developed in Sicily or Sardinia could only be stopped by a massive deployment of air forces. To this end, he had vainly requested the deployment of hundreds of additional German bombers and fighters. The Germans by July had provided additional aircraft but not nearly as many as requested by the *Comando Supremo*. Thus, Allied aerial superiority was going to be one of the factors influencing the campaign. Despite this numerical superiority the Axis aerial forces were committed "to throw in the battle every asset at their disposal to halt the invasion."[41]

Given the Axis's inferior forces especially in aircraft and tanks, the planners believed that only swift land based counter-attacks supported heavily by aerial power could push back the Allies into the sea. These were to be carried out immediately after an initial Allied bridgehead had been secured. "Axis strategists recognized that they did not have sufficient strength to hold Sicily should the Allies gain a firm foothold on the island. Their only hope of success lay in crushing the Allies on the shore before they had time to consolidate their beachhead. This was easier said than done, however, for most Axis units on the island lacked the mobility to launch a quick counterstrike. The Axis command was therefore forced to station its reserves as close as possible to the most likely landing places … Kesselring believed that the only way the Axis could repel the Allies was by having German forces ready to launch a quick counteroffensive at each of the potential landing sites."[42] These forces were to be backed up by heavy air attacks by Italian and German aircraft based in Italy. The role of the torpedo bombers specifically was to interdict Allied sea lanes through the Mediterranean by targeting both troop and ammunition transport ships as well as battleships. In a thirteen page report issued a few weeks before the start of Operation Husky *Tenente Colonnello* Muti discussed the low state of readiness of the RA especially in light of its new task which was to repel a potential enemy invasion of the peninsula. From an organizational perspective Muti argued that the RA had too many generals and too many office workers at its offices in Rome. A vast overhaul was proposed to retire some functionaries early. From a tactical perspective Muti argued that the RA had to convert its force toward the task at hand which was likely going to be repelling an Allied invasion. To this end the RA had to launch a vast modernization process aimed at doing three things: fitting the most advanced fighters with 20mm cannons, introducing in record time a new, more versatile torpedo bomber, and finally, to reconstitute the standard bomber units with new equipment. The first two things, according to Muti, were of critical importance since the Italian fighters fitted with 20mm guns were necessary to engage the Allied 'flying fortresses,' while the new, faster but more lethal torpedo bombers were to unleash their striking force against troop and ammunition/weapons naval carriers.[43]

41 Ufficio Storico Aeronautica Militare: Ufficio Aerosiluranti di Superaereo, "Azioni di aerosiluramento effettuate contro naviglio nemico dal 7 al 15 luglio 1943", 17 July 1943, p.4.

42 Ibid., p.12.

43 Ufficio Storico, Tenente Colonnello Ettore Muti, "Brevi cenni di critica alla Regia Aeronauitica", 20 June 1943.

The torpedo bombers achieved two hits in the days preceding Operation Husky. On 7 July two *Sparvieri* from 108° *Gruppo* flown by *Tenenti* Francesco Pandolfo and Bernardo Braghieri took off from Sardinia to scour the coast of Tunisia for potential targets at sea. At 2245 *Tenente* Braghieri spotted a 7,000 tons steamer navigating approximately 20 miles from Galite Islands. Seeing that the lone steamer was not protected by naval escorts the pilot immediately pounced by bringing down his aircraft and releasing the torpedo which sunk the ship. At almost the same time (2250) *Tenente* Pandolfo released his deadly warhead against a 6,000 tons steamer which also sank shortly thereafter.

At the start of the massive enemy operation on the night of 9/10 July, the *Raggruppamento Aerosiluranti* made one large sweep over the enemy naval deployment but was unable to score any hits. Successive attacks were made on the following nights but they also did not yield any positive results. Three *Sparvieri* were shot down and one flown by *Tenente* Egone Bucher had to be ditched after failing to strike a cruiser on the night of 11/12 July. On the same night together with *Tenente* Luigi Buonaiuto, *Capitano* Di Bella targeted a large enemy deployment that included US Navy destroyers USS Murphy and USS McLanahan and several other battleships and steamers. Both pilots released their torpedoes against a steamer and a cruiser but it's unclear whether they had any success as they were chased away almost immediately by enemy fighters. Another torpedo attack was conducted on that night by three *Sparvieri* from 132° *Gruppo*/278ª *Squadriglia* off the coast near Augusta. The team claimed one steamer which was observed in flames.

The next night attacks were made again but without any hits. On the night between 13/14 July sixteen *Sparvieri* were deployed. *Capitano* Di Bella claimed a 10,000 steamer at Augusta Bay, while *Capitano* Carlo Faggioni of 132° *Gruppo*/278ª *Squadriglia* claimed a hit against a destroyer. However, the most relevant success of the torpedo bombers during Operation Husky was the strike against the mighty Force H which was tasked with supporting the landings by fighting off any interference from the Italian surface fleet. Force H was led by Vice-Admiral Cunningham sailing on HMS *Nelson* and was comprised of three naval divisions: 1st Division with HMS *Nelson*, HMS *Rodney* and HMS *Indomitable*, cruisers *Cleopatra* and *Euryalus* and the destroyers *Offa, Panther, Quail, ,Queenborough, Qulliame,* and *Piorum*. The 2nd Division with the battleships HMS *Warspite* and HMS *Valiant*, aircraft carrier HMS *Formidable*, cruisers *Aurora* and *Penelope* and several destroyers: *Faulknor, Fury, Echo, Eclipse, Inglefield, Ilex, Raider, Queen Olga*. Finally, 3rd Division (Force Z), with the battleships HMS *King George V, Howe*, the cruisers *Dido, Sirius*, and six destroyers *Jervis, Panther, Pathfinder, Penn, Paladine* and *Petard*.

On July 16 a few hours before the onset of darkness, Force H was spotted by a reconnaissance aircraft 90 miles north-east of Malta protecting the landing operations on the southern beaches of Sicily. At midnight *Capitano* Carlo Capelli, commander of 41° *Gruppo* and *Tenente* Ennio Caselli, who had taken off with their S. 79s from the airport of Gioia del Colle, headed to southern Sicily. It was a clear night with a full moon and great visibility. They came over the enemy force and dove down from 2,000 meters to 60 meters above the sea level. By getting down quickly they managed to ascend below the flak. At 1225 the aircraft jointly attacked HMS *Indomitable* (a 22,637 tons modified Illustrious-class aircraft carrier) 50 miles east of Cape Passero. The torpedo fired by Capelli struck the ship's port side just below the cabin of the Commander, Captain Guy Grantham flooding the boiler room and killing seven sailors. As the pilot flew over the ship his plane attracted considerable fire from the anti-aircraft defense but ultimately Capelli was able to return home with only slight damage. Meantime, the carrier, after receiving the hit, sailed at 11 knots to Malta. The ship was out of action for many months as it went in for extensive repairs in Britain. The clean shot against the ship was achieved primarily because while HMS *Nelson* had spotted the Italian plane at a distance of 8 miles and well ahead of the attack, the officers on board had mistakenly taken it for one of the six Albacore aircraft of the No. 817 Squadron which were returning to the aircraft carrier from an anti-submarine night patrol flight. For this reason the ship's anti-aircraft defense was not activated. Both observers on HMS *Nelson* and HMS *Indomitable* carefully monitored the maneuver of the approaching aircraft, until an observer on Indomitable saw something that was being released from the aircraft. At that point, one of the observing officers gave the order to the engine room to pull over at maximum speed, but the command was given too late to avoid the torpedo. A few hours later at 0640 on the morning of 16 July the Italian submarine *Alagi* scored a hit on the destroyer HMS *Cleopatra* near Augusta. On the same night Di Bella was again involved looking for potential targets but it is unclear whether he did hit a 12,000 steamer as he reports in the post battle report. Nonetheless at the termination of Operation Husky *Capitano* Francesco Di Bella was awarded a gold medal of military valor. On the night between 18/19 July two S.79 (*Capitano* Ennio Marescalchi and *Tenente* Ferruccio Coloni) from 253ª *Squadriglia* took off from Lecce airport and attacked enemy ships shelling Italian positions near Augusta. While flying over the enemy ships, the *Capitano's* plane was attacked from behind by enemy fighters but ultimately made it back to base, *while Tenente* Coloni's plane received some many hits that it had to be ditched off Calabria. The crew survived and were rescued at sea two days later.

Operation Husky revealed that the Allies had achieved by mid-1943 such numerical superiority of both men and equipment that the RA and the *Luftwaffe* could at best interfere and cause some damage but could not halt the invasion. The few successful torpedo hits along with other limited successes by the RM were unable to significantly halt the invasion plans where the Allies operated hundreds of vessels of all kind. Ahead of the invasion, the Italians had asked the *Luftwaffe* to supply 500 additional aircraft to have any hope of stopping the Allies. But the Germans could only supply approximately 100 additional aircraft, many of which were put out of action by preliminary bombardments of Axis airfields prior to the start of Husky. The Axis crews suffered further losses during the operation and achieved some results but were ultimately unable to even slow down the pace of the landings. The RM did not deploy its battleships in an operation were the enemy fielded hundreds of aircraft and opted to interfere with the operation with small crafts that had only very limited success.

During Operation Husky 136 torpedo bomber attacks were carried out and according to RA records 39 torpedoes struck enemy ships while six crews and their aircraft failed to return home.[44] The 39 hits are largely unconfirmed and based exclusively on the rather optimistic reports of the crews during their debriefings at the conclusions of missions. It appears that the actual hits were much less and in the single digits. Despite their unwavering commitment, the crews of RA were unable to push back the invaders. Historian Giuseppe Santoro has argued that: "Almost immediately it became quite evident that bombers and torpedo bombers could not be deployed in daylight operations to risk being annihilated by the strong and continued defense of the beachheads and of the transport ships by the very effective enemy anti-aircraft fire. Thus, bombers and torpedo bombers were forced to operate at night but they still suffered

44 Ibid., p.14.

heavy losses inflicted especially by enemy fighters that attacked and pursued them all the way to their bases by machine gunning the planes when they landed. The few Italian forces, operating mainly from bases in Central Italy, operated very little, if not at all during moonless nights. The torpedo bombers suffered heavy casualties."[45]

The post Sicilian campaign phase of the war was the hardest for the RA since its force was reduced even further. It could count on 662 fighters of which only 359 were ready for combat. It possessed 253 bombers of which only 83 were deemed combat ready. Similarly, it possessed 85 torpedo bombers but only 22 could be deployed immediately.[46] Despite being mired in many more operational difficulties such as the longer distance of their bases of operation from the Mediterranean, the torpedo bomber units continued to mount strikes after the loss of Sicily. On the night of 12 August three S. 79s of 132° *Gruppo* departed from Littoria under the command of *Tenente Colonnello* Vittorio Cannaviello to search for and attack convoys in the waters of Sicily. Flying in bad weather, they failed to return to base. The cause of their demise was never determined. It is possible that they carried an attack against some enemy ships, but it is unclear whether the crews died because of the bad weather or because they were shot down by enemy fire. Cannaviello was granted posthumously a gold medal for military valor. A few months prior to his death he was taken away from active duty by becoming an RA attaché. But when the invasion of Sicily began, he volunteered to come back into active service and found death as a torpedo bomber pilot.

The first post-Husky success for the torpedo bombers was achieved by *Capitano* Carlo Faggioni, commander of the 278ª *Squadriglia*, which on the evening of 14 August had taken off from Littoria together with another S.79 piloted by *Tenente* Ottone Sponza. Upon his return to base Faggioni reported having struck a destroyer at 0015 on 15 August. In reality Faggioni, and co- pilot Leopoldo Ruggeri, torpedoed, near Cani Island (north of Bizerte), the British tank landing ship LST414 (Lieutenant Howard Baskerville Cadogan). The 1,780 tons ship was part of a small convoy bound for Malta and it was towing the twin ship LST 416. The torpedo caused flooding in the engine room and to prevent it from sinking, the ship had to be towed at the beach near Bizerte, where it was later abandoned. There were two more torpedo hits on the night of 16 August by crews of 132° *Gruppo*. These had flown from Littoria to Millis airport in Sardinia to take advantage of the full moon that allowed the pilots to locate enemy ships more easily. The war diary of *Aeronautica della Sardegna* states that:

> Between 0025 and 0100 5 S. 79s took off from Milis airbase in Sardinia to conduct an attacking sweep over the coast of North Africa. At 0110 one aircraft torpedoed a steamer of 12,000 tons that was part of a seven ship convoy navigating west of Cape Bougaroun. The crew observed the warhead striking the ship. Flying over the convoy a second time, the pilot then saw the ship veering. At 0246 a bomber torpedoed another 12,000 tons steamer that was part of a large 50 ship convoy. It was observed that the steamer was struck by the warhead and then it began to sink. At 0335 a third aircraft torpedoed another steamer of approximately 6,000 or 7,000 tons navigating north of Bizerte with a convoy of 4 ships. After observing the steamer sinking, the aircraft was struck by very strong anti-aircraft fire and sustained damage to its right wing. At 0340 the fourth aircraft attacked a destroyer

45 Giuseppe Santoro, *L'aeronautica Italiana nella Seconda Guerra Mondiale*, Vol. 1, p.213.
46 Gregory Alegi, "Le Operazioni in Tunisia", in: *L'Italia in Guerra, Il Quarto Anno, Parte I* (Rome: Ufficio Storico, 1993), p.81.

> or freighter that was about to anchor at Bone harbor. But due to the heavy defensive fire it could not be determined whether the torpedo had hit the ship. Finally the fifth aircraft piloted by *Tenente* Antonio Saccillotto and Sergente Franco Rava did not return to base. The last remaining aircraft returned to base between 0350 and 0700.[47]

The war diary overestimated the number of successful hits on enemy ships and their tonnage. There were four attacks made but only two were on the mark. At 0210 *Capitano* Cimicchi launched his torpedo against the British steamer Empire Kestrel (2,674 tons) which sank almost immediately after being hit. This transport ship was part of a large convoy (UGS 13) when it was struck 10 miles north of Cape Bougaroun. The second hit was made by *Tenente* Vezio Terzi at 0246 when his torpedo struck the American Benjamin Contee transport ship (7,126 tons) which was sailing from Bone and headed to Oran. The ship received severe damage with the water entering two compartments. It sailed at 4 knots to Bone where it was then dispatched to Brooklyn for extensive repairs. It stayed under repair for a year and it was then deployed in Normandy in June 1944. At 0335 Near Bizerte *Sottotenente* Carlo Bernocchi launched his warhead against a steamer but he failed to hit the target.

On 17 August at 2100 three 281ª *Squadriglia* S. 79s, took off from Milis airport to attack enemy shipping near the coast of Sicily, but one plane, slightly after takeoff was forced to make a hasty return to base given the malfunctioning of the instrumentation panel. A second plane was shot down by enemy fire killing the crew including the pilot *Tenente* Mario Jotta when he began his descent toward the target. The plane was shot to pieces by Flak. The last remaining aircraft flown by *Capitano* Cimicchi made a determined attack at 0315 against an enemy convoy navigating west of Cape Serrat but the torpedo missed the targeted ship. For his continuous service as a torpedo bomber lead pilot Giuseppe Cimicchi was awarded a gold medal of military valor which came on the heels of a German Iron Cross second class awarded by the *Luftwaffe* for the successful action against the Empire Kestrel. The 132° *Gruppo* on 19, 22, and 24 August conducted several attacking sweeps but they were all unsuccessful. The pilots involved *Tenenti* Irnerio Bertuzzi, Caio Tredici and Silvio Cella upon their return to base claimed to have scored hits, but their reports turned out to be inaccurate.

The last known success of the torpedo bombers took place the day before the armistice. At 2125 on 7 September 1943 a lone S.79 from 281ª *Squadriglia*/132° *Gruppo flown by Tenente* Vasco Pagliarusco departed from Littoria to conduct a sweep along the coast of Northern Sicily. His S.79 trimotor drowned ahead until the pilot pressed forward an attack near Termini Imerese against a convoy ferrying special forces troops such as Rangers and Commandos from Palermo to Salerno. The pilot was able to launch the torpedo at a very favorable distance striking the British LST 417 tank carrying ship (1,625 tons) of Captain Robert James William Crowdy. The warhead hit the stern of the ship blasting an 8 meters wide hole and causing the immediate flooding of the deck. Captain Crowdy was thus forced to bring the ship to the coast of Sicily. The next day it was brought back to harbor were it had to undergo extensive repairs. On the 8th a combat action by nine torpedo bombers was cancelled almost at the last minute upon hearing about the armistice. As of the beginning of September 1943 the force of the torpedo bomber specialty was organized as follows:

47 Francesco Mattesini, "Operazione Husky", *Bollettino della Marina Militare*, May 2011, pp.55-56.

Commanders of Gruppi and Squadriglie Aerosiluranti as of 5 September 1943
41° *Gruppo Autonomo Aerosiluranti*: *Maggiore* Massimiliano Erasi,
-204ª *Squadriglia Aerosiluranti*: *Capitano* Giuseppe Cipelletti
-205ª *Squadriglia Aerosiluranti*: *Capitano* Alberto Piacentino

104° *Gruppo Autonomo Aerosiluranti*: *Tenente* Colonnello Ubaldo Puccio
-252ª *Squadriglia*: *Capitano* Alfredo Reyer
-253ª *Squadriglia*: *Capitano* Enrico Marescalchi

108° *Gruppo Autonomo Aerosiluranti*: *capitano* Mario Spezzaferri
-256ª *Squadriglia*: *capitano* Pietro Greco
-257ª *Squadriglia*: *capitano* Giuseppe Zucconi

131° *Gruppo Autonomo Aerosiluranti*: *Maggiore* Paris Pernazza
-279ª *Squadriglia*: *capitano* Carlo Cerqueni
-284ª *Squadriglia*: *capitano* Michele Palumbo

132° *Gruppo Autonomo Aerosiluranti*: *Maggiore* Gabriele Casini
-278ª *Squadriglia*: *capitano* Carlo Faggioni
-281ª *Squadriglia*: *capitano* Giuseppe Cimicchi

According to *Superaereo* at 2000 on 7 September 1943 the *Raggruppamento Aerosiluranti* had two bases Pisa and Siena. It had a force of fifty-one S. 79 belonging to the following *Gruppi* 41°, 108°,131° and 104°. At Littoria airbase there were twelve S. 79 of the 132° *Gruppo*, while at Capodichino (Naples) there was one S. 79 of the *Sezione Autonoma Aerosiluranti*. In total there were 64 torpedo bombers, of which only 46 were deemed combat ready.

Summary and Conclusions

1. Despite an increase of the training of the torpedo bomber crews to fight at night in 1943 torpedo bomber activity decreased markedly due to a host of factors. The three most important being: 1. The reduced number of hours per day that attacks could be made relegated mostly to nighttime hours with a full moon or few hours at dusk or dawn. 2. The torpedo bomber fleet being much smaller versus 1941-42 due to high losses, lack of experienced crews and lack of available fighter escort. 3. The overwhelming enemy superiority which in many cases translated into enemy squadrons preempting torpedo bomber operations by carpet bombing their bases or by fighters chasing torpedo bombers all the way to their bases of operation after they had accomplished a combat mission.
2. In 1943 German torpedo bomber units came to the fore in the Mediterranean theatre often by achieving significant results in some cases much more significant than their Italian counterparts due to extensive training of the crews.
3. Overall the Axis military situation in the Mediterranean basin became much more precarious first by the loss of the Tunisian bridgehead and then by the Allied invasion of Sicily

which caused a shakeup in the Italian government thereby producing the armistice of Cassibile and Italy's exit from the war.

4. Both the RA and the *Luftwaffe* forces operating in the Mediterranean continued to wage their campaign against the Allied overwhelming superiority. Although they did achieve some success this was not enough to substantially alter the course of the fighting or to halt the Allied invasion and Italy's ultimate capitulation.

Conclusion and Final Assessment

Some military historians hold the RA's role in the Second World War in contempt. MacGregor Knox, for example, states that its airplanes were "more deadly to their crews than to the enemy."[1] While others have argued that the RA's force and its torpedo bombers, in particular, were generally less successful than those of the Royal Navy Fleet Air Arm: "The two principal torpedo planes in the Mediterranean in 1940 were the Swordfish and her Italian rival, the Sm.79 Hunchback. The latter had a longer range, twice the speed, and three times as many engines, but it was the Swordfish, and the men who flew her, that changed history."[2] Another historian argues that while the Italian torpedo bombers should not be discounted, the bulk of the ships damaged/sunk by the Axis in the Mediterranean were made by the *Luftwaffe*: "Italian torpedo bombers might be partially exempted from the claim that the Regia Aeronautica had no success after 1940. But of the 385 Allied merchant and naval vessels sunk by air attack in the Mediterranean between 11 June 1940 and 8 September 1943, only thirty-six were sunk by the Regia Aeronautica: the rest were sunk by the Luftwaffe."[3] Finally, Brian Sullivan has argued that the *Regia Aeronautica* and, hence its torpedo bomber units, was flawed from the beginning of the war because of Italy's limited industrial base, the delays in introducing newer, more modern aircraft, and most importantly the slow output which in periods of the conflict at best covered the combat losses. This position of weakness as Italy entered the war was its *d'origine sans* which limited its operational ability during the war to the point that even in the Mediterranean it was highly dependent upon the *Luftwaffe*. While it can be argued that all these arguments have merits the data tells a slightly different story. In the anti-shipping campaign in the Mediterranean the airmen were able for a significant amount of time to interfere with the British supply operations to the point that by mid-year in 1942 Malta was in a severe state of crisis. The Axis grip on the island fortress only relented after the Allies turned the tide in the Mediterranean/North African campaign. A key contribution was made by the German air force and the Kriegsmarine, especially in 1942, but the bulk of the effort especially between 1940-41, was made by the *Regia Aeronautica*. The British assessments of the campaign point to the fact that the RA's air reconnaissance was highly effective, its horizontal bombings not as effective but functional in destabilizing naval convoys, while the torpedo bombing was reputed a major threat although it was inconsistent. For the Royal Navy the two major results

1 Knox, *Hitler's Italian Allies*, p.43.
2 Thomas P. Lowry, The *Attack on Taranto*, p.27.
3 Stephen Harvey, "The Italian War Effort and the Strategic Bombing of Italy", *History*, Vol. 70, 1985, pp.32–45.

of the Axis anti-shipping campaign was the loss of merchant ships and their cargo, the loss of warships escorting the convoy and at times the elongated journey when convoys were not forced through the Mediterranean resulting in a loss of time and resources. Another key objective of the Axis air forces was to fight off a major Allied seaborne and airborne landing in North Africa and in Europe. In both Operation Torch and Husky the combined Axis air forces were able to interfere to some extent with these operations but in no way could they halt them. Here the decision by Axis command to do not deploy the full force of the Navy in halting the invasion of Italy in particular facilitated the Allied operation as air forces alone supported by small crafts (torpedo boats, submarines, etc..) proved ineffectual in halting the landings. A third operational responsibility of the Axis air forces, providing an escort to the Italian battleships, was fulfilled only in part and partly explains the timidity of the Italian Navy in major battles with the Royal Navy such as Operation Harpoon in mid-June 1942.

Although less spectacular, the S.79s and to a more limited extent the S.84s, influenced substantially the convoy war until 1943. As one aviation historian argues: "The S.79 was adopted by Italy on all fronts for the duration of the war, and although it had been created as a bomber, its true role became the more aggressive one of torpedo launcher in which it proved to be insuperable."[4]

For example, the *Luftwaffe* did provide in two periods (first half of 1941 and first half of 1942) of the conflict its key contribution in the Mediterranean especially by executing almost daily bombing forays against Malta. Not only did these two interventions proved essential in weakening Malta and in debilitating its offensive potential against Axis convoys, but they also created favorable conditions in the Mediterranean for the continuation of the Axis advance in North Africa. The *Luftwaffe* also proved to be very capable in executing torpedo bomber attacks, especially in 1942 and beyond, but one must also look at the qualitative differences between the *Luftwaffe* and the Regia *Aeronautica* torpedo bomber successes. First, Italian torpedo-armed S.79s either sank or damaged 22 warships, and over 21 enemy merchant ships were put out of action and their cargo destroyed. It is estimated that S.79s and S.84s were responsible for damaging or sinking as much as 290,820 tons of enemy naval assets (Mattesini has a slightly higher figure of 299,557 tons either sunk or damaged).[5] In turn the German torpedo bombers sunk or damaged 11 warships and 44 merchant ships for a total of 330,037 tons.[6] If we further breakout the numbers there are some qualitative differences that stand out. The Italian torpedo bombers primarily pursued warships and achieved relevant success there such as the damage to the battleship HMS *Nelson* and the carrier HMS *Indomitable* and the hits against cruisers such as HMS *Kent,* HMS *Liverpool* (torpedoed twice), Glasgow (struck by two torpedoes), HMS *Manchester* and HMS *Phoebe.* Meanwhile the *Luftwaffe* torpedo bombers only damaged one light cruiser, the HMS *Arethusa* and scored hits on nine smaller warships (*Escaut, Thomas Stone, Leedstown, Acute, Tasajera*, *Avon Vale* and *Louisburg*). The majority of strikes were made against merchant ships. Warships remained throughout the war a much harder target to strike for a torpedo or standard bomber pilot than merchant ships which were not as heavily defended

4 Enzo Angelucci, *World War Two Combat Aircraft*, p.211.
5 Alberto Santoni and Francesco Mattesini, *La Partecipazione Tedesca alla Guerra Aeronavale nel Mediterraneo (1940–1945)* (Rome: Ufficio Storico, 1980), pp.597–98. See also, Marco Mattioli, *Savoia-Marchetti S.79 Saprviero*, p.90, and Francesco Mattesini, *Luci ed ombre*, pp.551-557.
6 Ibid., p.557.

by the anti-aircraft fire and had also thinner armor protection. Primarily for this reason the *Luftwaffe* basic doctrine was the use of the torpedo bombers primarily against merchant ships, especially small convoys which were more vulnerable. Torpedo bombing against capital warships remained a highly dangerous mission throughout the war. Only the fact that the targets were extremely valuable justified the losses typically experienced by these aircraft. Another qualitative difference is that while the German torpedo bomber units began to operate after the Italians established the S.79 torpedo units, they managed to operate for another two years (Sept 1943 to 1945) after Italy's capitulation. Therefore they operated for a longer timeframe than the Italian torpedo bomber crews. Another factor that must be considered is the dearth of Italian torpedoes during periods of time in the Mediterranean campaign which acted as a restraint on operations and limited the amount of strikes especially upon less relevant targets such as transports.

The record of the *Sparvieri* bombers also compares favorably to the torpedo bomber operations of the British Royal Navy Fleet Air Arm. "Between 1 November 1942 and 30 April 1943, a total of 387 Axis merchant ships and tankers were sunk in the Mediterranean. Of the 387 sinking, 185 (48 per cent) were directly sunk by aircraft, the next highest total were submarines with 159 sinking (41 percent). The remaining 43 vessels were sunk by either warships or mining. In terms of the tonnages of sinking over this period, aircraft accounted for 292,485 (46 per cent) of the total 639,885 GRT sunk."[7] The data provided by aviation historian Richard Hammond does not include data from the early period of the conflict (for example the strike against the Italian Fleet at Taranto in November 1940) but it includes all standard RAF bomber and FAA strikes until the last stages of the war for Italy. The latter were extremely vulnerable. The Tunisian convoys for example, were extremely easy preys because the RM was overstretched and the escorts provided were insufficient and poorly armed.[8]

Numbers alone do not provide the full story. The best example of the efficacy of the Axis air forces in the Mediterranean, of which the torpedo bombers were one of its most relevant components, is the siege of Malta in the summer of 1942. The March and June convoy operations sustained by the Royal Navy to relieve Malta had been heavily interfered with by the Axis air forces to the point that few supplies made it through. As naval historian Vincent O'Hara asserts "By mid-1942 Italian and German forces had Malta tightly blockaded by sea and bombarded by air, and the British chiefs of staff believed that its supplies would be exhausted by July."[9] Malta's survival was in peril until August when the Pedestal convoy courageously fought its way through to resupply Malta. The arrival of the surviving convoy merchant ships along with the Ohio tanker saved Malta and slowly allowed for the restoration of its fighting capacity. "It is certainly likely that without the arrival of the convoy, the island would have fallen. The governor

7 Richard Hammond, "Air Power and the British Anti-Shipping Campaign in the Mediterranean, 1940-1944", p.60.

8 "Despite the efforts of the Italian navy, the escorts they were providing at this stage were often vessels pressed into service sporting damage that was not fully repaired, or a few new vessels that were not yet fully worked up. Thanks to the casualties suffered from a relatively small pool of experienced officers and men, the crews were often less experienced and in some cases lacked full training. Allied Italian warships lacked particularly effective anti-aircraft armaments in general, and it was the threat from aircraft they were least capable of dealing with. This made the lack of available escort aircraft all the more keenly felt." Richard Hammond, "Air Power and the British Anti-Shipping Campaign in the Mediterranean, 1940-1944", p.60.

9 Vincent O'Hara, *In Passage Perilous: Malta and the Convoy Battles of June 1942*, p.2.

of the island had estimated that when it arrived, they were just 10 days from surrender through lack of supplies."[10] Thus it can be argued that the two year campaign waged against Malta by the Axis was effective up until the turning points of Operation Pedestal and later the third battle of El Alamein.

Having established that the torpedo bombers influenced the convoy war in the Mediterranean there are two other important roles that were carried out by these units during the war. First, the constant threat of the torpedo bombers against British shipping and bases in the Mediterranean meant that they tied up a much larger enemy force than originally envisioned for the defense from these types of operations. For example many convoys were not forced through the Mediterranean but took the longer route around the Cape of Good Hope and harbor defenses were significantly scaled up after September 1940. Thus, these torpedo strikes tied up resources that could have been otherwise deployed for other purposes including offensive actions. Second, throughout the Mediterranean campaign various plans were made by the British Royal Navy for the seaborne invasion of Sicily or Sardinia as well as planned strikes against key ports such as Genoa and La Spezia. Some of these plans were promoted and pushed directly by Churchill who was adamant about taking Italy out of the war. However, the reluctance by the Royal Navy to put them into effect in 1941 and 1942 had to do with many factors including the potential interference of the Italian air units or the Navy against these actions. For example, a strike against the port of Livorno in 1941 was cancelled almost at the last minute because of the fear of exposing the battlefleet to Axis air and naval assets close to home. Another example, is that one key aspect of the planning for Operation Husky was the consideration that a very large American and British naval force was necessary to counter the threat of Axis strikes by air and by sea.[11]

Torpedo bombers contribution to the convoy war could have been even more significant if the technology for both aerial torpedoes and the aircraft had improved during the conflict. While Japan, Britain and the United States were successful in this endeavor, for Italy in the critical phase of the war between 1942-43 it was not possible to introduce a new, more efficient and modern monoplane for the torpedo bomber units. Many factors contributed to this result. First, throughout the period June 1940-July 1943 the domestic industry was barely keeping up in replacing the losses in the battlefield. It was at times in full production mode but it still focused almost all of its efforts on the assembly of older aircraft models such the S.79. The S.84, design work on which had commenced prior to the war, revealed itself to be a failure, while the S.79bis was only partially successful. The plane's basic design was improved along with the devices to aid the pilot in improving the accuracy of the torpedo launch. But apart from these improvements the aircraft still had most of the basic design and technology features of the S.79. Some of the S.79s that were being fielded for service were generally low in efficiency since they had been utilized extensively and had been serviced several times already. As the war progressed, fewer S.79s were combat ready on a daily basis and many required extensive maintenance in order to be fielded for combat thus reducing the overall combat efficiency of these units. By late 1942 the lack of a more modern torpedo bomber was keenly felt as due to the relative speed of the S.79, daylight operations became quasi suicidal. Thus a missed opportunity was

10 Ibid. p.60.
11 Richard Hammond, "An Enduring Influence on Imperial Defence and Grand Strategy: British Perceptions of the Italian Navy, 1935-1943", *International History Review*, vol. 39, n. 5, 2017, pp.810-835.

the adaptation of the *Reggiane* Re.2001 fighter to the torpedo bomber role. A prototype was readied in 1943 but the plane was never launched in large numbers as a torpedo bomber despite its potential. Meanwhile, the 450mm Whitehead torpedo remained the weapon of choice for the torpedo bomber units since industry had not been able to turn other smaller torpedo prototypes into viable production weapons. The *silurotto*, for example, paired with the *Reggiane* Re.2001 was another missed opportunity while the circular torpedo/bomb *Motobomba* FFF was used only sparingly because the leadership of the RA ordered very limited numbers of this worthy warhead. Radio controlled torpedoes, which could have contributed to reducing losses of aircraft and their crews and improve torpedo bomber accuracy, were used very sparingly, if not at all. Given the lack of the development of newer aircraft and weapons, the torpedo bomber units lost some of their lethalness, to the point that their successes in 1942-43 trailed those of 1940-41, despite the expansion of the torpedo bomber units. Losses also increased.

Another factor that debilitated torpedo bomber attacks were the measures instituted by the Royal Navy and the RAF to preempt such attacks which improved as the war evolved. These included an increase in the number and quality of anti-aircraft weapons on board ships. Radar also played a role in diminishing the element of surprise of torpedo attacks, while fire control and coordination tactics adopted by the Royal Navy gunner crews also improved. Lastly, the development of gun shells that exploded in proximity of their targets but were lethal enough to take them down also played a part in blunting torpedo bomber attacks. These measures taken by the Royal Navy during the escort of its convoys or to protect harbor infrastructures made the life of the torpedo bombers much more difficult. The RAF with its modern, faster fighter planes that were well armed and equipped with radar enabling them to fight at night also contributed to challenging the torpedo bomber units. This combination of more effective Royal Navy defenses and improved RAF effectiveness in downing the *Sparvieri* did much to sap the morale and the combativeness of the torpedo bomber pilots who bravely fought on against ever escalating odds.

A greater effectiveness by the torpedo bomber units could also have been achieved if they had been readied prior to the beginning of the war to conduct early and unexpected strikes against the enemy. The objectives of the RA bombing units, and of the *Sparviero* units in particular, were twofold: disrupt British naval operations and supply convoys and attack ports and unloading docks on the coasts of Egypt and later Cyrenaica to disrupt, interfere with and ultimately paralyze the operational activities of the Royal Navy. These were extremely ambitious objectives given the paucity of forces available to the air service in mid-1940. In order to have a more meaningful and strategic impact upon the course of the war the RA should have had a fully trained torpedo bomber unit as well as German dive bombers and heavy large load bombers at the beginning of the war. Such a striking force could have obtained significant results if deployed in surprise attacks early on in the conflict. Limitations to its effectiveness, however, would have hampered its degree of success such as the limited endurance of the S.79 when targeting enemy bases such as Gibraltar and Alexandria, the difficulty of achieving torpedo hits in shallow waters, and the general lack of penetrative power with 100kg bombs dropped from high altitude, horizontal bombing forays. But unexpected strikes against warships and merchant ships at sea from the onset could still have achieved significant results.

Another factor that hampered the air service effectiveness in the early stages was the lack of cooperation with the RM and their inability to fight together in a cohesive fashion. If this factor had been addressed early in the war perhaps the anti-shipping campaign could have been more successful.

When the two services fought in an integrated fashion in 1942 against operations Harpoon and Pedestal, they achieved significant successes but unfortunately it would take almost two years for the combined strength of both services to be felt. Both the Italian Navy and the RA could have been more effective if they had already incorporated the integrated, combined arms approach, prior to or early in the conflict. The British Fleet Air Arm, for example, proved to be a much more effective as well as fully integrated combat unit especially in the early stages of the conflict in the Mediterranean.

Certain improvements were made during the war which positively influenced operations and especially torpedo bomber strikes. These improvements increased the odds of survival for the torpedo bomber crews. First, the development of proper group attack tactics with the torpedo bombers mounting their attack shortly after attacks by dive bombers and fighters improved the overall RA effectiveness. These attacks not only ensured that the enemy faced almost at once a large number of aircraft attacking from multiple sides, thus increasing the likelihood of a strike because of the sheer quantity of the weapons hurled against the warships, but they also distracted the enemy and suppressed and diffused his anti-aircraft defenses increasing the likelihood that an able pilot could bypass the defensive screen and launch the torpedo from a favorable distance. Beginning in 1941 the group attack tactic was adopted by the RA whereby a combination of bombers, torpedo bombers and fighters was hurled at the enemy convoys with greater frequency and with a greater number of aircraft. This tactic, which mirrored what the Japanese and British torpedo bomber units were doing, proved effective although the Italians could never match the sheer numbers of aircraft deployed by Japan or the United States in single operations. In 1942 the tactic was further refined with the introduction of new weapons such as the radio controlled torpedoes, aircraft loaded with explosives, etc.. but unfortunately they never got beyond the prototype or experimental stage.

Second, the effectiveness of torpedo bomber attacks increased as the units were supplied with an adequate fighter escort, to drive off and engage the enemy's fighters trying to interfere with the torpedo launches. This factor was largely dependent upon the quality and the quantity of fighters a national state could field during war. Initially in 1940 there were 24 *Stormi* of bombers and only eight of fighters. The latter were primarily equipped with Fiat CR.42 biplane fighters, that incorporated some modern elements of fighter design, such as aluminum alloy and steel framing and streamlined fuselage but were overall inferior to British fighters. All metal monoplanes such as the *Macchi* C.200 and the Fiat G.50 were introduced in 1941 when they became the fighters of choice of the *Stormi* of the RA. Despite being superior to the Fiat biplanes they were under gunned and underpowered in relation to fighters being produced in Germany or Britain. The *Macchi* C.202 fighter was finally the aircraft that could go head to head against such enemy fighters as the Spitfire in 1942 on an equal footing as demonstrated during Operations Harpoon and Pedestal. Then the 5 Series of fighters produced by *Macchi, Reggiane* and Fiat offered even greater power and speed as well as a stronger defensive platform. As the quality of Italian fighters improved the torpedo bombers were aided in their attacks with greater protection, thus better enabling them to achieve their tasks. No major torpedo attack was made without fighter escort in 1942. The RA preferred cancelling planned operations in case the fighter escort was not available. In turn, Hughes states that early in the Pacific campaign an American torpedo bomber force attacked the enemy without adequate fighter escort and was shot to pieces.[12] But the major issue faced in 1942 and 1943 was the declining fortunes of the RA and especially the limited output of new aircraft in relation to the losses sustained in the campaign, which ensured that many operations were conducted with fewer aircraft, especially in 1943.

A third factor that could have increased torpedo bomber effectiveness was an aerial warhead that could be dropped at higher speed and from greater altitude and by developing more advanced torpedo bombers that could execute higher drops and at greater speed, while also increasing their sturdiness in order to increase the crews chances of surviving against up gunned antiaircraft defenses. If we take a comparative look at both the Mediterranean and the Pacific theatres during the Second World War we can point to both the American and Japanese cases and see how they transitioned toward better performing torpedo bombers during the conflict. In the early stages of the conflict the American torpedo squadrons, for example, flew aircraft with an overall modest speed and were equipped with a torpedo warhead that had to be launched at 120 feet (or less than 40 meters from the water). By contrast, the American torpedo squadrons during the naval battles of 1943 where much more effective because they flew a much improved aircraft and an aerial torpedo that was more lethal. The same can be said for the Japanese squadrons that transitioned from an already effective torpedo bomber (B5NS) to the faster and more maneuverable Nakajima B6N. As Mark E. Stille asserts with regards to the B5NS that: "its effectiveness declined throughout 1942 as Allied ship-borne and aerial defenses took an increasing toll of these aircraft. Even in the face of improving US Navy air defenses, the B5N2 was a deadly weapon when crewed by skilled aviators. The aircraft's weaknesses meant its days as a frontline aircraft were numbered by the fall of 1942, its principal vulnerability being a lack of protection for the crew and the fuel tank."[13] Similarly, the S.79 was innovative and effective during the first years of the Mediterranean campaign but lost its effectiveness over time. But unlike the Japanese military which harnessed its combat power demonstrating considerable military effectiveness during war with the introduction of an improved torpedo bomber in the form of the Nakajima B6N and a deadlier warhead with the Type 91 Model 3, the Italian air force and its technical staff at Guidonia together with the domestic industry (*Savoia Marchetti* and *Reggiane*) was not able to introduce an improved torpedo bomber or a deadlier warhead. Just like the case of Japan an improved torpedo bomber would not have turned the tide in the Mediterranean convoy war but would have likely reversed for a time the descending effectiveness of the S.79 torpedo bomber. Instead, the Italian air force planners introduced several interesting prototypes like the radio controlled torpedo but these efforts were half hearted due to the general lack of interest by the leaders of the service and the general lack of funds. These were all efforts spearheaded by engineers or pilots that worked on them during their free time as there was never an organizational push by the RA to support these initiatives in a major way due to the contingencies of war. This also explains why many of these new projects took so much time to be transformed from preliminary concepts into prototypes. The Second World War was unlike prior wars because much of the fighting was driven by high technology weaponry. Weapons considered to be technologically advanced in 1940 were obsolescent by 1943 and in all branches of the military new weapons continued to change the dynamics of the fighting.

12 Wayne P. Hughes, *Fleet Tactics* (Annapolis MD: Naval Institute Press, 1986), p.87.
13 Mark E. Stille, *US Navy Ships vs Japanese Attack Aircraft* (Oxford: Osprey, 2020), pp.28-29.

The Fairey Swordfish, Britain's torpedo bomber, for example, demonstrates how technological change maintained an aircraft relevant throughout the war. The Swordfish MKII, which appeared in 1943, was a great improvement over earlier versions of the plane with its metal covered lower wings, enabling it to carry rocket projectiles. In addition, the plane also carried ASV radar making it one of the deadliest and high technology aircraft of the war. Introducing new weapons required massive amounts of spending in R&D and a considerable reorganization and rationalization of the means of production together with abundant reserves of fuel, coal and other feedstocks. Few national States, mainly the United States, the Soviet Union, Britain and Germany and perhaps Japan, possessed the know-how and the resources to support a conflict of constant technological change paired with a high level of attrition, while the Italian aviation industry and its Ministry did not have the organizational structure to sustain it.

One last point must be made while making a comparative analysis regarding torpedo development and technological innovation prior to and during the war. In an important work on torpedo development Professor Katherine Epstein argues a key point while comparing U.S. Navy and Royal Navy naval torpedo development that the race to improve its underlying technology was one of the factors behind the rise of the military-industrial complex in the United States and Britain. No private industry was willing to spend time and financial resources to develop sophisticated torpedo technology without some guarantees from the government. In the national states were torpedo development was at the forefront this led to increasingly close collaboration between private industry and the military, whereby the national state invested heavily in torpedo development.[14] If one looks at the initial approach to torpedo development in Italy, one can understand why this weapon development ultimately faltered during the Second World War. The RM and the *RA* were never fully invested in its development and they let private industry take the lead in the form of the Whitehead firm in Fiume. Special projects such as radio controlled torpedoes or other special applications were not the result of an organizational push but primarily the work of gifted individuals and innovators. Thus, despite having a world class aircraft for its time in the *Sparviero* in 1940, the lack of a preponderant national state intervention in the development of the torpedo ultimately led to a situation where technological innovation lagged those of other nations.

14 Katherine C. Epstein, *Torpedo: Inventing the Military-Industrial Complex in the United States and Great Britain* (Cambridge, Massachusetts: Harvard University Press, 2014), *passim.*

Appendix

Warships and Merchantmen Sunk or Damaged by Italian Torpedo Bombers

---

Warships

1. HMS *Kent* (cruiser) 9,850 tons – Damaged North East of Bardia on 17 September 1940.
2. HMS *Liverpool* (cruiser) 9,400 tons – Damaged south of Crete on 14 October 1940.
3. HMS *Glasgow* (cruiser) 9,100 tons – Damaged Suda Bay on 3 December 1940).
4. HMS *Glenroy* (landing ship) 9,871 tons – Slightly damaged near Crete on 26 May 1941.
5. HMS *Manchester* (cruiser) 9,400 tons – Damaged near Galite Islands on 23 July 1941.
6. HMS *Fearless* (destroyer) 1,375 tons – Sunk near Galite Islands on 23 July 1941.
7. HMS Protector (net layer) 2,900 tons – Damaged near Port Said on 11 August 1941.
8. HMS *Phoebe* (cruiser) 5,450 tons – Damaged near Bardia on 27 August 1941.
9. HMS *Nelson* (battleship) 33,950 tons – Damaged south of Sardinia on 27 August 27 1941.
10. HMS *Glenroy* (landing ship) 9,871 tons- Damaged north of Mersa Matruh on 23 November 1941.
11. HMS *Jackal* (destroyer) 1,690 tons – Damaged near Mersa Luch on 1 December 1941.
12. HMS *Chakdina* (armored boarding vessel) 3,033 tons – Sunk near Mersa Luch, 5 December 1941.
13. HMS *Liverpoo*l (cruiser) 9,400 tons – Damaged south of Sardinia on 14 June 1942.
14. HMS *Bedouin* (cruiser) 1,870 tons – Sunk south of Pantelleria on 15 June 1942.
15. HMS *Malines* (escort) 2,969 tons – Damaged near Port Said on 22 July 1942.
16. HMS *Foresight* (destroyer) 1,350 tons – Sunk near Cani Island on 12 August 1942.
17. HMS *Ibis* (sloop ship) 1,250 tons – Sunk north of Algiers on 11 November 1942.
18. HMS *Tynwald* (anti-aircraft ship 2,375 tons – Sunk near on 12 November 1942.
19. HMS *Marigold* (corvette) 925 tons – Sunk near Algiers on 9 December 1942.
20. HMS *Pozarica* (anti-aircraft ship) 4,540 tons – Sunk Bougie Bay 29 January 1943.
21. HMS *Indomitable* (aircraft carrier) 23,000 tons – Damaged south of Cape Passero on 17 July 1942.
22. US LST-414 (landing ship) 2,750 tons – Sunk near Cani Island on 15 August 1943.
23. US LST-417 (landing ship) 1,625 tons – Beached near Termini Imerese on 7 September 1943.

Merchantmen

1. *British Science* (tanker) 7,138 tons – Damaged Aegean Sea on 18 April 1941.
2. *British Lord* (tanker) 6,098 tons – Sunk eastern Mediterranean on 21 April 1941.
3. *Rawnsley* (motorship) 4,998 tons – Beached south of Crete on 8 May 1941.
4. *Hoegh Hood* (tanker) 9,351 tons – Damaged near Galite Islands on 24 July 1941.
5. *Turbo* (tanker) 4,782 tons – Damaged north of Port Said on 20 August 1941.
6. *Deucalion* (steamer) 7,514 tons – Damaged south of Sardinia on 27 August 1941.
7. *Imperial Star* (steamer) 12,427 tons – Sunk near Skerki on 27 September 1941.
8. *Empire Guillemot* (steamer) 5,720 tons – Sunk near Galite Islands on 4 October 1941.
9. *Empire Pelican* (steamer) 6,463 tons – Sunk near Galite Islands on 11 November 1941.
10. *Empire Defender* (steamer) 6,649 tons – Sunk near Galite Islands on 15 November 1941.
11. *Stureborg (*steamer) 1,661 tons – Sunk south of Cyprus on 9 Jun, 1942.
12. *Tanimbar* (steamer) 8,169 tons – Sunk south of Sardinia on 14 June 1942.
13. *Burdward* (steamer) 6,069 tons – Sunk south of Pantelleria on 15 June 1942.
14. *Aircrest (*steamer) 5,237 tons – Sunk west of Jaffa on 30 June 1942.
15. *Port Chalmers* (steamer) 8,535 tons – Damaged near Malta on 13 August 1942.
16. *Scythia* (steamer) 19,716 tons – Damaged near Algiers on 23 November 1942
17. *Selbo* (steamer) 1,774 tons – Sunk near Cape Cavallo on 28 November 1942.
18. *Al Ameriaah* (motor sailing ship) 75 tons – Sunk near Alexandria on 6 February 1943.
19. *Empire Rowan* (motorboat) 9,545 tons – Sunk Gulf of Philippeville on 27 March 1943.
20. *Benjamin Contee* (steamer) 7,126 tons – Damaged off Bone on 16 August 1943.
21. *Empire Kestrel* (steamer) 2,700 tons – Damaged off Cape Bougaroun on 16 August 1943.

Bibliography

Archival Sources

Ufficio Storico Aeronautica Militare: Diario storico del 278ª *Reparto Sperimentale Aerosiluranti*, Gorizia, 7 August 1940.

Verbali delle riunioni tenute dal capo di stato maggiore generale, vol. I, (Rome: Ufficio Storico, 1992).

Verbali dellle riunioni tenute dal capo di stato maggiore generale, vol. II, (Rome: Ufficio Storico, 1983).

Ufficio Storico Aeronautica Militare: "Costituzione dei reparti aerosiluranti," lettera n. 4073/op dell'ammiraglio Domenico Cavagnari.

Ufficio Storico Aeronautica Militare: Ufficio Aerosiluranti di Superaereo, "Azioni di aerosiluramento effettuate contro naviglio nemico dal 7 al 15 luglio 1943," 17 July 1943.

Ufficio Storico Aeronautica Militare: Comando 280ª *Squadriglia*, "Relazione attacco aerosiluranti alla formazione navale nemica nel mare di La Galite alle ore 12.50 dello 8-5-41, " 18 August 1941.

Archivio Storico Aeronautica Militare: Comando Aeronautica della Sardegna, "Operazione Halberd," 29 September 1941.

Ufficio Storico: Comando Supremo, "Norme Generali per la Cooperazione Aeronavale nel Mediterraneo," 10 October 1941.

Archivio Storico Aeronautica Militare: "La situazione al 9 luglio 1943," 4° Reparto di Superaereo n. 7025077, 9 July 1943.

Ufficio Storico: Regia Marina, "Investimento di Malta," 18 June 1940.

Ufficio Storico: Archivio Storico Regia Marina "Relazioni sulle operazioni navali dei giorni 6,7,8 e 9, 10, 11 luglio 1940," 14 July 1940.

Archivio Storico Aeronautica Militare: Rivista Aeronautica, "Aerosiluro o bomba?," N. 3, 1934.

Archivio Storico Aeronautica Militare: Rivista Aeronautica, "Il siluro," N. 7, 1934.

Archivio Storico Aeronautica Militare: Rivista Aeronautica, "I propri metodi," N.10, 1934.

Archivio Storico Aeronautica Militare: fondo LT2, cartella 19.

Archivio Storico Aeronautica Militare: Superaereo "Direttive d'impiego aerosiluranti," 1B/18184, 20 October 1941.

Archivio Storico Aeronautica Militare: Ufficio Aerosiluranti, Colonnello Antonino Serra, "Visite ai reparti siluranti della Sardegna," 13 November 1941.

Archivio Storico Aeronautica Militare: Superaereo, "Azioni aeree dei giorni 13-14 Febbraio contro forze navali nemiche in navigazione fra Malta ed Alessandria," 20 February 1942.

Archivio Storico Aeronautica Militare: 1B/4400 – Superaereo, Punto Comando 36° Stormo, "Azione siluramento giorno 30," 2 April 1942.
Archivio Storico Aeronautica Militare: 1B/4580 Superaereo, "Punto sulla situazione siluri," 2 April 1942.
Archivio Storico Aeronautica Militare: Superareo, "L'azione del 30 Marzo contro convoglio nemico," 5 April 1942.
Archivio Storico Aeronautica Militare: Allegato numero 3 alla lettera di Superaereo, 18 April 1942.
Archivio Storico Aeronautica Militare: Comando Aeronautica della Sicilia, "Operazioni contro forze navali H provenienti da Gibilterra," 15 July 1942.
Archivio Storico Aeronautica Militare, Superaereo, "La Battaglia di Mezzo Giugno," 19 June 1942.
Archivio Storico Aeronautica Militare: 132° *Gruppo* Aerosiluranti Diario Storico, 18 June, 1942.
Archivio Storico Aeronautica Militare: Superaereo, "Ordine operativo contro convoglio scortato," GAM 6, 11 August, 1942.
Archivio Storico Aeronautica Militare, "Studio critico sulla battaglia aeronavale dell'agosto 1942," 27 August 1942.
Archivio Storico Aeronautica Militare: Superaereo, Prot. n.5 21774, "Aerosiliranti," 3 September 1942.
Archivio Storico Aeronautica Militare: Generale Urbani, "Reparto operazioni dell'Aeronautica della Sardegna", n. 27831, 30 September 1942.
Archivio Storico Aeronautica Militare: 3ª Squadra Aerea, "Lettera al Capo di Stato Maggiore," n. 9/4678, 26 September, 1942.
Archivio Storico Aeronautica Militare: Generale Ranza, "Lettera a Capo di Stato Maggiore," n. Op/00402, 1 October 1942.
Archivio Storico Aeronautica Militare: 132° *Gruppo* Aerosiluranti Diario Storico, "Operazioni 1942," 20 December 1942.
Ufficio Storico, Tenente Colonnello Ettore Muti, "Brevi cenni di critica alla Regia Aeronauitica," 20 Giugno 1943.
James Somerville, "Mediterranean Convoy Operations – Operation Halberd," Supplement to the London Gazette, n. 38296, 10 August 1948.
Supplement to the London Gazette n. 38073, 18 September 1947.
Operation "Pedestal" (Main Convoy), W.H. Case 8269, Part I and II, 2–16 Aug 1942, ADM 199/1243, Public Records Office (London).
US Military Intelligence Service, "Italian Circling Torpedo," *Tactical and Technical Trends*, No. 11, 5 November 1942.
US Military Intelligence Service, "Torpedo Bomber (Italian Savoia-Marchetti SM-79)," *Intelligence Bulletin*, May 1943.
US Military Intelligence Service, "Notes on Air Tactics Used by The Japanese," *Intelligence Bulletin*, December 1943.

Published Sources

Enzo Angelucci, *World War Two Combat Aircraft* (New York: Military Press, 1988).
Giorgio Apostolo and Giovanni Massimello, *Italian Aces of World War Two* (Oxford: Osprey, 2000).

Pietro Badoglio, *Italy in the Second World War* (London: Oxford University Press, 1948).
Fabio Bianchi, "Gli aerosiluranti italiani," *Storia Militare*, n. 14, June 2014.
M. A. Bragadin, *Che ha fatto la Marina*? (Milan: Garzanti, 1947).
Cajus Bekker, *The Luftwaffe War Diaries* (Garden City: Doubleday, 1968).
James Burgwyn, *Mussolini Warlord* (New York: Enigma, 2008).
Domizia Carafoli and Gustavo Bocchini Padiglione, *Ettore Muti* (Milan: Mursia, 1993).
Lucio Ceva and Andrea Curami, *Industria bellica anni trenta: commesse militari, l'Ansaldo ed altri* (Milan: Franco Angeli, 1992).
Mark Chambers and Tony Holmes, *Nakajima B5N Kate and B6N Jill Units* (Oxford: Osprey, 2017).
Giuseppe Ciampaglia, "La sorprendente storia della motobomba FFF," *Rivista Italiana Difesa*, July 1999.
Giuseppe Cimicchi, *I siluri vengono dal cielo* (Milan: Longanesi, 1964).
Wesley Frank Craven (ed.), *The Army and the Air Forces in World War II, Vol. I: Plans & Early Operations* (Washington DC: Office of Air Force History, 1983).
Andrew Cunningham, *A Sailor's Odyssey* (London: Hutchinson and Company, 1951).
Andrea Curami, "Piani e progetti dell'aeronautica italiana 1939-1943 Stato maggiore e industrie," *Italia Contemporanea*, N. 187, June 1992.
R.L. Di Nardo, *Germany's Panzer Arm in World War II* (Mechanicsburg: Stackpole, 2006).
Robert S. Dudney "Douhet,"*Air Force Magazine*, April 2011.
Chris Dunning, *Courage Alone: The Italian Airforce 1940-1943* (New York: Hikoki, 2009).
Katherine C. Epstein, *Torpedo: Inventing the Military-Industrial Complex in the United States and Great Britain* (Cambridge: Harvard University Press, 2014).
Carlo Favagrossa, *Perche' perdemmo la guerra* (Milan: Rizzoli, 1946).
David French, "Fighting Power" in Richard Overy, *The Oxford Illustrated History of World War II* (Oxford: Oxford University Press, 2015).
Albert N. Garland and Howard McGaw Smyth, *Sicily and the Surrender of Italy* (Washington, DC: US
Army Publications, 1965).
G. Getti and R. Capinacci, "Relazione sulla missione in Africa," Silurifico Whitehead, October 1940.
Giorgio Giorgerini, *Uomini sul fondo: storia del sommergibilismo italiano dalle origini a oggi* (Milan: Mondadori, 2002).
Giorgio Giorgerini, *La guerra italiana sul mare. La marina tra vittoria e sconfitta 1940–1943* (Milan: Mondadori, 2004).
Giulio Cesare Graziani, *Con bombe e siluri fra le cannonate* (Rome: Edizioni Graziani, 1982).
Orazio Giuffrida, *Buscaglia e gli aerosiluranti* (Rome: Ufficio Storico, 1988).
Jack Greene and Alessandro Massignani, *The Naval War in the Mediterranean* (Norfolk: Naval Institute Press, 2011).
Jack Greene, "Air Force, Italy" in Spencer C. Tucker, *World War II: The Definitive Encyclopedia* (New York: ABC-CLIO, 2016).
John Gooch, *Mussolini and His Generals* (Cambridge: Cambridge University Press, 2007).
John Gooch, *Mussolini's War* (New York: Simon and Schuster, 2020).
Richard Hammond, "Air Power and the British Anti-Shipping Campaign in the Mediterranean, 1940-1944," *Air Power Review, vol.* 16, n.1, pp. 50-61.

Richard Hammond, "An Enduring Influence on Imperial Defence and Grand Strategy: British Perceptions of the Italian Navy, 1935-1943," *International History Review*, vol. 39, n. 5, 2017, pp. 810-835.
Max Hastings, *Operation Pedestal* (New York: Harper Collins, 2021).
Keith Hayward, *The British Aircraft Industry* (Manchester: Manchester University Press, 1989).
Ian Hogg, *The Weapons that Changed the World* (New York: Arbor House, 1986).
Wayne P. Hughes, *Fleet Tactics* (Annapolis, Maryland: Naval Institute Press, 1986).
Angelo Iachino, *Guado e Matapan (*Milan: Mondadori, 1963).
Marco Innocenti, *L'Italia del 1940* (Milan: Mursia, 1996).
Robert Jackson, *Warplanes of World War II Up Close* (New York: Rosen, 2015).
Malcolm Llewellyn-Jones, *The Royal Navy and the Mediterranean Convoys: A Naval Staff History* (New York: Routledge, 2007).
Albert Kesselring, *A Soldier's Record* (New York: William Morrow and Company, 1954).
Mac Gregor Knox, *Hitler's Italian Allies: Royal Armed Forces, Fascist Regime, and the War of 1940–1943* (Cambridge: Cambridge University Press, 2009).
Nicola Labanca, "The Italian Wars," in Richard Overy, *The Oxford Illustrated History of World War II* (Oxford: Oxford University Press, 2015).
Daniele Lembo, "Le armi segrete della Regia," *Aerei Nella Storia*, No. 15, 2015.
Daniele Lembo, *Prototipi e progetti della Regia Aeronautica* (Milan: IBN Editore, 2010).
Sebastiano Licheri, *L'arma aerea italiana* (Milan: Mursia, 1986).
Sebastiano Licheri, "Le azioni di mezzo giugno ed agosto: L'aspetto aereo," *Italia in Guerra 1942*, Ufficio Storico, vol. 2, 1997.
Thomas P. Lowry, The *Attack on Taranto* (Mechanicsburg, Pennsylvania: Stackpole, 1995).
Laddie Lucas, *Malta The Thorn in Rommel's Side* (London: Penguin Books, 1993).
Ron Mackay, *Heinkel He 111* (Wiltshire: Crowood Press, 2003).
Donald Macintyre, *Sea Power in The Mediterranean* (London: Little Hampton Book Services Ltd, 1972).
Tulio Marcon, "Sul rendimento degli aerosiluranti italiani," *Storia Militare*, December 1997.
Francesco Mattesini, "L'operazione brittanica Tiger," *Bollettino d'Archivio dell'Ufficio Storico della Marina Militare,* May 2001.
Francesco Mattesini, "I successi degli aerosiluranti italiani e tedeschi in Mediterraneo nella seconda guerra mondiale," *Bollettino d'Archivio dell'Ufficio Storico della Marina Militare*, March 2002.
Francesco Mattesini, *Luci ed ombre degli aerosiluranti italiani e tedeschi nel Mediterraneo* (Rome: Ristampa SRL, 2019).
Francesco Mattesini, "Operazione Husky," *Bollettino d'Archivio dell'Ufficio Storico della Marina Militare,* May 2011.
Francesco Mattesini, "Le operazioni britanniche Substance e Style per il rifornimento di Malta (31 Luglio– 4 Agosto 1941)," *Bollettino d'Archivio dell'Ufficio Storico della Marina Militare,* May 2001.
Francesco Mattesini, *La battaglia aeronavale di mezzo agosto. Il contrasto delle forze italo-tedesche all'operazione britannica Pedestal 10-15 Agosto 1942* (Santa Rufina di Cittaducale: RiStampa Edizioni, 2019).
Thomas G. Mahnken, "Asymmetric Warfare at Sea: The Naval Battles off Guadalcanal, 1942–1943," *Naval War College Review*, Vol. 64, No. 1 (Winter 2011), pp. 95-121.

Marco Mattioli, *Savoia-Marchetti S.79 Sparviero Torpedo-Bomber Units* (Oxford: Osprey, 2010).

Allan R. Millett, Williamson Murray and Kenneth H. Watman, "The Effectiveness of Military Organizations," *International Security*, Vol. 11, No. 1 (Summer, 1986), pp. 37-71.

Fortunato Minniti, "La politica industriale del ministero dell'aeronautica," *Storia Contemporanea*, No. 1, 1981, pp. 11-22.

Ryan K. Noppen, *Malta 1940-42* (Oxford: Osprey, 2018).

Vincent P. O'Hara, *Six Victories* (Annapolis, Maryland: Naval Institute Press, 2019).

Vincent O'Hara, *In Passage Perilous: Malta and the Convoy Battles of June 1942* (Bloomington, Indiana: Indiana University Press, 2012).

Franco Pagliano, *Storia di 10,000 aereoplani* (Milan: Mursia, 2003).

Ray Panko, "Pearl Harbor: Thunderfish in the Sky," *Pearl Harbor Aviation Museum Magazine*, 28 December 2015.

Mark R. Peattie, *Sunburst: The Rise of the Japanese Naval Air Power, 1909-1941* (Annapolis, Maryland: Naval Institute Press, 2001).

Major-General I.S.O. Playfair, *The Mediterranean and Middle East Volume I: The Early Successes against Italy (to May 1941),* (London: HMSO, 1954).

Major-General I.S.O. Playfair, *Mediterranean and Middle East, Volume 2: The Germans Come to the Help of Their Ally, 1941* (London: HMSO, 1954).

Major-General I.S.O. Playfair, *Mediterranean and Middle East, Volume 3: British Fortunes Reach Their Lowest Ebb* (London: HMSO, 1954).

Major-General I.S.O. Playfair, *Mediterranean and Middle East, Volume 4: The Destruction of the Axis Forces in Africa* (London: HMSO, 1954).

Alfred Price, *Luftwaffe Handbook* (New York: Charles Scribner's Sons, 1977).

Francesco Pricolo, *La Regia Aeronautica nella seconda guerra mondiale* (Milan: Mondadori, 1971).

Gianni Rocca, *I disperati* (Milan: Mondadori, 2003).

Giorgio Rochat, *Italo Balbo aviatore e ministro dell'aeronautica 1926-1933* (Ferrara: Italo Bovolenta Editore, 1979).

Giorgio Rochat, 'Lo sforzo bellico 1940–43: Analisi di una sconfitta', *Italia contemporanea*, N.160 (September 1985), pp. 5-32.

Stephen Peter Rosen, "New Ways of War: Understanding Military Innovation," *International Security,*

Vol. 13, No. 1 (Summer, 1988), pp. 134-168.

Stephen Roskill, *Churchill and the Admirals* (New York: William Morrow, 1978).

Stephen Roskill, *The Period of Balance. History of the Second World War: The War at Sea 1939–1945. II* (London: HMSO, 1962).

James Sadkovich, *The Italian Navy in World War II* (Westport: Greenwood Press, 1994).

Alberto Santoni, *La seconda battaglia della Sirte* (Rome: Edizioni dell'Ateneo, 1982).

Alberto Santoni and Francesco Mattesini, *La partecipazione tedesca alla guerra aeronavale nel Mediterraneo (1940-1945)* (Rome: Edizioni dell'Ateneo, 1980).

Giuseppe Santoro, *L'aeronautica Italiana nella Seconda Guerra Mondiale* (Rome: Ufficio Storico, 1957).

Claudio G. Segre, *Italo Balbo* (Berkeley: University of California Press, 2004).

Maurizio Simoncelli, "L'Industria militare italiana nella seconda guerra mondiale," *Disarmo*, No. 1-2, January 1996.

A.J. Smithers, *Taranto 1940* (Annapolis, MD: Naval Institute Press, 1995).

Fredmano Spairani, *Una politica aeronautica* (Milan: Franco Angeli, 1995).
Mark E. Stille, *US Navy Ships vs Japanese Attack Aircraft* (Oxford: Osprey, 2020).
Mark E. Stille, *Imperial Japanese Aircraft Carriers* (Oxford: Osprey, 2005).
Mark E. Stille, *The Italian Battleships of World War II* (Oxford: Osprey, 2001).
Mark E. Stille, *Italian Cruisers of World War II* (Oxford: Osprey, 2018).
Mark E. Stille, *Pacific Carrier War: Carrier Combat from Pearl Harbor to Okinawa* (Oxford: Osprey, 2021).
Brian Sullivan, "Fascist Italy's Military Involvement in the Spanish Civil War," *The Journal of Military History*, Vol. 59, No. 4 (1995), pp. 697–727.
Brian Sullivan, "Downfall of the Regia Aeronautica," in Robin Higham (ed.), *Why Air Forces Fail* (Lexington, Kentucky: University Press of Kentucky, 2006), pp. 100-135.
Milan Vego, "Major Convoy Operation to Malta, 10–15 August 1942 (Operation Pedestal)," *Naval War College Review*, Vol. 63, No. 1, 2010, pp. 107-154.
John de S. Winser *Short Sea: Long War. Cross-Channel Ships' Naval & Military Service in World War II* (London: World Ship Society, 1997).
John Withson (ed.), *The War at Sea* (New York: William Morrow, 1968).
Richard Woodman, *Malta Convoys, 1940–1943* (London: John Murray, 2000).

Electronic Sources

Encyclopedia.1914-1918, "Air Warfare Italy" <https://encyclopedia.1914-1918-online.net/article/air_warfare_italy>
Extract From The Journal of Midshipman W. P. Hayes, RCN Aboard HMS Liverpool, October 1940 <https://web.archive.org/web/20120224025032/http://www.noac-national.ca/article/hayes/returntoalexandria_bywphayes.html >
National WW2 Museum, "Out-Producing the Enemy: American Production During WWII" <https://www.nationalww2museum.org/sites/default/files/2017-07/mv-education-package.pdf >
Commando Supremo, "S.M. 79 Torpedo Tactics" <https://comandosupremo.com/forums/index.php?threads/s-m-79-torpedo-tactics.62/>
Arthur Burke, Torpedoes <(https://apps.dtic.mil/dtic/tr/fulltext/u2/1033484.pdf >
Medaglie D'oro <https://www.quirinale.it/onorificenze/insigniti/13144>
Medaglie D'oro <https://www.quirinale.it/onorificenze/insigniti/13248 >
Medaglie D'oro <https://www.quirinale.it/onorificenze/insigniti/13248 >
Medaglie D'oro <https://www.quirinale.it/onorificenze/insigniti/45315>
Ufficio Storico: Italiani in Guerra <https://italianiinguerra.com/2019/07/25/i-bollettini-di-guerra-del-25-luglio-1940-41-42-43/>
BBC Southern Counties Radio, "Torpedoed on the Scythia," <https://www.bbc.co.uk/history/ww2peopleswar/stories/36/a4445336.shtml>
Bruno Petrucci, "The Italian period of the Whitehead Torpedo' <http://protorpedo-rijeka.hr/wp/wp-content/uploads/2018/04/22.pdf>
Francesco Mattesini, "La battaglia aeronavale di mezzo giugno, 2017" <https://www.academia.edu/34682676/LA_BATTAGLIA_AERONAVALE_DI_MEZZO_GIUGNO>
WW2 Cruisers, "HMS Bedouin 1942" <https://www.world-war.co.uk/bedouin.php>

HMS Glenroy, Some Personal Experiences of CPO John Priscott-Shipwright Glenroy 1940- 1942 <http://web.archive.org/web/20070630030940/glenroy.freeservers.com/custom2.html>
Uboat.net, "Allied Warships: HMS Fortune" <https://uboat.net/allies/warships/ship/4227.html >
Uboat.net, "Allied Warships HMS Foresight" <https://uboat.net/allies/warships/ship/4387.html>
Uboat.net, "Allied Warships, HMS Quentin" < https://uboat.net/allies/warships/ship/4502.html>